THE THEORY OF INSPIRATION

FOR JEMILA AND FOR CAITLIN

TIMOTHY CLARK

THE THEORY OF INSPIRATION

Composition as a crisis of subjectivity
in Romantic and post-Romantic writing

MANCHESTER UNIVERSITY PRESS
MANCHESTER AND NEW YORK

distributed exclusively in the USA by St. Martin's Press

Published by Manchester University Press
Oxford Road, Manchester M13 9NR, UK
and Room 400, 175 Fifth Avenue, New York, NY 10010, USA

Distributed exclusively in the USA by
St. Martin's Press, Inc., 175 Fifth Avenue, New York,
NY 10010, USA

Distributed exclusively in Canada by
UBC Press, University of British Columbia
6344 Memorial Road, Vancouver, BC, Canada V6T 1Z2

British Library Cataloguing-in-Publication Data
A catalogue record for this book is available from the British Library

Library of Congress Cataloging-in-Publication Data
Clark, Timothy, 1958–
The theory of inspiration: composition as a crisis of
subjectivity in romantic and post-romantic writing/Timothy Clark.
     p.   cm.
ISBN 0-7190-5064-2
1. Inspiration in literature. 2. Creation (Literary, artistic, etc.)
3. Literature, Modern—History and criticism. 4. Philosophy.
PN46.C53 1997
801'.92—DC21   96–29805

ISBN 0 7190 5064 2 *hardback*

First published in 1997
01 00 99 98 97   ,   10 9 8 7 6 5 4 3 2 1

Typeset by Action Typesetting Ltd, Gloucester
Printed in Great Britain
by Bookcraft (Bath) Ltd, Midsomer Norton

CONTENTS

ACKNOWLEDGEMENTS

This book is mainly the product of a year's visit in 1994 to the Humanities Research Centre of the Australian National University. My thanks above all to Iain McCalman, Grahame Clarke and all other staff at the HRC for their hospitality in Canberra. My thanks also to the Publications Board of the University of Durham for a subvention towards the cost of publishing a book of this size. Portions of chapters nine and ten first appeared in *Sub-Stance*, and portions of chapter eleven in the *Oxford Literary Review*.

Many people have helped with this project during its composition. Anthony Mellors and Nicholas Royle gave valuable advice in reading and commenting on a penultimate draft of the manuscript. Jennifer Ford advised helpfully with the English Romantic chapters; Seán Burke gave support with several chapters, as did Bridget Nichols and Annette Stewart at a decisive and earlier stage. For help with individual chapters or items thanks are due to Diana Collecott, Robin Dix, Paul Eggert, Jacqueline Hall, Anne Kukkonen, Richard Lansdowne, Isobel Maddison, Scott Masson, Elizabeth Minchin and Michael O'Neill. Finally I am indebted to the help and expertise of Anita Roy, Matthew Frost and Stephanie Sloan at Manchester University Press.

With so much work from friends and colleagues, any remaining flaws in the book must be entirely their responsibility.

All translations not otherwise acknowledged are my own.

Introduction

This is a study of theories of 'creativity' in Western literary theory since the Enlightenment; or, to be more precise, of the understanding of the process of composition as the site of a unique, valuable and rare transformation and even revolution of the psyche; in a word, 'inspiration'.

To anyone with knowledge of the current state of literary studies, nothing sounds more trite, mystifying and even embarrassing than talk of writers as 'inspired'. 'Inspiration' seems a spurious and exploded theory of the sources of literary power. It usually refers the reader to a privileged relation between the writer's act of composition and some transcendent principle such as the muse, Apollo, genius or the Romantic imagination. Edgar Allan Poe's 'The Philosophy of Composition' (1846) remains the most cited demolition of crude ideas of intuitive creativity:

> Most writers – poets in especial – prefer having it understood that they compose by a species of fine frenzy – an ecstatic intuition – and would positively shudder at letting the public take a peep behind the scenes, at the elaborate and vacillating crudities of thought ... at the cautious selections and rejections – at the painful erasures and interpolations ... which, in ninety-nine cases out of the hundred, constitute the properties of the literary *histrio*.[1]

Yet accounts of inspiration have persisted, ineradicably, as part of Western literary culture for more than three thousand years. They have provided a recurrent source of controversy, obfuscation, enthusiasm, wonder and even comedy throughout this time. No sooner is the term disqualified for various reasons than crucial aspects of it come back, sometimes from an unexpected direction. Jacques Derrida's answer to the question 'Che cos'è la poesia?' (1988) almost returns us to the language of Plato's *Ion*, the *locus classicus* for the notion of inspiration in aesthetic (as opposed to theological) debate. 'The poetic,' Derrida writes, 'let us say it, would be that which you desire to learn, but from and of the other, thanks to the other and under dictation, by heart'.[2]

Unlike other major literary terms, such as *mimesis* or imagination, inspiration (I will let scare quotes be understood from now on) has barely been part of a continuously sustained tradition of debate. Instead, it has remained as a pervasive myth for writers to draw on, attack or reformulate as they think fit. Some, like Poe or Paul Valéry, cast the notion as a popular or naive indulgence.[3] Others, like Shelley or the surrealists, see inspiration as something to be reclaimed and given a genuinely philosophical underpinning. The term now has so little status that, though part of the ordinary language and arguably the key term in the history of Western poetics, it almost never appears in guides to literary terms. This study is the first to make it the object of a sustained critical analysis.

At first sight the association of inspiration with the romantic idealization of personal creativity seems a paradox. In both the Platonic and the biblical traditions inspiration described the supposed possession of an individual voice by some transcendent authority. The muse speaks, and the poet is only her mouthpiece and servant; or in the medieval Christian tradition the human *scriptor* has authority only as a scribe of divine truth.[4] Both notions actually negate individual creativity. Inspiration there concerns matters of authority, the right to speak and the claim to speak in the name of the truth. Seán Burke observes that 'What distinguishes pre-modern conceptions of authorship is their assumption that discourse is an affair of public rather than private consciousness ... So far from endorsing an interiority that feeds from itself back into itself, the inspirational tradition affirms that discourse is not a private intuition but a public revelation'.[5] The writer gains authority by disclaiming personal authorship. Since the eighteenth century, however, classical and Renaissance conceptions of the *furor poeticus* have often given way to theories of individual 'creativity' in which inspiration has the status of a 'calculated madness' (Wolfgang Lange).[6] That is to say, a crucial part of the process of composition is understood as a desired or even calculated suspension of reasoning or deliberation, a temporary mania or insanity. This suspension is valorised as a mode of access to 'deeper' or spontaneously productive areas of the psyche. The irrationality that is inspiration, though analogous to a kind of insanity, is understood to be *sui generis*, a peculiar, unique and probably rare state of being. The creative is less irrational than, so to speak, 'supra-rational.' It achieves feats unattainable by any merely rational or procedural method.

The discourse of inspiration has often comprised a tight knot of different, even contradictory, claims about subjectivity, value and productivity. (1) '*In-spiration*' is originally a late Latin term, usually translating the Greek *enthusiasmos*. In its Latin etymology the word comports the notion of breathing, of an empowering breath or 'spirit', the communication of a sounding energy or power of speech. It thus imposes an oral model on the process of writing, which is troped as an animated voice. Yet this voice is not that of the normal person of the author but mysterious and other. (This is also true of the Greek and German terms for inspiration, *enthusiasmos* and *Begeisterung*, despite their different etymology). (2) Inspiration is held to blur conceptions of agency: the writer is possessed or dispossessed, and may undergo an extreme state of elation. Composition may seem to be effortless, even automatic. The writer is often astonished by what he or she has written, yet the result is also seen as a matter of personal credit. (3) Inspiration also comprises the claim that an inspired text is of superior value. Normal logics of accounting and of cause and effect seem undone: it is as if there were a something for nothing. (4) Unlike the closely related notion of the *furor poeticus* or 'poetic madness', inspiration is a rhetorical concept. To be inspired is, necessarily, to inspire others. Inspiration may bear a peculiar transitivity, one that confounds distinctions between self and other. The writer may seem to be passively inspired, as if by some hidden agent, yet the same writer is said actively to inspire auditors or readers. Inspiration, then, can denote both cause and effect, and its sense often plays deceptively between those poles. Agency is uncertain and mobile – we also speak of an inspired text, without reference necessarily to an author. (5) More oddly yet, inspiration brings with it a peculiar temporality: 'We say that poems *are* inspired, not just that they once were. We say that what is inspired is the poem itself, not just the poet'.[7] (6) Finally, Romantic conceptions of inspiration often wrestle with the most intractable feature of the archaic notion – that writers have most authority when they least know what they are doing. (This is that aspect which Coleridge found unacceptable. He is happy to appropriate notions of inspiration as enhanced creative power related to an intuitive conception of reason, but the idea of an automatic dictation is abhorrent to him.)[8]

In sum, inspiration has often named a series of seeming disjunctions in logic and causality – between the self that tries to write and the agency or seeming subject of writing, between what seems to be written and what there is to be read, between reading a text and seeming to be read by it and, finally, a disjunction between conscious effort and resulting value. Inspiration is bound up in an economy of thought that defies contradiction. It affirms a logocentric conception of a language of self-evident authority. Yet it also represents an automatization of the signifier, a speaking without thought or intention. Ideas that sound a little like accounts of aporias in deconstructive thinking merge in bizarre ways with notions that rest on a religious or magical world view.

The last attempt in English to give a philosophical defence of writers' accounts of being in an inspired state is Rosamund Harding's *An Anatomy of Inspiration*, first published as long ago as 1940.[9] A wayward and fascinating book, which nominally belongs to psychology, it actually provides a clear articulation of assumptions at work in the discourse of inspiration in Romantic and post-Romantic writers. The main interest of Harding's argument lies in the way in which, faced with its bizarre material, it effectively collapses. Harding's theory becomes little distinguishable from the mythical accounts of inspiration in Robert Graves's *The White Goddess* (1948),[10] William Oxley's *The Cauldron of Inspiration* (1983),[11] or in the work of C. G. Jung.[12]

The fascination of Harding's study lies in the diverse material she gathers, from composers as well as writers. One's first temptation is to make an anthology of these bizarre accounts of composition as a crisis of subjectivity:

> the wind plays my old harp as it lists. It has its *high notes*, its *low notes*, its heavy notes – and its faltering notes, in the end it is all the same to me provided the emotion comes, but I can find nothing in myself. It is *the other* who sings as he likes, well or ill, and when I try to think about it, I am afraid and tell myself that I am nothing, nothing at all. (Harding, p. 14)

In this letter of George Sand's to Flaubert, the act of writing is still being idealized in Romantic terms, as a singing. The writer herself is an aeolian harp over which the real agency of composition plays as a wind. The 'emotion' that comes is oddly liminal, almost an external force. Sand's figure recalls Shelley's attempt to idealize inspiration in *A Defence of Poetry*, except that, for her, the experience is frightening, a kind of death. Thought and consciousness, coming to themselves afterwards, are insecure precisely because they seemed so uninvolved, obliterated (Harding does not seem to see this recurrent association of inspiration with suicide). George Eliot remarked to J. W. Cross 'that, in all that she considered her best writing, there was a "not herself" which took possession of her, and that she felt her own personality to be merely the instrument through which this spirit, as it were, was acting' (p. 14). For some writers, like Thackeray or Southey, the mere taking up of a pen was sufficient to act as a mini-ritual of self-transformation. Likewise 'Madame de Stael found that when she took up her pen her brain seemed to become uncontrollable' (p. 49).

What on earth can one do with such accounts? One thing Harding does not consider is that, since the nineteenth century – from which most of her examples come – there has been a very ready market for these kinds of anecdote. They form part of bourgeois culture's sacralisation of the writer as unique individual that has made literary culture increasingly part of the tourist industry, in its most obvious form sending the droves up the hill to Haworth parsonage. Romanticism exalted creativity as the object of a new mythology. Anecdotal accounts of moments of sudden illumination in the life of a 'great man' have now become a mini-genre in their own right, cited again and again in discussions of creativity or invention: Mozart supposedly conceiving a piece of music in an instant (an anecdote now known to be fake);[13] Kekulé realizing the molecular structure of benzene from a dream about snakes;[14] Poincaré suddenly extending the domain of mathematics at the precise moment he steps on a bus ... (Ghiselin, pp. 33–42). One can find collections of these experiences, such as Brewster Ghiselin's *The Creative Process* (1952), or Maria Shrady's *Moments of Insight* (1972).[15] Such accounts, like many nineteenth-century accounts of inspiration, confirm a basically liberal conception of personhood – inspiration is invariably the 'liberation' of a supposedly truer or deeper self from out of the pressures of convention, cliché, tradition, false thinking or inauthenticity. The fascination of these episodes also lies in their seductive status as modern versions of miracle. Glimpses of the creative process remain like brief visions of a promised land. They are, in effect, secularized versions of religious conversion narratives such as those of St Paul and St Augustine, with their dramatic peripeteia and scenes of recognition.[16]

Harding's argument collapses in trying to defend two traditional assumptions about inspiration. The first is that these experiences – with rare exceptions – are the bearers of original work or of work of value. Inspiration seems to be an experience that is itself testimony to the value of its products, *a performative that ensures its own value.* The second assumption is that these experiences are to be grounded in a theory of creativity based on individual psychology.

Harding's method is to gather anecdotes from 'letters, autobiographies, and eye-witness accounts' of writers at work. These documents are taken to provide raw data which can then be treated inductively so as to produce a general account of inspiration, divided into several stages. The basic model is that inspiration is a problem-solving process aided by the effects of the association of ideas. This argument – that the moment of inspiration is the revelation of a previously hidden association of ideas – has been standard in this field since the Enlightenment first isolated inspiration as a 'problem' for study.[17] It is common for Harding's time in theories of creativity and it reappears, with Gestaltist additions, in the work of Arthur Koestler (see Schlanger, pp. 46–9, 58–63). G. Wallas, for example, in 1926 presents the reader with a creative problem-solving process divided into four stages: Preparation, unconscious Incubation, sudden Illumination and, finally, Verification.[18] For Harding, focusing on the moment of Illumination only:

> Inspiration may thus be defined as the result of some unknown factor accidentally met operating on the mind of the man of science or artist at that particular moment when it is pent up to a certain tension either by accumulation of 'visions, colours, forms,' or by facts and pondering over them in the unsuccessful attempt to solve a problem. Although inspiration can occur to anyone it will only be manifested in its highest degree in those persons who are capable of this emotional tension. (p. 99)

However, accounts of inspiration as a species of the 'moment of insight', in Harding or Koestler, blur distinctions between the arts and sciences in misleading ways that serve modernist narratives of progress. The scientist or mathematician is assimilated to a form of heroic quest narrative – the enlightened mind in its struggle to be liberated from darkness – while the writer becomes a kind of problem-solver whose work admits of sudden and quasi-deductive leaps, as in the capitalist cult of the great 'inventor'.

Another shortcoming in such work, or in the anecdotal material collected in Ghiselin's anthology or Shrady's *Moments of Insight*, is the lack of any account of the question of the link between individual creativity and issues of general or historical value. How can being 'inspired' be any sort of guarantee of quality?

The problem-solving model, of course, begs the question here: the solution to any problem worth posing is necessarily valuable. More fundamentally, the question is also begged by the way Harding assumes the 'creative' to be a 'natural' category, referable entirely to the individual mind. The artist, she argues, 'must follow the natural unfolding of his idea' (Harding, p. 45). Inspiration is such a natural unfolding, but happening at an unusual speed: it is a state in which the artist's 'own wishes and desires are overruled by his knowledge of *natural* sequences of events, colours, forms, rhythms, tones' (p. 99) (emphasis added). The word 'natural' surreptitiously does all the work in Harding's argument. The force of possession is finally, truth and nature, which the mind '*must* follow' (p. 99) (Harding's emphasis), as if inevitably written into the scheme of things. This evasion of the question of value leads Harding's individual psychology into Romantic cliché. In fact the book comes apart in its last crucial chapter: 'The truly inspired person creates through a kind of mystical union with the natural world' (p. 100). This is just the old myth of the mysterious genius.

Harding's difficulty – for a psychologist to write 'kind of mystical union' is a gesture of giving up – relates to misconceptions that are still very powerful in this field, even in work in psychoanalysis. The difficulty stems from focusing on a 'creative process' referred entirely to a process located in an individual mind, and which is then recognized by the rest of us through its products. To turn to recent work in the theory of creativity is to find a mini-discipline in a state of crisis. Mihaly Csikszentmihalyi writes:

> all of the definitions of creativity of which I am aware assume that the phenomenon exists, as a concrete process open to investigation, either inside the person or in the works involved.
>
> After studying creativity on and off for almost a quarter of a century, I have come to the reluctant conclusion that this is not the case. We cannot study creativity by isolating individuals and their works from the social and historical milieu in which their actions are carried out.[19]

Csikszentmihalyi then sketches a theory of creativity that would take into account social and cultural conditions, based on a recognition of what many literary critics have known for some time – that any evaluative term (such as 'creative') is only meaningful diacritically, in a process of cultural negotiation, and not solely through reference back to some mysterious process in an individual. The 'question of Creativity,' still a major topic in the discipline of psychology, is increasingly being recognised as a vestige of Romantic individualism.[20] To attempt to explain important moments of historical invention by reference solely to individual psychology is to produce a fallacious myth of creative power: 'In passing directly from individual mentality to famous historical examples, one gives oneself a legendary view, a heroic fresco of the great innovating intuitions of knowledge'.[21]

What is true of creativity in the field of innovation and invention generally may be even more so in the case of literary production. Anyone who has read Wordsworth's *The Prelude* will recall the mildly blasphemous passage in the third book in which it is claimed that, despite the lure of fashion and a trivial social life at Cambridge, Wordsworth the student retained his integrity:

> Of Genius, Power,
> Creation, and Divinity itself
> I have been speaking, for my theme has been
> What pass'd within me. Not of outward things
> Done visibly for other minds, words, signs,
> Symbols, or actions; but of my own heart
> Have I been speaking, and my youthful mind.[22]

One can only wonder what kind of thought experiment the Wittgenstein of the *Philosophical Investigations* might have devised in response to this passage, concerning as it does an undergraduate who had as yet to produce any work of value. It may have taken the characteristic form of an anecdote: 'I put my hand over my eyes, introspect with care, wait a while and then, suddenly seeming to descry something, exclaim, "Blimey! I'm a genius!"'. The point would be that creative 'power', conceived as something located privately within the individual mind, makes only limited sense in the abstract like this, and little more even when it is a matter of listening to oneself while improvising poetry, as is presented in the preamble to *The Prelude*. If it is a matter of the power of a poet, then, logically and empirically, it must ultimately be a matter of possible relations to readers. One cannot simply declare oneself to 'be' a poet, any more than one can say 'I now pronounce myself king', Even completion of a work is in itself insufficient to tell its producer 'you are a writer/poet': other people will have to think so too – in some numbers. Notions of the self-sufficiency of genius seem tantamount to a direct denial of the real insecurities of composition and reception.

In effect, while it makes sense for analyses of creativity to continue to examine whatever faculties are involved in invention, with the application of heuristics, computer modelling etc., any notion of a privileged creative faculty that in itself grounds the social or historical value of its products is incoherent and is deservedly abandoned.

Myths of genius and of privileged states of super-creativity no longer command intellectual respect. This has the effect, however, of rendering writers' accounts of inspiration no less striking or anomalous. George Sand, P. B. Shelley, William Blake, Friedrich Nietzsche, Boris Pasternak, Fernando Pessoa, Rainer Maria Rilke, H.D., Octavio Paz and George Eliot (for example) are surely not only playing up to Romantic idealizations of the act or process of writing, even if notions of the artist as cultural hero make available to them coherent ways in which to present a crisis of subjectivity undergone during composition. Writers' self-descriptions are notorious for accommodating romantic myths of creativity, yet, even taking this into account, these diverse and recurrent references to possession, strange scenes of empowerment, peculiar agencies etc. demand better consideration than the forms of dismissal or evasion they have hitherto received.

The structure of this book

This book aims to provide an analytical account of major theories of inspiration in Western poetics since the Enlightenment. The focus, throughout, is on the tradition of valorising the act of composition as philosophically significant, on writers for whom a conception of the metamorphosis undergone during composition, in inspiration, is central either to their self-conception or to their concept of subjectivity.[23]

The most novel, and no doubt most risky aspect of the methodology of this study is, with qualification, to take writers' claims to inspiration seriously, relating them to certain real effects of the varying material dynamics of the process of composition. The book opens with an introductory section of two chapters. The first is devoted to outlining a working concept of the 'space of composition'. As a space of the complex interaction of psyche and text, composition is the site of some peculiar effects which transgress the economy of the subject considered as unitary agency or intention. The model of composition elaborated in the first chapter will be implicit in the various individual studies which follow, though each is readable independently. A second chapter concludes the introductory section with a close reading of the concept of inspiration in Plato's *Ion*, especially as it relates to ancient Greek poetry as a predominantly oral practice of composition and performance.

The second section of the book will consist in a series of individual case studies. In treating so vast a topic as varying theories of inspiration, one cannot hope to be fully comprehensive. To offer a series of carefully chosen, detailed case studies provides, I hope, a representative sense of changing conceptions of inspiration, without the limitations of a survey. Any choice of individual writers must ultimately be a partial one. My selection downplays topics that have already received a lot of attention (e.g. Coleridge on inspiration, aspects of the question of a 'woman's writing') and foregrounds others that have received less, such as Hölderlin's extraordinary theory of composition; concepts of mass feeling in Wordsworth or Shelley that link their concepts of inspiration to the rhetorical tradition as much as to theories of imagination; the decisive place of surrealism in the emergence of anti-humanist notions of the psyche in composition.

The opening chapter of the second section ('Enthusiasm and enlightenment') is not itself a case study but a broad consideration of the emergence of modern conceptions of inspiration (or 'enthusiasm') in the rhetoric and poetics of the British eighteenth century. Accounts of inspiration emerge as a case of 'residual orality' in Walter J. Ong's sense of practices and assumptions that see composition, even with pen in hand, in primarily oral terms, i.e. as the power of a dictating or captivating voice. Yet the eighteenth century also sees the terminal erosion of oral and formulaic conceptions of composition dominant since Homer. Thence, in Romantic and post-Romantic theories of inspiration, writers attempt to conceive the act of *written* composition as a form of immediate power over an (unknown) audience, in terms that often explicitly evoke nostalgia for the oral model or the communal life of an idealised Greek world.

A recurrent argument of this book is that a writer's conception of a 'creative' 'inner' power is often an image of an anticipated rhetorical effect – e.g. Wordsworth's and Shelley's different accounts of the workings of the imagination in composition both draw on rhetorical (oral) conceptions of the contagiousness of 'enthusiasm' and present themselves in terms identical to those concerning the supposed power of the 'inspired' text upon others.

Hölderlin's complex doctrine of the '*Wechsel der Töne*' offers a theory of composition that merges the aim of rationalizing or demystifying inspiration with the idea of a *calculable* inspiration that would be a poet's equivalent of the dreams of the alchemists. Inspiration, in its Romantic form of a state of super-creativity, is an aspect of 'modernity' in the sense of that condition in which the writer 'no longer knows for whom he writes', a situation contemporary with the demise of patronage, the professionalisation of the writer and the emergence of mass audiences.[24] The history of the concept of inspiration in much Romantic and post-Romantic writing can be summed up as the attempt to locate or employ some privileged 'creative' faculty with the property of *a performative that (impossibly) ensures its own value* or which, in other words, projects and incorporates its own audience. We will see this in eighteenth-century conceptions of poetic enthusiasm, Romantic conceptions of imagination and H.D.'s conception of the 'womb brain'. Such a myth lingers even in Nietzsche's conception of the inspired body.

The aesthetic of inspiration has not always been the simplistic notion of heightened and immediate self-expression for which it is now usually taken. Instead, it often situates the act of composition as a space of division, rupture or possibility between the mundane subjectivity of the writer and alternative and usually unforeseeable modes of being or subjectivity to which the unique interaction and intercontamination of the psychic and textual seems to give access. Inspiration recurrently forms part of an anti-formalist aesthetic which renders composition a kind of experiment upon the writer's psyche and received determinations both of the human and of art. After the eighteenth century, inspiration is recurrently seen as futural, avant-garde and often utopian in its force. It may be transgressive, even to the point of becoming a form of death-drive.

It is with Nietzsche, and from some work of the Romantic period, especially in Shelley and Hölderlin, that the term inspiration comes increasingly to name a crisis of subjectivity at odds with any humanist mythology of psychic power. The process of composition may become a defamiliarisation of received categories of text, world and self so intense as to threaten the very sanity of the writer. Such anti-humanist conceptions of inspiration, already too intertwined with the logocentric conception to be named a counter-tradition, become dominant in the work of the surrealists, Blanchot, Celan and Derrida.

Notes

1 Edgar Poe, *The Fall of the House of Usher and Other Writings*, ed. David Galloway (1967; London: Penguin, 1968), pp. 480–92, 481.
2 Jacques Derrida, 'Che cos'è la poesia?', trans. Peggy Kamuf in *A Derrida Reader: Between the Blinds*, ed. Peggy Kamuf (London and New York: Harvester Wheatsheaf, 1991), pp. 221–37, p. 227.
3 Paul Valéry, 'Remarks on Poetry', in *The Art of Poetry*, trans. Denise Folliot (New York: Panther books, 1958), pp. 196–215, p. 215.
4 See A. J. Minnis, *The Medieval Theory of Authorship: Scholastic Literary Attitudes in the Later Middle Ages* (London: Scholar Press, 1984).
5 Burke, *Authorship: From Plato to the Postmodern: A Reader* (Edinburgh: Edinburgh University Press, 1995), p. xviii.
6 Lange, *Der Kalkulierte Wahnsinn: Innenansichten ästhetischer Moderne* (Frankfurt: Fischer Taschenbuch, 1992). Lange shows how even Poe belongs to this tradition (pp. 149–72).
7 Roger Nash, 'The Demonology of Verse', *Philosophical Investigations*, 10 (1987), 299–316, p. 303.
8 Ina Lipkowitz, 'Inspiration and the Poetic Imagination: Samuel Taylor Coleridge', *Studies in Romanticism*, 30 (1991), 605–31.
9 E. M. Rosamund Harding, *An Anatomy of Inspiration* (Cambridge: W. Heffer & Sons, 1940).
10 Robert Graves, *The White Goddess: A Historical Grammar of Poetic Myth* (London: Faber and Faber, 1948).
11 William Oxley, *The Cauldron of Inspiration* (Salzburg: Universität Salzburg, 1983).
12 In Brewster Ghiselin (ed.), *The Creative Process: A Symposium* (Berkeley: University of California Press, 1952), pp. 208–23.
13 Peter Kivy, 'Mozart and Monotheism: An Essay in Spurious Aesthetics', *Journal of Musicology*, 2 (1983), 322–8.
14 Margaret A. Boden, *The Creative Mind: Myths and Mechanisms* (London: George Weidenfeld and Nicholson, 1990), pp. 16ff.
15 Maria Shrady (ed.), *Moments of Insight: The Emergence of Creative Ideas in the Lives of Great Men* (New York: Harper & Row, 1972). See also John Press, *The Fire and the Fountain: An Essay on Poetry* (1955; London: Methuen, 1966).
16 See also Judith Schlanger, *L'Invention intellectuelle* (Paris: Fayard, 1983), pp. 33–52.
17 See ch. 3; also Alexander Gerard, *An Essay on Genius 1774*, ed. Bernhard Fabian (Munich: Wilhelm Fink, 1966), pp. 66–70.
18 *The Art of Thought* (London: Cape, 1926). Compare also the account of inspiration in Théodule Ribot's *Essay on the Creative Imagination* (Chicago: Open Court, 1906; trans. by Albert H. N. Baron from *Essai sur l'imagination créative*, 1900), pp. 50–64.
19 Mihaly Csikszentmihalyi, 'Society, Culture, and Person: A Systems View of Creativity', in *The Nature of Creativity*, ed. Robert J. Sternberg (Cambridge: Cambridge University Press, 1988), pp. 325–39, p. 325. For a useful survey of theories of creativity see Jock Abra, *Assaulting Parnassus: Theoretical Views of Creativity* (Lanham, MD: University Presses of America, 1988).

20 Robert W. Weisberg, *Creativity, Genius and Other Myths: What You Mozart, Einstein, Picasso Have in Common*, (New York: W. H. Freeman and Co., 1986).

21 Schlanger, *L'Invention intellectuelle*, p. 62.

22 *The Thirteen-Book Prelude*, 2 vols, ed. Mark Reed (Ithaca: Cornell University Press, 1991), I, p. 139.

23 For this reason less attention has been paid to thinkers whose work on inspiration is not closely bound up with the minutiae of the practice of composition, but rather to notions of genius or authoritative insight *per se* – the Kant, for instance, who expounds a notion of genius as the power of a paradoxically natural art whose products exceed the capabilities of any procedural rule or method; or the Coleridge who, partly following Kant, elaborates a transcendental concept of the imagination which enables him to reconcile traditional conceptions of the Bible as the word of God with an acknowledgement of the humanity of its immediate authors.

24 Jean François Lyotard and Jean-Loup Thébaud, *Just Gaming*, trans. Wlad Godzich (Manchester: Manchester University Press, 1985), p. 9.

A common phrase among poets is, 'It came to me'. So hackneyed has this become that one learns to suppress the expression with care, but really it is the best description I know of the conscious arrival of a poem ... Some poets speak of hearing a voice speaking to them, and say that they write almost from dictation. I do not know whether my early scientific training is responsible for my using a less picturesque vocabulary, or whether their process really differs from mine. I do not hear a voice, but I do hear words pronounced, only the pronouncing is toneless. The words seem to be pronounced in my head, but with nobody speaking them ... Suddenly words are there, and there with an imperious insistence that brooks no delay. They must be written down immediately or an acute sense of suffering comes on ... (Amy Lowell)

Inspiration is for me the feeling that I am everywhere at the same time, in space as well as in the various recesses of the heart and the mind. The poetic state creates in my mind a kind of magic confusion, during which ideas and images become alive, leaving their places either in order to connect with other images – in that world all things are close – or to undergo profound metamorphoses, which render them unrecognizable. (Jules Supervielle)

Rhythm, as it is felt in the act of writing, signifies the creation of a continuum, an imaginary space within which words and memories, the given and the possible, can be felt as co-present, held over against each other, yet constantly crossing one another's paths. As the mind attends to the pulsation of the growing poem, it is as if it enters and shared this created space, which, filled by the invitations of movements and sound, seems at once landscape and music, perhaps more music than landscape. (Charles Tomlinson)

you know my state of mind as well as I do...How I work, how I walk, how I shut myself up, how I roll down hills and climb up cliffs; how the new story is everywhere – heaving in the sea, flying with the clouds, blowing in the wind, how I settle to nothing, and wonder (in the old way) at my own incomprehensibility. (Charles Dickens)

I can say that the process, though it takes place in some secret region on the sheer edge of consciousness, is always illuminated by the full light of critical attention. What happens there is as real and tangible as my encounter with friends and neighbours...though on an entirely different plane. It produces in me great emotional excitement, quite unrelated to joy and sorrow caused by real happenings. (Edith Wharton)

CHAPTER I

Orientations: the space of composition

How do I know what I think until I see what I say (E. M. Forster)

The space of composition

Even if we cannot 'believe in' inspiration in an idealized sense, literary history remains full of variously bizarre and variously reliable accounts of the process of composition as a crisis in subjectivity.[1] These are simply too numerous and uncalculating to be explained away as a writer's bid for some vestige of a quasi-prophetic authority. Paul Eggert, surveying accounts of composition from ten modern Australian novelists,[2] observes how some 'reach for pseudo-Romantic phrasings in their interviews because they have all experienced the feeling, however briefly, of not being in control, of going with the flow, of writing almost from dictation.'[3] Eggert continues:

> Literary theory gives no way of which I am aware of developing this insight about writing practice. It is an extraordinary lacuna. Romantic explanations about the genesis of poetry have been quite widely replaced amongst literary critics and theorists by forms of discursive analysis. (p. 11)[4]

My attempt to fill this lacuna approaches accounts of inspiration by elaborating two factors that go to make up the act of composition, considered according to the model of *improvized performance mediated by self-reading* (I will defend my terms later). This chapter has two parts. The first offers some basic parameters for a theory of the process of composition, outlining a working concept of the *space of composition*. The second suggests some general features of the psychic transformation ascribed to inspiration, arguing that it may have the structure of a chiasmus between a scene of production and a scene of reception. Although an earlier version of this chapter rested heavily on Lacanian psychoanalysis and its account of the constitution of the subject in language, I confine myself to a broadly phenomenological reconstruction of a hypothetical act of composition (while acknowledging aspects that break from phenomenological assumptions of conscious access). This thesis runs throughout: the association of inspiration with an enhanced fluency, with a dictating voice, and with a dispossession that is also, paradoxically, a sense of empowerment – these are real properties of composition. However, contrary to the traditional dream of inspiration, no psychological state in itself guarantees the worth of its products to others.

Formal, semiotic and material considerations

A first consideration must be the material media of composition. In the poetic arts there may be two notional poles. At one extreme there is purely oral composition, as practised by a culture entirely without writing – as seems to have been the case with Homer. Composition here may often mean improvisation and it may take place in the very presence of its audience. It is an art of mnemonics, of the transmission and interweaving of voices. At the other extreme are artists who exploit writing considered as a medium in itself, other than as a representation of speech. Its element, whether we are talking of Mallarmé or of a concrete poem, is a blank page destined for the silent perusal of an absent and probably unknown reader. This extreme is a relatively recent development. The sway of the predominantly oral art of rhetoric or public speaking over European education for some two thousand years may partly explain the extent to which composition, until about the Romantic period, has been conceived in mainly oral terms, as the preparation of material as if destined for oral performance.[5] The forms of story-telling and romance remained structured in formulaic and episodic terms at least until the eighteenth century. The predominance in Western poetry of an oral mechanics of rhythm, metre, the use of rhyme and stanzaic forms, also testifies to the extent to which composition remained an oral and aural exercise, bound up with a lingering practice of mnemonic techniques. Composition is a matter of voices that dictate and, repeating themselves, are played back, assessed and reinflected. One's own voice is played with as if it were that of another.

Reading silently and in private has only been common since the advent of printing. Throughout the middle ages written manuscript was regarded as script and reading mainly meant reading aloud, *lecture*. Yves Delègue has traced the internalization of orality in the silent reading that became normal with the widespread use of printing in Europe. Literary writing henceforth involved the production in texts, from Montaigne to Samuel Beckett, of various effects of *trompe-voix*. These would range from voice as the illusion of a unified subjective origin expressing itself in a lyric to, contrariwise, the silent concert that was a poem for Mallarmé. Delègue concludes that modes of 'the dummy voice [have] constituted what we call "literature" for four centuries'.[6]

For writers who appear in the general orientation which follows, one can generalize that composition involves the interaction of the material limits and possibilities of a *written* practice, together with a predominant treatment of written texts as the transmission of effects of voice.

Let us turn now to a specific case. After a period in which John Berryman was not expecting to write any more verse, he tells us:

> suddenly one day last winter [1969-70] I wrote down a line; 'I fell in love with a girl.' I looked at it, and I couldn't find anything wrong with it. I thought, 'God damn it, that is a *fact*.' I felt, as a friend of mine says: 'I feel comfortable with that.' And I looked at it until I thought of a second line, and then a third line, and then a fourth line, and that was a stanza. Unrhymed. And the more I looked at it, the better I liked it, so I wrote a second stanza. And then I wrote some more stanzas, and you know what? I had a lyric poem, and a very good one. I didn't know I had it in me![7]

It's hard not to suspect that Berryman is mocking some of the demands of a writer-at-work interview ('second line, and then a third line, and then a fourth line, and that was a stanza'). The extract also emphasizes, however, the degree to which composition may work through self-reading (or, of course, self-listening), or, more precisely, through the unanticipated effects that arise from moving between writing as act and reading as openness to possibility. The hyphen in the term 'self-reading' becomes a token of that transition into what may be termed the space of composition, a space in which the writer must try to read, not what he or she wrote, but what there is to be read. The demands of this split-mindedness are what often renders composition so difficult, even paralysing, the essence of the various difficulties that lead to writer's block.[8] Blanchot goes so far as to say that the writer's relation to the work is the impossibility of reading it.[9]

David Goldblatt offers ventriloquism, and the relation of ventriloquist to dummy, as a useful analogy for the relations between writer and work-in-process:

> In a work in progress the artist will be dealing with something in another voice – music and literature are other voices, paint is another voice and so on. Yet the source of this voice is no ordinary other, since it is the voice of an ecstatic exchange – the voice, in some respect, of the artist him/herself.[10]

Goldblatt means 'ecstatic' in its precise sense, *ecstasis* as a standing outside oneself. The process of composition, for Goldblatt, moves between the questions 'What does *the work* say?' and 'What am I saying?' (p. 394).

Perhaps the model of self-reading can make the idea of an ecstatic exchange less impressionistic. I turn here to Derrida's 'Force and Signification'.[11] Derrida's topic, in the earlier passages of this essay, is the act of composition, an act to which he cautiously gives some philosophical privilege:

> To write is to not only to know that through writing, through the extremities of style, the best will not necessarily transpire ... It is also to be incapable of making meaning absolutely precede writing: it is thus to lower meaning while simultaneously elevating inscription.[12]

Derrida quotes Merleau-Ponty: '"My own words take me by surprise and teach me what I think"' (p. 11). By virtue of its very structure, writing, or any sign, already implies the agency of others in the scene of composition, even when it is a matter of composition 'in the head'. The writer undergoes an experience of being somehow secondary to the sources of the text:

> is not the experience of *secondarity* tied to the strange redoubling by means of which constituted – written – meaning presents itself as prerequisitely and simultaneously *read*: and does not meaning present itself as such at the point at which the other is found, the other who maintains both the vigil and the back-and-forth motion, the work, that comes between writing and reading, making this work irreducible. Meaning is neither before nor after the act (p. 11).

The word 'work' is prominent here and elsewhere through Derrida's essay. It engages a sense of agency 'behind' the effects of meaning, yet this agent, 'the other', is itself but an effect of the irreducible secondarity of the sign – that it is no sooner written than read, diverging from what may have been intended, suggesting unexpected directions for the text .... Self-reading here is coming to name a very fissure or hiatus in the structure of subjectivity, unassimilable to notions of the subject as reflexive consciousness or simple interiority. The experience that meaning is always elsewhere is said to be the source of a sense of divine agency in writers like Saint John Chrysostom. For others, however, such an experience is witness to the impossibility of the *Book* or a totalizing word.

The act of inscription not only produces effects which immediately, as their very condition of appearance, escape the intentional grasp of the consciousness that wrote them, it may do so, on some occasions, in ways that are themselves 'creative' or surprising in a valuable way. Derrida is interested in conditions of (im)possibility that cannot be fully conceptualized or become the correlate of any intentional act. Our more restricted ambition of sketching a theory of inspiration, however, demands that we look in more detail at effects of otherness, of other agencies, as they manifest themselves in the act of writing.

The way writers describe composition is often in a language of mild paradox. This may be seen even in so familiar statement as Brewster Ghiselin's, concerning the making of a rather poor poem, that 'Now I began to see more clearly and fully what I was trying to say' – there is an unacknowledged disjunction here between the first and second 'I.'[13] (Compare Virginia Woolf's diary entry: 'I begin to see what I had in my mind'.[14]) John Ashbery observes: 'If I did not write, I would have no idea of what I can write. I suppose that I write so as to find what I have to write.'[15] Whether it be a sense of taking dictation, or of the surprising effects of self-reading as a draft goes through several stage of revision, almost all the one hundred and fifty or so accounts of composition I have analyzed bear out Jean Cocteau's argument that 'it is not possible to do what one *intends* ... one cannot know, questions of formulation and art are too complicated for it to be possible for one to foresee, and one simply does not know.'[16] Alternatively, 'what one intends' is matter of retrospective construction through submission to the institution of authorship, i.e. what one intends is what it seems one accepts when finally prepared to commit a piece of writing to the chances of its readers.[17] The question 'who is speaking?' is not only a problem for modern critical interpretation, but also for writers themselves in the space of composition[18] as they work towards that dubious form of self-transcendence known as publication – a point that may pose some problems for any editor or reader still fixated on psychological notions of meaning as original or final intention.

Anyone who has read Jonathan Culler's *Structuralist Poetics* will remember a forceful experiment designed to demonstrate how 'literariness' lies partly in trained or acquired modes of reading. A newspaper clipping is taken and set into short lines as if it were a lyric poem. This effects for the reader a profound metamorphosis touching every term in the text: a word such as 'yesterday' will come to mean the past in general. Words like 'red', 'grass,' 'man' are transformed: they transcend their empirical referents to enter a new space of meaning, taking on possibilities of sense that exist only when read 'as literature'.[19] Culler also reproduces a sentence from W. V. O. Quine in a way that transforms it into a poem reminiscent of Marianne Moore:

From a Logical Point of View

A curious
            thing
about the
            ontological
problem
        is
its
        simplicity

(p. 163)

Without endorsing the notion of readerly competence that Culler deduces from such transformations (and which is not capable of doing justice to the effects of slippage and surprise at issue here), one can affirm that something analogous to this transformation takes place during the scene of composition, or even as the force of the conception of a possible work – tripping on an uneven flagstone in Guermantes courtyard, Marcel Proust stumbles into the altered space and time of a literary work, holistic and already forcefully emergent.[20] There is a passage from mundane space into the space of composition: the word 'rose' is not the same in this space as it is in a conversation. Berryman's line, 'I fell in love with a girl', may move from the banal to seeming forcibly direct. Lying now on the page, it projects a series of possibilities that the poet engages in self-reading. (Virginia Woolf: 'I have just typed out my morning's work; and I can't feel altogether sure. There is *something* there ... but I can't get at it, squarely' (*Diary*, p. 149).)

Stephen Spender's account of inspiration, an unusually sober one, is explicit about the futural modality of those lines of force that cross and define the emergent work. Spender's takes up Valéry's idea of *une ligne donnée*:

> My own experience of inspiration is certainly that of a line or a phrase or a word or sometimes something still vague, a dim cloud of an idea which I feel must be condensed into a shower of words. The peculiarity of the key word or line is that it does not merely attract, as, say, the word 'braggadocio' attracts. It occurs in what seems to be active, male, germinal form as though it were the centre of a statement requiring a beginning and an end, and as though it had an impulse in a certain direction.[21]

Although written composition is usually solitary, unlike the oral poet invoking the muse, it retains even in its privacy a minimal quality of ritual: it is the crossing of a psychic threshold in which, say, the word 'I' is no longer 'myself' but a signifier in the space of composition. The working-model of composition I propose is one of improvised performance, mediated by self-reading. Why 'performance'? Any performance, whether of a poem, a play or dance, takes place as the articulation of a set of possibilities from a historical discursive field with its own rules of interpretation, norms, and techniques which both define its intelligibility and provide a framework enabling any new statement to be understood. The privacy of the writing act – as compared to poetic performance in an oral culture – need not disguise its status as a kind of improvised performance, constructing and correcting itself for eventual publication, mediated by the literary, semiotic and linguistic codes of its day.[22]

Familiarity with current codes of performance will be a necessary element of a writer's competence if his or her work is to have a chance of seeming valuable to other readers. At one extreme, with a hackneyed writer, the sense of dispossession may merely be testimony to an uninteresting automatism of language (surrender to cliché, the trite phrase, the obvious rhyme). At the other, with a writer sensitive to current codes of performance, social context and constraints, it may render the hiatus in self-reading an openness to an eruptive or inventive leap, rendering the text an *event* in Lyotard's sense of an occurrence which 'disrupts any pre-existing referential frame within which it might be represented or understood'.[23]

The writer's sense of emergent possibility in composition surely comes from the constraints inherent in the generic, rhythmic and semantic codes as they intersect in a yet virtual space with other vectors, those that arise from the demands of the writer's own intentions, preoccupations, fantasies and somatic and rhythmic drives. 'Improvisation' is appropriate because the emergent text is not, as it would be according to a structuralist model, the *parole* of some *langue*: it arises from an incalculable multiplicity of lines of intersection between all the vectors that play across the blank page. Moreover, there is no simple principle to which the text can be referred as to some kind of 'explanation'. It is the incalculable effect of diverse and often contradictory factors: 'The writer's intention hasn't anything to do with what he achieves'.[24]

One easily graspable image for the space of composition has been the blank page itself. This may be taken superficially as a figure for the writer's 'imagination', but the blank page is far more evidently a virtual space whose locus is neither in the psyche of the writer nor yet outside it. It is a space of mediation in which what I write, no matter what intention or fantasy it may seem designed to express, is echoed back to me transformed. It may be even an experience of historical alienation, the manifestation in my 'inmost' speech of the social within or behind the individual. This effect is all the stronger given that literature, unlike some of the fine arts, has an irreducible referential dimension, one necessary even to the most concrete of concrete poems. The two-dimensional space of the page takes on inevitably and at once a 'three-dimensional' effect. Valéry refers to the act of composition as a kind of excavating, of trying to get at something beneath the surface of the words and of gaining access somehow to the space of possibilities upon which the page opens as a window.[25]

In modern poems that exploit the very layout of the page to structure the aesthetic and cognitive resonance of words, the blank page becomes a true descendent of the archaic muse, not a dictating voice which grants fluency and confidence, but an enabling space of different interacting frames of possibility. One only has to start experimenting with variant line-endings of William Carlos Williams's 'Red wheelbarrow' to see this.[26] Again, the effect is of a phantasmatic agent or agencies at work. Robert Pickering, writing of Valéry, refers to the page as 'the changing locus for experimentation and potentialization, the theatre for the coursing energies which make it vibrant with a sense of becoming'.[27] The invention of the typewriter may be the crucial material condition of these notions. In this case, unlike the muse or the Romantic imagination, the merely figurative status of the blank page as a creative agency is obvious – no one credits a piece of paper with 'coursing energies' and 'becoming'. The emptiness is vibrant as the place of intersection of the writer's intentionality with multiple possibilities of reading. The empty page is full of a sense of potential because it is really already a crowded page.

'Crowded', yes, but no-one is speaking. The language of dispossession and *ecstasis* is justified by the fact that there is a purely textual effect, an enunciation without a subject. The 'I' of 'I fell in love with a girl' seems to speak – to its own author – from out of a non-empirical space. The text projects or performs its own act of utterance: the utterer of 'I fell in love with a girl' is speaking from out of a non-existent place. The 'I' here cannot be called a persona or an implied author since these denote strategies of manipulation employed upon readers by writers. The phantasmatic scene of utterance, however, is an inevitable effect, encountered passively. It may come from an unforeseen direction, cutting across a writer's plans, or drawing them another way. A new event may emerge in the phantasmatic act of utterance, one that (to use Benveniste's formula for the performative) 'is the event because it *creates* the event'.[28]

Subjectivity, intentionality, language and codes of reading and interpretation are coimplicated in a space whose temporality is non-linear and discontinuous in ways that can sometimes lead to surprising, incalculable effects: 'The experience [of revelation in poetry] is given as a naming of that which, until it is named, properly lacks existence' (Octavio Paz).[29] For example: the chance addition of one word to an incomplete sentence, stanza or line may – just before it is almost crossed out – alter the possible orientation of the whole in which it appears, projecting simultaneously a new vector in the work's future becoming, one which, in turn, may perhaps alter the beginning in an exciting way. Even the very last sentence of a work can do this. The space of composition is 'chaotic' in the strict sense: a field all of whose parameters interact in ways that are both incalculable and also susceptible to surprising changes of state as a result of minute or unpredictable factors.

An act that says more or otherwise than was anticipated may transform in turn, however minutely, the subject of enunciation. Inspiration may give a sense of release, of ease and dispossession – something else is doing the work – as complex effects of non-personal agency interact with and reinforce a writer's personal desire, intention or fantasy. Subjective intentions may become increasingly an effect of the very material that may have seemed to be their object. The subject of enunciation is a multiply contaminated one: the source of the work is neither a commanding conscious intentionality, nor the impulses and drives of the somatic or the unconscious, nor the structures and constraints of the discourse at issue, but the temporary and incalculable co-working of all these factors in a non-linear space that, at its most extreme, may be experienced by the writer as a reversal of cause and effect.

Composition is often described as a form of reverie.[30] A dream-like easing of repression is achieved through the willing distractedness of consciousness, surrendered to the fluctuating woof of the text. Nevertheless, analogies with the dream state can be misleading. In so far as the space of composition embraces the ventriloquial effects of received literary codes and their constraints, as well as the exigencies of an individual fantasy-life, then *the agent or subject of composition cannot be simply identified with the empirical subject.* To make such an identification is the main fallacy of psychoanalytic theories of inspiration.[31] The *copia* or heightened fluency of inspiration remain *sui generis* as a psychic/textual state. The following account from Pasternak, though extreme, is only an intensification of the paradoxy of E. M. Forster's 'How do I know what I think until I see what I say':[32]

> After two or three stanzas and several images by which he himself was astonished, his work took possession of him and he experienced the approach of what is usually called inspiration. At such moments the correlation of forces controlling the artist is, as it were stood on its head. The ascendency is no longer with the artist or the state of mind he is struggling to express, but with the language, his instrument of expression. Language, the home and dwelling of beauty and meaning, itself begins to think and speak for man, and turns wholly into music, not in the sense of outward, audible sounds but by virtue of the power and momentum of the inward flow. Then, like the current of a mighty river polishing stones turning wheels by its very movement, the flow of speech creates in passing, by the force of its own laws, rhyme and rhythm and countless other forms and formations, still more important and until now undiscovered, unconsidered and unnamed.[33]

Such effects may be a condition of the sense felt by writers that their emergent text is taking on a 'life' or 'will' of its own. Consider the following passage from Dan Jacobson's *The Beginners* (1966):

> It was extraordinary, he said, the change that had taken place in his feeling about the work. A fortnight ago he'd felt like a man with a

flat tire and a pump in his hand; he had simply been pumping away, almost mechanically. But now there was nothing mechanical about what he was doing: he had to be alert, cautious, obedient to the demands that he could feel the work wanted to make of him. For the first time he'd realized that this was the 'escape' which his work offered and which people talked about without knowing what they meant by it. Once escaped from oneself, one submitted oneself to an impersonal will. And it didn't matter that the will had originated in oneself. Once it had reached a certain degree of detachment its existence was as objective as any other – at least as objective as all the other wills whose reality people never questioned, but which were also projections of themselves: the will of the state, or the will of industry, or the will of God.[34]

Jacobson draws on the language of organicism. He even recalls Coleridge's classic distinction between the organic (as possessing an inner teleology directing the form of the emergent work in a movement of self-realization) and the mechanical (in which the work is shaped 'from without' by a will acting upon it intransigent to its inherent finality). Such naturalizing language is recurrent in accounts of the process of composition, not just in notions of the work's 'growing', or possessing an alien will, or of a novel's characters somehow taking over their own plot etc., but also in such minutiae of expression as that of not looking at a manuscript for some time in order to allow it to 'mature' or become 'ripe'. Since Plato's *Symposium*, a common image for composition has been that of pregnancy and gestation, arguably sometimes as a male would-be appropriation of natural female creativity.[35] Another image is the ancient topos of composition as a voyage or seafaring.[36] Almost ubiquitous, however, though ignored by critics, is recurrent imagery that associates composition with fighting and the energies of battle. Along with images of the author as father, these metaphorical investments in the creative tend to appropriate its authority in masculinist terms.

Inspiration as a psychic chiasmus

I come to the second abstractable factor in accounts of inspiration: that of a transformation of the psyche, of a metamorphosis of identity. Again, since it is a matter of an encounter between psyche and text that must engage different kinds of ambition, personal fantasy and social context in every case, these orientations limit themselves, as before, to certain generalizable features of the process of composition.

In his survey of the failure of modern individualistic psycho-logical theories of creativity Mihaly Csikszentmihalyi observes that the question 'what is creativity?' might be better replaced with the question '*Where* is creativity?'[37] Maurice Blanchot sees this question as the very difficulty of the writer in front of the empty page:

> from his very first step, Hegel virtually says, a person who wishes to write is stopped by a contradiction: in order to write, he must have the talent to write. But gifts, in themselves, are nothing. As long as he has not yet sat down at his table and written a work, the writer is not a writer and does not know if he has the capacity to become one. He has not talent until he has written, but he needs talent in order to write.[38]

The space of composition may be an encounter with what might be called a *phantasmatic author*, i.e. that transformed sense of identity that arises from interaction with the various phantasmatic agencies at work in the space of composition. It is recorded of Keats that

> he has often not been aware of the beauty of some thought or expression until after he has composed and written it down. It has then struck him with astonishment – and seemed rather the produc-tion of another person than his own.[39]

A phantasmatic agent, the 'another person' in Keats's account, is constructed in a specular movement in which consciousness encounters an image of 'itself' as read, or as seemingly reflected back from others. A phantasmatic figure or power seems to become the very source of the emergent work, whether this is constructed as one's skill when aided by a 'muse', possession by some inscrutable facet of one's mind, surrender to 'negative capability' (as for Keats) or, as for Wordsworth, a 'true' self. The transformed identity 'known' in inspiration is not then the self as the subject of self-expression which might precede the act of writing or the gift of 'voice' in inspiration but a textual effect, a place or instance of writing.

A study can be made of how different poets and writers confront and conceptualize the phantasmatic agency in inspiration, a figure as unreal as it is often powerful. Some writers may not always take profound notice of these effects – Woolf employs a recurrent and mildly facetious terminology from horse riding, of having a gallop or taking fences.[40] For others, the space of compo-sition as a scene of encounter with this phantasmatic agency, however interpreted or constructed, is at the centre of their very self-conception as writers and the vocation of writing itself. Little can be more vital to writers than their relation to their seeming sources of power. To a qualified degree, one can assert that arguably the most important literary movements of the nineteenth and twentieth centuries, namely Romanticism and Surrealism respectively, base themselves on the promises that seem to beckon from cultivating a relationship with these seemingly mysterious sources of power. Modern women writers have drawn strength from constructing inspiration in terms drawn from naturalizing analogies between composition and giving birth. The muse has also been refigured as an image of feminine authority.[41] For Milton in *Paradise Lost*, the favour of the heavenly muse, seen as a sign of divine grace, was bound up with the very question of personal salvation. Led 'upwards' by Urania, the poet's sense of transport, exaltation and (implicitly) of election, can also become one of fear:

> Least from this flying Steed unrein'd (as once
> *Bellerophon*, though from a lower Clime)
> Dismounted, on the Aleian Field I fall
> Erroneous there to wander and forlorn.
>
> (VII, ll. 17–20)

'Fall' and 'error' are terms that need not be further emphasized in an epic or the Fall of Man.[42] Less extreme than Milton, Wordsworth sees his relation to these states of empowerment as one to his 'true self', located both backwards in childhood and forwards in the poet he may become. ... But let us not anticipate later chapters.

This brings us to consider why traditional Romantic and post-Romantic notions of the imagination or creativity will not do in trying to understand what happens in the space of composition. This space is potentially transgressive: it skews distinctions of inner and outer, conception and reception. It is a place of unlocatable agencies, with their effects of surprise or disappointment, agencies that skew seeming boundaries between self and other, act and passivity, paralysis and gift. Writers have often referred, with varying degrees of seriousness, to the mediations of a muse – as a liminal figure presiding unpredictably over the genesis of a text or oral composition. Oddly, this reference to an ambiguously external agency may be more accurate, despite its mystification, than the Romantic reference of all the active forces at play in composition to the writer's 'Imagination'. Coleridge writes in *Biographia Literaria*:

intuitively will [the poet] know, which differences of style it [the
excitement produced by the very act of poetic composition] at once
inspires and justifies; what intermixture of conscious volition is
natural to that state; and in what instances such figures and colors
of speech degenerate into mere creatures of an arbitrary purpose of
cold technical artifices ... Could a rule be given from *without*,
poetry would cease to be poetry, and sink into a mechanical art ...
The *rules* of the IMAGINATION are themselves the very powers
of growth and production.[43]

Coleridge's organicism provides one of the most exalted idealizations of the act of composition in secular Western thought – an
idealization painfully at odds with Coleridge's actual practice:[44] it
enacts a principle of creativity (the 'Imagination') that supposedly
reconciles inner and outer, subject and object, freedom and necessity, impulse and purposiveness. The term 'organic' in Coleridge's
thinking is not a metaphor. He derives from German thinkers such
as A. W. Schlegel and F. W. J. Schelling the notion of the work of
art as manifesting a hidden productivity, also at work in nature but
present in human genius in its highest form. Creativity is thus
valorized as the self-knowledge of a transcendental subjectivity, as
an opening of the finite ego to modes of the divine and infinite.
Even writers ignorant of German idealism tend, writing of inspiration, to produce what read like detached fragments of
Naturphilosophie.

This Romantic idealization arises partly on the basis of an
internalization of all the constraints and forces playing across the
space of composition. These become reified or misconstrued as a
process referred totally to the individual mind, rather than to a
complex event that plays, in multiple ways, across the space
between self and other. The writer's sense of a certain force of auto-
genesis in an emergent text, read on the basis of this presupposition,
is then credited to a mysterious faculty of mind. Such an idealization of creativity thus seems credible mainly on the basis of a fallacy
about the nature of meaning: that language means because it is the
making-outward of an idea *in* the mind.[45] Hence for Coleridge:
'Poetry is purely *human* – all its materials are *from* the mind, and all
the products are *for* the mind.'[46] Inspiration thus comes to seem an
inner *dynamis*, not an *ecstasis* in which individual intentions may be
an effect of the space of composition. Harding, whose analysis relies
on an idea of the 'natural' workings of the creative mind in composition, commits a similar fallacy of total internalization.

Transcendental models of subjectivity offer an attractive way of conceptualizing the more striking effects of the space of composition, not as the workings of an external agency but as the manifestation of hidden 'depths' of the mind, depths that might also be accessible perhaps in dreams or through experiments with drugs. This mystification tends to deprive the work of art its status as a cultural product. It is taken to embody a privileged mode of consciousness that overcomes Cartesian dualism. The poem comes to be read in relation to some mysterious faculty of 'creativity', testimony to a union between the mind and some more universal principle of life, a lost human possibility to which writers have access in a heroic *katabasis* into the psyche – the artist as possessor of a unique power that may hold the key even to the underworld. This Romantic Orphism remains the dominant way in which poets have tried to understand inspiration. Again and again writers have searched for some mysterious technique or hidden faculty of mind with the rhetorical properties traditionally ascribed to inspiration – that of a creative *fiat* that somehow guarantees its own overwhelming power and value in the eyes of others. Wolfgang Lange, in readings of Poe, Baudelaire, Hölderlin, Clemans Brentano, Flaubert, Rimbaud and others, has shown how the notion of a deliberately contrived or calculated delirium was at the centre of creative practice throughout the nineteenth century.[47] Hence also Coleridge's attempt to link the composition of 'Kubla Khan' to the mysteries of the dream process, H.D.'s notion of the 'womb brain' or Henri Michaux's experiments with mescaline. The work of Octavio Paz is a more recent instance of this would-be secularized Orphism (see chapter 9).[48]

A final decisive factor structuring the space of composition for a writer is the possible stance towards an audience available in his or her culture, whether this be that of the writer as humble artisan or as divine magus. Let us imagine that during composition, or even while otherwise engaged, something occurs to the writer that has sufficient force to take the writer – as reader – by surprise. The excitement, force and sense of power here may be understood to be the writer's sense of, or even conscious anticipation of, the possible impact of the emergent text on a notional or ideal audience of his or her day (to which, as reader, the writer also belongs). Inspiration here may be described as a chiasmatic structure in which the scene of composition is already a prolepsis of reception, a scene in which the writer recognizes in his or her emergent material such apparent force that it seems to be coming from another and to be part of a work which is somehow both already-read and also yet to emerge. The work thus announces itself as a certain compulsion-to-be. It is as if the emergent text were a quotation from a possible work that the writer must try to realize – 'a dim cloud of an idea which I feel must be condensed into a shower of verse' (Spender; quoted above). The force and excitement with which the text or voice is 'heard' may stem from the fact that, in recognizing something that seems of value in what is emerging, the writer is already, at the work's very inception, projected into a scene of its reception, undergoing, in anticipation, a sense of the potential force of the emergent work upon the readers of his or her time and the publicly-sanctioned identity or role that accompanies such a relation to an audience. It is perhaps a short step from Dickens's being excitedly possessed by the voices of his characters and the impulse of his writing (and even trying out faces in the mirror)[49] to Dickens as the actual performer-out-loud of his texts to massed audiences all over the country.[50]

What a writer may perceive as a potential power or transformed self must depend upon possible relations to an audience. Inspiration may be experienced as the bestowal of a seeming identity arising not only from the actual work, but from the complex chiasmatic structure of anticipation and projection, a something 'evermore about to be' that empowers the writer in the emergent work. For Romantic and post-Romantic writers the image of the writer as hero, sage or prophet, or as an initiate into mysteries of creativity, becomes the compelling way of presenting what is undergone in the space of composition. 'Image' here should be understood in the sense of Lacan's imaginary, viz. as a fantasy of identification with an image of control, reflected back from others and which serves to deny and repress a sense of fragmentation and powerlessness. The sense of simultaneous empowerment and dispossession in inspiration may partly come from this peculiar temporal structure in which the writer identifies with an imaginary audience, readership or posterity as the ground of value, even as the feeling that the emergent words are already elsewhere also makes this a scene in which agency and authorship are experienced as uncertain.[51]

What then of the received wisdom that, when inspired, writers are 'filled with an unaccountable power which enables them *to create not only more easily but better than at any other time*' (Maurice Bowra; emphasis added)?[52] This description accords with what many writers claim to have experienced. However, there is a questionable notion of causality at work here: inspiration is said to *cause* enhanced creativity. Bearing in mind the complex temporality of the space of composition, a more plausible explanation would be that any transformed state of mind accompanies or follows the emergent words and the sense of proleptic reception that they produce. That is to say that any emergent material that seems of a quality to trigger some sense of anticipation, the corroborating of personal fantasy, intention or ambition, will necessarily be accompanied by a sense of ease and confidence. The crucial affective dimension of inspiration, I believe, should be characterized in privative terms, i.e. as the removal of blocking agents.[53] There may be a release from inhibitions, possibly accompanied by a sense of speed or of being overwhelmed by all the emergent possibilities that proliferate in the space of composition.

Other emotional states that accompany the sense of proleptic reception and released inhibition must vary from writer to writer. At its most intense inspiration may bear comparison to aspects of states of ecstasy studied by psychoanalysts of religious experience, states constituting a regression to an infantile sense of seeming total self-repletion and omnipresence, the sense of objectlessness or fusion known in the earliest stages of involvement with the mother, before any differentiation of self and object.[54] This seems to be a crucial feature of Rousseau's experience, triggered by the conception of his prize-winning discourse on the effects of the sciences and the arts. At the same time, however, inspiration may involve, as well as intense regression, both that release of inhibition and also, paradoxically, that sense of ego expansion that accompanies an excited anticipation of fulfilled ambition:

> If ever anything resembled a sudden inspiration, it was the commotion which began in me as I read this. All at once I felt myself dazzled by a thousand sparking lights, crowds of vivid ideas thronged into mind with a force and confusion that threw me into unspeakable agitation. I felt my head whirling in a giddiness like that of intoxication. A violent palpitation oppressed me; unable to walk for difficulty of breathing, I sank under one of the trees of the avenue, and passed half an hour there in such a condition of excitement that when I arose I saw that the front of my waistcoat was all wet with tears, though I was wholly unconscious of shedding them. Ah, if ever I could have written a quarter of what I saw and felt under that tree, with what clearness should I have brought out all the contradictions of our social system ...[55]

More common, however, seems to be a less extreme sense of release and empowerment, manifest in a sense of the ubiquity of thought. This may be found in Wordsworth, Dickens or, more recently, in Jules Supervielle: 'the feeling that I am everywhere at the same time, in space as well as in the various recesses of the heart and the mind.'[56] The experience of empowerment and enhanced fluency can seem contradictory and elusive, as is witnessed by the masculine myth of the fickle muse. It may juxtapose a sense of futural achievement with a sense of insecurity and urgency, for without intense labour the work that already somehow exists may never yet be at all. Inspiration is not only, for the writer, a proleptic sense of what he or she might become, but also a frustrating confrontation with what could have been, as the work reveals itself repeatedly in the role of just having vanished: 'when composition begins, inspiration is already on the decline'.[57] Frustration and aggressivity are never far away, as is witnessed by Dickens's furious forty-mile walks or the recurrent complaint of writers that composition makes them ill.

Of course, the excitement of anticipation in inspiration must, in itself, be fantasy. An element of narcissism, however, is not always so apparent as it is in the following extract from Woolf's *The Waves*, dramatizing a young man's interior speech:

> Boats float past, through the red, through the green ... Oh, I am in love with life ... Now begins to rise in me the familiar rhythm; words that have lain dormant now lift, now toss their crests, and fall and rise, and fall and rise again. I am a poet, yes. Surely I am a great poet. Boats and youth passing and distant trees, 'the falling fountains of the pendant trees'. I see it all. I feel it all. I am inspired.[58]

Woolf's sketch is a mildly satirical one. It recalls the classic satire on male creativity as a destructive fantasy of power, the account in Mary Shelley's *Frankenstein* of Victor Frankenstein's conception of the monster, an egotistical appropriation of natural (female) creative power in which he anticipates becoming as a god to a new race of creatures. These satirical sketches of inspired men may underline the difficulties that the possibility of feeling 'inspired' may have represented for women in the past. Seán Burke writes that 'It would scarcely be an exaggeration to say that the struggles of feminism have been primarily a struggle for authorship – understood in the widest sense as the arena in which culture attempts to define itself.'[59] So far in this chapter I have used excerpts from writer's accounts of composition without regard to gender. Both sexes testify to a sense of dispossession and uncertainty of agency during composition. However, it is overwhelmingly among male writers that this sense of composition as a crisis of subjectivity has been recuperable in terms of a stance of inspired, even prophetic authority. Images of women as prophets, on the other hand, have often been marked by an extreme ambivalence and misogyny in our culture.

If inspiration is anything like the model I am suggesting here, it may well not have been available to women for a long time in terms so easily recuperable as a stance of public authority. Unable to foresee recognition or fair reception, and with few socially-sanctioned images of authorship available to her, a woman writing may have experienced not 'poetic fire' but a sense of blockage, a sense of dispossession but not necessarily of empowerment, as with the account from George Sand quoted earlier.[60] Such a sense of being possessed by some 'external' power may be experienced as a form of rape.[61] The woman writer may even have been swayed to interpret this in terms of lack of talent or ability, or in terms of the supposed inferiority of women. Alternatively, she may resort, like 'George Eliot' or 'Currer Bell' to writing under a male pseudonym, finally finding perhaps, as did Mary Ann Evans, that to be ventriloquized by such a persona becomes necessary in order to able to write with fluency.

More recently, as public life has become less exclusively the rule of men, the discourse of inspiration has become one of genuine empowerment for women, i.e. a source of publicly recognised authority. Marguerite Duras argues that 'The writing of women is really translated from the unknown: 'I know that when I write ... I let something take over inside me that probably flows from my femininity ... everything shuts off – the analytical way of thinking, thinking inculcated by college, studies, reading, experience ... It's as if I were returning to a wild country.'[62] Duras gives what is recognisably still a Romantic notion of inspiration as the release of a hitherto suppressed potential. In its overt emphasis on inspiration as transgressive of received discourse, her account is also close to thinking in modern French feminism. Helène Cixous, Luce Irigaray and Julia Kristeva, in their different ways, affirm a mode of writing that transgresses what is seen as the linear rationality of patriarchal language in favour of a fluid, pre-Oedipal or non-logical 'feminine' or sexually unmarked form of language. They recover its potentially transgressive force as a public stance of rejection of certain dominant modes of discourse, as an affirmation of the bodily or material against the patriarchal valorization of instrumentalist forms of consciousness. This is to rewrite radically the ancient discourse of inspiration, redeploying the sexualized metaphorics of creativity in liberating ways. By providing one way in which a woman writer can affirm herself in the space of composition, effects of dispossession become affirmable as a form of *public* empowerment – another variant of the traditional paradox of inspiration.

More problematic, however, is the attempt, in the work of Cixous and Irigaray, to trace such transgressive effects to female physiology. As Domna C. Stanton writes of a related valorization of the 'maternal' as a mode of discourse, such notions are best seen in terms of an enabling mythology, one which undoes the masculinist bias of dominant metaphors of creativity.[63] The woman's body here becomes a late addition to the list of mysterious sources of creativity in the Romantic-idealist tradition (see chapter 7).

Notes

1 This includes many of the one hundred and fifty or so writers, mainly from the twentieth century, whose testimonies I have worked through for this general chapter.

2 Sue Woolfe and Kate Grenville, *Making Stories: How Ten Australian Novels were Written* (St Leonards, New South Wales: Allen and Unwin, 1993).

3 'Social Discourse or Authorial Agency?: Bridging the Divide between Editing and Theory', unpublished paper, The Australian Defence Force Academy, p. 11.

4 Compare also Richard Ederhart in *The Writer's Mind: Interviews with American Authors*, 3 vols, ed. Irv. Broughton (Fayetteville and London: University of Arkansas Press, 1989), I, 218; Thornton Wilder in *Writers at Work: The* Paris Review *Interviews*, ed. George Plimpton, 1st series (New York: Viking, 1958), p. 96.

5 Walter J. Ong, *Orality and Literacy: The Technologizing of the Word* (London: Routledge, 1988), p. 26.

6 'La Littérature ventriloque,' *Poétique*, 18 (1987), 431–42, p. 440.

7 *Writers at Work: The* Paris Review *Interviews*, ed. George Plimpton, 4th series (New York: Viking,1976), p. 315.

8 See Mike Rose, *Writers' Block: The Cognitive Dimension* (Edwardsville and Carbondale: Southern Illinois University Press, 1984), p. 4.

9 *The Space of Literature* [1955], trans. Ann Smock (Lincoln: University of Nebraska Press, 1982), pp. 23–4.

10 'Ventriloquism: Ecstatic Exchange and the History of the Artwork', *Journal of Aesthetics and Art Criticism*, 51 (1993), 389–98, p. 394.

11 A note of caution. Derrida has complained of the dangers of conflating empirical writing with what he terms 'archi-writing'. In this essay, however, the empirical act of composition *is* given an existential privilege as a mode of conceiving the effects of what Derrida was later to term

différance. The 'anguish' of writing, we read, is 'not [essentially] an empirical modification or state of the writer' ('Force and Signification', in *Writing and Difference*, trans. Alan Bass (Chicago: University of Chicago Press, 1978), 3–30, p. 9). I replace the word 'essentially' (*essentiellement*) omitted from the published translation. Derrida's choice of 'anguish' retains a privileged relation between that state of mind and the more essential non-experiential 'anguish' of writing.

12 Derrida, 'Force and Signification', p. 10.

13 *The Creative Process: A Symposium*, ed. Brewster Ghiselin (Berkeley: University of California Press, 1952), p. 132

14 *A Writers' Diary*, ed. Leonard Woolf (London: Hogarth Press, 1954), p. 159.

15 John Ashbery, 'Pourquoi Écrivez-vous?', *Libération*, March 1985, p. 47.

16 *Writers at Work: The* Paris Review *Interviews*, ed. George Plimpton, 3rd series (New York: Viking, 1967), pp. 69–72.

17 My argument takes issue with the model of the act of writing as a recursive cognitive process dominant in studies of composition and 'rhetoric' in the U.S. For a related critique, see Marilyn M. Cooper, 'The Ecology of Writing', *College English*, 48 (1986), 364–75, p. 366. For a survey of theories of composition directed towards the mainly expository wiiting of composition classes see Lynn Faigley, 'Competing Theories of Process: A Critique and a Proposal', *College English*, 48 (1986), 527–42.

18 See also, for example, Joan Didion, *Women Writers at Work: The* Paris Review *Interviews*, ed. George Plimpton (New York: Viking, 1989), p. 330; John Steinbeck, *Writers at Work*, 4th series, p. 197.

19 Jonathan Culler, *Structuralist Poetics: Structuralism, Linguistics and the Study of Literature* (London: Routledge and Kegan Paul, 1975), pp. 161–3.

20 See Maurice Blanchot, *The Sirens' Song*, trans. Sacha Rabinovitch (Sussex: Harvester, 1982), p. 67.

21 In Ghiselin, *The Creative Process*, p. 118. Compare also Alan Tate in *The Writer's Mind*, I, 58; Ghiselin, *ibid.*, p. 151. See also the accounts of inspiration as conception in chapter 1 of John Press, *The Fire and the Fountain: An Essay on Poetry* (1955; London: Methuen, 1966).

22 See Robert P. Crease, 'The Improvisational Problem', *Man and World*, 27 (1994), 181–93.

23 See Bill Readings, *Introducing Lyotard: Art and Politics* (London: Routledge, 1991), p. xxxi.

24 Lilian Hellman in *Women Writers at Work*, p. 143.

25 Robert Pickering, 'Writing and the Page: Rimbaud, Mallarmé, Valéry', *Modern Language Review*, 87 (1992), 56–71. For a reading of some latent sexual dynamics in the image of the 'virgin' page see Susan Gubar, '"The Blank Page", and Issues of Female Creativity', in *Writing and Sexual Difference*, ed. Elizabeth Abel (Brighton: Harvester Press, 1982), pp. 73–93.

26 Williams, *Selected Poems*, ed. Charles Tomlinson (London: Penguin, 1976), p. 57.

27 Pickering, 'Writing and the Page', p. 71.

28 Emile Benveniste, *Problèmes de linguistique générale* (Paris: Editions Gallimard, 1966), p. 273.

29 Octavio Paz, *The Bow and The Lyre*, trans. Ruth L. C. Simmons, 2nd edn (Austin: University of Texas Press, 1967), p. 140.

30 The association of dreams and hidden, perhaps prophetic, powers of mind is ancient, but two anecdotes overshadow post-Enlightenment attempts to harness dreams for the purposes of enhanced individual creativity: Coleridge's dubious account of the composition of 'Kubla Khan' and the violinist Giuseppe Tartini's supposed pact with the devil to create his *Devil's Sonata* in his sleep. For more detailed accounts see Jennifer Ford, *Coleridge on Dreaming: Romanticism, Dreams and the Medical Imagination* (Cambridge: Cambridge University Press, 1997); Tony James, *Dreams, Creativity, and Madness in Nineteenth-Century France* (Oxford: Clarendon Press, 1995).

31 See the section on inspiration in Ernst Kris, *Psychoanalytic Explorations in Art* (New York: International Universities Press, 1952). Kris, like Freud, cannot finally account for the difference between the product of an artist and the fantasies of a neurotic. My own theory incorporates the element of a writer's anticipating the effects of the emergent work upon others. However, no psychological state in itself ensures the worth of its products. The plurality of the space of composition also contradicts the simplistically bipolar structure of Harold Bloom's notion of creative power as the 'repression' of a precursor text. See his *The Anxiety of Influence; A Theory of Poetry* (New York: Oxford University Press, 1973).

32 Quoted by Saul Bellow in *Writers at Work*, 3rd series, p. 184. According to Forster, the creative state lets down 'buckets into the subconscious. It does not conceive in sleep, or know what it has said after it has said it. Think before you speak is criticism's motto; speak before you think creation's.' *Two Cheers for Democracy* (1951; London: Edward Arnold, 1975), p. 112.

33 Boris Pasternak, *Dr. Zhivago* (London: Collins, 1961), p. 427. My thanks to Richard Lansdowne for drawing my attention to this passage and also the one from Jacobson that follows.

34 Dan Jacobson, *The Beginners* (New York: Macmillan, 1966), p. 146.

35 Nina Auerbach responds to Sandra M. Gilbert and Susan Gubar's analysis of metaphors of literary paternity: there is 'an equally timeless and, for me, even more oppressive metaphorical equation between literary creativity and childbirth', review of *The Madwoman in the Attic, Victorian Studies*, 23 (1980), p. 506. However, by the early twentieth century, the notion of the 'womb' of creativity, given more than metaphorical status by vitalist thought, could cause problems for male writers. See Helen Sword, *Engendering Inspiration: Visionary Strategies in Rilke, Lawrence and H.D.* (Ann Arbor: University of Michigan Press, 1995).

36 See E. R. Curtius, *European Literature and the Latin Middle Ages*, trans. Willard R. Trask (London: Routledge and Kegan Paul, 1953), pp. 128–30.

37 'Society, Culture, and Person: A Systems View of Creativity', in *The Nature of Creativity*, ed. Robert J. Sternberg (Cambridge: Cambridge University Press, 1988), pp. 325–39, p. 325.

38 'Literature and the Right to Death', in *The Gaze of Orpheus and Other Literary Essays*, trans. Lydia Davis (New York: Station Hill, 1981), p. 23.

39 Hyder E. Rollins, *The Keats Circle: Letters and Papers, 1816–1878*, 2 vols

(Cambridge, Mass.: Harvard University Press, 1948), I, p. 128.

40 See Mary Ann Caws, 'The Conceptions of Engendering: The Erotics of Editing', in *The Poetics of Gender*, ed. Nancy K. Miller (New York: Columbia University Press, 1986), pp. 42–62, 46–50.

41 See Mary K. DeShazer, *Inspiring Women: Reimagining the Muse* (New York: Pergamon Press, 1986).

42 See Walter Schindler, *Voice and Crisis: Invocation in Milton's Poetry*, (Hamben, Connct.: Archon Books, 1984), p. 48.

43 S. T. Coleridge, *Biographia Literaria 1817: Or Biographical Sketches of My Literary Life and Opinions,* 2 vols, ed. James Engell and W. Jackson Bate (Princeton, New Jersey: Princeton University Press, 1983), II, 83–4.

44 See Norman Fruman's account of Coleridge's exaggerated claims about writing when inspired and his concealment of sensual as opposed to would-be transcendental aspects of the imagination, 'Creative Process and Concealment in Coleridge's Poetry', in *Romantic Revisions*, ed. Robert Brinkley and Keith Hanley (Cambridge: Cambridge University Press, 1992), pp. 154–68.

45 For Wittgenstein on this fallacy, see G. P. Baker, *Insight and Illusion: Themes in the Philosophy of Wittgenstein*, rev. edn (Oxford: Clarendon Press, 1986), pp. 129ff.

46 *The Notebooks of Samuel Taylor Coleridge*, 8 vols, ed. Kathleen Coburn (Princeton: Princeton University Press, 1973), III, 4397.

47 Lange, *Der Kalkulierte Wahnsinn: Innenansichten ästhetische Moderne* (Frankfurt: Fischer Taschen, 1992).

48 See also William Oxley, *The Cauldron of Inspiration* (Salzburg: Universität Salzburg, 1983); Ghiselin, *The Writer's Mind*, I, 136. For a broad survey see Walter A. Strauss, *Descent and Return: The Orphic Theme in Modern Literature* (Cambridge, Mass.: Harvard University Press, 1971).

49 See Richard Lettis, '"Hard Work": Dickens in the Writer's Chair', *The Dickensian*, 89 (1993), 5–24.

50 'Self-reading' as a model may account for some of the more peculiar aspects of what is experienced as 'inspiration'. To illustrate this I must allow myself a brief digression into the phenomenology of reading, focusing on Garrett Stewart's *Reading Voices: Literature and the Phonotext* (Berkeley: University of California Press, 1990). Stewart's study offers a revaluation of notions of voice that have been too rapidly caricatured or rejected in the wake of a certain misunderstanding of Derrida's grammatology. What is the 'voice' one hears, silently yet truly, in one's head as one reads? This is not voice understood as the mysterious anthropomorphized origin of the text, but the opposite, signalling the very *destination* of the text in the reading act, its realization in a silent voicing:

> It is because we hear overtones of our voice when reading to, and out of, ourselves – I have argued – that we are tempted to posit a sense, or sanctify a relic, of voice in text. It is because we have an 'articulated' anatomy, upon which are strung vocal chords, that we read in this way, read in our own voice. (p. 137)

Even the internal 'voice' of silent reading is not really silent, the reader of these very words, for example, is hearing them in a sense, or imagining hearing them (the oddness being that there is no difference). The reading voice is, grammatically speaking, akin to a middle voice, between the passive and the active. What one 'hears' – or imagines hearing – is an aphonic voice that is both one's own yet also one in which the text inhabits the reading psyche in a ventriloquizing fashion. The act of reading, while I read, occupies and possesses me, drawing me into the text so that 'there is no stable position left from which an implied I can be said to *have been reading* all along. Literature thus takes (its) place "in" the reader to the exclusion of the existential self' (p. 24).

What has this to do with inspiration? Let us return to Amy Lowell's account – 'Some poets speak of hearing a voice speaking to them, and say that they write almost to dictation ... I do not hear a voice but I do hear words pronounced, only the pronouncing is toneless' (Ghiselin, *The Creative Process*, p. 110). My hypothesis is that the voice which the poet 'hears' is his or her own 'reading' voice, emerging either haphazardly or directly out of the labour and the chances of composition, but 'pronouncing' text that may not have been read anywhere, though echoes and transformations of the previously read must make up the substance of the voice (as Deleuze and Guattari remind us, 'Language in its entirety is indirect discourse' (*A Thousand Plateaus: Capitalism and Schizophrenia*, trans. Brian Massumi. Minneapolois: University of Minnesota Press, 1987), p. 84). This aphonic voice may acquire suddenly an especially 'loud' or inspired quality when it initiates a proleptic sense of reception – the sense of coming-from-elsewhere, or having the force of being quotation from something which one might want to read.

51 It is this 'imaginary' aspect of the contaminated subjectivity of inspiration that prevents any simple identification of it with notions of *jouissance* or Kristeva's notion of the semiotic (i.e. the infusion of received symbolic codes by rhythmic drives of the pre-Oedipal body). Julia Kristeva, *Revolution in Poetic Language*, trans. Margaret Waller (New York: Columbia University Press, 1984).

52 C. M. Bowra, *Inspiration and Poetry* (London: Macmillan, 1955), p. 2.

53 The sense of speed, pressure or sometimes irritability described by writers superficially resembles the state psychologists term 'hypomania'. For a survey of work on hypomania see Aktar Salman Aktar, 'Hypomanic Personality Disorder', *Integrative Psychiatry*, 6 (1988), 37–52. However, inspiration, in the sense of some subjective effects of the psychic and textual in the space of composition, remains *sui generis*, and is, at most, an artificially-induced state of hypomania. Modern research has not validated the traditional association between psychosis and genius: see Albert Rothenberg, *Creativity and Madness: New Findings and Old Stereotypes* (Baltimore: Johns Hopkins University Press, 1990).

54 See Bertram D. Lewin, *The Psychoanalysis of Elation* (New York: The Psychoanalytic Quarterly Inc., 1961), pp. 146–50; also W. W. Meissner, *Psychoanalysis and Religious Experience* (New Haven and London: Yale University Press, 1984), p. 151. Lewin sees states of 'visionary' elation as an extreme reaction to a sense of helplessness – a thesis that correlates well

with the relation between the poetics of inspiration and writers' sense of uncertainty about readership.

55 Requoted from Maria Shrady (ed.), *Moments of Insight: The Emergence of Creative Ideas in the Lives of Great Men* (New York: Harper & Row, 1972), pp. 42–3.

56 Requoted from Joseph Chiari, *Contemporary French Poetry* (1952; rpt. Freeport New York: Books for Libraries Press, 1968), p. 69.

57 *A Defence of Poetry*, in *Shelley's Poetry and Prose*, ed. Donald H. Reiman and Sharon B. Powers (New York: W. W. Norton, 1977), p. 504. Tchaikovsky commented that, 'If that condition of mind which we call inspiration, lasted long without intermission, no artist could survive it', requoted from E. M. Rosamund Harding, *An Anatomy of Inspiration* (Cambridge: W. Heffer & Sons, 1940), p. 12.

58 *The Waves*, ed. James M. Haule and Philip H. Smith (Oxford: Blackwell, 1993), pp. 51–2.

59 *Authorship: From Plato to the Postmodern: A Reader* (Edinburgh: Edinburgh University Press, 1995), p. 145.

60 Nicole Mozet compares the writing practices of George Sand and Balzac: 'everything happens as if George Sand had been obliged to pay for creative force by a violent refusal of femininity' ('Pour une Histoire des Pratiques d'écriture: Peut-on Comparer les Manuscrits de Balzac et ceux de George Sand?', in *Sur la Génétique textuelle*, ed. D. G. Bevan and P. M. Wetherill (Amsterdam; Atlanta, Ga: Ropodi, 1990), pp. 33–53, p. 40). Sandra M. Gilbert and Susan Gubar write of the woman writer that, 'In order to define herself as an author she must redefine the terms of her socialization' (*The Madwoman in the Attic: The Woman Writer and the Nineteenth-Century Imagination* (New Haven and London: Yale University Press, 1979), p. 49).

61 For the sense of inspiration as violent assault see DeShazer, *Inspiring Women*, pp. 30–1; Susan Gubar, '"The Blank Page" and the Issues of Female Creativity', in *Writing and Sexual Difference*, ed. Elizabeth Abel (Sussex: Harvester Press, 1982), pp. 73–93.

62 'From an Interview' [1975], *New French Feminisms*, ed. Elaine Marks and Isabelle de Courtivron (Brighton: Harvester, 1981), pp. 174–5.

63 'Difference on Trial: A Critique of the Maternal Metaphor in Cixous, Irigaray, and Kristeva', in *The Thinking Muse: Feminism and Modern French Philosophy*, ed. Jeffner Allen and Iris Marion Young (Bloomington: Indiana University Press, 1989), pp. 156–79, p. 170.

CHAPTER 2

Enthusiasmos: archaic Greece and Plato's *Ion*

> Everything ... begins in a way as it does in the *Iliad*, with an invo-
> cation of the muse, a call to voice and the desire to give oneself
> over to this speech of the outside that speaks everywhere.
> (Blanchot, *The Infinite Conversation*)

There are two reasons for starting a study of the concept of inspiration in Romantic and post-Romantic writers with a reconsideration
of Plato's *Ion*. This minor dialogue is, along with parts of the
Phaedrus, the *locus classicus* for the notion of artistic inspiration in
Western culture. Secondly, Plato's concern is poetic practice in an
oral tradition – Ion's performance necessarily takes place in the very
presence of his auditors – and the divergence between this practice
and the material technology of modern writing will serve to introduce a point that recurs again and again in this study. This is the
degree to which effects that seem psychic, internal or psychological
are often determined by the material parameters of composition.

The term *enthousiasmos*, translated as inspiration, first appears
gnomically in Fragment 18 of Democritus in the sixth century BC.[1]
In the *Laws* (719c) Plato refers to the notion of a poet's possession
by 'divine madness' as an 'old story'.[2] Oddly, however, there is no
real proof to back up this assertion – the notion of 'madness' only
appears in Democritus by questionable report,[3] '[I]t is impossible to
find in Greek literature before Plato any indisputable proof of the
truth of Plato's assertion.'[4] Moreover the analogy Plato makes
between poetic inspiration and divine madness draws on aspects of
Bacchic maenadism, a cult only known in Greece since the fifth
century. It was also at this period that the cult of Orpheus was
established in Athens.[5]

It is possible, however, to overstate the degree to which the
notion of *furor poeticus* is Plato's invention, part of his tortured rela-

tion to the poetic. If archaic poets do not speak of themselves as divinely insane, they do not depict themselves as in a normal or a detached frame of mind either. What was Plato reacting to?

The greatest gulf between archaic Greece and ourselves is that this was a culture almost without writing. Scholars are still in the process of recognising just how fundamentally different in individual psychology, cultural practices and values an oral society must be compared to a literate one. Without going again over ground covered by Walter Ong, Eric Havelock and others,[6] let us limit ourselves to the specific question of 'literary' production in such a society. How does one compose a poem, not only without writing, but with no sense at all that language might be able to exist in some stable, visible and relatively impersonal form, in something other than in the elusive and time-bound media of sound? Composition, in such circumstances, takes the form of dictating to oneself, of employing skills of memorising and improvising – or making oneself ready to improvise – variant patterns of received formulae acquired through a process of oral training. The poet must give his or her psyche over to voices, to voices overlapping, interacting and weaving themselves together and becoming internalized in the automatism of mnemonic technique.[7]

The Muses in Homer are inseparable from the authority of tradition and memory in an oral tradition. The archaic Greek term for poet is *aoidos* (singer), not the classical *poietes*.[8] Verse, in its capacity of mnemonic, is the very medium of cultural transmission, the sole guarantor of mediation between the ephemeral or immediate and the general life, history and posterity of the community. Verse, in pre-literate Greece, was not only the bearer of epics but of any message of importance. It was used by judges, princes and generals, to ensure maximum transmissibility of a message without loss. In Hesiod's *Theogony* the muse Calliope is an assistant of kings (line 80) as well as poets. Archaic Greek verse, transmitted to us in written form, had no need of writing to ensure its perdurability. The evidence is that the alphabet was introduced in Greece circa 700 BC but that little general use was made of writing until late in the fifth century BC, so strong and effective were the institutions of an oral culture.[9] As the bearers of oral tradition the Muses are the repositories of cultural truth. Havelock goes so far as to describe Homer as being for archaic Greece a sort of cultural encyclopaedia.[10] It was not to be until the establishment of the library at Alexandria that poetry came to be grounded institutionally in the archiving of written texts, in the late fourth and early third centuries BC.[11]

The oral poet, addressing the Muse rather than those auditors immediately in front of him, conjures a situation that at once negates some features of the immediate environment and offers the poem as the result of a double enunciation. The song comes from both the poet and the divinity. It is a situation that seems paradoxical, even self-contradictory, to modern thinking, for no sharp contrast is made in this process between divine agency and human skill (cf. *Iliad* 2, 484, 761; 11, 218; 14, 508; 16; 112; Hesiod, *Theogony* verse 114).[12] It is this paradox that Plato's *Ion* effectively exorcises.

As inhabitants of Olympus and the daughters of Zeus and Mnemosyne, according to Hesiod (*Theogony*, 54), the Muses link the authority of the tales they transmit to the ruling principles of order and authority in the Greek world. The poetic performance is not a matter of 'fiction' in our sense (there is no such word in Greek). Mnemosyne, according to the Homeric *Hymn to Hermes*, is first among the gods (line 429). The poet's cooperation with and partial surrender to the Muses is the guarantee of a truth that transcends poet and auditors, and of the fulfilment of the traditional function of celebrating the gods and the renown of heroes. Without their help, we read in the *Iliad* Book Two, he would be limited to mere report or 'rumour' (*kleos*) and, 'As for the mass of men, I could not tell of them or name them'.[13]

The space of composition, as I argued in the previous chapter, is one of transformation: the 'I' of mundane life becomes the 'I' projected by the discourse, the seeming focus of the novel possibilities of meaning and authority. In archaic oral composition, movement into this space is an explicit crossing of a threshold. This is signalled by such meta-narrative devices as the invocations to the muse.[14] Memory is not primarily an individual faculty in this context, but a function of a communal transformation (so it is dubious to describe the Muses as 'personifications' of a poet's memory). Memory does not call to the mind an image of the past. It names a general transformation that carries poet and auditor to another, co-temporal aspect of reality, the realm of myth, legend, fame – not so much the past as the realm of all meaning *per se*, of all that perdures in the space where the language of cultural self-definition continually speaks itself. The poets are 'masters of the truth' (Marcel Detienne).[15] Jean-Pierre Vernant argues of memory:

> It does not reconstruct the past; nor abolish it either. In overcoming the barrier which separates the present from the past, it throws

a bridge between the world of the living and that beyond to which return all who have quitted the light of the sun. It realises for the past an 'evocation' comparable to that which the Homeric ritual of '*ékklesis*' effects for the dead: the appeal among the living and the coming to the light of day, for a brief moment, of someone deceased, raised up from the infernal world.[16]

Our terms 'knowledge' and 'truth' are rather anachronistic here. The Muses do not transmit knowledge in the sense of objective detachment in relation to a representation whose accuracy they secure. They grant a knowing guaranteed by the poet's affective surrender to the mnemonic legacy, to theatre, and to *mimesis* in the sense of impersonation (see below).

Marcel Detienne's work in this field bears critically on Heidegger's idealization of the Greek word for truth, *aletheia*, as meaning 'unconcealment', affirmed against notions of truth as correct representation, an unconceptualizable realm of a more primordial, phenomenologically fundamental openness to being that is the condition of subjective thought and representation.[17] Certainly *aletheia* is in conflict with the notion of truth as correspondence but, *pace* Heidegger, it names a certain primacy of the performativity of language, not a primordial 'unconcealment' (Detienne, p. 27). It is a performativity that exceeds and conditions subjective thought, not as a primordial phenomenological realm but the agency of the signifier as the basis of a culture whose element is oral mnemonics.[18] *Aletheia*, as the realm of what means and perdures, is a condition for individual subjectivity, yet hardly in Heidegger's sense.

The poet, as first performer of the poem, participates in a quasi-ritual transformation that already embraces the poem's auditors. Movement into the space of composition is a communal event. Joseph Russo and Bennett Simon write of the recitation setting up 'a kind of common "field" ' in which poet, audience and the characters within the poems are all defined, with some blurring of the boundaries that normally separate the three.[19] This blurring appears in the indeterminacy as to the degree to which the poet is being dictated by the Muse or is an active participant, and in the fact that the Muses are also themselves auditors and addressees of the verse, as well as its supposed provenance. Dichotomies of making and receiving, active and passive, cause and effect, first and second, are skewed in the overall transformation that is the poem itself as an unusual form of event.

Oral performance here may be approached through analogy with or as a form of *ecstatic* ritual.[20] The Muses conjure up past, present and future and, by the same token, bring a forgetfulness of self, oblivion of ills and miseries (Hesiod, *Th.* 38, 55, 98ff). Divine memory was equated with human oblivion, an effect which was also held to lend genuine therapeutic qualities to poetry.[21] Plato's *Ion*, in an account of lyric poetry, presents both poet and auditors as taken forcibly out of themselves, voluntarily surrendering to an external compulsion that is the poem's unfolding:

> just as the worshipping Corybantes are not in their senses when they dance, so the lyric poets are not in their senses when they make these lovely lyric poems. No, when once they launch into harmony and rhythm, they are seized with the Bacchic transport, and are possessed – as the bacchants, when possessed, draw milk and honey from the rivers, but not when in their senses. So the spirit of the lyric poet works, according to their own report. (534)

Socrates, and the poets themselves, compare the situation of performance to that of ecstatic ritual. Gorgias the rhetorician uses similar terms.[22] The Corybantian rituals to which Socrates refers did not exist in Greece at Homer's time, yet his epic work also makes recurrent correlations between the power of poetry and song, enchantment and magic.[23] What is striking to the modern reader is the extent to which relations between poet and audience, poem and addressee, are conceived not in terms of imaginary identification or empathy but as modes of power of the one over the other. Song, *aoide*, is closely connected to *ep-aoide*, enchantment.[24] The song of the sirens in the *Odyssey* enacts such *thelxis* or enchantment at its most powerful, acultural and dangerous, combining as they do the height of technical artistry with association with all that is wild, marine and deadly (*Od.* 12, 36–58).[25]

Havelock's reconstruction of the 'Psychology of the Poetic Performance'[26] traces the poem's appeal to and instrumentation of speech rhythms and bodily reflexes; it is both mnemonic and dance ('speaking dance' – a name one finds in Plutarch for one form of poetry, the *hyporcheme*, *Table Talk IX*, 15, 748a). The Muses are dancers as well as singers.[27] The captivation and manipulation of bodily rhythms effects a relaxation of tensions akin to hypnosis and a temporary oblivion of anxieties. Havelock's terminology is from physiology ('motor system', 'motor reflex') and can be supported by more recent work on the physiological transformation undergone in ritual.[28] Havelock reminds us of how far 'thinking' in this context, as a giving oneself up to mnemonics and formulae, is a bodily affair in a way that cuts across familiar dualisms.[29] What would be even

more useful, however, would be an account related to a phenomenology of the process, since this would explicate the experience of
the world projected by the poem, its effects of reference, as well as
its formal properties. Emmanuel Levinas's essay 'Reality and its
Shadow' (1948), while not focused specifically on archaic cultures,
offers one such account. Levinas writes of the transformation of the
psyche in ecstatic ritual as a means of understanding some effects of
rhythm in art in ways directed against some modern conceptions of
the aesthetic:

> The idea of rhythm, which art criticism so frequently invokes but
> leaves in the state of a vague suggestive notion and catch-all, desig-
> nates not so much an inner law of the poetic order as the way the
> poetic order affects us, as a closed whole, whose elements call for
> one another like the syllables of a verse, but do so only insofar as
> they impose themselves on us, disengaging themselves from reality.
> *But they impose themselves on us without our assuming them.*[30]

Levinas is attacking the notion of intentionality in Husserlian
phenomenology and, beyond that, the heritage of the Cartesian
model of subjectivity as an autonomous self-presence standing in a
relation of transcendence and of instrumentalizing opposition to
language or an object world. Poetic practice in archaic Greece
already reads as a practical refutation of such a notion of the subject
as self-standing interiority.[31]

The decisive feature in Levinas's account of rhythm is *reversed
intentionality*, a transformation in which 'we cannot speak of consent,
assumption, initiative or freedom, because the subject is caught up
and carried away' by the situation. It may even seem to become part
of the representation. The experience is *ecstatic*, but in no way is
there an obliteration of consciousness. Rather consciousness
persists, slightly paralysed, as in a waking dream, absorbed in the
transformed realm around it, of which it is but a part, no longer able
to pose as the transcendent consciousness or detached master of the
scene. Relations of 'interior' and 'exterior' are transformed. The
conscious subject:

> is exterior to itself, but with an exteriority which is not that of a
> body, since the pain of the I-actor is felt by the I-spectator, and not
> through compassion. Here we have really an exteriority of the
> inward. It is surprising that phenomenological analysis never tried
> to apply this fundamental paradox of rhythm and dreams, which
> describes a sphere situated outside of the conscious and the uncon-
> scious, a sphere whose role in all ecstatic rites has been shown by

> ethnography; it is surprising that we have stayed with metaphors of 'idea-motor' phenomena and with the study of the prolongation of sensations into actions. (p. 4)

A transitional conclusion presents itself: 'to be inspired' in its archaic Greek context means to enter voluntarily into a shared transformation of language, action and individual psychology that embraces both performer and audience. This transformation is signalled, and occasionally reinforced, by use of such liminal language as invocation to the Muses or to some other presiding deity. The transformation is akin in some respects to the experience of ecstatic ritual and is vehicled by a modulation of language into chant or *mousike*. The effect is that the poem has a double scene of enunciation, both human and divine. It enacts and seems to confirm an anti-humanist model of subjectivity as a heteronomy. It may enact a disorientation of seeming distinctions between self and other, hearing and reciting, past and present, mythical and mundane. However, this enchantment is not without its dangers. Poetic power is open to abuse. Ideally, however, this power is seen as supportive of the poem's fidelity to supposed real events, the truths of myth, and the celebration of the renown of heroes.

Let us move now some generations forward to a poem by Sappho, her first fragment, the so-called 'Hymn to Aphrodite', with these conclusions in mind. This will lead us into Plato on inspiration:

> Immortal Aphrodite, elegant daughter
> Of Zeus, goddess of guile, I pray to you
> Do not, my lady, break my heart with sufferings,
>
> But come to me, if once before you heard
> My voice from afar, and listened to my speech,
> And left your father's house and yoked your car
>
> And came. Beautiful, lightning – swift they were,
> The sparrows that drew you over the black earth,
> With wheeling wings, from heaven through the fiery air.
>
> Suddenly they were here. But you, my lady,
> Turned on me your immortal face and smiled,
> And asked, why was I calling you again, and what
>
> Was my complaint and what did I have in mind
> For my grand passion? 'Who is it now that I
> Must lure into your arms? Who is the culprit, Sappho?

If she's fleeing, soon she'll be in pursuit;
If she is rejecting gifts, she'll be the giver;
If she does not love, soon she will, despite herself.'

Come now again, my lady, and set me free
From anxious troubles, and help me to achieve
The longings of my heart! Be my ally in person![32]

Although we term this a lyric, many of the connotations of this term (not yet established by Sappho's time c. 600 BC) are misleading. The fragment, if it is not indeed a complete poem as many critics think, is a monody, a song to be performed solo for a lyre accompaniment, not like Homer, something recited or chanted.[33] Modern conceptions of lyric would be unhelpful here in projecting on to this text distinctions of public and private, 'inner' and 'outer' that it would be misplaced to assume in this context. Although very little is known about the circumstances of Sappho's compositions, it seems likely that Sappho was a figure of authority in an institute of girls' education of some kind[34] and that poems were part of the adjuncts of a general activity in which all were 'servants of the Muses' as overseers of learning. The voice of the hymn is a choral one. The singer, addressed in the hymn itself as 'Sappho' (line 15), is a solo voice speaking from out of a choral group.[35] A ritual function or origin for the hymn appears in the fact that it is an *epiklesis* in form, an invocation of a deity before a statue of that deity – much of the controversy surrounding the text focuses on the issue of how genuine an *epiklesis* it is, or whether Sappho is not employing a religious form in a context of personal seduction, secularizing it to a degree.[36] It is, nevertheless, an *epiklesis* in the ritual epithets bestowed on the deity, the solemn tone of address and other formal characteristics.

My reading of this hymn concentrates on the words of Aphrodite in response to the poet's invocation: 'Who is it ... now that I / Must lure into your arms? ...' This is what we would nowadays, in our highly literate culture, call a 'quotation'. In Sappho's predominantly oral context, however, it would seem to be a matter of *mimesis* in what is perhaps its oldest sense as impersonation or mimicry (see the *Homeric Hymn to Apollo*, 163; Plato, *Republic*, Bk. 3).[37] This *mimesis* works to a multiple, complex effect. Strictly a repetition of a speech-act that Sappho is recalling from previous occasions, the *mimesis* is so modulated and is of such a length, that for the reader, half-forgetting the original past tense, it becomes an answer to the present invocation too. This effect also intensifies the

47

irony of the goddess, who is in effect saying 'what is it this time?' ('this time' [*deute*] occurs on three occasions). The poem, then, seems to represent its own act of enunciation within itself, yet this hardly makes its status problematic in accordance with the epistemological bind that Hillis Miller calls a 'linguistic moment' – that moment in which the poetic medium, reflexively taking itself as its object, renders itself or its referentiality opaque or problematic.[38] The apparent reflexivity of this text is, on the contrary, the effect of a heteronomic movement that is the opposite of the poem closing upon itself. Instead, the 'reflexive' elements in Sappho's text, its formal properties as well as the use of the words of Aphrodite, signify – along with the whole defining context of performance on the lyre – a metamorphosis of language into a mode akin to ritual action. Sappho's poem, exploiting as it does a speech-act with a self-fulfilling structure in a ritual situation heightened by music, gives itself over to the effect of *reversed intentionality* in which the singer and auditors become partly possessed by the representation. It renders itself a form of charm which one does not need to believe in Aphrodite to appreciate. The pace of the song's opening lines serves to heighten its ritual qualities by depicting the journey in several stages (the goddess leaving the house of Zeus, yoking her chariot ...) drawn out through seven lines to the effect that, exploiting the real time of the performance, the delayed line 'Suddenly they were here' also has the force of an epiphany in the present, as the face of the goddess turns towards the poet. Charles Segal argues that the incantatory rhythm of Sappho's verse seeks 'to create a verbal equivalent to the magnetic, quasi-magical compulsion which the ancient poets called *thelxis*, "enchantment," or *peitho*, "persuasion". The repetitions and recurrent rhythms of the poetic language evoke the magical effect of eros itself; and this "magic" is also the mysterious *peitho* or *thelxis* which the archaic poet undergoes when gripped by the beauty of a young girl.'[39] The words become, produce, or transfer (the structure is complex enough to require all these terms together) a ritual-mimetic emotion that may possess or *en-thuse* those whom it may encounter.

Poetry here is not so much a matter of expressing subjective states or composing fictions as it is of negotiating the fragile divisions between 'self' and 'other', and attempting to exploit that fragility in effects of power, recognition or love, as in the image of *eros* in fragment 112: 'Graceful your figure, sweet your eyes, *eros is poured over your face*. Aphrodite holds you in honour' (emphasis added). The hymn to Aphrodite is partly, it seems, a seduction poem. It ends 'Come now again, my lady, and set me free / From anxious troubles, and help me to achieve / The longings of my heart: Be my ally in person!' It concludes where it began, as if the whole poem were an invocation to its own effect, *and* the effect of this invocation.

Aphrodite is directly invoked to affect the auditors of the poem, in a way the Muses in Homer never are, and this invocation itself becomes the fascination of her power and the enactment of her voice. The penultimate line envisages Aphrodite and Sappho acting together, in concert: 'help me to achieve/ The longings of my heart.'[40] By including her own name in the poem, as she does also in fragments 94 and 65, Sappho identifies with and partially appropriates this power in a way reminiscent of that scene in Hesiod's *Theogony* where the poet describes an encounter in which the Muses both insult his rivals and explicitly name him as their pupil (*Th.* 22–35).

Why need the name matter? Segal suggests that use of the name implies a 'nascent critical attitude', a distance from total absorption in the song.[41] It is also possible that Sappho's use of her own name relates to the growing effect of writing and literacy on the culture of the sixth century. Her poems exploit effects of parallelism in their construction which are only conceivable, Ong suggests (after Berkeley Peabody), in a mind influenced by the new technology of writing and the possibilities of detachment and manipulative control it made available.[42] The long enactment of the journey of Aphrodite, while it recalls accounts of divine journeys in Homer, might be seen as a virtuoso exploitation of effects made possible by the tension between the detachment and longer term control made possible by writing – the use as a pacing device of a relatively complex grammar of subordination over a considerable length of the poem – and the expectations of simple, immediate presentation dominant in a mainly oral culture.[43]

Other aspects of the text back up the view of Sappho as a transitional figure. Jesper Svenbro has recently drawn attention to some peculiar effects that befall personal pronouns when, coming from the oral tradition, the poem is entrusted to writing.

> What happened when the bard's narrative was committed to writing ? I would say that, from the point of view of the speech-act, the *egó* that was pronounced out loud by the bard and that referred to himself was written down so that it could be repronounced by the reader (the reciter of the narrative) who, for his part, could not lay claim for that *egó* despite the linguistic definition

according to which 'the *ego* is the one who says "ego"'. [Benveniste, *Problèmes de linguistique générale*, 1:260]. In truth, transcription produces paradoxes that are sometimes difficult to resolve.[44]

One point here might be that, *pace* Svenbro, these are effects that apply just as well to the oral performance of poems when the performer is no longer the poet in person. A fuller argument might be that Sappho is exploiting, in a still oral situation, effects that may have first become manifest with inscriptions. The effects at issue, though most apparent in written texts, also arise in oral performance by a rhapsode or reciter. Anyone performing Sappho's hymn, including as it does Aphrodite's address to 'Sappho' as speaker of the poem, is in effect being ventriloquized by Sappho with effects of possession and appropriation of voice of just the kind that Svenbro shows at work in early Greek inscriptions.[45] The poem's scene of enunciation becomes one of possession by what the previous chapter called a 'phantasmatic author,' a figure which is an ineluctable textual effect. Unlike Homer, who seems content to remain nameless, Sappho explicitly expects not to be forgotten after her death (*Fr.* 55). The Muses become the bestowers of immortality as well as being immortal themselves. *Mimesis*, in what is perhaps its earliest sense as impersonation, comports a ventriloquizing series that extends through Aphrodite, Sappho, the later performer of the song and, on all occasions, its auditors. The poem enacts a seizure of psychic power oriented towards the future. Pindar's poems, from some generations later, are replete with effects of the bestowal and transference of power of this kind, now on hire to whoever wished to employ the poet's services.[46] Socrates' account, in *Ion*, of the magnetic chain of inspiration that extends from muse to poet to rhapsode to audience, is clearly not an *ad hoc* description thrown up by debate with the recalcitrant Ion:

> As I just now said, this gift you have of speaking well on Homer is not an art; it is a power divine, impelling you like the power in the stone Euripides called the magnet, which most call 'stone of Heraclea.' This stone does not simply attract the iron rings, just by themselves; it also imparts to the rings a force enabling them to do the same thing as the stone itself, that is, to attract another ring, so that sometimes a chain is formed, quite a long one, of iron rings, suspended from one another. For all of them, however, their power depends upon that loadstone. Just so the Muse. She first makes men inspired, and then through these inspired ones others share in the

enthusiasm, and a chain is formed (533 d–e). One poet is suspended from one Muse, another from another; we call it being 'possessed,' but the fact is much the same, since he is *held*. And from these primary rings, the poets, others are in turn suspended, some attached to this one, some to that, and are filled with inspiration, some by Orpheus, others by Musaeus. But the majority are possessed and held by Homer (536 a–b).

It is notable here that poets themselves have now become sources of inspiration for others, as well as being inspired themselves. This passage also bears out how closely the *Ion*, unlike the *Phaedrus*, follows the technics and psychology of composition at this time.

There is no contradiction in a poet in archaic Greece claiming both to be inspired and to possess a genuine technical skill (*Od.* 8, 44–5), as in Sappho's hymn, where they are inseparable. A situation of performance is set up in which the modality of reversed intentionality embraces and seizes the poet, even as he or she is also the partial technician of this *ecstasis*. In Pindar's 'Nemean III' we read 'grant me an abundant flow of song welling from my own thought'.[47] It is in Plato's *Ion* that one meets the argument that *techne* and inspiration are incompatible alternatives. Here too inspiration becomes mere possession and 'divine madness'. In fact, despite the huge influence of the *Ion* on subsequent idealizations of the poet, 'inspiration' in this dialogue is a deeply ambivalent if not downright ironic notion.

The terms of the argument into which Ion the rhapsode is forced by Socrates are these: he can either admit that he is being deceitful when he boasts his knowledge in speaking of Homer or accept that he speaks wholly by divine dispensation (541e, 542). How does Socrates come to work this double-edged compliment, one whose ambiguity was often ignored in subsequent accounts of the poet as inspired?

Ion is a rhapsode, a reciter or performer of poetry, not a poet. The rhapsodes succeeded, or derived from, poets who, like Pindar, both composed and performed their own work. Though rhapsodising is the lesser task it seems to have involved little loss of prestige for the performer.[48] The rhapsode remained master of ceremonies in a ritual event. The rhapsodes not only recited poems to large audiences, they also delivered encomia upon them and provided 'interpretation' or a *belle-lettrist* kind of appreciation. The context would be one of competition between rhapsodes for prizes and honours – Ion has come to Athens to compete in the Panathenaea, having just won first prize at Epidaurus.

The dialogue with Socrates moves elusively between the rhapsode's two activities of recitation and interpretation. Socrates hypothesizes that 'one never could be a rhapsode if one did not comprehend the utterances of the poet, for the rhapsode must become an interpreter of the poet's thoughts to those who listen' (530c). The terms of debate thus slip, almost imperceptibly, from a discussion about the kind of knowledge implicit in the ability to give good performances to the need for knowledge of the topic at issue *in* the performance and thus in the poem itself, e.g. when Homer speaks of the art of the seer or of the doctor who, Socrates asks, is it who has most authority to speak knowledgeably on these matters, a rhapsode like Ion, whose art is confined to reciting and speaking well of Homer, or the practitioners of such arts themselves, the seer and the doctor? Of course, Ion, a thespian as unintelligent as he is conceited, has no answer to such an argument.

Much of *Ion* bears on the problem of what is specific to poetry as a field of skill and a supposed mode of knowledge. Firstly, there is the mystery that Ion's ability as a rhapsode is limited to one poet: 'When anyone discusses any other poet, I pay no attention, and can offer no remark of value. I frankly doze. But whenever anyone mentions Homer, immediately I am awake, attentive, and full of things to say' (532). Ion is a drearily familiar kind of literary specialist. Yet how, Socrates, asks, can it really be possible to speak well of Homer on various topics without being able to discuss those topics themselves in general or even what other poets have had to say about them? Ion knows only the Homeric viewpoint on any topic: 'Like someone who understands the effect of a drug by seeing what it does to every aspect of experience – its distortion of colours, shadows, motion and time – Ion learns about Homer by virtue of misperceiving the world.'[49]

Socrates' theory of inspiration in the *Ion* testifies to the power of the poet and rhapsode. This is never denied. The Muses are invariably objects of respect in Plato and in the *Phaedrus* both poet and the philosopher are said to be divinely mad, though only the philosopher who knows is the most truly 'possessed'. In fact the contrast between the *Ion* and the *Phaedrus* suggests a reading of *enthusiasmos* in Plato in terms similar to those of Derrida's analysis of the doubleness in the term *pharmakon*.[50] In the *Phaedrus* the philosopher is inspired through a vision of beauty and truth that elevates the soul and becomes part of a process of individual growth and aspiration. In the *Ion* on the other hand inspiration is a passive surrender to an exterior voice and the transmission of sensual effects of transport. Socrates elides the fact that poetry and rhapsody are arts in themselves in order to deny that there is any *techne* in the epistemic content of what they are saying.

Havelock's *Preface to Plato* (1963) argues that, in banishing the poets from his republic, barring a few residual functions, Plato's target is the entire mind-set associated with the place of poetry in Greek education, the oral transmission of culture through a mnemonic technique that promulgated impersonation, performance and seduction as the basis of its power and durability – everything I have been comparing to a mode of ecstatic ritual. Plato's use of the word *mimesis* supports this thesis.[51] In *Republic* Book III it refers both to the act of composing a poem and to impersonation, the performance of an actor or a rhapsode. One instance of this last sense is a poet's dramatization of the speech of a figure in a poem as opposed to narration *in propria persona* (the example here is from Homer, though the argument could apply to Sappho's 'quotation'/ impersonation of Aphrodite). In Book 10, however, *mimesis* names more than dramatic impersonation. Now it refers to the whole status of the poetic performance itself (*viz.* more familiarly *mimesis* = imitation = representation). However, there is further semantic slippage here: *mimesis* is also, in this discussion, the lure of personal empathy or identification that draws an audience into a performance and holds them there, spell-bound. In sum, very disparate senses of *mimesis* are at work. Taken together, however, all these seemingly exclusive senses of *mimesis* do demonstrate a common field of reference, the situation of oral performance itself as a scene of, often simultaneously, composition, imitation, impersonation and ecstatic identification.

Havelock ties the development of the possibility of detached rationality in Greece to the progress of literacy. His thesis has been criticized on several points.[52] Nevertheless, his analysis of the term *mimesis* bears helpfully upon the concept of inspiration in the *Ion* and elsewhere (e.g. *Laws* 719c), for it is the effects of poetry upon its auditors that lead Socrates to describe the notion; inspiration is not, despite appearances, an issue primarily of the genesis of poetry, rather of the power, knowledge and authority at work in the poetic performance.

Everything proceeds as if Socrates believed that there was a specific kind of knowledge inherent in poetic practice and that, in questioning Ion, he was trying to isolate it. There are, Michel Charles suggests, two ways in which to interpret Ion's inability to reply.[53] Firstly, and familiarly, it is a mark of Socrates' victory in deriding the cognitive claims of poets and poetry. Secondly, however, this inability can itself be read as a genuine response to the questioning: it pertains to the nature of poetic art to be unable to ground its effects in a conscious unified agency capable of conceptualizing the practice in which it is involved. Socrates' notion of inspiration thus moves, as a pseudo-explanation, into the gap between performance and knowledge (*Apology*, 22a–c).

Let us look at this second possibility more closely. Plato has no concept of 'fiction' to draw on in this debate, only the psychic notion of theatricality. There is what we might call a disjunction between theory and practice in the rhapsode's art. Ion does speak well of Homer – he wins prizes – but he cannot translate the speech-act of this performance into terms that satisfy Socrates in the discipline of dialectic. Socrates allows Ion to recite some Homer (537a–b) but, on two occasions, he avoids letting Ion give any direct demonstration of his art of speaking of Homer (530d, 536d). Socrates seems unable to admit that various modes of discourse might bear different claims to different effects and to a real authority without being translatable into each other. Instead he works here with an extreme and restrictive dichotomy of rational self-possessed knowledge and divine possession. Might not, however, an 'impersonation', as a case of blurred agency, be the vehicle of abilities and knowledge unavailable to the impersonator *in propria persona*? Although the theory sketched in the introduction applied to accounts of inspiration in modern literate cultures, the notion of a 'phantasmatic author' is all the more clearly applicable in an oral context. Ion's skill may be said to lie in his maintaining, simultaneously, an intense sensitivity to immediate audience reactions, even as he gives himself over to the role in which he identifes with the phantasmatic source of these effects projected by the text (and is thus 'ventriloquized' by Homer even in his encomia). This double-mindedness is precisely the quandary which the Socratic notion of inspiration both describes and disguises – for Ion has in fact denied that he is possessed, offering to give an example of his skill to Socrates: 'I should be much surprised if by your argument you succeeded in convincing me that I am possessed or mad when I praise Homer, nor do I think that you yourself would find me so if you heard me speaking upon Homer' (536d). Socrates also never finishes the argument about Ion's claim that his skill is the same as that of a general exhorting and galvanizing his troops before battle (540e–541c). This association of eloquence, leadership and war will recur in later accounts of the process of composition. Socrates, however, is not interested in a demonstration of Ion's practice and the rhapsode, painting himself into a corner with his answers, finally comes to accept the hypothesis of inspiration as at least 'nobler' than that of being thought a charlatan.

The unstated assumption throughout the *Ion* is that a definite effect must imply an identifiable agency. The affect must come from somewhere, it seems, while for us, as a modern commentator observes (surely rather problematically), 'We could become enthralled by *Hamlet* even if the script has somehow been worked up by monkeys.'[54] Socrates may envisage the enraptured spectator as the last in a chain of magnetized rings extending from Muse to poet to rhapsode to auditors, but the effect on the spectator is really what is at stake throughout. It is a matter of effects of knowing that have no source:

> Imitation in our language is governed by the presupposition that there is a separate existence of an original which is then copied. The essence of Plato's point, the raison d' être of his attack is that in the poetic performance as practiced hitherto in Greece there was no 'original'.

Readers of Derrida's essay on the *Phaedrus* may be surprised to discover that this quotation is not Derrida on 'writing' as the danger of supplanting true memory with a mere mnemonic device, but Havelock on the oral frame of mind.[55] The oral situation, with its deliberately cultivated *ecstasis*, its partial surrender to mnemonics and impersonation, already exemplifies all the effects for which writing as a signifier of the signifier also seems a scapegoat in the *Phaedrus*. Socrates' notion of inspiration is a response to these effects. It emerges then, surprisingly, as part of an attempt to demystify poetry, to fix effects of meaning without a simple or identifiable origin that the oral situation had brought about programmatically. The issue is that of the determinacy or indeterminacy of agency and hence responsibility. Socrates' argument ironically situates the poet as a mere mouthpiece for some deity – the Muses or the newly fashionable Orpheus. The fact that this position also enforces a simple notion of agency, unlike the paradoxical structures to be found in archaic poetry, renders it a smaller step than might appear to the tendency in Hellenistic poets to subjectivize the sources of the poetic and appropriate this agency in or as the poet's own psyche.[56]

In sum, Plato's notion of inspiration as divine madness originally stems from a crisis in the oral tradition, at a moment in which emergent models of rationality wish to challenge the hitherto intimate connection between citation or *mimesis* and authority in the interests of a new ideal of the psyche as a detached self-governing subjectivity. 'Inspiration' simultaneously names and masks a crisis of subjectivity associated with the process of composition, a crisis difficult to reconcile with models of the subject as a responsible, self-possessed agency: 'a man must not suffer the principles in his soul to do each the work of some other and interfere and meddle with one another, but he should dispose well of what in the true sense of the word is properly his own.' Such a man is 'a unit, one man instead of many, self-controlled and in unison' (*Republic*, 443d). All the terms, however˅ describing Ion's multiple relations to the muse, Homer and the spectators suggest dispersal and plurality. Ion rhapsodizing is less a unified person than the focal point of an ecstatic group psychology, which he manipulates and intensifies. It is hugely ironic therefore, that the reception of Plato's doctrine of inspiration in the Neoplatonic tradition which Marsilio Ficino's commentaries transmitted to Renaissance writers should conflate the poetic act with the authority of a philosophic contemplation of the ideas[57] – an identification of the very two things, philosopher and poet, that the *Ion* is striving to prise apart.[58]

Notes

1 H. Diels ed., *Die Fragmente der Vorsokratiker*, 6th edn, rev. W. Kranz 3 vols, (Berlin: Weidmann, 1952). Kathleen Freeman, *Ancilla to the Pre-Socratic Philosophers* (Oxford: Clarendon Press, 1946), p. 97.

2 References to Plato are to *The Collected Dialogues of Plato, Including the Letters*, ed. Edith Hamilton and Huntingdon Cairns (Princeton: Princeton University Press, 1961). Translations from Homer are from *The Iliad: A New Prose Translation*, trans. Martin Hammond (London: Penguin, 1987); *The Odyssey*, trans. Robert Fitzgerald (London: Collins Harvill, 1988).

3 See V. Delatte, 'Les Conceptions de l'enthousiasme chez les philosophes présocratiques', *L'Antiquité Classique*, 3 (1934) 5–80, pp. 28–35.

4 E. N. Tigerstedt, '*Furor Poeticus*: Poetic Inspiration in Greek Literature before Democritus and Plato', *Journal of the History of Ideas*, 31 (1970), 163–78, p. 165; see also Penelope Murray, 'Homer and the Bard', in *Aspects of the Epic*, ed. Tom Winnifrith, Penelope Murray and K.W. Gransden (London: Macmillan, 1983), pp. 1–15; Penelope Murray, 'Poetic Inspiration in Early Greece', *Journal of Hellenic Studies*, 101 (1981), 87–100.

5 Bernard C. Dietrich, 'Oracles and Divine Inspiration', *Kronos*, 3 (1990), 157–74, p. 159; Robert McGahey, *The Orphic Moment: Shaman to Poet-Thinker in Plato, Nietzsche & Mallarmé* (Albany: State University of New York Press, 1994), pp. 6–12.

6 Walter J. Ong, *Orality and Literacy: The Technologizing of the Word* (1982; London: Routledge, 1988); Eric A. Havelock, *The Literate Revolution and its Consequences* (Princeton: Princeton University Press, 1981).

7 See Albert B. Lord, *The Singer of Tales* (Cambridge, Mass.: Harvard University Press, 1960), pp. 13–29.

8 Gregory Nagy, *Pindar's Homer: The Lyric Possession of an Epic Past* (Baltimore and London: The Johns Hopkins University Press, 1990), pp. 18–24.

9 See Eric A. Havelock, *The Literate Revolution; The Muse Learns to Write* (New Haven: Yale University Press, 1986).

10 Eric A. Havelock, *Preface to Plato* (Oxford: Basil Blackwell, 1963), pp. 61–86.

11 Peter Bing, *The Well-Read Muse: Present and Past in Callimachus and the Hellenistic Poets* (Göttingen: Vandenhoeck & Ruprecht, 1988), pp. 14–15.

12 See W. J. Verdenius, 'The Principles of Greek Literary Criticism', *Mnemosyne* 36 (1983), 14–59, pp. 38–40

13 When Odysseus, being entertained by the Phaecians, hears the poet Demodocus perform a poem on Troy, it is the accuracy of his account, *kata kosmon* ('according to the order of things', l. 489) that so affects him and which leads him to attribute this power to the Muses or to Apollo (*Od.* 8, 487–91). Alcinous, Odysseus' host, distinguishes a genuine poet by the fact that he speaks the truth (*Od.* 11, 363–8). See also Hesiod, *Th.* 36–40; Hesiod, *Th.* 97ff; Homer, Il. 2, 485.

14 Elizabeth Minchin, 'The Poet Appeals to his Muse: Homeric Invocations in the Context of Epic Performance', unpublished paper, The Australian National University, p. 9.

15 *Les Maîtres de vérité dans la Grèce archaïque* (Paris: François Maspero, 1967), pp. 3–27.

16 *Mythe et pensé chez les Grecs: Etudes de psychologie historique*, 2 vols (Paris: François Maspero, 1971), I, 87.

17 See John D. Caputo, 'Demythologizing Heidegger: *Aletheia*, Metaphysics and the History of Being', *Review of Metaphysics*, 41 (1987–88), 519–46.

18 See Ong, *Orality and Literacy*, p. 75.

19 Joseph Russo and Bennett Simon, 'Homeric Psychology and the Oral Epic Tradition', *Journal of the History of Ideas*, 29 (1968), 483–98, p. 492.

20 One has of course to distinguish between the portrayal of the poets at work in Homer from the actual circumstances of the performances of Homer from the eighth century onwards. Homer's depiction of the poet, which may already be a traditional anachronism, situates oral performance mainly in social gatherings of the evening (see Colin Macleod, 'Homer on Poetry and the Poetry of Homer', in *The Collected Essays of Colin Macleod* (Oxford: Clarendon, 1983), pp. 1–15). Actual performances of Homer tended to become more highly ritualized and ceremonial, as parts of Pan-Hellenic festivals or related events (Gregory Nagy, *Greek Mythology and Poetics* (Ithaca: Cornell University Press, 1990), pp.38ff). For some suggestive analogies between acting and ritual transformation see David Cole, *The Theatrical Event: A Mythos, A Vocabulary, A Perspective* (Middletown, Connct.: Wesleyan University Press, 1975).

21 Pedro Laín Entralgo, *The Therapy of the Word in Classical Antiquity*, ed., trans. L. J. Rather and John M. Sharp (New Haven and London: Yale University Press, 1970), pp. 1–31.

22 Freeman, *Ancilla*, pp. 132–3.

23 *The Odyssey*, although it contains only one ritual invocation to the Muses (the opening) repeatedly draws attention to the various powers and possibilities of deception in the poet's performance in this respect. The verb *thelgein*, to put a spell on, to fascinate, recurs. It refers to the seductiveness of Calypso's language as she attempts to induce in Odysseus forgetfulness of his home (*Od.* 1, 56–7) as well as the effect of Circe's sexuality (*Od.* 10, 213, 291; 318; 326) or Penelope's (18, 212).

24 Entralgo, *Therapy of the Word*, p. 21ff.

25 The song of the sirens likewise 'enchants,' *thelgein* (12. 44–5). Stories and speeches can call for related references to enchantment – when Odysseus closes his story to the Phaecians we read 'no one stirred or sighed/ in the shadowy hall, spellbound as they all were' (*Od.* 13, 1–2; see also 17, 521). Poetry is also compared to Helen's drugs in *Odyssey* 4, 219–34; it casts a spell and thus removes pain (*Od.* 1, 337–8). Helen's drug itself was administered so that her household and their guests (including Telemachus) would be able to listen to tales of Odysseus without being embittered by a sense of his loss (*The Odyssey* contains other instances of poetry failing to enchant because the auditor is too close to the matter of the song, as when Odysseus, incognito, breaks down while listening to a poem about Troy (*Od.* 8, 521–31)).

26 Havelock, *Preface to Plato*, pp. 145–64.

27 Nagy, *Pindar's Homer*, p. 351.

28 See Eugene G. d'Aquili, and Charles Laughlin Jr., 'The Biopsychological Determinants of Religious Ritual Behaviour', *Zygon*, 10 (1975), 32–58; Barbara Myerhoff, 'The Transformation of Consciousness in Ritual Performance: Some Thoughts and Questions,' in *By Means of Performance: Intercultural Studies of Theatre and Ritual*, ed. Richard Schechner and Willa Appel (Cambridge: Cambridge University Press, 1990).

29 See also Ong, *Orality and Literacy*, p. 35, p. 67.

30 'Reality and its Shadow', in *Collected Philosophical Papers*, trans. Alphonso Lingis (Dordrecht: Martinus Nijhoff, 1987), pp. 1–13, pp. 3–4.

31 In such modes of experience as Levinas describes, subjectivity is revealed in its constitutive structure, not as a punctual consciousness or 'mind' but in relation to exteriority and an impersonal spontaneity that yet inhabits, exceeds and envelops it.

32 This translation of Sappho fragment 1 is by T. G. Rosenmey, in J. R. Johnson, *The Idea of Lyric: Lyric Modes in Ancient and Modern Poetry* (Berkeley: University of California Press, 1982), p. 45. I have adapted the penultimate stanza, omitting personal pronouns not justified by the Greek, so as not to rule out a plausible alternative reading offered by Anne Giacolmelli, 'The Justice of Aphrodite in Sappho Fr. 1', *Transactions of the American Philological Association*, 110 (1980), 135–42.

33 See Nagy *Pindar's Homer*, p. 340. Sappho's poems display the marks of having been written in the oral tradition, though hers was a period of tran-

sition to the use of writing to preserve poetry. For a speculative reading of Sappho in this context see Jesper Svenbro, *Phrasikleia: An Anthropology of Reading in Ancient Greece* (Ithaca, New York: Cornell University Press, 1993), pp. 145–59.

34 François Lasserre, *Sappho: une autre lecture* (Padua: Editrice Antenore, 1989), p. 114.

35 Nagy, *Pindar's Homer*, p. 37.

36 See e.g. D. Page, *Sappho and Alcaeus* (Oxford: Clarendon Press, 1955), p. 16; Charles Segal, '*Eros* and Incantation: Sappho and Oral Poetry', *Arethusa*, 7 (1974), 139–60, pp. 148–9; R. L. Fowler, *The Nature of Early Greek Lyric: Three Preliminary Studies* (Toronto: University of Toronto Press, 1987), pp. 56–7, 65–6.

37 See Nagy, 'Early Greek Views of Poets and Poetry', in *Cambridge History of Literary Criticism*, I, Classical Criticism, ed. G. Kennedy (Cambridge: Cambridge University Press, 1989), pp. 1–77, pp. 47–51. Nagy's analysis of the performance of Pindar's choral lyrics concludes: 'In all these models, the common point of departure is that the person of the composer can be reenacted by the performer or performers. In other words the performer may impersonate the composer as well as the character represented as speaking within the composition. Such reenactment or impersonation is the essence of *mimesis*' (*Pindar's Homer*, p. 381).

38 *The Linguistic Moment: From Wordsworth to Stevens* (Princeton: Princeton University Press, 1985), pp. 1–15.

39 Segal, '*Eros* and Incantation', p. 139.

40 See Nagy, *Greek Mythology*, pp. 59–60.

41 Segal, '*Eros* and Incantation', p. 56.

42 Ong, *Orality and Literacy*, p. 147; also C. Calame, 'Entre Oralité et écriture: Enonciation et énoncé dans la poésie greque archaïque', *Semiotica*, 43 (1983), 245–73, p. 250ff.

43 Compare Havelock's analytical juxtaposition of the oral Homeric 'Hymn to Aphrodite' and Callimachus' written 'Hymn to Zeus' (*The Muse Learns to Write*, pp. 107–10).

44 Svenbro, *Phrasikleia*, pp. 27–8. Svenbro demonstrates how early Greek inscriptions were understood as a form of latent speech-act that, when activated by being read aloud, was seen to temporarily dispossess the reader of his or her own voice.

45 Svenbro, *ibid.*, pp. 26–43.

46 Nagy, *Pindar's Homer*, pp. 146–98.

47 Translation from E. R. Dodds, *The Greeks and the Irrational* (Berkeley: University of California Press, 1951), p. 22.

48 Nagy, *Greek Mythology*, p. 42.

49 Nickolas Pappas, 'Plato's *Ion*: The Problem of the Author', *Philosophy*, 64 (1989), 381–9, p. 385.

50 Jacques Derrida, 'Plato's Pharmacy', in *Dissemination*, trans. Barbara Johnson (Chicago: University of Chicago Press, 1981), pp. 63–172.

51 Havelock, *Preface to Plato*, pp. 20–31. Socrates' treatment of Ion may be compared to his reading of a poem by Simonides in the *Protagoras* (338e–348a). He interrogates the poem for philosophical content that might

aid the discussion in hand, but, frustrated by the incapacity of a written text to answer back and explain itself, he interprets the text in terms that force it to back up his own argument, ignoring in the process parts of it that don't fit. It is a matter only of the truth which can be extracted from the text – there is no question of giving an interpretation or elucidation of the text in its singularity. The result is that 'In order to derive true statements from a poem, Socrates is positively compelled to attribute his own beliefs to every author' (Nickolas Pappas, 'Socrates' Charitable Treatment of Poetry', *Philosophy and Literature*, 13 (1989), 248–61, p. 256).

52 Arthur W. H. Adkins, 'Orality and Philosophy', *Language and Thought in Early Greek Philosophy*, ed. Kevin Robb (La Salle, Illinois: The Hegeler Institute, 1983), pp. 207–27; Friedrich Solmsen, rev. of Havelock, *Preface to Plato*, *American Journal of Philology*, 87 (1966), 99–105.

53 Michel Charles, *Rhétorique de la lecture* (Paris: Editions du Seuil, 1977), p. 70.

54 G. R. F. Ferrari, 'Plato and Poetry', *The Cambridge History of Literary Criticism*, I, 92–148, p. 98.

55 Havelock, *Preface to Plato*, p. 159.

56 Verdenius, 'Principles of Greek Literary Criticism' p. 456. The tendency may be already apparent in Aristotle *Poetics*, 17: 'poetry is the work of a genius rather than of a madman.'

57 See Michael J. B. Allen, *The Platonism of Marsilio Ficino: A Study of his Phaedrus Commentary, its Sources and Genesis* (Berkeley: University of California Press, 1984); Joel F. Willcox, 'Ficino's Commentary on Plato's *Ion* and Chapman's Inspired Poet in the *Odyssey*', *Philological Quarterly*, 64 (1985), 195–209.

58 My thanks to Elizabeth Minchin of the Australian National University for her invaluable advice during the writing of this chapter.

CHAPTER 3

Enthusiasm and enlightenment

If the discourse of inspiration proved so ineradicable in the millennia subsequent to Plato it may not only be because it made available to writers an unrivalled claim for authority. It also continued to correspond well with the technics of composition and reception. Until the Romantic period these remained predominantly oral/aural and formulaic in nature. Poetry, whether in the broad sense of imaginative writing or the narrow one of metrical composition, remained predominantly a case of *residual orality* in Walter Ong's sense of techniques, assumptions and practices based on the 'supposition that the paradigm of all expression is the oration'.[1] Poetic composition, destined often for recital rather than silent reading, remained overwhelmingly the technique of producing effects of voice, whether real or imagined.

Poetry's residual orality was also sustained by school and university studies in Latin composition and oration, which was usually the only training in composition available to the (male) population. Ong writes, of the late eighteenth century in England, 'In Coleridge's day boys were still being trained to compose as they did because a continuing tradition dating back to ancient oral culture and changing only with glacial slowness favored composing the way Homer did (and Virgil perhaps thought he was doing), that is, in formulary fashion' (pp. 275–6).

The subject of this chapter is the demise of the oral/rhetorical notion of composition and the emergence of modern concepts of inspiration as super-creativity. It may be regarded as trying to answer the following incomplete formulation of Derrida's:

> At a certain moment in history, for reasons to be analyzed, the poet ceased being considered the prey of a foreign voice, in mania, delirium, enthusiasm, or inspiration. Poetic 'hallucination' is then accommodated under the rubric of the 'regime': a simple elaboration of hearing-oneself-speak ...[2]

Inspiration becomes a personal power, the individual property of a writer now working, with the end of systems of aristocratic patronage, increasingly in his or her own name. My focus is on the British eighteeenth century, for it was mainly in Britain that concepts of 'poetic enthusiasm' emerged which were to be decisive for later conceptions of inspiration as a form of super-subjectivity, both in Britain and in the *Sturm und Drang* movement in Germany.[3]

By the seventeenth century it had become common to state the contradiction between poets' professed Christianity and the custom of invoking the pagan muses.[4] Thomas Hobbes derides the habit of 'almost all the approved Poets' of ascribing their work to the agency of a heathen muse. This is

> a foolish custom by which a man, enabled to speak wisely from the principles of nature, and his own meditation, loves rather to be thought to speak by inspiration, like a bagpipe.[5]

For Christian writers, moreover, the notion of inspiration cannot but be fraught with questions about authority. The main reason for this, of course, is the overwhelming authority of the Bible as an inspired text, as the very word of God. Inspiration there concerns above all the truth of the Bible, and the authority or otherwise of the Church or individuals to mediate that truth.

In a social context in which Christianity is bound up with social authority, any individual's claim to be inspired is necessarily contentious. Renaissance writers of diverse sects often showed great anxiety to reconcile claims to poetic inspiration with the demands of their Christian faith. Boccaccio's *De genealogia* (XIV.8) had drawn a clear distinction between the inspiration of the Bible and that of the pagan poets. On the other hand, the poets of the Pléiade, in the French sixteenth century, were anxious to adapt Ficino's commentaries on Plato to a Christianised notion of divine inspiration.[6] Increasingly, just as the emergence of the novel was to turn around the narrative stance of a non-transcendent subject, claims to inspiration came to be confined largely to texts with a religious subject-matter, such as Tasso's *Gerusalemme Liberata* (1581) or Milton's *Paradise Lost* (1667)

Enthusiasm and Disorder

A first point about most post-Renaissance notions of inspiration is that, stressing a writer's unique power and insight, they imply a form of individualism. One of the effects of the religious wars of the late Renaissance was to intensify the controversial status of claims to personal inspiration in societies riven by sectarianism and competing forms of authority. Such claims are potentially a rejection of church and civil authorities in favour of one's supposedly more immediate access to the divine.[7] In the British Isles for a century and a half after the civil wars of 1640–60 this issue is at the heart of the controversy about the nature of 'enthusiasm'. Enthusiasm has the predominant sense of a deluded claim to inspiration. The word enters English from French usage in the late Renaissance, though the use of the Greek *enthousiasmos* to mean deluded inspiration dates from the early Christian period. Figures as diverse in their beliefs as Meric Casaubon, Thomas Hobbes, Henry More, Alexander Ross and Jonathan Swift all attack enthusiasm as an irrationalism and a threat to civil peace.[8] Fear of enthusiasm is fear of mass cults, of crowd behaviour, of popular delusions or even insurrections. Elusive and unobjectifiable, enthusiasm may be as invisible and insidious as a rumour, and yet capable of galvanizing multitudes. Writers often figure it in images of disease as a 'contagion' or a 'pestilence'. It is too elusive to admit of being an object of clear legislation. In societies that are mainly non-literate enthusiasm is associated mostly with the power of speech, of incendiary sermons or the exhortations of demagogues and itinerant preachers: 'one mad man can infect a whole province', wrote Casaubon.[9] Samuel Parker, an Anglican royalist, wrote 'what pestilential influence the genius of enthusiasm or opinionative zeal has upon the public peace is so evident from experience that it needs not to be prov'd from reason.'[10] Enthusiasm also had gender connotations. Male enthusiasts were seen as pathologically feminized or unmanly in their apparent lack of self-control. Female enthusiasts were seen as possessed by an unseemly and ranting power of speech and evoked reactions of the most virulent misogyny.

Enthusiasm was especially linked to the activities of extreme Protestant sects. Alexander Ross, in his *A View of All Religions of the World* (1654) lists as enthusiasts the Adamites, Anabaptists, Antinomians, Brownists, Familists, Independents, Quakers, Ranters and Socinians. By the late eighteenth century many people would also have included the Methodists.[11] Enthusiasm, then, is not primarily an issue because one or two people claim to prophesy or to speak for God, it is because it relates to the power of mass psychological movements, to sectarianism, to fear of the 'mob'. In the French *Encyclopédie* (1751), Diderot's entry for enthusiasm describes it as 'a living fire which prevails by degrees, which feeds from its own flames and which, far from becoming feebler as it expands, acquires new strength in proportion to the extent that it spreads and communicates itself.'[12] There is a paradoxical relation between the individualism of claims to personal inspiration and the spectre of contagious irrational feeling.[13]

The Restoration of 1660 had reacted severely, in the name of notions of rationality and order, against deviant religious claims and enthusiasts. Enthusiasm is often presented as a pathology of the passions. Its symptoms in an individual are primarily linguistic – a seductive eloquence and the wild use of figurative language, especially in the interpretation of contemporary events through extravagant and often subversive forms of biblical typology. From the second half of the seventeenth century, published studies of individual and mass psychology are responding to a sense of social crisis: 'Psychology', writes Frank E. Manuel, 'was ... the consequence of a need for an objective criterion to evaluate aberrant religious experience.'[14] Similarly there emerged a deep suspicion of figurative and merely persuasive language, most famously in the dreams of linguistic reform associated with the new Royal Society. For men such as Samuel Parker and Thomas Sprat figurative speech *per se* bore connotations of social disorder.[15]

In Germany enthusiasts were often known as '*Schwärmer*', loosely translated as swarming fanatics. The tendency in German pietism to make faith a matter of individual feeling was perceived as a threat to social discipline as well as to orthodox Lutheranism. *Schwärmerei*, in the sense of fanaticism or dangerous utopianism, remained a term of contempt in Germany during the controversy surrounding the French Revolution. Fanaticism, utopianism and millenarianism are contentious features of the hopes and terrors of the revolutionary 1790s. Kant termed *Schwärmerei* a 'disease' and followers such as Jacobi, Schelling and Fichte each felt compelled to address the issue in some way or another.[16]

'Poetic enthusiasm'

A decisive event for later concepts of inspiration was a growing acceptance of some aspects of enthusiasm in early eighteenth-century Britain, especially in the newly prominent concept of 'poetic enthusiasm'. This comes to be opposed to the religious fanaticism with which it nevertheless shares key features. In the work of John Dennis, Joseph Addison, Isaac Watts, Sir Thomas

Blackwell and others, notions of enthusiasm become increasingly appropriated by high cultural discourse. Critics of enthusiasm such as Casaubon and the Cambridge Platonists Henry More and Ralph Cudworth had distinguished a 'true' from the false enthusiasm.[17] In the work of Dennis in particular there emerges a view of poetic creativity as a carefully-regulated form of frenzy, analogous to the delirium of religious enthusiasm but capable of acceptable insight into the cosmic order – 'poetic enthusiasm'.[18]

Henry More's *Enthusiasmus Triumphatus* (1656) had already claimed that 'A Poet is an *Enthusiast in Jest*, and an Enthusiast is a *Poet in good Earnest.*'[19] During the eighteenth century 'poetic enthusiasm' takes up, in regulated form, two key characteristics of religious enthusiasm. Firstly it is associated with the eloquence of passion. Secondly, this in turn is said to manifest itself in deviant or figurative language. In the influential poetry of James Thomson's *The Seasons* (1730) and Edward Young's *Night Thoughts* (1742–5),[20] poetic enthusiasm forms the basis for a deployment of rhapsodic poetic language as the vehicle of privileged insights into the order and meaning of Nature. Thomson even assimilates the scientific work of Bacon and Newton to the discourse of election, revelation and inspiration ('Summer', lines 1535–63) – an instance of those muted conversion narratives that still structure accounts of the 'moment of insight' to this day. Even for theorists who do not subscribe to the bardic claims of Thomson or Young, 'enthusiasm' may lose the sense of delusion inherent in religious and social contexts, leaving the notion of extreme states of mind, power of insight, and a heightened figurative eloquence of unusual contagiousness. Enthusiasm is a notion of passion *and* of its communicability.

The radical religious associations of enthusiastic discourse persisted into the work of Christopher Smart and, arguably, William Blake in the late eighteenth century.[21] Elsewhere, however, 'enthusiasm' becomes increasingly secularized and divorced from mass politics. Key characteristics of the notion of enthusiasm became free to function in a theory of communication. Voltaire, in his *Philosophical Dictionary* (1764) argues that 'Rational enthusiasm is the attribute of great poets'.[22] Diderot tries to reconcile the workings of seeming inspiration in artists with a form of psychology. Enthusiasm is the vivacity of representation itself, forceful to the point of delusion.[23] In Britain, as we shall see, enthusiasm is appropriated by arguments that would affirm impassioned language as an ideal of natural communication, transcending the arbitrariness of signs.

It is primarily in the sense of contagious rhetorical power that enthusiasm becomes assimilated to notions of the sublime in eighteenth-century treatises of poetics and rhetoric. The rediscovery of Longinus' first-century treatise of rhetoric and poetics *Peri Hypsous* or *On the Sublime* at the end of the seventeenth century provided, in effect, a neutral or secularized theory of inspiration.[24] Now people could refer to both Homer and the Book of Genesis as possessing or communicating 'sublimity', without implying a particular religious position. (This is just what one finds, for instance, in the rhetorician Hugh Blair's lecture 'The Sublime in Writing'[25]). At the same time Longinus' conception of the sublime as a mobile, possessing, self-duplicating and disseminating power itself belongs to the tradition of classical concepts of inspiration.[26] In *Peri Hypsous*, however, the notion of an inspired/inspiring force is part of a detailed rhetorical study of specific textual effects, and how they are produced. Five sources of *hypsos* or the sublime are given. They are: (1) the ability to conceive great thoughts; (2) the stimulus of powerful or 'inspired' (*enthusiastikon*) feeling; (3) the appropriate function of certain figures of thought and of speech; (4) nobility of diction and lastly; (5) composition (*sunthesis*). *Peri Hypsous* has been accused of blurring incoherently notions of the agency of the author, of the text and of the audience. Yet this mobility is a resource in notions of the transitivity of inspiration that partly look to Longinus. The section that would have elucidated an explicit reference to inspiration is missing. In what remains, however, inspiration is a primarily rhetorical concept – the stress is on a writer's or orator's means of achieving power over an audience.

Poetic enthusiasm is comparable to Longinian *hypsos* in that both are modes of rhetorical coercion. Longinus distinguishes between merely persuasive language, which an auditor is free to resist, and the sublime itself, which is irresistible: 'sublime passages exert an irresistible force and mastery, and get the upper hand with every hearer' (ch. 1, p. 100 in Dorsh). The terminology of the sublime is one of psychic violence. Longinus writes of Democritus that 'The orator is doing ... exactly what the bully does – hitting the jury in the mind with blow after blow' (ch. 20, p. 130 in Dorsh; trans. modified).

It is through the appropriation of notions of enthusiasm to an aesthetic of sublimity that many critics come to understand or define their concept of inspiration. John Dennis, in his works *The Advancement and Reformation of Modern Poetry* (London: 1701) and *The Grounds of Criticism in Poetry* (London: 1704) assimilates

Longinus' sublime to a notion of the Christian marvellous.[27] Dennis dismisses religious enthusiasm with its figurative and typological excesses as the effects of a deluded passion. The notion of passion, however, provides a bridge into the more psychologized notion of 'poetic enthusiasm'. Dennis writes, 'figurative Language is but a Consequence of the Enthusiasm, that being the natural Language of the Passions.'[28] Dennis becomes the first thinker in Britain to argue that poetry's traditional aims of pleasure and instruction can be achieved by exciting passion. His notion of poetic enthusiasm also transposes from the religious variety the idea of a peculiar contagiousness of passion. Enthusiasm is, transitively, both cause and effect: enthusiasm in the poet is also 'the Elevation, and Vehemence, and Fury' created in the reader (*Critical Works*, I, 222–3). Disassociating enthusiasm from fanaticism to produce a new conception of poetic enthusiasm, Dennis distinguishes between 'vulgar Passion' and 'Enthusiastic Passion'. The former is 'that which is moved by the Objects themselves, or the Ideas in the ordinary Course of Life' (*Critical Works*, I, 338); the latter is that which is 'moved by the Ideas in Contemplation or the Meditations of things that belong not to common life' (*Critical Works*, I, 338). Enthusiasm, at its most uplifting or sublime, retains its relation to the divinity, but this relation is reconfigured in a subtle and decisive manner:

> as great Elevation must be produced by a great Admiration, as every Passion which the Poet excites ought to be just and Reasonable, and Adapted to its Object, it is impossible that any one, who is not stupid, can seriously contemplate his Maker, but that his Soul must be exalted and lifted up towards its Primitive Objects, and fill'd and inspired with the highest Admiration. For 'tis then that the Enthusiasm in Poetry is wonderful and Divine, when it shows the Excellence of the Author's Discernment, and the Largeness of his Soul: now all the Ideas of God are such, that the more large and comprehensive the Soul of a poet is, and the more it is capable of receiving those Ideas, the more is it sure to be raised and filled and lifted to the Skies with Wonder: The Spirit or the Passion in Poetry ought to be proportion'd to the Ideas, and the Ideas to the Object ... But nothing but God, and what relates to God, is worthy to move the Soul of a great and a wise Man. (*Critical Works*, I, 345).

Inspiration is no longer the fanatic's notion of a direct impulse from God. It is heavily mediated as a poetic enthusiasm that responds to and is fired by the *idea* of God in the psyche. Here it is all part of an internal economy of the psyche, of the mind's relation to its own representations, not of a transgressive or disruptive infringement of otherness. Dennis celebrates the passion of poetry as a kind of therapy for psychic imbalance, working in the interests of virtue and piety. His view of poetry as reformative passion effectively reinforces the norms of the Whig and Anglican establishment at the same time as it allows an exalted idea of poetry itself: 'The great Design of Arts is to restore the Decays that happen'd to human Nature by the Fall, by restoring Order' (*Critical Works* I, 336). This kind of millenarianism marries a carefully mediated inspirational aesthetic to a politically conservative notion of harmony. Such a strategy also characterizes some of the rhapsodic poetry of the early and mid eighteenth century.

Hobbes had dismissively ascribed claims to religious inspiration to the delusion of intense passion.[29] However, Dennis, and thinkers such as William Duff, Alexander Gerard and the Wordsworth of the Preface to *Lyrical Ballads* are elaborating what might be termed a philosophy of composition. Within this context 'enthusiasm', in the sense of an intense passion that is unusually communicable or contagious, works as a transitional term in the shift from religious or Neoplatonic ideas of inspiration to secularized theories of 'creativity' that would ground themselves on the postulate of a shared or universal human nature. Universalism and 'Nature' replace direct reference to God as the trans-individual ground upon which a writer or speaker can achieve psychically charged modes of language that are held to be necessarily repeated in other minds.

Enlightenment treatises that offer a rational explanation for claims to inspiration superficially resemble twentieth-century accounts of creativity, such as those by Poincaré or Koestler.[30] However, the notions of reason and passion at issue in Enlightenment theories of 'genius' often function normatively and are at once implicated in debates about concepts of decorum and order in ways alien to the later attempts to provide supposedly rational accounts of privileged moments of insight. The association of enthusiasm with irrationalism, 'womanly' lack of self-control and social disorder make even 'poetic enthusiasm' an object of circumspection. In works of poetics, 'poetic enthusiasm' is always strictly policed and guided by notions of judgement, taste and reason. '[M]ear Enthusiasm', Dennis wrote, 'is but Madness' (Preface to *Miscellanies in Verse and Prose* [1693]; *Critical Works*, I, 6–10, p. 6).

The most influential revalorization or appropriation of enthusiasm was that of Lord Shaftesbury, "Europe's Plato" as J. G. Herder named him.[31] Shaftesbury's version of the dichotomy of true and false enthusiasm depends on a divorce of the true variety from any crude supernaturalism. It becomes the response of disinterested rapture to a sense of divine order, fitness or beauty in people or things. False enthusiasm is associated once again with the melancholia of a disordered or diseased imagination. Both true and false enthusiasm make up a drive of self-transcendence or self-sacrifice, but true enthusiasm devotes itself to enlightened and socially sanctioned ends, such as the heroism of the battlefield. It thus affirms a providentially sanctioned ideal of order quite opposite to the associations of enthusiasm with social breakdown:

> all sound *Love* and *Admiration* is ENTHUSIASM: The transports of *Poets*, the sublime of *Orators*, the Rapture of *Musicians*, the high strains of the *Virtuosi*; all mere ENTHUSIASM! Even *Learning* itself, the love of *Arts* and *Curiosity*, the Spirit of *Travellers* and *Adventurers*; *Gallantry*, *War*, *Heroism*; All, all ENTHUSIASM! – 'tis enough: I am content to be this new *Enthusiast* ... ('The Moralists, a Philosophical Rhapsody')[32]

Enthusiasm may become the self-transcendence of a form of Platonic eros, drawing us out of our concern with ourselves to a love of the good and beautiful in others and even, ultimately, to a love of the cosmos itself. Such self-transcendence is an essential element of Shaftesbury's Neoplatonic notion of poetic genius as 'a second *Maker*; a just Prometheus under Jove' (*Characteristics*, I, 136). Unlike the wild verbal creations of the religious enthusiast, this second maker produces a proportionally ordered microcosm, 'with due subjection and subordinacy of constituent parts' (*Characteristics*, I, 136)

In the 'A Letter Concerning Enthusiasm' (1708) (*Characteristics*, I, 3–39) Shaftesbury relates enthusiasm in its pejorative sense to the mass emotions and delusions of crowd behaviour. It is a species of 'panic', This is a state in which 'very looks are infectious. The fury flies from face to face: and the disease is no sooner seen than caught' (p. 13). Later, Shaftesbury compares such enthusiasm to a raging, uncontrollable fire:

> No wonder if the blaze rises so of a sudden; when innumerable eyes glow with the passion, and heaving breasts are labouring with inspiration; when not the aspect only, but the very breath and exhalations of men are infectious, and the inspiring disease imparts itself by insensible transpiration. (p. 32)

69

Such language is cliché by this time. Shaftesbury is attacking the Camisards, a sect of French enthusiasts in London. However, the letter also gives a theory of literary inspiration (a combination of religious polemic and advanced poetics bizarre to us but common at this time). According to Shaftesbury the poet, orator or writer is inspired or empowered by the thought of an addressee, whether real or imaginary. Thus the ancients, with their belief in and devotion to the Muses or Apollo, could be animated by the very supposition of divine agency: 'It was never surely the business of poets in those days to call *revelation* in question, when it evidently made so well for their art' (pp. 7–8). In effect, whether inspiration was credited in literal terms or not, to indulge it as a supposition was, in effect, to realize its power. Even 'the cold Lucretius', he observes, who wrote against inspiration, 'is forced to raise an apparition of Nature, in a divine form, to animate and conduct him' (pp. 36–7). The inspiration derived from the thought of one's addressee, Shaftesbury observes with courtesy, is his own reason in addressing his own 'letter' to 'My Lord Sommers' (though that name was not to appear on the title page until the edition of 1737). This argument is linked to Shaftesbury's observations on the contagion of enthusiasm in crowds. He writes that when a party is affected by some apparition, whether true, false or imagined, 'there follows always an itch of imparting it, and kindling the same fire in other breasts' (p. 36). It is this 'innocent kind of fanaticism' (p. 36) that renders poets 'fanatics too' (p. 36), whether from a real belief in the working of some divine presence upon them *or* from the empowering effects of such a supposition. In effect, meditation upon some of the more striking phenomena of crowd behaviour allows Shaftesbury to construct a theory of inspiration as a psychological structure that effectively creates its own value, whatever the status of its cause.

Rationalizing appropriations of enthusiasm are also a feature of attempts to analyse the psyche of the 'genius'. In his *An Essay on Original Genius* (1767), a study of genius in both sciences and arts, William Duff affirms enthusiasm both as a principle of the communicability of affect and as an energising passion. This acts as a catalyst upon the originating faculty of imagination, as this in turn is regulated in its ideas by Nature and Reason. Duff's notion of enthusiasm gives a precise form to the 'madness' traditionally allied to genius,[33] enabling him to offer a rationalizing interpretation of the *Ion*:

> A glowing ardor of Imagination is indeed (if we may be permitted the expression) the very soul of Poetry. It is the principal source of

INSPIRATION; and the Poet who is possessed of it, like the Dephian Priestess, is animated with a kind of DIVINE FURY. The intenseness and vigour of his sensations produce that ENTHUSI-ASM of Imagination, which as it were hurries the mind out of itself; and which is vented in warm and vehement description, exciting in every susceptible breast the same emotions that were felt by the AUTHOR himself. It is this ENTHUSIASM which gives life and strength to poetical representations, renders them striking imitations of nature, and thereby produces that inchanting delight which genuine poetry is calculated to inspire. Without this animating principle, all poetical and rhetorical compositions are spiritless and languid, like those bodies that are drained of their vital juices ... [34]

Enthusiasm here, is an intensifier and disseminator. Later in the treatise Duff celebrates visionary/allegorical poetry as the most inventive. Working as a principle of communicability, enthusiasm excites 'in every susceptible breast the same emotions that were felt by the AUTHOR himself.' The vivacity it gives to the products of genius is a considerable part of their originality. Genius, Duff writes, is 'the vital principle which animates every species of composition' (p. 25). It is a source of 'that inchanting delight which genuine poetry is calculated to inspire.' Duff's account here bears out the transitivity of inspiration as a chiasmatic structure – this second use of the word refers to the affect undergone by the reader. As in Longinus it is a matter of an energy that slides swiftly between enthused author, inspiring text and inspired reader or auditor – a power transmits itself with peculiar immediacy through each, as if linked by some common medium. Duff's emphasis on how the human pysche engenders its own inspiration make this account of inspiration markedly different from Platonic or biblical conceptions. It was after all no part of claims that the Bible is inspired that God had to experience a particular form of passion that is then duplicated in his text and its readers.

Rhetoric

Duff's account, and the many like it in other treatises of this time, are effectively a description of magic. Their seeming plausibility may lie in the fact that, though ostensibly about writing, they draw hugely on an implicit and unacknowledged oral or rhetorical model of composition and affect. One of the striking features of eighteenth-century theories of poetry is their proximity to contemporary thinking in rhetoric. George Campbell's *Philosophy of Rhetoric* (1776) (the most popular book of rhetoric at this time) states simply that 'Poetry indeed is properly no other than a particular mode or form of certain branches of oratory.'[35] Despite the long tradition of discussion on stylistic issues in prose composition, the tendency with poetry was to assimilate composition as only a stage towards oral performance. P. W. K. Stone observes, in his survey of this material, that oratory and poetry are usually classed 'neatly under one head'.[36] An instrumentalist model of communication predominates in both disciplines. Both poet and orator are 'conceived of as pursuing a specific aim, inventing, elaborating and ordering a subject-matter in accordance with that aim, then clothing his notions in suitable language. This view of the matter, where it is not explicit, is everywhere implicitly accepted – in the arguments of theoreticians as in the *obiter dicta* of practical critics' (Stone, p. 36).

Despite his references to the *Ion*, Duff's notion of enthusiasm is closer to contemporary works of rhetoric than to any form of Platonism. In fact, after archaic Greece and the *Ion*, it was less in poetics than in treatises on the art of rhetoric or public speech-making that a close connection survived between notions of inspiration and detailed consideration of the techniques of composition.[37] Duff's account of inspiration compares closely with contemporary revisions of rhetorical notions of *inventio*. Traditionally, *inventio*, one-fifth of the art of rhetoric as classically defined, had involved mastery of certain *topoi* or *loci communes*, ready-made devices or turns of thought that could be applied to any appropriate occasion. These were probably a residue from the practices of composition in a predominantly oral culture, forming as they did internalized sources of reference and a repertoire of techniques to be drawn on from memory: 'Rhetorical culture,' Ong argues is basically 'oral culture shrouded in writing.'[38] The seventeenth and eighteenth centuries had seen repeated attacks by rhetoricians on the *topoi* as outmoded, limited and unnecessary. The most dramatic rejection of the commonplace tradition took place in 1759, with the publication of Edward Young's hugely influential *Conjectures on Original Composition*, with its advocacy of individualistic notions of genius and originality in literary production.[39] Duff's essay also breaks from rhetorical culture, presenting a theory of the imagination of genius as selecting and combining its ideas into original forms. A contemporary of Duff's, the rhetorician Hugh Blair, attacks the *topoi* as 'mere art', a servile imitativeness, compared to the more forceful and individualized effects of 'Passion'.[40] 'Passion' takes up many of the characteristics of enthusiasm, i.e. it is not only a catalyst to the powers of invention, it may also be immediately persuasive.

Ong is overwhemingly convincing in his argument that the death of rhetorical culture and the commonplace tradition must be largely owing to effects of increased literacy and the psychological transformations wrought by print culture (pp. 255–83). Nevertheless, Duff's counter-advocacy of 'Passion' and enthusiasm still deploys one traditional aspect of *inventio*. 'INVENTION', he writes, is a 'vital spark' which is 'the very soul of all poetical composition', 'the source of that inchanting delight, which the mind receives from its perusal' (pp. 125–6). If we turn to Cicero's *De Oratore*, we find the advice that young orators search in themselves to excite that anger, grief or admiration which they would like to produce in their auditors. *Inventio* may include the art of inciting oneself by use of the commonplaces, so producing passion as a supplementary power. Antonius, a speaker in Cicero's dialogue, refers this practice to the notion of *enthousiasmos* in Democritus and Plato, suggesting his own account of passion as a demystification of ancient claims to divine *afflatus* (Bk. II, xlv–xlvi). Horace's much quoted *dictum*, '*Si vis me flere dolendum est primum ipse tibi*' ['If you want me to weep you must first be in tears yourself'] almost certainly relates to the rhetorical conception of *inventio* and is not the notion of spontaneous sincerity it may appear to be. Quintilian also elaborates the same argument in Book Ten of his *De Institutione Oratoria* about the orator working upon himself to produce a real, if worked-up and histrionic passion.[41] He also discusses those moments in the performance of a speech when the orator, warmed to an unusual passion and fluency, may launch into improvisation. Both Cicero and Quintilian offer accounts of the *copia* achievable in forms of hard-earned moments of improvisation in terms that also rationalize the notion of a *furor poeticus*. Quintilian writes: 'if a speaker is swept away by warmth of feeling and genuine inspiration (*calor et spiritus*), it frequently happens that he attains a success from improvisation which would have been beyond the reach of the most careful preparation' (*Inst.orat.* X. vii, 13). In fact, as Terence Cave has demonstrated, in classical and Renaissance rhetoric 'the notions of improvisation and inspiration mirror one another.'[42] Improvisation is seen as a becoming spontaneous or self-generating of deeply-ingrained skills in thought or practice; it is thus to be carefully distinguished from mere logorrhoea, empty babble or any mere automatism of the signifier.

The notion of enthusiasm, then, in Duff and others, is conceived as a natural energy of the mind which ensures its vigour and inventiveness as opposed to the outmoded and servile machinery of the *topoi*. Hugh Blair's account of the contagion and self-duplication of poetic passion grafts those characteristics of enthusiasm into a theory of invention in a similar way:

> A man, actuated by a strong passion, becomes much greater than he is at other times. He is conscious of more strength and force ... But chiefly, with respect to persuasion, is the power of passion felt. Almost every man, in passion, is eloquent. Then, he is at no loss for words and arguments. He transmits to others, *by a sort of contagious sympathy*, the warm sentiments which he feels; his looks and gestures are all persuasive; and Nature here shows herself infinitely more powerful than all art. (Blair, *Lectures*, II, 6–7; emphasis added; see also I, 60)

The subject of this extract is oratory, not poetry; hence the assumption that the auditors are immediately present. In the orator's case, of course, performance and affect are effectively simultaneous. Blair goes on: 'hence, the universally acknowledged effect of enthusiasm, or warmth of any kind, in public Speakers, for affecting their audience' (Blair, *Lectures*, II, 7; cf. Priestley, *Lectures*, pp. 114–15). Yet this argument that passion is also a poet's most reliable source of power reads as an abbreviated version of the portrait of oratorical enthusiasm:

> [The poet's] mind is supposed to be animated by some interesting object which fires his Imagination, or engages his Passions; and which, of course, communicates to his Style a peculiar elevation suited to his ideas; very different from that mode of expression, which is natural to the mind in its calm, ordinary state. (Blair, *Lectures*, II, 312)

This argument borrows much of its plausibility, in effect, from an oral model that Blair's other passage makes explicit.

Adam Smith's lectures on rhetoric also deploy the psychology of orality in referring to the immediate 'sympathy' established between author and audience 'When the sentiment of the speaker is expressed in a neat, clear, plain, and clever manner, and the passion of affection he is possessed of and intends, *by sympathy*, to communicate to his hearer, is plainly and cleverly hit off, then and then only the expression has all the force and beauty that language can give it.'[43] George Campbell, Robert Lowth and others make similar statements about 'sympathy'.[44] Such sympathy, in the sense of shared feeling, would also have been reinforced by body language, intonation, gesture, and by that general lowering of thresholds of emotional resistance always associated with large gatherings. In effect, notions of 'passion' and 'sympathy' (the principle according to which a person is spontaneously compelled to conform to the feeling of others) often simply transpose characteristics of enthusiasm, while this term itself comes to appear with less frequency after about 1770: 'All passions are communicative, and are universally propagated by the genuine expressions of them'.[45]

Biblical inspiration/enthusiasm

The valorization of oral models of communication was also a prominent part of that idealization of ancient and primitive cultures that characterizes the middle of the eighteenth century.[46] Thomas Blackwell's *Enquiry into the Life and Writings of Homer* (London: 1736) celebrated Homer's power as that of a poet who worked in a culture where letters were little known and in which poetry was the main medium of cultural transmission. More decisively for subsequent views of poetry, Bishop Robert Lowth celebrated the stylistic features of ancient Hebrew poetry. His influential *Lectures on the Sacred Poetry of the Hebrews* (first published in Latin in 1753) assimilates the Bible to notions of an enthusiastic poetry, rhapsodic and powerfully figurative.[47] For centuries the Bible's blatant divergence from the stylistic norms of classicism had made it almost a matter of stylistic embarrassment to the educated. Calvin, for example, had seen the Bible's supposedly lowly language as a kind of trial of faith to penetrate to the genuinely inspired meaning.[48] It was in the seventeenth century that the Bible's language came to seen as a possible model of style. Such views culminate in Lowth's celebration of the Bible as a model of sublimity and rhetorical power. Lowth praises the particular sublimity of Hebrew poetry as impassioned, 'irregular' from the viewpoint of neoclassical models.[49]

Lowth's analysis tries to maintain a strict dichotomy between Christian 'inspiration' and pagan or secular 'enthusiasm', reserving the former for the Bible, while giving the conventional view of enthusiasm as an extreme form of passion that is also a principle of immediate communication. Lowth's notion of enthusiasm remains close to the rhetorical notions of worked-up emotion. His ascription of the sources of poetry to impersonated passion is also similar to the rhetorical notions of *inventio* and improvisation.

> Every affection of the human soul, while it rages with violence, is a momentary frenzy. When, therefore a poet is able, by the force of genius, or rather of imagination, to conceive any emotion of the mind so perfectly as to transfer to his own feelings the instinctive passion of another, and, agreeably to the nature of the subject, to express it in all its vigour, such a one, according to a common mode of speaking, may be said to possess the true poetic enthusiasm, or, as the ancients would have expressed it, 'to be inspired; full of the god'. (Lowth, pp. 183–4).

Lowth's work, ironically, tends towards a secularization of the very biblical inspiration which he is trying to defend. He insists that the Hebrew poets did not lose their individuality in divine inspiration. For Moses and others it was rather a case of 'the natural powers of the mind' being 'in general elevated and refined' (p. 174). It is, in fact, only an ultimate reference to God that differentiates such inspiration from mere enthusiasm. Lowth's defence of the Bible as sublime poetry, then, tends to collapse the very distinction it tries to maintain between inspiration and enthusiasm, and facilitates, despite itself, a secularized view of the Bible as literature. In Germany Lowth's approach to the Bible as a Hebrew cultural document was to become radicalized as the controversial 'higher criticism'.

Lowth's book becomes, contrary to its own programme, a pointed instance of a transition from notions of inspiration based on revelation to notions grounded in the conception of universal nature:

> The origin and first use of poetical language are undoubtedly to be traced into the vehement affections of the mind. For, what is meant by that singular frenzy of poets, which the Greeks, ascribing to Divine inspiration, distinguished by the appellation of *enthusiasm*, but a style and expression directly prompted by nature itself, and exhibiting the true and express image of a mind violently agitated? (p. 50)

What is true of this passage is true of all those quoted in this chapter: enthusiasm is an overwhelming case of residual orality. Clearly, such orality is largely incongruous for a poet in a sophisticated literate society – poetry no longer serves as the mnemonic repository of culture. Instead, the stress on passion and enthusiasm enables a theory of poetic communication as engaging an audience through affective as well as rational appeals. Poetic inspiration is becoming the 'natural' insistence of more genuine modes of language, token of a 'truer' or deeper self which addresses, and

depends upon, an ideal of bonding communal feeling. It thus functions to bolster emerging liberal conceptions of the individual,
conceived as struggling for self-realization against the restraints of
unnatural rule or custom. In effect, with the decline of patronage,
the idealization of orality and communality provides writers with a
new stance of general authority: as at once communal voice and
original individual. Leo Braudy writes:

> With originality, in the double sense of the unprecedented and a
> return to roots, becoming a prime criterion of value in art, artistic
> creators turned against centuries of works that freely admitted their
> commissioned, collaborative and externally inspired status.
> Inspiration, like the muse and the patron, had become aspects of
> the artist's own being.[50]

The Hebrew poets celebrated by Lowth were seen, like
Homer, as communal voices. It was, however, the German theorist
and admirer of Lowth, Johann Gottfried Herder, who expressed
most fully the ideal of the poet as a national or communal voice. His
work contributed to the idea of the need to emulate, in modern
conditions, the art of ancient Greece as an embodiment of unalienated humanity.[51] Such ideals of a genuine poetry of the *Volk* were to
inform the communal ideals of German Romanticism, a subject to
which we will return in the fifth chapter.

The probable sign

Theories of composition until the late eighteenth century tend to be
strongly instrumentalist in nature. Such instrumentalism found one
basis in what has been termed the doctrine of the 'probable sign'.[52]
A probable sign is one which is read as *an effect from which a cause can
be inferred*. For example, hyperbole is seen as the natural expression
of anger and the appearance of that trope allows the reader to infer
anger as its source. Such a doctrine, Patey shows, formed the basis
for theories of the arts of communication in the eighteenth century
until the 1790s.

> 'Probable signs' are effects which lead the mind to infer to their
> causes; probable signification, we might say, is a causal relation in
> reverse. Until well into the eighteenth century, it was through
> probable signs that reasoning from effect to cause, from the 'mani-
> fest' (outer) properties of objects to their 'occult' or 'hidden'
> (inner) properties was understood ... the theory of the literary
> work as a structure of probable signs, of interpretation as a proba-

bilistic process of sign-inference, of criticism as an attempt to formulate general rules of literary probability, and even of rhetoric and the theory of acting as formularies for the deployment of probable signs, was the property of the Augustan age as a whole. It was, in short, the Augustan theory of literature. (Patey, pp. 35–89)

The instrumental use of signs of passion in oratory is one instance of this doctrine at work, another is the deployment of gesture and expression in acting. Once one is alert to it, one notices this rhetorical anthropology at work in the minutiae of many texts of this period. Lowth, for instance, adds to the ancient maxim that each emotion has its visual sign the view that each has also its characteristic linguistic sign: 'Every impulse of the mind ... has not only a peculiar style and expression, but a certain tone of voice, and a certain gesture of the body adopted to it' (Lowth, p. 50). Such accounts of visual and verbal signs were ubiquitous (Patey, p. 96). Rhetorical effects are taken as immediate evidence of a psychic condition, whether imitated or sincere.

It is a short step from a view of composition as the instrumental use of probable signs, in oratory or acting, and the techniques of calculated or indulged illusion, to the view that the best way to evoke the response one wishes is be genuinely impassioned oneself. Duff gives the following account of Plato's inspiration:

> He was indeed animated with all that ardor and enthusiasm of Imagination which distinguishes the Poet; and it is impossible for a person, possessed of any degree of sensibility, to read his Writings without catching somewhat of the enthusiasm. (Duff, p. 104)

Passages like this seem at first to conform to empiricist notions of observation or inductive enquiry. But the sole evidence for Plato's inspiration is his text, read according to certain assumptions about passion and its transitivity. It is one thing to argue that passion in composition may be an energising force with unusual communicative properties, it is quite another to argue from the passion received from the text that the author's psyche must have been in a particular state. This is to make a metaphorical identification between the texts of a writer and the authorial voice projected as the virtual or seeming origin of those writings.[53] A great deal turns around the pivotal and seemingly innocent word 'and' ('and it is impossible ... to read his [Plato's] Writing without catching somewhat of the enthusiasm'). There is a slight, unobtrusive but quite decisive shift here from the rhetorical/instrumental to a 'psychological' frame of reference. To be more precise a 'psychological' conception of inspiration as a natural psychological state emerges from an internalization or automatization, under the categories of the natural or spontaneous, of procedures previously considered a matter of instrumental technique.

Lowth's definition of sublimity is a particularly striking instance of the erosion of rhetorical modes of thought. The terminology of his passage wavers uncertainly between differing senses. For Lowth the sublime is

> that force of composition, whatever it be, which strikes and overpowers the mind, which excites the passions, and which expresses ideas at once with perspicuity and elevation; not solicitous whether the language be plain or ornamented, refined or familiar. (Lowth, p. 155)

The first half of this extract could be concerned entirely with the rhetorical effects of a text. Thus one would read 'composition' in its ancient sense as referring to the organization of the material (*compositio, sunthesis*). The rest of the clause would thus be a dramatization of the reader's or auditor's experience as the sublime 'strikes and overpowers the mind' and 'excites the passions'. Yet the way the sentence continues makes this reading uncertain. It becomes clear that 'composition' here also means a psychic process, albeit one presumably inferred from the text. It can only be the author's mind that is not 'solicitous whether the language be plain or ornamental, refined or familiar.' At the same time, Lowth is arguing on the basis of a rhetorical anthropology which tends to identify or conflate the affects of composition and the affects of reception, so that his account of sublimity may still be read as dealing with either or both. 'Every masterly Composer of Music', writes Duff, 'must feel, in the most intense and exquisite degree, the various emotions, which, by his compositions, he attempts to excite in the minds of others' (Duff, p. 250).[54]

In sum, accounts from this time which purport to describe the workings of the psyche during the process of invention or composition are not always the psychological analyses they purport to be. Statements of the poet's creative frenzy during composition are constructions or projections, enabled by a reasoning backwards from 'effect' to 'cause'. Thus exalted images of Milton are produced from out of the sublime effects of reading *Paradise Lost*. An 'imaginative confusion between authorial identity and creative artefact ... characterizes the reception of Milton more than any other poet in the [English] literary canon.'[55] Writers thus become the figures of secular myth, as in the busts of Dryden, Milton and Shakespeare that Alexander Pope kept near his desk.

In this way, with questions of technique and effect down-played by a rhetorical anthropology of the passions with their 'natural' indices, and with the effects of the composition reflected back to construct a virtual scene of invention, the artist's psyche becomes conceived as the arena of intense and peculiarly contagious affects, an inner theatre of proto-rhetorical energies. The artist, seen now as also the first recipient or audience of these forces, comes to seem a curiously passive figure, mediating energies from seemingly hidden depths. This idealization of the artist as cultural hero, the genius whose products exceed all craft, thus goes hand in hand with the image of the artist as a humble servant of the very forces the reader feels in response to the work.

Conceptions of written composition

Until the latter half of the eighteenth century, it is rare to find accounts of poetic composition that deal with written composition at all as something distinct from an oral affair. When such a distinc-tion is acknowledged, it can cause problems. Blair's work is a case in point. He not only stresses the oral nature and origins of poetry as a form older than prose (II, 314–18), but his advocacy of sincere passion in written composition, as we have seen, is an internaliza-tion of a scene of oral performance. In one passage Blair admits the difficulty of forcing an oral model upon written composition. Defending what he calls the 'Vehement' in style he writes:

> It has a peculiar ardour; it is a glowing Style; the language of a man, whose imagination and passions are heated, and strongly affected by what he writes; who is therefore negligent of lesser graces, but pours himself with the rapidity and fulness of a torrent. (Blair, *Lectures*, II, 399; cf. Lowth, p. 174)

At this point the inappropriateness of the oral model seems to strike Blair, who continues, 'It [the vehement] belongs to the higher kinds of oratory; and indeed is rather expected from a man who is speak-ing, than from one who is writing in his closet.' Blair confronts the difficulty by drawing on notions of natural signification, arguing that passion in written composition expresses itself in certain intensifying figures of speech, such as apostrophe and exclamation, and that these, appealing to the reader's faculty of sympathy, will excite an analogous passion there. Yet the very example Blair chooses to illustrate the power of sympathy again contradicts his avowed topic of written composition – he falls back on the enthusiasm of crowd-psychology:

> Sympathy is a very powerful and extensive principle in our nature, disposing us to enter into every feeling and passion, which we behold expressed by others. Hence, a single person coming into company with strong marks, either of melancholy or joy, upon his countenance, will diffuse that passion, in a moment through the whole circle. Hence in a great crowd, passions are so easily caught, and so fast spread, by that powerful contagion which the animated looks, cries, and gestures of a multitude never fail to carry. (Blair, *Lectures*, II, 357)

The next sentence, about written figures, is almost a *non sequitur*: 'Now, interrogations and exclamations, being natural signs of a moved and agitated mind, always, when they are properly used, dispose us to sympathize with the dispositions of those who use them, and to feel as they feel' (II, 357). Blair can only, it seems, fall back on those aspects of a text that mark a sort of ghost-drama. He concludes that 'the writer' should always attend to the genuine expressions of passion and never 'affect the style of a passion which he does not feel.' The writer must 'attend to the manner in which nature dictates to us to express any emotion or passion' (II, 357). An ethic of sincerity is bolstered by the implicit image of the space of written composition as the site of an imaginary audience or crowd. The space of composition in Blair is still one of a latent rhetorical drama. Likewise, the notion, dating from this period, that sincere passion is the poet's most reliable inspiration was to become such a cliché that we forget how odd, and even inappropriate, it is for the heavily mediated act of written composition. A similar uncertainty about orality characterizes and, to modern tastes, mars the style of the poetry of this time. In *Night Thoughts*, for instance, or several of the odes of Collins, the poet's stress on the solitude and interiority of religious meditation rests incongruously with a heightened rhap-sodic style whose loudness casts its reader amidst virtual crowds.

Theorists who dwell in a more focused way on the constraints and effects of written composition valorize it in an unprecedented form. Two points are striking. The first concerns the absence of an immediate audience for written composition, which is thus seen as demanding less attention to rhetorical affect and more to the subject matter itself. Such attention to the text itself as object facilitates modes of thinking, such as the ideal of 'organic' form, that under-stand the work as the manifestation of its own, inherent properties.

Secondly, theorists who discuss the particular demands and resources of written composition tend to express them in terms of a doctrine of associationism. This is true of Joseph Priestley, Alexander Gerard, William Hazlitt and, most famously, the Wordsworth of the Preface to *Lyrical Ballads*.

A rather forced analogy between the oral and the written (similar to Blair's) plays a crucial structuring role in Priestley's advocacy of 'ardour' in written composition. It is the act of inscription that is analogous to the orator's moment of delivery. The writing should be a *mimesis* of that ardour, preserving 'the very *order* and *connexion*' of the sentiments and sensations of the time of composition: 'For, such is the similarity of all human minds, that when the same appearances are presented to another person, his mind will, in general, be equally struck and affected with them ...' (Priestley, *Lectures*, p. 31). The text thus becomes a double *mimesis*, communicating the passion of the time of composition itself as well as the matter of the discourse.

For Priestley, however, the act of composition is also an essentializing process. Whatever the initial looseness of first ideas, the 'close attention to a subject which [written] composition requires, unavoidably warms the imagination: then ideas crowd upon us, the mind hastens, as it were, into the midst of things, and is impatient till those strong conceptions be expressed' (p. 31). Written composition is superior to the arts of public speaking because of the way it brings to bear the mind's powers of association. It forces a 'nicer discernment' of 'the relations and connexions of things' and is thus more suitable for people of exact judgement. For others, however, public speaking is more suitable, for there minor lapses of logic or coherence tend to go unnoticed (p. 30).

Alexander Gerard's account of great scientists and artists at work relates the 'enthusiastic ardour' that arises from the exertions of genius to an enlivening of the mind's powers of associating ideas and of judging the possible efficacy of new associations (*An Essay on Genius*, p. 69). Gerard also implicitly valorizes non-oral composition for its enforced attention on the subject matter rather than immediate effect: 'It is reported of Marini, that he was so intent on revising some stanzas of his Adonis, that he suffered one of his legs to be burnt for a considerable time, before he was sensible of it' (p. 69). Gerard's attempt to find a rational explanation for what people claim to have experienced as inspiration rests on the doctrine of association of ideas, as does his whole theory of the nature of genius.

When an ingenious track of thinking presents itself, though but casually, to true genius, occupied it may be with something else, imagination darts alongst it with great rapidity; and by this rapidity its ardor is more inflamed. The velocity of its motion sets it on fire, like a chariot wheel which is kindled by the quickness of revolution (pp. 67–8)[56]

Although it is not commonly read as such, William Wordsworth's 1802 Preface to the *Lyrical Ballads* is a crucial document in the emergence of notions of inspiration explicitly related to writing. Nevertheless, Wordsworth was an oral poet in a restricted sense: 'He never wrote down as he composed, composed walking, riding, or in bed, and wrote down after ...'[57] Moreover, Wordsworth's debt to rhetorical culture was immense. Quintilian's argument on heightened passion as a natural source of eloquence is echoed in the Preface. It also quotes Quintilian book ten as its motto. Yet one way to read the famous doctrine of 'emotion recollected in tranquillity' (or in bed) is as adjusting a model of inspiration as sympathetic passion to the more mediated conditions of producing written manuscript in solitude. Wordsworth goes further than Priestley in his focus on the essentializing and intensifying effects to be found in the passion uniquely associated with the act and time of composition itself. The concept of *inventio* as a working of the mind upon itself receives a philosophical underpinning in Wordsworth's modifications of associationism:

I have said that poetry is the spontaneous overflow of powerful feelings: it takes its origin from emotion recollected in tranquillity: the emotion is contemplated till, by a species of re-action, the tranquillity gradually disappears, and an emotion, kindred to that which was before the subject of contemplation, is gradually produced, and does itself actually exist in the mind. In this mood successful composition generally begins ... (*Prose*, I, 149)

This passage recalls Wordsworth's admiration for Dennis's distinction between vulgar or non-reflective passion and enthusiastic passion.[58] Poetic enthusiasm has been revised in terms of the intensifying and purifying effects of reflection. Wordsworth depicts the process of composition as one in which received language is radically metamorphosed, removed from its relatively arbitrary or parochial associations, and rendered universal. This ideal he then grounds (controversially) in his defence of the language of supposedly timeless rural communities.

One of the best essays on Wordsworth from his own day concentrates entirely on the contrasted kinds of power and self-conception available through oral and through written modes of composition. This is William Hazlitt's 'On the Difference between Writing and Speaking' in *The Plain Speaker* (1826).[59] Though it nowhere mentions Wordsworth by name, Hazlitt's language recalls the Preface to the *Lyrical Ballads* in a way that recurrently suggests Wordsworth as one model for the writer in this account. This is a figure pictured, according to Wordsworth's public image, as a solitary in meditation, brooding upon an inner imaginative power capable of transforming its perceptions into forms that, as writing or poetry, may endure across wide stretches of space and time.

Orality, for Hazlitt, is the medium of immediate effect, of 'rhetoric' in its pejorative sense. Oral power is associated with the career politician, the demagogue and mob psychology. Hazlitt writes of the 'most dashing orator' he ever heard: 'He was the model of a flashy, powerful demagogue – a madman blessed with a fit audience. He was possessed, infuriated with the patriotic *mania* ...' (p. 264). He seems the centre of a mass hysteria, which he inflames, feeds off and manipulates: 'The lightning of national indignation flashed from his eye; the workings of the popular mind were seen labouring in his bosom ...' (p. 264). These 'electrical fusions' however are lifeless in print – 'In speaking, he was like a volcano vomiting out *lava*; in writing, he is like a volcano burnt out' (p. 264). Hazlitt contrasts this figure with Edmund Burke, whose speeches, on delivery, were appreciated by only four or five people in the House.

It is writers, not orators, who are more truly inspired:

> They are never less alone than when alone. Mount them on a dinner-table, and they have nothing to say; shut them up in a room by themselves, and they are inspired. They are 'made fierce with dash keeping.' In revenge for being tongue-tyed, a torrent of words flows from their poems, and the storm which was so long collecting comes down apace. (p. 278)

This recalls those passages in the Preface to *Lyrical Ballads* in which the poet is said to be distinguished by a greater propensity to think, feel and become empowered in expression without the occasions of external circumstances[60] – power is said to come from independent, internal sources. Like Wordsworth, Hazlitt characterizes the long-term business of written composition as a process of intensification and reduction to the essential. Both employ the terminology of associationism. A writer, unlike a public speaker, Hazlitt observes, can afford to wait for the precise word: 'his associations are habitually intense, not vague and shallow, and words occur to him only as *tallies* to certain modifications of feeling. They are links in the chain of thought' (Hazlitt, pp. 277–8).[61] Writing, as the product of long study and profound thinking, is more concerned, in Wordsworth's terminology, with 'passions and thoughts and feelings' that are 'the general passions and thoughts and feelings of men' (Preface to *Lyrical Ballads*, *Prose*, I, 142).

All the Romantic (male) poets were educated not only in the art of rhetoric as a staple part of their curriculum, but also in the composition of Latin verses. Coleridge describes such training in his *Biographia Literaria* (I, 8–12). Central to the practice of Latin versifying was the so-called *Gradus ad Parnassum*, the much reprinted compendium of 'places' for use in compositions, i.e. stock epithets, phrases, synonyms, paraphrases and quotations to be worked into new compositions. As Ong observes: 'Books in which commonplaces in the sense of cullings or excerpts were gathered could be anything from collections of moderately lengthy passages of several words on set subjects, such as heroism or treachery or a description of a storm at sea, to lists of mere epithets or stock phrases ...'[62] In the Preface to *Lyrical Ballads* Wordsworth set himself against an anglicized form of this tradition of composition in rejecting a poetic diction caricatured as laden with tautologous epithets and redundant abstractions ('In vain to me the smiling mornings shine / And reddening Phoebus lifts his golden fire' (Thomas Gray, quoted by Wordsworth (Preface, *Prose*, I, 132)). This sort of language is to be replaced by one supposedly more 'natural'. In effect, a notion of inspiration and composition structured by the reflective effects of explicitly written composition goes hand in hand with a rejection of residually formulaic modes of expression.[63]

According to Hazlitt's essay, a chief requisite for the writer is 'patience of soul, and a power increasing with the difficulties it has to master' (p. 262). By 'power' Hazlitt means not only the supposed universality of what a writer produces, but an experience of empowerment undergone in the act of composition.[64] Again echoing Wordsworth's description of the poet in the Preface (*Prose*, I, 288–9), Hazlitt locates this power in the writer's introspectiveness:

> The whole of a man's thoughts and feelings cannot lie on the surface, made up for use; but the whole must be a greater quantity, a mightier power, if they could be got at, layer under layer, and

brought into play by the levers of imagination and reflection. Such
a person sees farther and feels deeper than most others. (Hazlitt, p.
279)

Yet this 'power' is still – even in the 1820s – recognizably an internalization of a speaker's power over a crowd: '[Writers] are never
less alone than when alone' (p. 278); while they 'look into their
own minds, not in the faces of a gaping multitude' (p. 279) yet their
internal power may be a 'storm' lashing itself 'into a foam' (p. 278),
just as a public speaker had been 'like a volcano vomiting out *lava*'
(p. 264). Writing is an act of internalized oratory, the oral become
meditative, essential and potentially ubiquitous; populism become
universalism. The associations of enthusiasm with popular leadership and personal charisma are internalized. In Wordsworth's *The
Prelude*, subject of the first of our individual case studies, such
connections remain both legible and decisive.

Notes

1 Walter Ong, *Rhetoric, Romance, and Technology: Studies in the Interaction of
Expression and Culture* (Ithaca and London: Cornell University Press, 1971),
p. 3. To turn to the sixteenth-century Pléaide poet, Pontus de Tyard, is to
find an account of the process of composition that seems to merge the
claim that the source of one's work is divine, with details of an experience
of composition that bespeak a predominant orality. Pontus writes, in his
Solitaire Premier, ou, Discours des Muses, et de la fureur poëtique (1552):

> La fureur Poëtique procede des Muses (dy-je) et est un ravissement
> de l'Ame, qui est docile et invincible: au moyen duquel elle est
> esveillée, esmuë, et incitée par chants, et autres Poësies, à l'instruc-
> tion des hommes. Par ce ravissement d'Ame, j'enten que l'Ame est
> occupée, et entierement convertie, et intentive aux saintes et sacrées
> Muses, qui l'ont rencontrée docile et apte à recevoir la forme,
> qu'elles impriment, c'est à dire, l'ont trouvée preparée à estre esprise
> de ce ravissement, par lequel estant esmeuë, elle devient invincible,
> et ne peut estre souillée, ou vaincue d'aucune chose basse et terrestre
> ... D'avantage elle est esveillée du sommeil et dormir corporel à
> l'intellectuel veiller, et revoquée des tenebres d'ignorance à la
> lumiere de verité. (*Oeuvres: Le Solitaire Premier*, ed. Silvio F. Baridon
> (Geneva: Droz, 1950) pp. 21–2)

Pontus's claim to inspiration is scarcely part of what we would nowadays
recognise as a theory of the process of composition. The stress is mainly on
the content of the verse, on the divine insight granted the poet by the
Christianized Muses. Nevertheless, the traditional claim that inspiration is
transmitted from the muses and the poets to 'ceux qui les recitent et inter-
pretent' and thence to their audience, may testify how far poetry, though

it was archived as writing, was still primarily a matter of oral recitation.

2 Derrida, 'Qual Quelle: Valéry's Sources', in *Margins of Philosophy*, trans. Alan Bass (Chicago: University of Chicago Press, 1982), pp. 273–306, p. 298.

3 For the decisive place of British writers on enthusiasm and genius in Germany see Hans-Jürgen Schings, *Melancholie und Aufklärung: Melancholie und ihre Kritiker in Erfahrungsseelenkunde und Literatur des 18. Jahrhunderts* (Stuttgart: J. B. Mezlersche, 1977).

4 E. R. Curtius, *European Literature and the Latin Middle Ages* [1948], trans. William R. Trask (London: Routledge & Kegan Paul, 1953), pp. 238–44.

5 'The Answer of Mr. Hobbes to Sir William Davenant's Preface before Gondibert', in *The English Works of Thomas Hobbes of Malmesbury*, 11 vols ed. Sir William Molesworth (1839–49; np: Scientia Aalen, 1962), IV, pp. 443–60, p. 448.

6 See Grahame Castor, *Pléiade Poetics: A Study in Sixteenth-Century Thought and Terminology* (Cambridge: Cambridge University Press, 1964), pp. 24–50.

7 See Susie I. Tucker, *Enthusiasm: A Study in Semantic Change* (Cambridge: Cambridge University Press, 1972), p. 27.

8 See Truman Guy Steffan, 'The Social Argument Against Enthusiasm (1650–1660)', *Texas Studies in English* (1941), 39–63.

9 Casaubon, *A Treatise Concerning Enthusiasm* (London: 1655).

10 Parker, *A Free and Impartial Censure of the Platonick Philosophie* (Oxford: 1666), p. 73.

11 See Steffan, *The Social Argument*, p. 39. See also Mary R. Ryder, 'Avoiding the "Many-Headed Monster": Wesley and Johnson on Enthusiam', *Methodist History*, 23 (1985), 214–22. 'Enthusiasm' retains pejorative overtones until well into the nineteenth century. Coleridge, in *Aids to Reflection* (1825) (ed. John Beer, vol. 9 of *The Collected Works of Samuel Taylor Coleridge*, gen. ed. Kathleen Coburn (London: Routledge, 1993)) merely makes up a late member of a series of thinkers who feel bound to perform a gesture of disassociation between a truly visionary enthusiasm and enthusiasm in the pejorative sense of fanaticism or *Schwärmerei* (p. 389, 393).

12 'Enthousiasme' in *Encyclopédie ou Dictionnaire Raisonée des Sciences, des Arts et des Métiers* (Paris: 1755).

13 G. W. Leibniz gives a succinct history of the semantics of 'enthusiasm' in Western Europe in his *New Essays on Human Understanding* [1765], trans. Peter Remnant & Jonathan Bennett (Cambridge: Cambridge University Press, 1981), pp. 505–6.

14 Frank E. Manuel, *The Eighteenth Century Confronts the Gods* (Cambridge, Mass: Harvard University Press, 1959) p. 71.

15 See Shaun Anthony Irlam, 'Unworlding and Otherworldliness: Enthusiasm, Epiphany, and Typology in the Poetry of James Thomson and Edward Young', Diss. Johns Hopkins University, 1993, pp. 42–4.

16 For an argument on the concepts of *Schwärmerei* and *Enthusiasmus* in the German lands comparable to that given in this chapter concerning Britain see Schings, *Melancholie und Aufklärung*; Jonathan P. Clark, 'Beyond Rhyme or Reason. Fanaticism and the Transference of Interpretive Paradigms from

the Seventeenth-Century Orthodoxy to the Aesthetics of Enlightenment', *MLN*, 105 (1990), 563–82.

17 See Michael Heyd, 'The Reaction to Enthusiasm in the Seventeenth Century: From Anti-Structure to Structure', *Religion* 15 (1985), 279–89; also Irlam, 'Unworldling', pp. 53–172.

18 Devotional poets, like the Anglican Thomas Traherne or the Royalist Henry Vaughan (in *Silex Scintillans* (1650)), had deployed in their work the vocabulary and visionary claims associated with enthusiasm and its drive to transgress or transcend the limits of the finite self. The association of enthusiasm with poets could entail a non-pejorative sense of the word even prior to the eighteenth century, as its relation to Plato's vocabulary must suggest to any educated reader. John Dryden, in 'The Author's Apology for Heroic Poetry and Poetic License' (1677) writes that 'Imaging is, in itself, the very height and life of Poetry. It is, as Longinus describes it, a discourse which, by a kind of enthusiasm or extraordinary emotion of the soul, makes it seem to us that we behold those things which the poet paints' (*Essays of John Dryden*, 2 vols, ed. W. P. Ker (Oxford: Clarendon Press, 1926), I, 178–90, p. 186). See also Michael Ponsford, '"Poetical Fury": The Religious Enthusiasts of the Late Seventeenth Century', *Christian Scholar's Review*, 16 (1986), 24–39.

19 More, *Enthusiasmus Triumphatus* (London: 1656), p. 20.

20 James Thomson, *The Complete Poetical Works*, ed. J. Logie Robertson (1908; London: Oxford University Press, 1963); Edward Young, *Night Thoughts*, ed. Stephen Cornford (Cambridge: Cambridge University Press, 1989). See Irlam, 'Unworldling'; Michèle Plaisant, 'La Poésie de la nature et le concept d'enthousiasme (1726–1750): Redécouverte, évolution et transformations', *Bulletin de la Société d'Etudes Anglo-Américaines de XVII et XVIII Siècles*, 38 (1994), 171–82.

21 See Clement Hawes, *Mania and Literary Style: The Rhetoric of Enthusiasm from the Ranters to Christopher Smart* (Cambridge: Cambridge University Press, 1996); John Mee, *Dangerous Enthusiasm: William Blake and the Culture of Radicalism in the 1790s* (Oxford: Clarendon Press, 1992).

22 Voltaire, *Philosophical Dictionary* [1764], ed., trans., Theodore Besterman (London: Penguin, 1971), p. 188.

23 See Kineret S. Jaffe, 'The Concept of Genius: Its Changing Role in Eighteenth-Century French Aesthetics', *Journal of the History of Ideas*, 41 (1980), 579–99, pp. 595–8.

24 *Aristotle, Horace, Longinus: Classical Literary Criticism*, trans. T. S. Dorsch (London: Penguin, 1965). See Richard Macksey, 'Longinus Reconsidered', *MLN*, 108 (1993), 913–34.

25 Blair, *Lectures on Rhetoric and Belles Lettres*, 2 vols, ed. Harold F. Harding (Carbondale and Edwardsville: Southern Illinois University Press, 1965), I, 57–79.

26 See George A. Kennedy, 'Hellenistic Literary and Philosophical Scholarship', in *The Cambridge History of Criticism*, I, Classical Criticism, ed. George A. Kennedy (Cambridge : Cambridge University Press, 1989), pp. 200–14, p. 213.

27 See Douglas Lane Patey, *Probability and Literary Form: Philosophic theory and*

literary practice in the Augustan Age (Cambridge: Cambridge University Press, 1984), pp. 174–80.

28 *Grounds*, in *The Critical Works of John Dennis*, 2 vols, ed. Edward Niles Hooker (Baltimore: The Johns Hopkins Press, 1939–43), I, 325–73, p. 359.

29 Hobbes, *Leviathan, or The Matter, Form, and Power of a Commonwealth, Ecclesiastical and Civil* [1651], *Works*, III, 63–41.

30 In *Les Beaux Arts réduits à un même principe* (Paris: 1746) Abbé Charles Batteux argues that genius is entirely an affair of learning and rationality. What seems like inspiration is merely a response of joy at what one's reason has produced. A comparable argument appears in William Sharpe's *A Dissertation upon Genius* [1755], (facsimile edition; Delmay, New York: Scholars' Facsimiles, 1973. For D'Alembert, writing in the *Encyclopédie* (1755), genius is merely reasoning taking place at an unusual speed. For these and related arguments see Jaffe, 'The Concept of Genius'. Alexander Gerard's influential *An Essay on Genius* (1774) employs the principles of associationism to argue along similar lines.

31 See Stanley Grean, *Shaftesbury's Philosophy of Religion and Ethics: A Study in Enthusiasm* (n.p.: Ohio University Press, 1967), p. 27. For Herder's comment see Schings, *Melancholie und Aufklärung*, p. 183. See also E. Casati, 'Hérauts et commentateurs de Shaftesbury en France', *Revue de la Littérature Comparée*, 14 (1934), 615–45.

32 Shaftesbury, *Characteristics of Men, Manners, Opinions, Times* [1711], 2 vols, ed. John M. Robertson (London: Grant Richards, 1900), II, 3–156, p. 129.

33 See Frederick Burwick, *Poetic Madness and the Romantic Imagination* (University Park: University of Pennsylvania Press, 1996), pp. 21–42.

34 Duff, *An Essay on Original Genius and its Various Modes of Exertion in Philosophy and the Fine Arts, Particularly Poetry* [1767], ed. John L. Mahoney (Delmar, New York: Scholar's Facsimiles, 1978), pp. 171–2.

35 George Campbell, *Philosophy of Rhetoric*, 7th edn (London, W. Bayne, 1823), p. 7.

36 P. W. K. Stone, *The Art of Poetry 1750–1820: Theories of Poetic Composition and Style in the Late Neo-Classic and Early Romantic Periods* (London: Routledge and Kegan Paul, 1967), p. 16.

37 The arts of rhetoric carried over into literate cultures many of the skills and techniques first associated with orality and extempore performance. See Frank D'Angelo, 'The Evolution of the Analytic Topoi', in *Essays on Classical Rhetoric and Discourse*, ed. Robert J. Connors, Lisa S. Ede, and Andrea Lunsford (Carbondale: Southern Illinois University Press, 1984), pp. 50–68.

38 Ong, *Rhetoric, Romance and Technology*, p. 261.

39 Young, *Conjectures on Original Composition, in a letter to the Author of Sir Charles Grandison* (London: 1759).

40 'If it shall now be enquired, What are the proper sources of the Sublime? My answer is, That they are to be looked for every where in nature. It is not by hunting after tropes, and figures, and rhetorical assistances, that we can expect to produce it. No: it stands clear, for the most part, of these laboured refinements of art. It must come unsought, if it come at all; and be the natural offspring of a strong imagination' (Blair, *Lectures*, I, 75). See

also *Lecture XXXII*. Joseph Priestley sees the *topoi* as suitable for novices only or for set declamations, not original matter; *A Course of Lectures on Oratory and Criticism* [1777], facsimile edition (Menston: The Scholar's Press, 1968), p. 24.

41 See Terence Cave, *The Cornucopian Text: Problems of Writing in the French Renaissance* (Oxford: Clarendon, 1979), pp. 126–34.

42 Cave, *The Cornucopian Text*, p. 125.

43 Adam Smith, *Lectures on Rhetoric and Belles Lettres ... Reported by a Student in 1762–3*, ed. John M. Lothian (London: Thomas Nelson and Sons, 1963), pp. 22–3.

44 See Stone, *The Art of Poetry*, pp. 64–76.

45 Priestley, *Lectures*, p. 110. See also Stone, *The Art of Poetry* (on Lord Kames), p. 75; Duff, *An Essay on Original Genius* (on oratory), p. 205; Gerard, *An Essay on Genius*, p. 66. Not surprisingly, ideas of effective eloquence as the contagious impersonation of passion in poetics and rhetoric are matched almost exactly in theories of acting. See Earl Wasserman, 'The Sympathetic Imagination in Eighteenth-Century Theories of Acting', *Journal of English and Germanic Philology*, 46 (1947), 264–72. The Wordsworth of the Preface to *Lyrical Ballads* also sees the ideal poet as such an universal impersonator, one who must actually create and feel within the passion to be communicated (*The Prose Works of William Wordsworth*, 3 vols, ed. W. J. B. Owen, and Jane Worthington Smyser (Oxford: Clarendon Press, 1974), I, 118–88, p. 138).

46 See Scott Harshbarger, 'Robert Lowth's *Sacred Hebrew Poetry* and the Oral Dimension of Romantic Rhetoric', in *Rhetorical Traditions and British Romantic Literature*, ed. Don H. Bialostosky and Lawrence D. Needham (Bloomington: Indiana University Press, 1995), pp. 199–214.

47 Robert Lowth, *Lectures on the Sacred Poetry of the Hebrews*, trans. G. Gregory (London: S. Chadwick and Co., 1847).

48 David Norton, *A History of the Bible as Literature*, 2 vols (Cambridge: Cambridge University Press, 1993), I, 194–5.

49 Stephen Prickett describes Lowth's *Lectures on the Sacred Poetry of the Hebrews* as 'the book that was to transform biblical studies in England and Germany alike, and which was to do more than any other single work to make the biblical tradition [the poet taking a prophetic stance], rather than the neo-classical one, the central poetic tradition of the Romantics' (*Words and the Word: Language, Poetics and Biblical Interpretation* (Cambridge: Cambridge University Press, 1986) p. 105.

50 Leo Braudy, *The Frenzy of Renown: Fame and its History* (New York: Oxford University Press, 1986), p. 419. The odd conjunction of professional self-promotion and the claim to the authority of embodying a communal *ethos* manifests itself in the bizarre careers and forgeries of James Macpherson and Thomas Chatterton, both trying to pass off their work as the redis-covered product of an idealized past.

51 See F. M. Barnard, *Herder's Social and Political Thought: From Enlightenment to Nationalism* (Oxford: Clarendon Press, 1965).

52 Patey, *Probability and Literary Form*.

53 A notable exception is Henry Home, Lord Kames's *Elements of Criticism*, 2

vols (Edinburgh: 1761) which limits itself with unusual strictness to analysis of works only and their effects: when Kames writes of a piece of writing 'expressing' an emotion his use of the shifting term 'express' is confined solely to the affects produced by the text upon a reader.

54 Likewise, in the following quotation from Coleridge the little word 'and' again does an enormous amount of hidden work: 'The very assumption that we are reading the work of a poet supposes that he is in a continuous state of excitement; *and* thereby arises a language in prose unnatural but in poetry natural' (*Shakespearean Criticism*, 2 vols, ed. T. M. Raysor (London: Constable, 1930), II, 42; emphasis added.

55 Lucy Newlyn, Paradise Lost *and the Romantic Reader* (Oxford: Clarendon Press, 1993), p. 27.

56 Compare Duff's account of the composition of his own treatise on genius, *An Essay on Original Genius*, p. iv.

57 From *The Greville Memoirs*, requoted from *The Critical Opinions of William Wordsworth*, ed. Markham L. Peacock Jr. (Baltimore: Johns Hopkins University Press, 1950), p. 23. For Wordsworth's habits of oral composition see Andrew J. Bennett, '"Devious Feet": Wordsworth and the Scandal of Narrative Form', *ELH*, 59 (1992), 145–73.

58 See W. J. B. Owen, *Wordsworth as Critic* (London: Oxford University Press, 1969), pp. 215–21.

59 *The Complete Works of William Hazlitt*, 21 vols, ed. P. Howe (London and Toronto; J. M. Dent, 1931), XII, 262–79.

60 *Prose Works of William Wordsworth*, I, 138, 142; see also Paul Magnuson, 'Wordsworth and Spontaneity', in *The Evidence of the Imagination*, ed. Donald H. Reiman. (New York: New York University Press, 1978), pp. 101–18, pp. 103–7.

61 Compare the Preface, *Prose Works of William Wordsworth*, I, 127.

62 Ong, *Rhetoric, Romance and Technology*, p. 262.

63 See Ong, *Rhetoric, Romance and Technology*, pp. 255–83.

64 Compare the Preface, *Prose Works of William Wordsworth*, I, 283.

CHAPTER 4

The fantasy crowd 1: 'Power' in Wordsworth's *The Prelude*

We have done with patronage ... An author leaves the great and applies to the multitude (Johnson)

Introduction: composition as self-totalization

William Wordsworth's autobiographical epic, *The Prelude*,[1] presents itself as growing out of what has become one of the famous instances of writer's block. Unable to make headway with an over-ambitious philosophical poem to be called 'The Recluse', Wordsworth recalls with frustration the seeming promise of his childhood: 'Was it for this / That one, the fairest of all rivers, loved / To blend his murmurs with my nurse's song ...?' (Bk. 1, ll. 269–70). The text then moves fluently into memories of infancy, and becomes, in effect, a new and different poem from that first envisaged. Wordsworth's solution to his writing block then is to present his text as enacting the space of composition itself. The act of writing is valorized as the poet's search for the sources of his power, located in a process of repeated meditation upon formative experiences. Progression becomes a matter, paradoxically, of retro-spection and reflective appropriation as the poet narrates his own life. Existing in possibly some twenty versions, and unpublished until after its writer's death, *The Prelude* becomes an exercise in self-definition. The poem takes up the epic theme of a hero's ordeal and applies it to the vicissitudes of the poet's own imagination. Conceived by Wordsworth as a trial of his poetic strength, *The Prelude* is less a chronological account of a life than an attempt to depict a personal essence.

The Prelude employs structure of crisis and recovery reminis-cent of the tradition of spiritual autobiography, but it largely secularizes notions of divine election and inspiration to put them at the service of a form of individualism. The poet emerges from the despair caused by the failures of the revolutionary politics of his day through conversion to a cult of self-discovery and development, with meditations on the nature of a poet's possible fame and power. The poem is already, in effect, a book-length version of the more banal narratives of the 'moment of insight' that still recur in accounts of creativity to this day.

The process of composition is one in which the poet tries to 'enshrine the spirit of the past/For future restoration' (Bk. 11, ll. 341–2). The arduous process of writing, self-reading and revision is seen as one of self-refinement and self-appropriation, in which the writer attempts to assume the character of an essentialized figure whose efforts may transcend parochial limitations of time and space. *The Prelude* sets up its own text as the self-reflection of a subject-object engaged in a progressive dialectic between unreflected spontaneous experience and its transmutations and intensification through meditation.[2]

This conception of the space of composition marries the minutiae of Wordsworth's practice of writing and repeated revision to his theory of subjectivity.[3] The space of composition forms a space of self-appraisal and self-transcendence that draws the writing of the poem into the workings of the theory it describes, with its exalted conception of human subjectivity. Following Isobel Armstrong, I know of no better introduction to Wordsworth's concept of subjectivity than a passage in Goethe's *The Sorrows of Young Werther*. There Werther speaks of the joys of growing one's own cabbages:

> Oh, how thankful I am that my heart can feel the simple, harmless joys of the man who brings to the table a head of cabbage he has grown himself, and in a single moment enjoys, not only the vegetable, but all the fine days and fresh mornings, since he planted it, the mild evenings when he watered it, and the pleasure he felt while watching it grow.[4]

Werther's sentimentalism is at the same time a Romantic conception of experience as the labour of the mind upon the objects of perception, a labour that is also, dialectically, an act of self-definition and self-creation – to eat the cabbage is to consume and totalize one's own past experiences in watching it grow. The thing or object in such a relation is not merely posited, it is partly constituted by consciousness and by all the emotions and associations vested in it over time. Experience is a metamorphosis, a dialectic of self-making through relation to an object world that reflects back the subject in its very act of totalizing its previous instantiations. This schema is already an account of the imagination as a principle of psychic growth in *The Prelude*. Likewise, in Wordsworth's infamous encounter with those daffodils ('I wandered, lonely as a cloud'), the memory of the experience becomes more powerful than the experience itself: 'I gazed and gazed, but little thought/What wealth the show to me had brought.' At issue here is an individualistic notion of subjectivity as the accumulator of internal property in the precise sense of that which is, or which becomes, one's own.

The processes of composition – or later revision – are themselves acts within this dialectic. Two of the poem's most striking scenes on an influx of poetic 'Power' are presented as having taken place during composition itself. Composition is not the representation of a subjectivity already there, but part of a process which institutes, sustains and enacts a higher self. For Wordsworth those aspects of invention or composition that surprise a poet in the space of composition are to be appropriated in a scene of self-constitution – as the result of sub-conscious processes of mind suddenly bearing fruit. Drawing on German Romantic-idealist thinking mediated through Coleridge, Wordsworth affirms these influxes of spontaneous power as the access to modes of the psyche inaccessible to the merely ratiocinative faculty. The psyche of the poet seems thereby confirmed as a power whose scope always transcends any one moment of self-reflection or introspection. Inspiration or 'Power' is not the irrationality of mere passion but the supra-rationality, so to speak, of the 'creative'.

This is the distinguishing feature of Romantic conceptions of inspiration: they are simultaneously theories of creativity and an active critique of received conceptions of rationality and normality. It is one of the ironies of *The Prelude*, however, that it should eulogise the values of small rural communities at the same time as promulgating an individualistic ethos of continuous self-development far more obviously appropriate to the urban capitalism it seems to attack.

Power as mass enthusiasm

Genealogies of the Romantic imagination have focused mainly on philosophical issues. They trace the emergence of theories of mind opposed to Enlightenment models based on 'mechanistic' or narrowly associationist arguments. Against these the mind is seen as itself a principle of active synthesis in relation to sense-data, a free, creative and active agent, and not the merely calculable product of environmental factors. Coleridge, elaborating his version of post-Kantian idealism, characterizes the imagination as a faculty of intuitive rather than merely discursive reason.[5] The importance to Wordsworth of these ultimately German ideas is indisputable. Nevertheless, Wordsworth's conception of inspiration cannot be wholly subsumed by this Romantic-idealist notion of the creative. Crucial aspects of it draw heavily on older and primarily rhetorical (as opposed to the philosophical) conceptions of poetic power – the focus is on enthusiasm, rhetorical affect and the contagiousness of passion as a transforming force upon a body of auditors or readers.

Book Nine of *The Prelude* recounts the young Wordsworth's ecstatic conversion-experience in France during the early days of the revolution. Wordsworth recalls conversations with Michel Beaupuy about their mutual hopes for the long-term effects of the revolution. Wordsworth considers the power of popular leaders. They talk

> Of single Spirits that catch the flame from Heaven,
> And how the multitude of men will feed
> And fan each other, thought of Sects, how keen
> They are to put the appropriate nature on,
> Triumphant over every obstacle
> Of custom, language, Country, love, and hate,
> And what they do and suffer for their creed,
> How far they travel, and how long endure,
> How quickly mighty Nations have been form'd,
> From least beginnings; how, together lock'd
> By new opinions, scatter'd tribes have made
> One body, spreading wide as clouds in heaven.
>
> (Bk. 9, ll. 376–87)

The implicit dynamic in this piece of proto-sociology lies in notions of contagious enthusiasm and 'sympathy'. An enthusiastic leader, catching 'the fire from heaven' may inspire, galvanize, unite and transform a multitude in a manner akin to the Pentecostal miracle. Beaupuy himself, a revolutionary possessed with all the traditional chivalric virtues, is described as 'Meek, though enthusiastic' (Bk. 9, l. 300). A similar passage on the early days of the revolution, extracted from drafts of *The Prelude*, was published in 1815 under the ambivalent title of 'French Revolution, As It Appeared to Enthusiasts at Its Commencement.'[6] In both texts the discourse of religious conversion has been reapplied as an account of mass social change, and depicted as a power strong enough to sweep away normal ties of custom, blood and country.

This aspect of *The Prelude* may be placed between seventeenth- and eighteenth-century notions of enthusiasm as a social force and the late nineteenth-century studies of political and religious fanaticism, the so-called 'crowd psychology' of Gustave Le Bon or Emile Durkheim's sociology of collective behaviour. Le Bon's work, and Freud's later study of mass hypnosis carry over many aspects of the earlier 'non-scientific' depictions of mass group phenomena, its class prejudice for instance.[7] Nevertheless, a common set of images and representations links these texts, earlier notions of mass enthusiasm and *Schwärmerei* and even contemporary studies of 'patterns of social action that are spontaneous and unstructured in as much as they are not organized and are not reducible to social structure.'[8] A crowd may take on characteristics quite different from that of any of the individuals composing it. A new and unified entity may form, together with a heightened sense of receptivity, an intensification of emotion, and a lowering of critical faculties – 'There is no question that, taken herdwise, people are less sane and sensible than they are dispersed.'[9] They may also be more idealistic or heroic. There is, simultaneously, a lowering of forces of psychic repression and an intensification of feeling, with 'casual stimuli making for enormous effects, by the avalanche-like growth of the most negligible impulses of love and hate' (Ross, p. 42). 'Contagion' – a term familiar from accounts of enthusiasm – recurs in texts on spontaneous mass psychology. Impulses emanating from the mass may spread rapidly to others. Much of the combined sense of glamour and apprehension felt by an observer of mass behaviour comes from this impulse to let go and to become part of it, to lose individuality in some more potent body.[10] One theorist fortuitously recalls the *Ion*: 'The mass draws us as the magnet polarises iron filings and holds us by its affective and irrational energy' (Moscovici, p. 93). In such conditions the performative power of language may reach almost a magical intensity, blurring the distinction 'between expressed and suggested reality' (Moscovici, p. 86). Above all, individuals may be 'out of themselves' (Ross, p. 51), possessed by a contagious and centripetal group-force: 'the release of impulses and feelings which encounter no restraint, which come to possess the individual, and which acquire a quasi-sanction through the support of other people, gives the individual a sense of power of ego-expansion, and of rectitude.

Thus he is likely to experience a sense of invincibility ... in his actions' (Blumer, p. 74). As critics of enthusiasm knew, it is invariably in large groups or meetings that people exhibit peculiar, seemingly visionary behaviour such as speaking-in-tongues, or manifest heightened oratorical power and fluency – effects exploited by religious leaders and revivalists. The release of being 'carried away by a spirit whose source is unknown' (Blumer, p. 76) may be cathartic in nature. It may even become an experience of conversion, of human nature seeming born again.[11]

It is striking and puzzling that accounts of the social action of enthusiasm and continuing studies of the phenomena of mass psychology should both recall Wordsworth's accounts of the imagination. It is a matter of a power that may arise from a central source or voice and which emits an energy which can infuse itself over a distance, transforming, unifying and energizing what it touches in ways that release hidden or pent-up qualities. Wordsworth, with Charles Lamb, defines the imagination as 'the power which ... draws all things to one; which makes things animate or inanimate, beings with their attributes, subjects with their accessaries, take one colour and serve to one effect.'[12] Might there be a coherent rationale for this parallelism? In theorizing about the imagination, we tend to focus on the philosophical genealogy of conceptions of mental power, reflecting modern psychology's concern with a realm of internal representations. However, poets and orators at this time conceived whatever powers were within them in mainly rhetorical terms, i.e. in terms of their effects on others. In the poetics of Duff, Lowth, Blair and others, the space of composition is, despite its seeming interiority, a virtual public drama, an arena of implicit rhetorical influence and emotion. What presents itself as an account of the psychology of composition, as we saw, is often merely a transposition of those effects supposedly felt by the reader or auditor. Analogously, Crabb Robinson observed how Wordsworth valued his poems as *agents*, looking 'to the powers of the mind his poems call forth, and the energies they presuppose and excite, as the standard by which they are to be estimated.'[13] 'Power', for Wordsworth, his word for the mind's sublimity, still functions frequently as a rhetorical term. It reads as a reformulation of the notion of poetic enthusiasm in terms that recall and appropriate the mass enthusiasm of the revolutionary politics that had overwhelmed him in the early 1790s.

It is not difficult to trace Wordsworth's intense and ambivalent familiarity with mass psychology, both from his conversion-like experience of the early, festive activities of the French Revolution in 1790 (Bk. 6, ll. 354–356; also Bk. 9, ll. 391–6), and then of the early Terror, in 1792 (Bk. 10, ll. 38–81), followed by his intense sense of alienation as a French sympathizer amidst the hysterical war-fever in Britain after the outbreak of war with France in 1793.[14] The radical popular culture of the 1790s saw various millenarian movements, outbursts of radical enthusiasm and subversive claims to prophesy. Wordsworth would also have been only too aware of food riots,[15] king-and-country mobs and the propaganda of Pitt's oppressive regime, and then, conversely, the threatening armies of Napoleon's imperialism. Merely living in a city as large and volatile as London had made Wordsworth an ambivalent witness of 'times when half the City shall break out / Full of one passion, vengeance, rage, or fear, / To executions, to a Street on fire, / Mobs, riots, or rejoicings ...' (Bk. 7, ll. 646–9). These are all communal instances of 'the spontaneous overflow of powerful feelings' (*Prose*, I, 126, 148).

Wordsworth's recurrent term for inspiration is 'Power', one of the most peculiar terms in his oeuvre. One peculiarity is that it is often employed *in abstracto*: it is not power to do x or power *of* anything, e.g. of persuasion or of numbers, nor is the term often qualified as, say, 'political power' or 'poetic power'. Frequently it is simply 'Power' with a capital P. Examples can be listed copiously.[16] At what is generally regarded as the climax to *The Prelude*, Wordsworth celebrates chosen creative spirits: 'they are Powers; and hence the highest bliss / That can be known is theirs, the consciousness / Of whom they are habitually infused / Through every image, and through every thought ...' (Bk. 13, ll. 107–10). Most famous perhaps, is the account of Imagination as a power in Book Six: 'Imagination ... here that Power, / In all the might of its endowments, came / Athwart me' (Bk. 6, ll. 525–29). In his *A Course of Lectures on Oratory and Criticism* (1777) Joseph Priestley lists '*power*' among a series of abstract terms that, though they have no force of the sublime in themselves, 'inspire that sentiment by their association with others that are capable of it.'[17] The associations of 'power' are 'ideas of the good or evil it may produce, and of the multitudes which are subject to its control' (Priestley, p. 157). Similar associations between crowds and the latent violence of the sublime appear in Edmund Burke's influential *A Philosophical Enquiry into the Origin of our Ideas of the Sublime and Beautiful* (1757).[18] For Wordsworth too, 'Power' names, as well as the imagination, the sense of the presence of vast numbers of people, of a multitude so big, so unknowable and in mass so powerful that even the mere thought of it is a source of the sublime. A sonnet of 1811 links the unseen presence and power of masses of people to the sublime:

> The power of Armies is a visible thing,
> Formal, and circumscribed in time and space;
> But who the limits of that power can trace
> Which a brave People into light can bring
> Or hide, at will – for freedom combating
> By just revenge enflamed? No foot can chase,
> No eye can follow, to a *fatal* place
> That power, that spirit, whether on the wing
> Like the strong wind, or sleeping like the wind
> Within its awful caves ... [19]

Such power may seem for the good when it is a matter of the English people under threat of invasion.[20] The glamour of invisible multitudes, however, becomes sinister once it is a matter of the opposing side: 'The Coast of France, the Coast of France how near! / Drawn almost into frightful neighbourhood. / I shrunk ... yet what power is there! / What mightiness for evil and for good!' ('September, 1802. Near Dover').[21] Power comports the mixed glamour and horror of mass violence. In the patriotic sonnet on the power of the people the language is legibly that more familiarly linked to individual poetic or visionary power ('That power, that ..., whether on the wing / Like the strong wind, or sleeping like the wind / Within its awful caves ...'). It is invisible, unpredictable, and from a mysterious source with oracular connotations – 'awful caves'. Being ubiquitous, it cannot be traced by the eye to 'a fatal place'. The contrast between the outward, visible power of armies and this mysterious, hidden power also recalls aesthetic distinctions. The poetic diction of the commonplaces so vehemently rejected in the Preface to *Lyrical Ballads* (1802), as well as the cult of the picturesque satirized in *The Prelude*, are both characterized by their stress on the visible – the despotism of a sense directed outward.[22] Such modes are 'Formal and circumscribed in time and space', as distinct from genuine poetic force which, like the power of the people here, knows neither limits nor definable origins and cannot be easily predicted, controlled or measured. The association of winds, a potentially contagious *afflatus*, and large multitudes of people is also a recurrent one in *The Prelude* (see e.g. Bk. 7, l. 187; Bk. 7, l. 473; Bk. 10, l. 11; Bk. 10, l. 70; Bk. 10, l. 313).

Enthusiasm is, by definition, the duplication of the author's passion in the psyche of those it touches. 'Power' in *The Prelude* names at once a force both in the genesis of poetry and its reception by a reader. The affinity with notions of enthusiasm is partly disguised, however, by the fact that Wordsworth often treats 'Power' or 'powers' *in abstracto*, viz. as a potential faculty divorced from actual exercise upon an audience, and the hero of a narrative of education and development. Wordsworth often displaces relations to possible audiences into relations with natural phenomena. Consider the following passage for example: 'I had come with holy powers / And faculties, whether to work or feel: / To apprehend all passions and all moods / Which time, and place, and season do impress / Upon the visible universe; *and work / Like changes there by force of my own mind*' (Bk. 3, ll. 83–88; emphasis added). This is, of course, a bizarre vaunt for a poet, who might be expected to be more concerned with affecting other people than with his perceptions of the weather, unless one accepts that the *ultimate* claim being made here relates to a power that will, in due course, perhaps in the projected 'The Recluse,' manifest itself in a text and its effects on others.[23]

The climax of *The Prelude* instantiates a similar displacement and abstraction. A 'mighty Mind', Wordsworth claims in the episode of the climbing of Snowdon in the final, summarizing book, possesses a power analogous to that of the most powerful natural phenomena. Yet the latter 'circumstance most awful and sublime' (Bk. 13, ll. 76) is described in terms at least equally suited to mass enthusiasm:

> That domination which she [Nature] oftentimes
> Exerts upon the outward face of things,
> So molds them, and endues, abstracts, combines
> Or by abrupt and unhabitual influence
> Doth make one object so impress itself
> Upon all others, and pervade them so
> That even the grossest minds must see and hear
> And cannot choose but feel.
>
> (Bk. 13, ll. 77–84)

These lines refer back to a description of the moon above Snowdon suddenly illuminating and animating an illusory sea formed by the tops of clouds. It is first useful, however, to ask oneself a simple, even banal question: as an image of a poet's power, which is the more credible, certain meteorological phenomena or the way a large gathering may be galvanized by oratorical force? The latter image seems implicit in this account of natural force. Wordsworth describes a force that transmutes the individuality of what it touches, a domination that may be abrupt and unpredictable but which unifies those it moves into a more powerful mass, drawing even the least sensitive into itself. The image of the spreading mass of clouds, touched into life by the moon, recalls accounts of oratorical power infusing, transforming and unifying its audience:

> I look'd about, and lo!
> The Moon stood naked in the Heavens, at height
> Immense above my head, and on the shore
> I found myself of a huge sea of mist,
> Which meek and silent, rested at my feet.
> A hundred hills their dusky backs upheaved
> All over this still Ocean, and beyond,
> Far, far beyond, the vapours shot themselves
> In headlands, tongues, and promontory shapes
> Into the Sea, the real Sea, that seem'd
> To dwindle and give up its majesty,
> Usurp'd upon as far as sight could reach.

(Bk. 13, ll. 40–51)

The passage offers the scene as an analogue of the power of the human imagination. The figure of the clouds also recalls the scene of mass enthusiasm in the passage on Beaupuy. A unifying force of emotional transformation spreads through a people and makes 'One body spreading wide as clouds in heaven' (Bk. 9, ll. 387). This potentially revolutionary force is the analogue of the 'glorious faculty / Which higher minds bear with them as their own' (Bk. 13, ll. 89–90) and of the transformations they can send abroad. In short, the qualities of a virtual, fantasy crowd give structure here to the notion of imagination as an active, synthetic, and individual power, that Wordsworth and Coleridge worked out from eighteenth-century British aesthetics and German idealism. The penultimate book of *The Prelude* claims that Wordsworth could never have been fully happy through involvement with the 'tumultuous world', 'How far soe'er transported and possess'd' (Bk. 12, l. 115), yet the inner Power which is supposed to answer this sense of lack is itself modelled on that same transport and possession.

One oddity in the quoted passage is that, although the scene of the moon above the mist is presented as an analogue of the mind's poetic power (and other seemingly incongruent analogies were drafted),[24] Wordsworth explains this analogy not by reference to specific workings of the mind, but, tautologically, to Nature once more (Bk. 13, ll. 77ff)! The crucial term of the comparison (the poet's power *qua* poet) is actually elided, nor is it fulfilled by the later focus on the influences that go to form a mighty mind (ll. 91–110). W. J. B. Owen attempts to fill this gap by mapping this passage onto accounts of the imagination in Wordsworth's prose.[25] The fantasy of an animated crowd, however, also seems a plausible answer to the problem, and one model for the imagination itself. Later lines bear out this reading, especially in the fourteen-book version:

> through a rift
> Not distant from the shore whereon we stood,
> A fixed, abysmal, gloomy, breathing-place,
> Mounted the roar of waters – torrents – streams
> Innumerable, roaring with one voice!
> Heard over earth and sea, and in that hour,
> For so it seemed, felt by the starry heavens.
>
> (Bk. 14, ll. 56–62)

The transitivity inherent in Wordsworth's inspirational notion of Power enables an easy transposition of internal and external spaces. Hence this passage is at the same time, without contradiction, an image of the poet's inner power and of his relation to an audience. More paradoxically, however, the implicit egalitarianism of this entity 'roaring with one voice' is, simultaneously, an image of a higher mind's possible fame or effect on others. Poetic power is an internalized or essentialized demagoguery. Read as a proleptic fantasy of reception the lines on Snowdon anticipate a later prose passage on a true poet's audience – the 'People' as the inspired *Vox Populi* of the 1815 'Essay, Supplementary to the Preface.' According to the adage '*vox populi, vox dei*' the People here possess a voice that proclaims a true poet and which issues from the 'Spirit' of human knowledge, itself described, as moving (as if on wings) over past and future (*Prose*, III, 55–107, p. 84).

Fame and audience

Changed conceptions of a poet's 'inner' power may be correlated to changing possibilities of audience. One major condition for the emergence of the exalted conceptions of the poet that accompany the Romantic notion of imagination may lie simply in the way notions of 'fame' altered during the eighteenth century. The imagination, as a notion of self-transcendence, finds one of its conditions in and may, to a surprising degree, be defined by changing notions of fame, i.e. the new self-conceptions made available by a writer's potential relation to an audience at this time. Leo Braudy argues that the eighteenth century sees the emergence of distinctively modern ways of being famous. With the growth of secularism, individualism, the erosion of fixed social hierarchies, and with the spread of literacy in Europe, notions of fame undergo a transformation. 'Fame' may become a way of achieving self-definition in forms that transcend the limitations of one's family, caste or position in society. Individualistic notions of fame increasingly replace classical ideas of civic fame and religious ideas of spiritual fame.[26] Literary fame is perhaps the most cited exemplar – Shakespeare is famous as Shakespeare, not for reasons of inherited privilege or civic virtue. The possibility of fame of this kind may become a new way of defining one's identity while alive. For a writer freed from the pressures but also the securities of patronage, it may involve a complex relation to a possible audience. Jean-Jacques Rousseau is already Romantic in his seeking out of a solitude for writing, away from one public, to be able to reveal himself as he 'truly is' to another, envisaged as a posterity of readers: 'I am leaving behind in my writings a witness in my favour that will sooner or later triumph over the machinations of men.'[27] Wordsworth makes a similar statement of self-definition in 1799 by establishing his household in the remote Lake District. This gestures towards an audience that transcends the limits of his immediate time and culture. The space of composition becomes, oxymoronically, one of a publicly-staged solitude and self-transcendence.

There is a paradox in this conception of the solitary writer fleeing society to become (in writing) a self that transcends the limitations of his or her time: such stress on solitude and the inner life is an option viable only within a context of increased literacy, widely-based and efficient means of publication, improved communications and a multitudinous audience (Braudy, p. 376). Rousseau and Wordsworth bear out Walter J. Ong's paradox that the Romantic stress on solitary interiority is a by-product of technology.[28]

Comparison between the conceptions of a possible reader offered by Samuel Johnson and by Wordsworth illuminates the different conceptions of a poet's power that become available through relation to an audience over this period. The reader in Johnson is 'the common reader'.[29] This common reader rises above the provincial and topical, belonging seemingly to no particular space or time, is both ordinary and representative. Johnson also calls this figure the 'public': 'from the public, and only from the public is the writer to await a confirmation of his claim, and a final justification of self esteem.'[30] The terms, 'writer' and 'poet' are here explicitly acknowledged to be claims made upon a readership. Moreover Johnson's sentence also suggests that a writer may await an answer to this claim in an unspecified period, but one certainly less than a lifetime. Wordsworth, in 1815, reaffirms the position that only posterity bestows true fame (*Prose*, III, 83–4). Writing becomes increasingly no longer only an object to circulate in the cultural networks that had largely defined it during the Augustan period, with their relatively shared civic, aesthetic and ethical norms. It becomes more 'open', increasingly destined towards an addressee defined less totally or surely in social or geographical terms – posterity, the 'people', 'mankind'. In the Preface to *Lyrical Ballads* Wordsworth pictures a readership which embodies universal human nature, yet envisaged more anonymously than for Johnson, over vaster and more daunting stretches of space and time:

> Emphatically may it be said of the Poet, as Shakspeare hath said of man, 'that he looks before and after.' He is the rock of defence for human nature; an upholder and preserver, carrying everywhere with him relationship and love. In spite of difference of soil and climate, of language and manners, of laws and customs: in spite of things silently gone out of mind, and things violently destroyed; the Poet binds together by passion and knowledge the vast empire of human society, as it is spread over the whole earth, and over all time. (*Prose*, I, 118–88, p. 141).

This is an audience considered so much in the abstract as to become almost disembodied, an element of reception, participation and communication so ubiquitous as to seem no longer dependent on particular technologies or media, such as means of publication or transport or even paper and ink.[31] It enables a conception of the poet as an egalitarian, unifying power in this etherealized medium of other consciousnesses: 'The objects of the Poet's thought are every where; though the eyes and senses of man are, it is true, his favourite guides, yet he will follow wheresoever he can find an atmosphere of sensation in which to move his wings' (*Prose*, I, 141). The ancient topos of creativity as a poetic 'flight' or 'transport' finds new expression in this last sentence, recognisably a variant of the characteristic Wordsworthian fantasy of an omnipresence of thought.[32] In relation to such notions of audience, the self-conceptions open to a writer become correspondingly transformed. One's text may project a 'phantasmatic author' correspondingly mysterious, vast and powerful. Wordsworth idealizes the act of composition as a form of spiritual leadership. Composition becomes a negotiation with a possible identity or a power one might become.[33]

I turn now to another passage on Power, one originally drafted for 'The Pedlar' but reincorporated into the earliest *Prelude* and all subsequent versions. In the 1805–6 *Prelude* it reads:

> I would walk alone
> In storm and tempest, or in star-light nights
> Beneath the quiet Heavens; and at that time,
> Have felt whate'er there is of power in sound
> To breathe an elevated mood, by form
> Or image unprofaned: and I would stand
> Beneath some rock, listening to sounds that are
> The ghostly language of the ancient earth,
> Or make their dim abode in distant winds.
> Thence did I drink the visionary power.
> I deem not profitless those fleeting moods
> Of shadowy exultation: not for this,
> That they are kindred to our purer mind
> And intellectual life; but that the soul,
> Remembering how she felt, but what she felt
> Remembering not, retains an obscure sense
> Of possible sublimity, to which
> With growing faculties she doth aspire,
> With faculties still growing, feeling still
> That whatsoever point they gain, they still
> Have something to pursue.

(Bk. 2, ll. 321–41)

This passage describes Nature as a sort of sublime poet. Book one also described the influence of the natural world upon the boy Wordsworth as one of 'forms' and 'images,' and used the same terms to name rhetorical devices at the service of the adult poet: 'Nor am I naked in external things, / Forms, images, nor numerous other aids / Of less regard ...' (Bk. 1, ll. 165–7). In the passage from Book Two just quoted, it is a matter of an energy or breath which is abstracted from form or image (Bk. 2, ll. 325–6), a pure power of transformation and enthusing that has no specific content or referent. Modes of power and subjective coercion which the rhetorical tradition would have conceived instrumentally, as a supplementary power of expressiveness, a catalyst, have here become themselves the main topic. Thus abstracted from any immediate circuit of communication, modes of subjective power become themselves the crucial concern. It is as if Wordsworth were presenting the force of powerful language upon a massed and susceptible crowd, yet, removing 'form' or 'image' of either people or language, has abstracted from the whole exultant and yet potentially violent experience an atmosphere only.[34] As a Pentecostal experience of 'visionary power' this force is explicitly staged as a prolepsis of what the poetic spirit may become:

> With growing faculties she doth aspire,
> With faculties still growing, feeling still
> That whatsoever point they gain, they still
> Have something to pursue.

(Bk. 2, ll. 38–41)

The scene is so denuded of particular nouns that almost nothing is said beyond the delineation of a mode of, simultaneously, ego-expansion and dispossession by more powerful circumambient force, with undertones of both excitement and hidden violence. These are images of rhetorical power that again conflate a virtual audience – a space of shadowy, ubiquitous affects without definite or specific embodiment – with fantasies of individual transformation and fame. Wordsworth's hedging syntax ('not for this ...') allows him to suggest possibilities even in their very denial – that the moods are akin to the spiritual life. The distinction between the soul remembering 'how she felt' but not ' what she felt' is obscure again because of its degree of abstraction. Wordsworth's visionary power, understood as a proleptic image of the poet-to-be, will consist in a disembodied force of sound, transcending limitation in particular form or image, broadcast upon the wind with a kind of ghostly ubiquity that combines the potency of a storm with an association with what is permanent and elemental ('The ghostly language of the ancient earth'). Perhaps a sense of possible power – fame – is all that is at issue, with no more particular image than that of some potentially violent or revolutionary disturbance. This sense of self-transcendence is then located in the future as the object of a continuing aspiration.

The transitivity of inspiration or Power reappears in the way the passage on Power at the end of Book five, an account of reading, explicitly recalls the scene with the 'ghostly language of the ancient earth'. The account of the influx of Power in the poet is simply transposed into an account of the reader's experience of the poet's work:

> Visionary Power
> Attends upon the motions of the winds
> Embodied in the mystery of words.
> There darkness makes abode, and all the host
> Of shadowy things do work their changes there,
> As in a mansion like their proper home: –
> Even forms and substances are circumfus'd
> By that transparent veil with light divine;
> And through the turnings intricate of Verse
> Present themselves as objects recognis'd
> In flashes, and with a glory scarce their own.

(Bk. 5, ll. 619–29)

The peculiarity of this passage is that it combines images of external and possibly disruptive forces – winds, darkness, shadowy things – with internal affects. By means of the powerful psychic transformation embodied in words, phenomena reappear in this medium with a 'glory scarce their own'. The text takes up the sense of an oratorical force and of mass feeling from the earlier passage and recasts it as a metamorphosing energy that is the power encountered in reading. Linguistic power is associated again with a virtual multitude, a 'host' of shadowy things working their changes. To read is to be affected by a force that is that of one poetic voice taking on the power of a multitudinous presence. This is a recurrent image in Wordsworth – a voice or wind becoming multiplicitous voices or winds, voices at once ubiquitous, 'homeless' or 'unfathered' yet also peculiarly internal, as if they were already voices in the mind.[35]

Let us turn finally to one of the most famous passages on the imagination in English Romantic writing – Wordsworth's affirmation of that 'infinitude' associated with the upsurging of 'Power' in the Simplon Pass passage in Book Six. Having recounted how, on a walking tour, Wordsworth and a friend had crossed the Alps unawares, a great anti-climax, the verse seems to interrupt itself:

> Imagination! lifting up itself
> Before the eye and progress of my Song
> Like an unfather'd vapour; here that Power
> In all the might of its endowments, came
> Athwart me; I was lost as in a cloud,
> Halted without a struggle to break through,

> And now recovering to my Soul I say
> I recognize thy glory; in such strength
> Of usurpation, in such visitings
> Of awful promise, when the light of sense
> Goes out in flashes that have shewn to us
> The invisible world, doth Greatness make abode,
> There harbours whether we be young or old.
> Our destiny, our nature, and our home
> Is with infinitude, and only there;
> With hope it is, hope that can never die,
> Effort and expectation, and desire,
> And something evermore about to be.
>   The mind beneath such banners militant
> Thinks not of spoils, trophies or of aught
> That may attest its prowess ...

> (Bk. 6, ll. 525–45)

Wordsworth dramatizes this event as taking place in the time of composition itself – 'Now' and 'Here'. The passage is an unusually explicit idealization of the space of composition as one of subjective transformation. It is a crisis of self-recognition. These lines epitomize Wordsworth's strategy of idealizing the act of composition as one of struggle and heroism in a paradoxically public solitude. The Simplon Pass passage alludes implicitly to scenes of battle. The passage as a whole may, as Alan Liu and Nicholas Roe argue, allude to the actions of the French revolutionary army[36] and Napoleon's emulation of Hannibal's crossing of the Alps. Wordsworth thus redeploys the ancient association, dating back to the *Ion* itself, between powers of composition and the arts of generalship. He describes the experience of Power as one of paralysis until the identification made between Power and the inner soul interprets the sense of ambush or usurpation as the affirmation of an identity not bound to empirical sense. The claims made for this sense of transcendent destiny are again elusive, as if Wordsworth were grasping for some way to articulate an experience he himself cannot interpret. Despite the reference to 'The invisible world' as home of 'Greatness', 'Effort, and expectation and desire' are more surely images of this-wordly aspiration. The power of imagination, it is implied as in the sonnet of 1811, is at least equal to that of armies, but without militarism.[37]

Wordsworth's language may be non-particular, not from vagueness, but from multiplicity of implication. This passage engages a doubleness and transitivity similar to that in the other extracts. Once again, the conception of the mind's internal power is an image of an anticipated and massive rhetorical effect. If we turn to the 1815 prose essay we find that Wordsworth there deploys the image of Hannibal crossing the Alps as a metaphor for the task of the modern poet, his need to create his own audience (*Prose*, III, 80). Inspiration, in effect, is auto-legitimation, a power that should be performative of its own value and reception. The Simplon Pass apostrophe to the imagination, often read as relating an experience of Power undergone during composition,[38] also forms a close parallel to Wordsworth's memory of entering the peopled mass of London and feeling, not at the time but while writing the recollection itself, 'weight and power,/Power growing with the weight' (Bk. 8, ll. 705–6). This would suggest a sense of in-finitude not as any definite transcendent realm but simply the feeling that the subject of inspiration achieves an identity bound to no particular place or time. The space of composition is a scene of self-transformation or reconfiguration, an encounter with a vaguely defined power which one may 'recognise' or 'become' through the act of writing.[39] The act of composition may itself form a rite-of-passage. In fact, the temporality of the written text suggests itself as the implicit model here for the enormous claims made on behalf of the poet's psyche, as an entity whose 'here' and 'now' are always renewed with each act of reading, even as they transcend it in their movement towards an indefinite posterity: 'Effort, and expectation, and desire,/And something evermore about to be' (Bk. 6, ll. 541–2).

The experience of self-transcendence, Wordsworth claims, is its own reward, without thought of trophies or recognition, yet this is already an image of self-legitimation so intense as to transgress itself and suggest itself as really a gesture of denial. Wordsworth's notion of inspiration as a virile self-possession of powers nurtured in uncorrupted solitude reads partly as a defensive denial of the insecurities of the act of writing – as if questions of value, reception and rhetorical power could all be decided at the time of inscription. Wordsworth's strategy of self-legitimation depends, like Rousseau's conception of his true self, on a division of possible readers into two classes: a distinction between the present reading public, with its distorted taste, and an abstraction which the essay of 1815 terms the 'People', whose recognition is granted infallibility. Great poetry survives among the People. Wordsworth quotes himself on the *Vox Populi* that proclaims a true poet: '"– Past and future, are the wings/On whose support, harmoniously conjoined,/Moves the great

Spirit of human knowledge –" The voice that issues from this Spirit, is that Vox Populi which the Deity inspires. Foolish must he be who can mistake for this a local acclamation ...' (*Prose*, III, 84). It is striking, however, that this same essay should conjoin the notion that a true poet is *self-inspired* (*Prose*, III, 72) with a statement that a poet's audience itself needs inspiration in its choice!

Notes

1 All incorporated references are to *The Thirteen-Book Prelude*, 2 vols, ed. Mark Reed (Ithaca and London: Cornell University Press, 1991), I.

2 Cyrus Hamlin has drawn parallels between the poetics inherent in *The Prelude* and notions of composition as a process of self-reflection and total-ization found in a contemporary German poetics, *Genre*, 6 (1973), 142–77. Wordsworth knew of German thought through the mediation of Coleridge. In addition, late eighteenth-century German thinkers 'quite literally stand in the tradition of Hume, Shaftesbury, Addison, Hutcheson and so on' (David Simpson, introduction to *German Literary and Aesthetic Criticism: Kant, Fichte, Schelling, Schopenhauer, Hegel* (Cambridge: Cambridge University Press, 1984), pp. 1–24, p. 21).

3 Contrast the difficulties Coleridge experienced transferring his famous oral, impromptu conversational abilities into finished, written structures. See Mark L. Waldo, 'Why Coleridge Hated to Write: An Ambivalence of Theory and Practice', *The Wordsworth Circle*, 16 (1985), 25–9.

4 *The Sorrows of Young Werther*, ed. Hermann J. Weigand (London: Signet, 1962), p. 43. *Language as Living Form in Nineteenth-Century Poetry* (Sussex: Harvester, 1982), p.1. For Wordsworth's presentations of the influence of natural phenomena as in-spirations within this teleogical notion of educa-tion, see M. H. Abrams, 'The Correspondent Breeze: A Romantic Metaphor', in *English Romantic Poets: Modern Essays in Criticism*, ed. M. H. Abrams (New York: Oxford University Press, 1960), pp. 37–54; Michael Edwards, *Poetry and Possibility* (London: Macmillan, 1988), pp. 60–89.

5 See James Engell, *The Creative Imagination: Enlightenment to Romanticism* (Cambridge, Mass and London: Harvard University Press, 1981).

6 William Wordsworth, *Poems*, 2 vols, (London: 1815), II, pp. 69–71. For 'enthusiasm' in Wordsworth and Coleridge see Stephen Prickett, *England and the French Revolution* (London: Macmillan, 1989), pp. 105–111.

7 For Le Bon, Freud, Durkheim and also Bataille on group psychology see Michèle Richman, 'The Sacred Group: a Durkheimian Perspective on the Collège de Sociologie', in Georges Bataille, *Writing the Sacred*, ed. Carolyn Bailey Gill. (London: Routledge, 1995), pp. 58–76.

8 Robert R. Evans(ed.), *Readings in Collective Behavior* (Chicago: Rand McNally & Co., 1969), p. 11. The term 'crowd' is used in the following account to name spontaneous mass-psychological phenomena in general (such as epidemics of fear or exultation in a population during times of war or revolutionary turmoil), and is not limited to groups in immediate phys-ical contact with each other.

9 Edward Alsworth Ross, 'Collective Social Psychology', in *Collective Behavior*, ed. Evans, pp. 46–64, p. 48.

10 Herbert Blumer, 'Outline of Collective Behavior', in *Collective Behavior*, ed. Evans, pp. 65–88, p. 70; see also Serge Moscovici, *The Age of the Crowd*, (Cambridge: Cambridge University Press, 1985), pp. 15–17.

11 See Elias Canetti, *Crowds and Power*, trans. Carol Stewart (London: Gollancz, 1962), pp. 58–62.

12 Preface to *Poems* (1815), *The Prose Works of William Wordsworth*, 3 vols, ed. W. J. B. Owen and Jane Worthington Smyser, (Oxford: Clarendon Press, 1974), III, 23–52, p. 34.

13 *Henry Crabb Robinson on Books and their Writers*, requoted from *The Critical Opinions of William Wordsworth*, ed. Markham L. Peacock Jr. (Baltimore: Johns Hopkins University Press, 1950), p. 111.

14 For Wordsworth's experiences in France and engagement with radical politics at this time see Nicholas Roe, *Wordsworth and Coleridge: The Radical Years* (Oxford: Clarendon Press, 1988), pp. 38–83, pp. 118–44. For the revolutionary *fête*, see Frank Kennedy, *A Cultural History of the French Revolution* (New Haven: Yale University Press, 1989), pp. 329–53. For the decisive interventions of crowds during the Revolution itself, see George Rudé, *The Crowd in the French Revolution*, 2nd edn (Oxford: Oxford University Press, 1972).

15 See Alan Liu, *Wordsworth: The Sense of History* (Stanford Calif.: Stanford University Press, 1989), pp. 342–3.

16 See W. J. B. Owen, *Wordsworth as Critic* (London: Oxford University Press, 1969), pp. 195–228.

17 Priestley, *A Course of Lectures on Oratory and Criticism* (New York: Garland Inc., 1971), p. 157.

18 Edmund Burke describes 'the shouting of multitudes' as sublime: 'by the sole strength of the sound, [it] so amazes and confounds the imagination, that in this staggering, and hurry of mind, the best established tempers can scarcely forbear being borne down, and joining in the common cry, and common resolution of the croud.' *A Philosophical Enquiry into the Origin of our Ideas of the Sublime and Beautiful* [1757], rev. edn, James T. Boulton (Oxford: Basil Blackwell, 1987), p. 82. See also Hugh Blair, *Lectures on Rhetoric and Belles Lettres*, 2 vols, ed. Harold F. Harding (Carbondale and Edwardsville, Southern Illinois University Press, 1965), I, 47–8.

19 Wordsworth, *Shorter Poems, 1807–20*, ed. Carl H. Ketcham (Ithaca: Cornell University Press, 1989), p. 74.

20 Moscovici writes that 'When many thousands of people read the same newspaper and books and feel that they are the same public, they acquire that feeling of omnipotence proper to the crowd' (*Age of the Crowd*, pp. 188–9). For the emergence in this period of that mass feeling known as nationalism see Benedict Anderson, *Imagined Communities: Reflections on the Origin and Spread of Nationalism*, rev. edn (London: Verso, 1991).

21 William Wordsworth, *Poems in Two Volumes, and Other Poems, 1800–1807*, ed. Jared Curtis (Ithaca: Cornell University Press, 1983), p. 163.

22 W. J. B. Owen, 'The Most Despotic of Our Senses', *The Wordsworth Circle*, 19 (1989), 136–44.

23 Wordsworth's account of his youthful enraptured relation to Nature, later to be tempered by 'reason', also recalls the *fête* (cf. also Bk. 3, ll. 121–31)

> '... the deep enthusiastic joy,
> The rapture of the hallelujah sent
> From all that breathes and is ...' (Bk. 13, ll. 261–3).

24 These discarded analogies comprise natural scenes as well as anecdotes of heroism, violence and danger. See J. F. Kishel, 'The Analogy Passage from Wordsworth's Five-Book *Prelude*', *Studies in Romanticism*, 18 (1979), 271–85. Manuscript MS D testifies that Wordsworth once thought of describing Nature's domination in this section in terms of 'mutual domination' and 'interchangeable supremacy', *The Fourteen Book Prelude*, ed. W. J. B. Owen (Ithaca and London: Cornell University Press, 1985), p. 1127.

25 W. J. B. Owen, 'The Perfect Image of a Mighty Mind', *The Wordsworth Circle*, 10 (1979), 3–16.

26 Leo Braudy, *The Frenzy of Renown: Fame and its History* (New York: Oxford University Press, 1986).

27 Quoted in Braudy, *The Frenzy of Renown*, p. 376.

28 Walter J. Ong, *Rhetoric, Romance, and Technology: Studies in the Interaction of Expression and Culture* (Ithaca and London: Cornell University Press, 1971) pp. 255–83.

29 Robert DeMaria Jr., 'The Ideal Reader: A Critical Fiction', *PMLA*, 93 (1978), 463–74. See also Jon P. Klancher, *The Making of English Reading Audiences, 1790–1832* (Wisconsin: University of Wisconsin Press, 1987).

30 Quoted in DeMaria, 'The Ideal Reader', p. 464.

31 Such issues are also reflected in the way so many Romantic texts dramatize themselves as addressed to an idealized, imaginary listener. Mary Jacobus writes of 'Coleridge' as the addressee of *The Prelude*: 'to have an imaginary auditor is to fantasize the reproduction of one's speech in another without external mediation or deferral, and so create the illusion of mastery over the process of signification', Mary Jacobus, *Romanticism, Writing and Sexual Difference: Essays on* The Prelude (Oxford: Clarendon Press, 1989), pp. 181–2.

32 The same tendency to abstract and etherealize a potential readership as the poet's element may be found in *The Prelude* (Bk. 5, ll. 198–222) Wordsworth also describes how, as a youth in London, he sought 'not then/Knowledge; but craved for power, and power I found in all things' (Bk. 8, ll. 754–6). Here the obscure term 'power', naming Wordsworth's response to various monuments to human achievement, includes an imaginary identification with fame. Wordsworth prizes the sense of power arising from identification with objects understood as 'capacious' in proportion to their transcending the limited or the circumscribed: 'all objects, being/Themselves capacious, also found in me/Capaciousness and amplitude of mind:/Such is the strength and glory of our Youth!' (Bk. 8, ll. 604–7).

33 'Nature' often functions in Wordsworth as the ground and guarantee of a universal communicability. He writes of 'The great Nature that exists in

words/Of mighty Poets' (Bk. 5, ll. 618–20). This universalism, reflected back as an exalted image of a poet's possible identity, contrasts with the more strictly socially-defined notions of a previous generation: 'To ask the question why write does not make much sense in Augustan ideology because the function of writing is assumed to be a socializing process that, through socio-conventional genres and addresses and styles, overdetermines the individual urge to write. In other words, the question can only be asked in purely social terms, and the answer is ready-made: to please and to instruct' (Marlon B. Ross, *The Contours of Masculine Desire: Romanticism and the Rise of Women's Poetry* (New York: Oxford University Press, 1989), p. 64). It is certainly not to transcend oneself.

34 In *Crowds and Power* Canetti lists a series of natural phenomena termed 'crowd symbols' which, though 'never made up of men, are ... *felt* to be a crowd' (p. 75). Of wind he writes:

> Wind is invisible, but the movement it impels to clouds
> and waves, leaves and grass, makes its multiplicity
> apparent ... The age-old identification of mind and breath
> is proof of how concentrated wind is felt to be; it
> has the density of breath. Its invisibility, on the
> other hand, enables it to stand for invisible crowds,
> and thus for spirits. (p. 86)

35 J. Douglas Kneale suggests that Geoffrey Hartman's beautiful aphorism should be modified: not '*In the imagination of Wordsworth everything tends to the image and sound of universal waters,*' but, '*In the language of Wordsworth the sound of waters tends to the image of voice*' (*Monumental Writing: Aspects of Rhetoric in Wordsworth's Poetry* (Lincoln and London: University of Nebraska Press, 1988), p. 82)

36 See Liu, Wordsworth: *The Sense of History*, pp. 23–31; Roe, *The Radical Years*, pp. 61–2.

37 Teresa Kelly writes: 'If at first the mind is submerged beneath its sublimity, those "banners militant," it is soon submerged beneath an "access of joy/Which hides it like the overflowing Nile" ... The uncontained, destructive power of floods and deluge, which is in this and other poems a figure for revolution and the sublime, is here contained by a tamed version of itself – the annual overflow of the Nile – not a catastrophe but an anticipated and welcome irrigation" (*Wordsworth's Revisionary Aesthetics* (Cambridge: Cambridge University Press, 1988), p. 11) Kelly's study is particularly strong on Wordsworth's association of the sublime with revolutionary energies. These, she demonstrates, are regarded with deep ambivalence and tempered by cultivation of the 'feminine' values of the 'beautiful'.

38 For the fullest and latest version of this reading see Keith Hanley, 'Crossings Out: The Problem of Textual Passage in *The Prelude*', in *Romantic Revisions*, ed. Robert Brinkley and Keith Hanley (Cambridge: Cambridge University Press, 1992), pp. 103–35.

39 Compare the passage in which Edward Young, defending an individualistic notion of original genius, offers his own rationalization for 'the fable of poetic inspiration':

a man may be scarce less ignorant of his own powers,
than an oyster of its pearl ... that he may possess
dormant, unsuspected abilities, till awakened by loud
calls, or stung up by striking emergencies, is evident
from the sudden eruptions of some men, out of perfect
obscurity, into publick admiration, on the strong
impulse of some animating occasion; not more to the
world's surprise, than their own. Few authors of
distinction but have experienced something of this
nature, at the first beamings of their yet unsuspected
genius on their hitherto dark Composition: The writer
starts at it, as at a lucid meteor in the night; is
much surprized; can scarce believe it true. During his
happy confusion, it may be said of him, as to Eve at
the lake,

What there thou seest, fair creature, is thyself.
                    MILT.

... This sensation, which I speak of in a writer, might favour, and so
promote, the fable of poetic inspiration (*Conjectures on Original
Composition* [1759], ed. Edith J. Morley (Manchester: Manchester
University Press, 1918), p. 23).

CHAPTER 5

Infinite inspiration: Hölderlin and Schelling

Introduction

Friedrich Hölderlin has served modern Europe as the archetype of the inspired poet. There is a Hölderlin myth. It is that of a young poet, destitute, painfully in love and grief-stricken, who loses his mind through too immediate a contact with the language of the gods. This myth has been reworked many times in the twentieth century – in Hölderlin's appropriation by Stefan George, by Heidegger, and by existentialists and theologians.[1] In his *Blanche ou l'oubli* (1967) the surrealist Louis Aragon places Hölderlin with Arthur Rimbaud: 'Two poets have pushed the spiritual existence to its extreme. One threw his message in the face of the world and broke his pen; the other became mad. At the borders of intelligence and reason, they made the same discoveries' (Lernout, p. 23).

Hölderlin's image remains thus deeply enmeshed with those idealized conceptions of creativity that, together with F. W. J. Schelling, Novalis and others, he had helped to establish. Yet he has also become a hero of modern anti-humanist thought. For Michel Foucault and Maurice Blanchot he is the poet who, like Antonin Artaud and Georges Bataille in the twentieth century, took language to the limits of its possibility, opening himself in the process to forms of experience that exceed the grasp of humanist conceptions of 'man' (Lernout, pp. 71–3). Philippe Lacoue-Labarthe and Jean-Luc Nancy have discovered in Hölderlin a thinker who was already far in advance of his contemporaries the Jena Romantics (Novalis, the Schlegels). He is celebrated as working through a deconstruction of the systems of German idealism which, as a friend and fellow student of both Schelling and G. W. F. Hegel, he had helped to construct.[2]

The fascination of Hölderlin for us lies similarly in the tension between a conception of *Begeisterung* or inspiration as the super-subjectivity of the creative, and the growing dominance in his work after 1800 of darker and arguably anti-humanist conceptions that link the compulsion to write with a form of death-drive. Despite the Hölderlin myth, his work reacts sharply against the cult of unregulated genius that had characterized the *Sturm und Drang* movement of the late eighteenth century. As Gerhard Kurz writes: 'There is scarcely another poet who taught the necessity of objective rules for poetic production as severely as Hölderlin did.'[3]

Although it remains little known in the Anglophone world, Hölderlin's theory of inspiration forms perhaps the most ambitious and extraordinary enterprise of its kind in Western poetics. Its relation to the traditional status of inspiration, as a performative that ensures its own value, is a rather paradoxical one. On the one hand he would demystify the notion by producing a calculable theory of inspiration. On the other hand, the quest for such a calculus, for a reconciliation of *ars* and *ingenium*, is a poet's equivalent of the ambitions of the alchemists.

The Romantics were often to be caricatured as advocating an uninhibited creativity and the cult of spontaneous genius. In fact Hölderlin and the Jena Romantics modify to the point of inverting the terms of Kant's notion of genius as the innate disposition through which nature gives the rule to art.[4] Hölderlin's notion of a calculated inspiration sounds oxymoronic. In fact, it might serve as the title for the neglected tradition of conceiving inspiration as a carefully studied, planned or cultivated delirium – an artificially induced Orphic power, akin to madness or the state of dreaming, perhaps involving drugs (as in Baudelaire's experiments with hashish),[5] but ultimately *sui generis*, and irreducible to the reductive categories with which medical science would describe aberrant psychic states.

Hölderlin's contemporary Novalis describes the artist as the *Kunstler des Wahnsinns* (Lange, p. 79). He also argued that 'To dream and not to dream simultaneously is, synthesized, the operation of genius.'[6] For Friedrich Schlegel and Novalis poetic madness is to be mediated into a carefully reckoned or calculated delirium that reconciles or transcends the distinction of art and nature (Lange, pp. 78–80). Gerard de Nerval, also discussing the dream life, talked of conquering it and bringing it to order.[7] Rimbaud proclaimed that 'The Poet makes himself into a *seer* by a long, tremendous and methodical derangement of all the senses.'[8] Such a notion of inspiration as technique culminates, as we will see in chapter eight, in the surrealist experiments with the act of composition.[9] Lange writes:

In distinction from the Cartesian type of rational subject, radical-aesthetic consciousness does not seek to exclude or negate the irrational: the concern is not to discriminate madness for the purpose of banning it from the public domain, but, above all, its mimetic transformation. (p. 112)

This notion of a deliberately-induced simulation of the irrational at first sight resembles rhetorical conceptions of enthusiasm or worked-up passion. There is a crucial distinction, however. The notion of enthusiasm or rhetorical passion lacks two critical features of these later conceptions of inspiration. It neither (a) forms part of a project to totalize the various levels, conscious and unconscious, of the psyche with the ideal of realizing an unalienated humanity; nor (b) is the state of inspiration held to form a critique of dominant conceptions of normality, sanity or rationality.

Jena

The decisive event in Hölderlin's intellectual formation was his brief period of study at the University of Jena with Johann Gottlieb Fichte in 1795, and the repercussions of this encounter in discussions with his friends Schelling and Hegel. Concepts of inspiration become suddenly crucial to major philosophical issues. The process of composition is idealized in terms of the synthesizing and totalizing ambitions that characterize German idealism in the period immediately after Kant.

Hölderlin's own aim to synthesize technical virtuosity and enthusiasm is only in fact part of a much more far-reaching programme to reconcile the perceived dualism of subjectivity and objectivity. At Jena, Fichte had elaborated a philosophy of idealism according to which the object world is merely a form of the self-intuition of an absolute subject, positing itself in the alienated form of exteriority. For Fichte this absolute I is self-grounded and self-positing, i.e absolutely free or self-determining. The object world is merely a 'check' (*Anstoß*) on the activity of the absolute subject in which we all participate, i.e. the subject is active in constituting not only the forms of cognition, as Kant had argued, but also the content of sensation:

> The matter of sensation is explained here, not in terms of a thing's activity upon the self, but rather as the result of an 'infinite' activity on the part of the subject that is 'checked,' or blocked, by the inert, wholly passive *Anstoß* and then reflected back to the subject.

The reflection that the subject's activity undergoes is intended to explain why the perceiving subject normally takes what is actually its own activity to be affection by an external independent thing.[10]

Experience for Fichte is the reciprocal interaction between two definitive capacities of the self, unreflecting intuition and active reflection. The individual finite subject is engaged in an open-ended struggle towards an unconditional freedom, the self-realization of an absolute I. It was this affirmation of a striving towards an unconditioned freedom that led to analogies between Fichte's thought and French revolutionary politics. He was eventually to leave the University of Jena in a controversy about the proximity of his thinking to atheism.

The decisive move in the appropriation of Fichte's thinking in poetics concerns the identification of the formative principle in art with a principle of selfhood. The structures of poetic form are seen as essentially structures of mind.[11] The I is seen as both positing and reflecting itself in a movement of self-determination in or through the art-work. The kinds of art-work, previously conceived in terms of genres defined through the description of received works, become understood as the manifestation of philosophical principles. Composition becomes valorized as an act of supreme philosophical significance: it is the writer's struggle to overcome his or her own limits and finitude. Moving between the act of *poiesis* and critical acts of self-reading and revision, the writer confronts in this process an intense sense of his or her limits. This sense of 'irony', however, need not be negative. It may lead to demands for new and less restrictive forms of determination and self-representation (*Darstellungen*).

Fichte's *Reflexionstheorie* is a decisive influence on Friedrich Schlegel's formulations on composition. Schlegel describes the interaction between the writer's consciousness and the formal and other constraints in the emergent work. The writer's drive for self-realization and freedom sets up a dialectic between formal constraint and an enthusiastic transgressive drive. Gerald Izenberg writes:

> as totality, form is the principle to which the writer subordinated him- or herself, the external norm by which the writer is compelled in the very work he or she is ostensibly freely creating. The author's freedom becomes a prisoner of itself, of its own aesthetic choices, servant to a structure beyond choice even though that

structure emerges from its choices ... Thus on the one hand, form is the very embodiment of absolute human freedom, and, on the other, it is an external totality that contains and constrains the author, making demands of its own.[12]

The valorization of the literary text as a process of psychic transformation, an Odyssey of the spirit, finds its most philosophically coherent formulation at Jena. Each work is a critical act of reflection upon its own process or principle of productivity. It is 'neither mere "literature" ... nor simply a "theory of literature" ... Rather it is theory itself as literature or, in other words, literature producing itself as it produces its own theory.'[13]

After Jena, European aesthetics and poetics may be said largely to comprise debate on the borders between a finite conscious self and its others as these same borders implicate themselves in the various determinations of the work. The text's status is be poised upon this border in diversely challenging ways – whether it be in relation to Fichtean conceptions of an absolute I, idealist conceptions of *Geist*, notions of the 'surreal', or psychoanalytic conceptions of sublimation or the unconscious.

The young Hölderlin, before the encounter with Fichte's thinking, had written hymns that take up pantheistic and Neoplatonic conceptions of love and harmony. Here the notion of inspiration is reminiscent still of the Spinozist pantheism of the *Sturm und Drang*, such as in Johann Gottfried Herder's 'Shakespeare' (1773) and other texts.[14] In Herder the recuperation and idealization of aspects of *Schwärmerei* in theories of genius produced a celebration of a Dionysian poetry of the passions and senses. Herder understood Dionysian inspiration among the Greeks as the realization of a communal spirit or essence.[15] In a text of 1764 he describes an animal-like and sensual language of wine and dancing, rising to the status of a certain mystical-sensual language of the gods.[16] Although his own thought was spare in its nostalgia, Herder's view of the Greek festival opens the space for Richard Wagner and the early Nietzsche with their theories of genuine inspiration as arising from communal festivals and the 'spirit of the people' (see chapter seven). For the young Hölderlin, in the revolutionary years of the early 1790s, poetic enthusiasm participates in the unifying principle of life, the *en kai pan*: it also enacts a communal spirit that serves to harbinger a future liberated society, one partly modelled on Rousseau's idealization of the festival or on the *fêtes* of the young French republic.[17] These hymns present themselves as 'enthusiastic' in the strict sense of *en-theos* (the god within). They seek to transmit this enthusiasm to others as a unifying, egalitarian force. 'Their wilful ecstacies have thus a quasi-liturgical function and are not meant to be confessions of private feeling.'[18] The Hölderlin of these hymns was seen as a revolutionary *Schwärmer*.

After Jena, Hölderlin's conceptions of enthusiasm receive a grounding in idealist philosophy. Yet they also change drastically in ways that question that philosophy. Hölderlin sees the notion of the *en kai pan* as inaccessible to any immediate approach. He treats with a new ambivalence the very idea of an individual's unification with a universal spirit; such unification would be a personal death. Representation and figuration, with their inherent structures of substitution and distantiation, come to be conceived as a safeguard and protection against the very spiritual incineration they mediate. Composition becomes an experiment with one's own mind.

Friedrich Schlegel idealizes romantic poetry as alone universal, infinite and free. Its first commandment is 'that the will of the poet can tolerate no law above itself' (*Athenaeum Fragment* 116).[19] Hölderlin's distinction is to elaborate a theory of inspiration that does not exalt so individualistic a notion of the subject but which openly takes issue with its voluntarism. He saw Fichte's conception of the primacy of an absolute I as an inherent assault upon the otherness of nature and elaborates in response a critique of the ambitions of philosophic reason. Andrew Bowie, in a discussion of Novalis, outlines a response to Fichte that was equally Hölderlin's:

> The idea is that philosophy sees things the wrong way round because it relies on reflection. The inability of the I to grasp itself as the highest principle is a *result* of its trying to make itself into an object. Philosophy since Fichte begins with reflection upon the activity which is required for reflection to take place at all: the action of the I. The I is, therefore, already subsequent to its basis: without some *prior* sense of the I there would be no reason to reflect at all, as there would be nothing to reflect upon.[20]

The goal of philosophical reflection, the union of knower and known in '*intellectual intuition*', is unattainable by philosophy as such, for by rendering the knowing consciousness an object of thought the act of reflection divides it from itself and alters its nature. The pre-reflexive basis of consciousness cannot be grasped in this way. Hölderlin thus reaches a conclusion superficially similar to some modern deconstructive thinking: that the philosophical or the theoretical is itself the condition of the impossibility of its own ambitions. The self, for Hölderlin correspondingly, in his difference from Fichte, is not an origin. The I is already subsequent to its basis. Any Fichtean act of self-positing is inconceivable without a constitutive relation to an alterity whose necessity must challenge the egocentricity of Fichte's thought. The relation of I to the not I (*Anstoß*) that determines and limits it is only conceivable on the basis of an underlying ground which embraces both.[21] This ground is what Hölderlin's 'Judgement and Being' [Über Urteil und Sein'] terms 'being', though he also speaks of Nature and the 'gods'.[22]

This argument may be seen as the basis of Hölderlin's turn to aesthetics. It is in an 'aesthetically' mediated non-conceptual structure of consciousness, not in philosophical conceptualization, that Hölderlin seeks a mode of thinking/action that addresses this impasse. In the late summer of 1795 Hölderlin wrote to Schiller outlining his own newly-developed philosophical programme. Here, his use of Fichte's terminology is already becoming anachronistic:

> I am attempting to prove that what must be continually demonstrated of any system, the union of the subject and object in an absolute I (or whatever name one gives it), is undoubtedly possible on the aesthetic level, in intellectual intuition, but not on the theoretical level except by means of an infinite approximation, like that of the square of the circle. (Sept. 4, 1795; VI: 1, pp. 180–1, p. 181)

Hölderlin's solution to the aporias of reflection turns to the aesthetic as a superior and non-reifying mode of knowing. 'On the Operations of the Poetic Spirit' ('Die Verfahrungs weise des poetischen Geistes') contains the following proposal as a response to the aporias of reflection:

> What everything depends on, then, is that the 'I' remain not merely in reciprocal activity, from which it cannot abstract without superceding itself, but that it freely choose an object from which, if it wants, it can abstract without cancelling itself in order to be adequately determined by it and determine it. (IV: 1, p. 254).

As Bowie glosses the argument, '*only* the I, as free spontaneity, can see nature aesthetically or produce aesthetic objects.'[23] In relating thus to an object of its own making, such as a work of art, the subject may grasp the form of an unalienated relationship, that the division of subject and object in self-consciousness need not be a form of reification. As Gerhard Kurz describes: 'The completed poem, the free poetic representation, is for Hölderlin anticipation and the promise of a free human life' (pp. 89-90).

These concerns may seem arcane and marginal to the revolutionary times in which Hölderlin lived. Yet his concern is with a conception of the poetic that would present his contemporaries with a reconfiguration of nothing less than the meaning of their communality. The term *'poetische'* in Hölderlin's title ('Die Verfahrungsweise des poetischen Geistes') is to be taken in the Greek sense of *poiesis* as referring to the realm of making and creation in general as the principal agent of human culture or *Bildung* (see Kurz, p. 78). Hölderlin's formulation of the rule of the progression for the poetic spirit refers not to poetics in any narrow sense, but to human self-determination in general through relation to some communal myth, shared religion or the structures of thought embodied in public and governmental institutions. The poet's task, in the very crisis of subjectivity undergone in *poiesis*, is to struggle to find newly-liberating determinations of communality.

Perhaps the most significant result of Hölderlin's disagreement with Fichtean notions of the subject is the view that the subjectivity of the writer is radically at stake in the space of composition. Adorno writes: 'Hölderlin's procedure takes into account the fact that the subject, which mistakes itself for something immediate and ultimate, is something utterly mediated.'[24] The modernity of Hölderlin's thinking on the process of composition partly lies in the fact that he was the first thinker to contest Kant's thesis that philosophy should take the unity of consciousness as its first and fundamental principle.[25] The self is other to itself as its very condition of being, a condition experienced as a deep sense of mortality, mutability, finitude and longing (IV:1, p. 235). Hölderlin's work, accordingly, cannot but be a rejection of any poetic of self-expression and of 'the type of subjective lyric that had become the norm since Goethe's early work' (Adorno, p. 143). The poet is rather a translator or mediator of the 'divine', not in the sense of a personal god but as the ground and determinant of our being.[26]

Poetic composition for Hölderlin then, as with Wordsworth in England, is an act of spiritual heroism and leadership. The space of composition is one in which the writer's subjectivity, textual form, subject matter and a possible reader emerge and interact in a movement of mutual determination, one that ideally bears a privileged relation to the project of realizing the human *Geist* in a revolutionary and newly-fulfilling form. For Hölderlin, however, our own

time is one of difficulty and aridity for poets. In contrast he idealizes the communal authority bestowed on their poets by the Greeks
and their seeming favour with Dionysus as the God of wine and
public festivity

> and who wants poets at all in lean years?
> But they are, you say, like those holy ones, priests of the wine-god
> Who in holy Night roamed from one place to the next.
> ('Bread and Wine' ['Brot und Wein'])[27]

In the act of poetic composition the poet must work to render his
psyche the site of a reversal, changeover or revolution that mediates
the present night of wandering with the day of a coming god.[28]

Enthusiasm and suicide

Hölderlin's thinking compares closely to other attempts in the
German lands in the 1790s to appropriate the intertwined conceptions of enthusiasm, *Begeisterung* and *Schwärmerei* for a system of
poetics that looks to the thought of Kant. Thinkers attempt both to
explain the 'disease' of irrationalism and fanaticism and to appropriate their energies as a fully-understood moment in their own
system.[29] In Friedrich Schlegel, Novalis and Schiller enthusiasm is
conceived in terms of a principle of the human psyche that strives
to overcome or transgress the boundaries of its finitude. Schiller's
dichotomy of the naive and the sentimental places enthusiasm as a
perversion of the sentimental:

> The sentimental genius ... is exposed to the danger, due to the
> effort of removing all limitations from it, of suppressing human
> nature altogether, and not only, as it may and should, elevating or
> *idealising* itself above and beyond all determined and limited actual-
> ity to absolute possibility, but rather of going still further beyond
> possibility, but rather of going still further beyond possibility or
> otherwise falling into extravagant *enthusiasm*.[30]

Hölderlin writes, analogously, 'One can fall upward just as well as
downward' (IV:1, p. 233). If the poetic act is not to lose itself in an
emptiness, he argues, it must be engaged in a technique and discipline of restraint.

Schiller's view here may be compared to the rather darker
idealizations of suicide to be found in Hölderlin, Novalis and
Friedrich Schlegel. Suicide, as an extreme act of reflexivity, may be
conceived as self-transcendence of the empirical ego as it unites

itself with its transcendental ground. Its moment may seem to combine and reconcile the contraries of activity and passivity, necessity and freedom. As Simon Critchley observes: 'The romantic affirmation of suicide is an attempt at the appropriation of *time*, to gather time into the living present of eternity at the moment of death.'[31] For Schlegel all artists make a sacrifice of themselves; 'the enthusiasm of annihilation' is one in which 'the meaning of the divine creation is revealed for the first time. Only in the midst of death does the lightning bolt of eternal life explode.'[32]

The topic of suicide is inseparable from controversies about the nature and dangers of *Schwärmerei*. In the eighth letter of *Philosophical Letters on Dogmatism and Criticism* (1795; 2nd ed. 1804) Schelling offers a philosophical deduction of 'the principle of all eccentric fantasy [*Schwärmerei*]' (182).[33] It is to be seen as a form of what Schelling terms 'dogmatism', that is a limited kind of thinking that takes as its ground a merely posited reality, without taking into account the freedom of the positing I. The crux of the argument is that what the enthusiast perceives as a self-annihilation in some Godhead is a misinterpretation:

> It is not likely that any enthusiast [*Schwärmer*] would ever have taken delight in the thought of being engulfed in the abyss of the deity, had he not always put his own ego in the place of the deity. It is not likely that any mystic could have conceived of himself as annihilated, had he not always, in his thought, retained his own self as the substratum of the annihilation. (p. 181; trans. modified)

For Schelling, desire for annihilation is inconceivable *per se*. It must really be a misrecognised desire for self-transcendence. The *Schwärmer*'s drive to self-immolation thus becomes for Schelling an aspect or 'moment' in the life of the autonomous principle – in this case the still Fichtean absolute subject of Schelling's thought in 1795 before the development of his philosophy of identity.

Schelling's argument exemplifies beautifully Joseph L. Esposito's generalization about post-Kantian idealism as 'marked by a continual process of seeking out what had hitherto been considered a source of heteronomy and incorporating those sources into a larger, autonomous framework.'[34] Nevertheless, for any finitely-determined individual, transcendence into an absolute or in-finite freedom still remains tantamount to death:

> Where all resistance [*Widerstand*] ceases, there is infinite expansion. But the intensity of our consciousness is in inverse ratio to the extension of our being. The supreme moment of being is, for us,

transition to not-being, the moment of annihilation. Here in this moment of absolute being, supreme passivity is one with the most unlimited activity. Unlimited activity is absolute repose – perfect Epicureanism.

We awaken from intellectual intuition as from a state of death. (p. 185)

The transgressive drive which finds one manifestation in the *Schwärmer* must be disciplined to the necessity of limitation and the determination of the *I* through its relation to otherness. Pure intellectual intuition – the union of knower and known – would be an immolation – 'with absolute freedom no consciousness of self is compatible. An activity without any object, An activity which encounters no resistance, never returns to itself. Only a restricted reality [*Realität*] is an actuality [*Wirklichkeit*] for us' (p. 184). Schelling will later turn to the aesthetic as answering this demand for a mode of absolute consciousness which is neither nihilism (the I seen as mere epiphenomenon of objective substance) nor the empty mysticism of an I conceived, impossibly, with no defining object.

Hölderlin's abandoned project, moving through three unfinished drafts, to write a poetic drama on the suicide of Empedocles instantiates related ideas on intellectual intuition and the process of composition. Empedocles' suicide seems to have been conceived as one of a Christ-like self-sacrifice. An individual who sums up all the various and conflicting exigencies of his epoch would achieve, through his death, a major and irreversible change in the human *Geist* in general.[35] The text itself would be the mediation of this sacrifice and of the revolution it accomplished. It is thus 'the justification of speculative suicide.'[36] But it is also its mediation, for it is an inherent and necessary part of the revolutionary status of Empedocles' act that it be communicated and known.

However, it was to be Hölderlin's younger friend Schelling, who was to work out the best-known and most influential version of *Begeisterung* as a suicide mediated into a form of self-transcendence, perhaps as a direct result of debates with Hölderlin at this time.[37] Schelling's *Naturphilosophie* and *The System of Transcendental Idealism* of 1800 explicate 'for the first time one of the most influential ideas in modern thinking: the idea that self-consciousness has to develop in stages from a point where it did not exist as such.'[38] It also comprises the most exalted account in Western thought of the process of artistic composition as a philosophically significant act. (The work is best-known to many readers of English through

Coleridge's plagiarism of its arguments in the *Biographia Literaria*). Although, Schelling argues, the I cannot conceptualize its own act of positing without at the same time reifying or objectifying that act, perverting it from its true nature, the artistic process seems to offer a privileged mode of experience in which the finite self may achieve an awareness of it without losing consciousness of itself. Schelling refers to the sense, during inspiration, of being simultaneously free, in command of intention, and yet also impelled by a sense of necessity. Autonomy and heteronomy seem reconciled in a unique experience of harmony. Schelling interprets this as the coming to consciousness of the productivity of nature itself, not in opposition to but as fully realized in a conscious human activity. Aesthetic intuition is thus intellectual intuition rendered into an objective form. Genius is valorized as the achievement of a resolution of contradictions unresolvable by any sort of training or *techne*:

> Just as the man of destiny does not execute what he wishes or intends, but rather what he is obliged to execute by an inscrutable fate which governs him, so the artist, however deliberate he may be, seems nonetheless to be governed, in regard to what is truly objective in his creation, by a power which separates him from all other men, and compels him to say or depict things which he does not fully understand himself, and whose meaning is infinite. (Schelling, p. 223)

Inspiration in this work is not only a notion of genius as a principle of productivity inexplicable by any sort of procedural rule, it is nothing less than the self-intuition of the absolute. It reconciles the demands of two possible foundationalist metaphysical arguments, the one which starts from the certainty or the givenness of the object and attempts, as did Spinoza, to explain all things (including consciousness) as the modification of an absolute substance, and the other which starts from the certainty of self-consciousness and attempts, as did Fichte, to deduce all phenomena as the modifications of an absolute subject. Inspiration becomes in Schelling what it remains in the surrealists, the resolution of contradictions that defy reason: 'art ... achieves the impossible' (p. 230). Schelling's argument is, in effect, a philosophical defence of Orphism: just as Orpheus could enchant the animals and plants, so the poetic process is that which energizes and informs the cosmos.

One correlate of the *Naturphilosophische* concept of inspiration is the argument that the work of art must exceed conceptualization not only in its genesis but also in its reading or interpretation. It is a mode of disclosure that does not lend itself to conceptual totalization, its meaning cannot be captured in any finite series of propositions:

> in the product which merely apes the character of a work of art, purpose and rule lie on the surface, and seem so restricted and circumscribed, that the product is no more than a faithful replica of the artist's conscious activity, and is in every respect an object for reflection only, not for intuition, which loves to sink itself in what it contemplates, and finds no resting place short of the infinite. (p. 225).

Schelling's transcendental conception of genius was to inform such dichotomies as that of Coleridge's 'fancy' and 'secondary imagination', Schopenhauer's *Idea* and *Concept*,[39] De Quincey on 'talent' and 'genius'.[40] In Eduard von Hartmann's influential *Philosophy of the Unconscious* in 1869,[41] the *Naturphisophische* conception of the unconscious productivity of nature reappears as, simply, the Unconscious. (It was von Hartmann's work which text introduced the substantive *l'inconscient*, into French).[42] Von Hartmann's Unconscious is simultaneously the universal formative principle in living things and the ground of the *a priori* nature of spontaneous aesthetic feeling. This hidden and dynamic congruence between personal feeling and the general principles of life is held to account for such phenomena as a sudden inspiration coming 'quite unexpectedly, as if fallen from heaven on journeys, in the theatre, in conversation, everywhere where it is least expected' (von Hartmann, p. 278). Von Hartmann also argues that such conceptions are holistic in nature, i.e. they are a preconception of the whole work in its unity. It is the organic or holistic nature of such conceptions that directs, teleologically, the unfolding of the artistic process, even when 'rational work alone is to fill up the entire interval between the first conception and the completed work' (p. 281). Such conceptions of the inherent rightness of unconscious artistic labour were to be become a cliché of late nineteenth and early twentieth century accounts of inspiration, even in work which, like that of the surrealists, would seem outwardly to eschew the metaphysics of Schelling and von Hartmann.[43]

Reflection

For a more detailed account of Hölderlin's work on the minutiae of the process of composition I turn to 'Reflection', a text of Spring

1799. Whereas Schelling came to see the aesthetic as the culmination and completion of a philosophical system, for Hölderlin art is not the self-realization of the absolute, but a measure and determination of finite human spirit. Philosophy and theory are not grounded in art, but shown to be themselves the very conditions for the impossibility of their ambitions for intellectual intuition.

'Reflection' (not Hölderlin's title) makes up a series of *Kurze* or brief texts that form an implicit dialogue with Longinus on the sublime, even though Longinus is never explicitly named.[44] Longinus had been appropriated by the *Sturm und Drang* movement of the late eighteenth century as the champion of unregulated natural genius and against the supposed constraints of neoclassical rules and Aristotelian poetics. Hölderlin, however, goes beyond the simplistic dichotomy of rules and genius, art and nature, to formulate a kind of transcendental 'psychology' of composition, a reworking of Longinus on the need for sobriety and control in inspiration.

Longinus, whose rhetorical theory of *hypsos* offers a series of techniques for achieving effects of inspiration, is an apt precursor. Longinus writes of an orator's art of calculating ends and means in an immediate relation to an audience, and the dangers of being 'over-inspired' and losing one's hold over them. Chapter 16 analyses the occasion and exact wording of Demosthenes' use of an oath – his swearing by the heroes of Marathon – in support of a campaign against Philip of Macedon: 'he keeps on the safe side and measures every word, showing that even in orgies of the imagination it is necessary to remain sober.'[45] Elsewhere he associates excessive emotionalism with frenzy and drunkenness. Hölderlin's stress is on the writer's need for self-observation during the emotional drama of written composition. *Peri Hypsous* refers sublimity to what now reads as a peculiar mixture of psychological states and rhetorical devices. 'Reflection', while repeating this variety of reference, rests on a sophisticated philosophical theory which grounds as it interrelates states of emotion and calculable, rhetorical procedures. Hölderlin's second section, in particular, recalls chapter 22 of *Peri Hypsous*, 'The Figure of Hyperbaton, or Inversion', in its discussion of the stylistic issue of the use of inversion and the various effects it may produce.

Hölderlin begins:

> There are degrees of enthusiasm. From gaiety, which is probably the lowest, up to the enthusiasm of the general who in the midst of the battle maintains his genius with presence of mind, there exists

an infinite ladder. To mount up and down on this ladder is the vocation and delight of the poet. (IV:1, p. 233; trans. modified)

Enthusiasm, rather than inspiration, remains the preferred translation of *Begeisterung* here since the passage recalls the debate on the nature of enthusiasm as self-abandonment and self-dedication, either in mundane affairs, in religious fervour or – as here – on the battlefield. Hölderlin's relation to Longinus here is to internalize a predominantly oral model of communication (still legible in his own image of the general commanding his troops) into a quasi-dialectical conception of written composition. Hölderlin anticipates Blanchot's meticulous work on the space of composition as one in which the writer, resisting the desire for mere self-expression, must open his or her psyche to the mutually-antagonistic demands of the linguistic material and the drive of a totalizing principle that often manifests itself as a nihilating impatience with finite determination (see ch. 10).

Longinus's Platonic or Neoplatonic notion of *eros* as the love of what is greater or more divine than ourselves is comparable to the German idealist programme of assimilating *Schwärmerei* to systematic idealist thinking. It is a drive to transcend the limits of our mortality, its force revealing that the supersensible is our true destination: 'the entire universe does not satisfy the contemplation and thought that lie within the scope of human endeavour; our ideas often go beyond the boundaries by which we are circumscribed' (ch. 35, p. 146). Such a transgression of finitude, however, is for Hölderlin one of the dangers of enthusiasm. Its annihilating fire is one facet only of his account of poetic composition as the determination of *Geist* from out of a three-way relation between the emergent textual material, the im-mediating exigencies of the divine and the emotional state of the writer. The writer must remain sober and detached at the crossroads of these different factors in order to gauge the correct 'measure of enthusiasm' for the work at hand:

> Once feeling is [unnerved through lack of a sense of restraint and direction], the poet, because he knows it, can do nothing better than to never let himself be frightened by it and to respect it only insofar as he proceeds somewhat more restrained and uses his understanding as readily as possible in order to immediately correct the impression that it [feeling] be restricted or liberating, and – once he has repeatedly helped himself out in this manner – to restore to feeling the natural certainty and consistency. (IV:1, p. 234)

This passage advocates a minutely attentive process of introspection during composition. The poet should learn to read what might seem mere swings of mood as signalling or steering devices. While writing, the poet confronts the human *Geist* in the externalized form of the work, a form that, although it has its empirical origin in the poet's own act, also transcends the subjective life of its maker. The emergent work is an unstable structure that may induce a disparate series of emotional states: self-recognition, self-alienation and self-transcendence.

For Longinus, poets and orators who do achieve a sublimity unattainable by mere art are risk-takers, risking not personal derangement but sudden fallings-off in their power: 'Both Pindar and Sophocles seem at times in their impetuous career to burn up everything in their path, although their fire is often unaccountably quenched, and they lapse into a most miserable flatness' (ch. 33, p. 144). Hölderlin considers a similar danger:

> If the spirit restricts itself, then it [feeling] senses too anxiously the momentary restriction, becomes too warm, loses clarity [*verliert die Klarheit*], and impels the spirit with an incomprehensible restlessness into the unlimited; if the spirit is more free, and if it lifts instantly above the rule and the subject matter, then it [feeling] becomes likewise anxious, fears going astray as before it feared the restrictedness; it [feeling] becomes cold and dull, wears on the spirit so that it sinks, hesitates and labours under superfluous doubts. (IV:1, pp. 233–34; trans. modified)

The poet's emotional reactions during composition are both a source of energy and a kind of gauge whereby the poet can measure and guide the relation of spirit or *Geist* and the emerging work. Feeling, writes Hölderlin, 'is the spirit's bridle and spur. It impels the spirit with warmth, [and] it defines its boundary with tenderness, authenticity, clarity and restrains it so that it does not go astray and thus it is at once understanding and will' (IV:1, p. 233; trans. modified). In effect, Longinus's model of calculated inspiration, which implied an immediate relation of orator or poet to audience, has become internalized in Hölderlin to the dynamics of a writer's solitary mental struggle over a blank page. The drive or energy of composition stands in a relation of antagonistic yet mutually-defining determination with the restrictions and laws of the formal and thematic material. Enthusiasm's drive to unmediated self-realization is inherently transgressive of empirical limitations, potentially annihilating of any particular text. *Begeisterung*, at an extreme, would be a mode of fruitless self-expenditure.

In a letter of early 1798 Hölderlin describes the extraordinary difficulty of maintaining that emotional equilibrium that is the gauge of successful composition, the effort of trying to give the appropriate determinate form to as yet undetermined material. Sometimes he may do too little from a fear of doing too much and, at others, do too much from fear of doing too little (VI:1, pp. 262–5, p. 262). Such lack of equilibrium may also become what we would call writer's block. This is subject to a similar kind of transcendental deduction. In a letter to his half brother of 4th June 1799 Hölderlin writes:

> when we only feel a lack as infinite, we are naturally inclined to want to eradicate this lack in an infinite fashion; in this manner our powers in such cases find themselves involved in a undetermined, fruitless and exhausting wrestling, for they have no definite knowledge where the lack lies and how this, and precisely this lack, is to be rectified and completed. As long as I encounter no check [*Anstoß*] in my work, everything makes vigorous progress, but the least mistake, which I at once feel too vividly to see clearly, sometimes drives me into a state of useless tension. What goes for my work also goes for my life and my dealings with other people, aged child that I am. (VI:1, pp. 326–7; my translation).

'Reflection' only adumbrates Hölderlin's byzantine and almost incomprehensible theory of calculating composition through what he terms the 'alternation of tonalities'.[46] Composition is the complex determination of the text in reciprocal interaction with the writer's psyche. The text becomes a subject-object in which the conflicting exigencies of that interaction – the various moods, tones and formal and material demands – achieve a relation of 'harmonious opposition', i.e. one in which the contrasting interaction brings each into its own in a harmonious whole. The process is one of a reciprocal determination of language and *Geist*, in which the seemingly irreconcilable (or merely 'directly opposed') states of *Geist* and the material and forms of representation resolve themselves in a complex and multiply-chiasmatic structure in which the exigencies of spiritual form, spiritual content and material form and material content – each only perceptible through its very conflict with its counterparts – compensate each for the deficiencies or lack of representability in the other. In retrospect, Hölderlin's theory might be termed that of a technics of 'sublimation'. So convinced was

Hölderlin of the efficacy of this theory that he seems to have employed it in painstaking detail in the making of his poems.[47]

Hölderlin writes finally of the achievement of an *'infinite unity'*. This is (in the obscure notation of his theory):

> the point of separation for the unified as such, but then again also point of union for the unified as the opposed, finally it is also both at once, so that what is harmoniously opposed within it is neither opposed as something unified nor unified as something opposed but as both in One, is felt as opposed in unified manner as inseparable and is invented as something felt. This sense is veritably poetical character, neither genius nor art, but poetic individuality, and *it alone is given the identity of enthusiasm [Begeisterung], the perfection of genius and art*, the actualization of the infinite, the divine moment. (IV:1, p. 251; emphasis added).

The text, that is, forms a non-alienating mode of spirit's self-reflection, a unification that does not obliterate the self; it achieves 'the highest opposition and unification of the living and the intellectual [the unreflected and the reflected], of the formal and material subject-object' (IV:1, p. 262). Thus the poet may feel 'himself comprehended in his entire inner and outer life by the pure tone of his primordial sensation' (IV:1, p. 263). This moment of intuited totalization is a beautiful defamiliarization, a kind of rebirth:

> the sum of all his experiences, of his knowledge, of his intuition, of his thinking, art and nature, as they present themselves within him and outside of him, everything exists, as it were, for the first time and for that reason is uncomprehended, undetermined, dissolved into pure matter and life, present to him. (IV:1, p. 263).

The fantasy crowd

Despite the solitude of composition, enthusiasm for Hölderlin remains the exigency, demand and promise of a *communal* transformation and reconciliation.[48] The poet may thus be a figure of revolutionary unrest, like the Empedocles of the second version of Hölderlin's play. The individual's unique access to divine enthusiasm is also an inspiration of others. This familiar transitivity (legible in the very words *Geist* and *Begeisterung*) is reworked here into an idealist system of thought. Received figures of an enthused audience undergo a like transformation. The play would have opened as follows:

MECADES: Do you hear the frenzied crowd?
    ...
    The spirit of that man
    Persuades, pervades them.
HEMOCRATES: I know, like withered grass
    The minds of men catch fire.

(Poems, p. 267)

Hölderlin's more peaceable ideal for his own time is that the poet should be the mediator of a 'mythology of reason' a religion without superstition that would present modern Europe with an achievable ideal of a non-alienated individuality and community. The poetic is the vanguard against increasing social tendencies towards alienation and reification.

With this communal function in mind, Hölderlin treats with intense suspicion that sense of individual exaltation usually associated with poetic enthusiasm. He sees it as false inspiration and self-aggrandizement, a mode of denial and evasion. Its intensity of feeling is proportional merely to the limits it would deny. It is the escapism of the unhappy consciousness, 'an exorbitant consciousness of shortcoming and a divinization of the self in the very sensation of its finitude'.[49] Its correlate, in the field of human action is the unreformed *Schwärmer* and *Schwärmerei*. We read in the penultimate section of 'Reflection':

> The deep sense of mortality, of change, of his temporal limitations enflames man so that he attempts much; [it] exercises all his powers, and prevents him from idleness, and one struggles for chimeras so long until again something true and authentic is found for cognition and occupation. In good times there are seldom any *Schwärmer*. Yet when man lacks great, pure objects then he creates some phantom out of this or that and closes the eyes in order to be able to take an interest in it and live for it. (IV:1, pp. 235–6; trans. modified).

The impulse in *Schwärmerei* is a potentially revolutionary one, but diverted into a mere utopianism. Alternatively, as in the poem 'Voice of the People' ['Stimme des Volks'] it can become a tragically heroic response to an impossible situation. The poem's title surely recalls the adage *vox populi, vox dei*, and must be read as part of Hölderlin's response to the terrors of the French Revolution, perhaps as 'a positive reception of "chaos" as a necessary element in the over-all process' of history.[50] This extraordinary text correlates mass enthusiasm and a death-drive as violent as the headlong plunge of rivers to the sea:

> Only too gladly will mortal beings
>
> Speed back into the All by the shortest way;
>   So rivers plunge – not movement, but rest they seek –
> Drawn on, pulled down against their will from
>   Boulder to boulder – abandoned, helpless –
>
> By that mysterious yearning toward the chasm;
>   Chaotic deeps attract, and whole peoples too
>   May come to long for death, and valiant
>   Towns that have striven to do the best thing,
>
> Year in, year out pursuing their task – these too
>   A holy end has stricken ...

(*Poems*, p. 179)

However attractive this Empedoclean drive to return directly to the origin, the poet, *qua* poet, is of necessity a mediator. 'Voice of the People' ends, quietly, 'yet there's also need of/One to interpret these holy legends.'

The social correlate of the successfully achieved poetic text as a harmonious opposition of unity and plurality is, throughout Hölderlin, the *Festtag* or *fête*. In the model of the festival Hölderlin expresses a revolutionary utopian ideal of community. It is one in which people form a transindividual unity, yet without the effacement of their difference. They are in a relation of 'harmonious opposition' to each other, i.e. a sublation of unity and difference into a third condition in which both are conserved. Hölderlin's idealization of ancient Greece sees that country itself as a festal hall, whose floor is the ocean ('Bread and Wine', *Poems*, pp. 242–253, p. 246–7). One embodiment of this communal transformation, in Hölderlin's rationally grounded appropriation of Greek myth, is Dionysus, both as the god of wine, a communal spirit, and as a traditional source of poetic inspiration. In the elegy 'Stutgard' (II:1, pp. 86–9) an autumn festival is presented as a foretaste of a fuller relation, yet to come, between gods and mortals: 'the communal god is a wind in our hair, is a garland,/And our selfhood, each one's melts, as a pearl does, in wine' (ll. 31–2; p. 87).

Let us take stock at this point. For all its extraordinary intelligence, Hölderlin's theory of inspiration surely rests on an uneasy assumption – that one can work out in one's own head, prior to any actual response from readers, the precise effectivity of one's own work. Hölderlin postulates that his own reactions, as first reader of the emergent material, provide a reliable general gauge – that all the multiplicitous factors that play across the space of composition can be reckoned up. Peter Bürger might be writing of the dilemma facing Hölderlin when he argues: 'It is the status of their products, not the consciousness artists have of their activity, that defines the social effect of works.'[51] Andrew Bowie suggests that one reason Hölderlin lost his mind was the increasingly intolerable discrepancy between his practice of composition and its social or historical context: 'the objective political and social world makes it harder and harder to believe in the possibility of realizing this vision [of the poetic process as reconciling art and nature, genius and technique, ancient and modern]: it will more and more take on the attributes of autonomous art in its growing complexity and lack of immediate accessibility.'[52] This conflict drove Hölderlin into further contradictions both with himself and with his environment. He was pushed, finally, into the quiescence of forty years of insanity.

Tragedy: 'infinite inspiration'

Since Aristotle's *Poetics* tragedy has always been the most philosophical of the literary kinds. In associating inspiration with the dangers of hubris, Hölderlin in effect aligns it with the issues of self-transcendence, transgression and danger that distinguish tragic action. A conception of inspiration as self-sacrifice also formed part of the development of a modern philosophy of tragedy in the thought of Schelling and Hegel. In the tenth of his *Philosophical Letters on Dogmatism and Criticism* in 1795 Schelling assimilates the paradoxes of the tragic to his burgeoning system of idealism:

> Many a time the question has been asked how Greek reason could bear the contradictions of Greek tragedy. A mortal, destined by fate to become a malefactor and himself fighting *against* this fate, is nevertheless appallingly punished for the crime, although it was a deed of destiny! The ground of this contradiction, that which made the contradiction bearable, lay deeper than one would seek it. It lay in the contest between human freedom and the power of the objective world in which the mortal must succumb *necessarily* if that power is absolutely superior, if it is fate. And yet he must be punished for succumbing because he did not succumb *without a*

struggle. That the malefactor who succumbed under the power of fate was punished, this tragic fact was the recognition of human freedom; it was the *honour* due to freedom. By suffering punishment willingly for an inevitable crime, the Greek hero affirms human freedom in its very loss. (pp. 192–3)

This structure of thought gives the paradoxy of the tragic a crucial place in the genesis of speculative dialectics.[53] It also anticipates Schelling's later notion of inspiration as enacting and resolving contradiction. Tragic representation achieves a conflictual unification of the subjective and objective, of the free and the necessary. It is a human defeat that yet affirms the human spirit.

When Hölderlin comes to put into practice ideas on inspiration and composition closely related to Schelling's, it is to tragedy that he turns, either in his own unfinished tragedy on Empedocles, or his later studies of Greek tragedy. Lyric, he writes in 'On the Difference of Poetic Modes' [*Über die verschiedene Arten, zu dichten*], is 'a continuous metaphor of feeling', epic is 'the metaphor of great aspirations', but the tragic is 'the metaphor of an intellectual intuition' (IV:1, p. 266), a metaphor, that is, for union with the ground of consciousness itself.

Philosophic thought, for Schelling in 1800, finds its precondition in the infinite division inherent to life. Art, however, reconciles division and establishes, in objective form, a harmonious intuition of the whole. For Hölderlin it is tragedy that focuses on 'the ideal of a living whole as briefly and, at the same time, as completely and perfectly as possible.'[54] Unlike Schelling, however, Hölderlin sees the tragic in essentially historical terms, as a catastrophic change in the determinations of human *Geist* at a particular juncture. It is only in a movement of the disappearance of one epoch and the emergence of another that the whole becomes intuitable:

> the world of all worlds, the all in all which always *is*, only *presents* itself in time – or in the downfall or in the moment, more genetically, in the becoming of the instant and in the beginning of time and world, and this downfall and beginning is – like Language – Expression, Sign, Representation of a living yet particular whole. ('Becoming in Dissolution', IV:1, p. 282; trans. modified)

Schelling's account of art as reconciling division, intuiting a timeless harmony etc., may sound to us merely escapist, a case of the 'ideology of the aesthetic'. In Hölderlin, however, the tragic is a catastrophic reversal in the relation of human and 'divine', a violent reconfiguration of the basic parameters of human culture. This may take the form of a profound conflict of values, of a 'revolt,' as in the conflict between Antigone and Creon in *Antigone*. The break in received determinations is irreversible. It discloses no clear new measure of human finitude. There is no self-recovery in the tragic experience, as Hölderlin underscores when he writes that 'man forgets himself'.[55]

In the 'Remarks on "Antigone"' Hölderlin writes:

> As has been hinted at in the remarks on 'Oedipus,' the tragic representation has as its premise that the immediate god is all at one with man ... that the *infinite* enthusiasm/inspiration [*Begeisterung*] conceives of itself *infinitely*, that is, in consciousness which cancels consciousness, separating itself in a sacred manner, and that the god is present in the figure of death. (V, 269; trans. modified)

Pure immediacy, as a form of access so total as to exclude any mediation by concept or thought, is paradoxically the most remote of relations. It is not a form of knowledge, but a catastrophic alteration in the would-be subject of knowlege – a 'consciousness which cancels consciousness' and hence also a recoil, 'separating itself in a sacred manner, ... the god is present in the figure of death.' Tragedy is the union of human and divine in the form of monstrosity.

Hölderlin's idea of the sacred entails a strict differentiation of human and divine: the monstrosity of their union is inherently unstable, one in which 'the infinite unification purifies itself through infinite separation' ('Remarks on "Oedipus"', V, 201; trans. modified). Thus the sacred, to preserve the separation of human and divine, may even be preserved by an act of blasphemy: 'It is a great resource of the secretly working soul that at the highest point of consciousness, it avoids consciousness; and before the manifest Divinity overwhelms it, it frequently opposes him with a bold, often with a blasphemous word, and so preserves the sacred and living possibility of the spirit' ('Remarks on "Antigone"', V, 267, trans. modified). Infinite *Begeisterung* entails the overwhelming of all the finite bounds that determine an individual identity. For the human being it is a movement of near annihilation and fearful recoil. Oedipus, through his transgression, is thrown into a space of double exile, for he is separate from both gods and from humanity. In the case of Antigone, the catastrophe or revolt takes the form of a language of defiance, one that effectively condemns its speaker to death, a verbal equivalent of Empedocles' act of self-annihilation.

Such action is not, of course, a matter of 'real' people or experiences that Sophocles is being seen to re-present, but of a profound conflict of values and meaning which the work creates and moves through in the theatre, and which the dramatist, according to Hölderlin, should be able to produce according to certain calculable procedures. For both dramatist and audience, 'infinite inspiration' might be termed an *oxymoron*, not as a logical or verbal contradiction in terms but as a state of existence that must be undergone in all its violence:

> the tragic *transport* is actually empty and the least restrained.
>
> Hence the rhythmic sequence of the ideas, wherein the *transport* presents itself, demands a counter-rhythmic interruption, a pure word, *what in poetic metre is called cesura*, in order to confront the onrushing alternation of ideas at its highest point in such that very soon not the alternation of the idea, but the idea [*Vorstellung*] itself emerges. ('Remarks on "Oedipus"', V, 196; trans. modified).

The structure of chiasmus and of the reciprocal determination of elements that defined the emergence of the poetic work in Hölderlin's other essays is transformed here. They become, as it were, a knot of radical indetermination. In the cesura, the normal interplay of representations that make up the work gives way to a moment that foregrounds the totality itself as suddenly at issue. Here, Hölderlin sees art less as a mode of human self-transcendence than as articulating – in this crisis – the boundaries of our finitude, the formal structure of a kind of 'limit-experience'.

Hölderlin's conception of the cesura, as a deeply enigmatic or undecipherable measure of human finitude, refractory to representation is less close to Schelling than it is to Blanchot's notion of a writer's inspiration as radical existential exile. Sophocles' 'true language' is praised as depicting 'man's understanding as wandering under the unthinkable' (V, 266; trans. modified). However, from out of the *nefas*, the catastrophe of received laws of being, a new dispensation may emerge. In Antigone's sacrifice and opposition to Creon, Hölderlin saw the affirmation of modern 'Hesperian' notions of community and fraternity: 'The form of reason which takes shape here as a tragic one is political, namely republican ...' (V, 272).[56]

Notes

1 See Geert Lernout, *The Poet as Thinker: Hölderlin in France* (Columbia, South Carolina: Camden House, 1994), pp. 3–17.

2 Philippe Lacoue-Labarthe, 'The Caesura of the Speculative', *Glyph*, 4 (1978), 57–84; Jean-Luc Nancy, 'Hyperion's Joy', trans. Christine Laennec

and Michael Syrotinski, in *The Birth to Presence*, trans. Brian Holmes *et al.* (Stanford: Stanford University Press, 1993), pp. 58–81.

3 Gerhard Kurz, *Mittelbarkeit und Vereinigung: Zum Verhältnis von Poesie, Reflexion und Revolution bei Hölderlin* (Stuttgart: J. B. Metzlersche Verlagsbuchhandlung, 1975), p. 94.

4 Wolfgang Lange, *Der Kalkulierte Wahnsinn: Innenansichten ästhetischer Moderne* (Frankfurt: Taschenbuch, 1992), p. 80.

5 See Claire Lyu, ' "High" Poetics: Baudelaire's *Le Poème du hachisch*', *MLN* 109 (1994), 698–740.

6 *Novalis: Werke*, ed. Gerhard Schulz (Munich: C. H. Beck, 1969), p. 433.

7 See Tony James on de Nerval's *Aurélia*, in *Dream, Creativity, and Madness in Nineteenth-Century France* (Oxford: Clarendon, 1995), pp. 131–44. See also Jean Paul Richter's conceptions in *Horn of Oberon: Jean Paul Richter's School for Aesthetics (1804)*, trans. Margaret R. Hale (Detroit: Wayne State University Press, 1973): 'It is a misunderstanding and a prejudice to infer from [the writer's reflectiveness] any limits to the poet's enthusiasm. For he must simultaneously cast flames upon the least detail and apply a thermometer to the flames; he must in the battle heat of all his faculties maintain the subtle balance of single syllables ... Inspiration produces only the whole; calmness produces the parts' (p. 37; see also p. 216).

8 See James, *Dream, Creativity*, pp. 250–61.

9 It also informs Ludwig Börne's eccentric essay 'The Art of Becoming an Original Writer in Three Days', in *Sämtliche Schriften*, 5 vols, ed. Inge and Peter Rippmann (Düsseldorf: Joseph Melzer, 1964–8), I, 740–3. This essay, which was admired by Freud, advocates that the would-be original writer undergo three days of enforced seclusion, writing down automatically, without censorship, everything that comes to mind. See Henri Ellenberger, *The Discovery of the Unconscious* (1970; London: Fontana, 1994), pp. 466–7.

10 Frederick Neuhouser, *Fichte's Theory of Subjectivity* (Cambridge: Cambridge University Press, 1990), p. 48.

11 See Cyrus Hamlin, 'The Origins of a Philosophical Genre Theory in German Romanticism', *European Romantic Review*, 5 (1994), 3–14. In 'On the Spirit and the Letter in Philosophy' (In a Series of Letters, 1794, trans. Elizabeth Rubenstein, in *German Aesthetic and Literary Criticism: Kant, Fichte, Schelling, Schopenhauer, Hegel*, ed. David Simpson (Cambridge: Cambridge University Press, 1984), pp. 74–93) Fichte takes up a standard enlightenment account of inspiration and reworks it in terms of his own theory of *Geist* and of the human drive of self-determination towards complete freedom. The moment of inspiration is that of a progressive revelation within this narrative of spirit. It is, once more, a performative that is testimony to it own truth: the artist does not need 'the approval of the crowd to believe what is revealed to him through an irresistible feeling at the moment of inspiration – a feeling as irresistible as that of his own existence' (pp. 88–9). The desire to communicate, for Fichte, is a form of self-assertion – 'the drive to make the people round us as like ourselves as possible, and to duplicate ourselves in them' (p. 89).

12 Gerald N. Izenberg, *Impossible Individuality: Romanticism, Revolution, and the Origins of Modern Selfhood, 1787–1802* (Princeton: Princeton University

Press, 1992), pp. 60–1.

13 Philippe Lacoue-Labarthe and Jean-Luc Nancy, *The Literary Absolute: The Theory of Literature in German Romanticism*, trans. Philip Barnard and Cheryl Lester (Albany: State University of New York Press, 1988), p. 12.

14 J. G. Herder, *Sämtliche Werke*, 33 vols, ed. Bernhard Suphan, (1877–1913; Hildesheim: Georg Olms, 1967–8), V, 208–31; see Frederick Burwick, *Poetic Madness and the Romantic Imagination* (University Park: Pennsylvania State University Press, 1996), pp. 23–5. See also J. G. Hamann, *Aesthetica in Nuce: A Rhapsody in Cabbalistic Prose*, in H. B. Nisbet (ed.), *German Aesthetic and Literary Criticism: Winckelmann, Lessing, Hamann, Herder, Schiller and Goethe* (Cambridge: Cambridge University Press, 1985), pp. 139–50.

15 See Max L. Baeumer, 'Nietzsche and the Tradition of the Dionysian', in *Studies in Nietzsche and the Classical Tradition*, ed. James C. O'Flaherty, Timothy F. Sellner and Robert M. Helm (Chapel Hill: University of North Carolina Press, 1979), pp. 165–89.

16 'Aus dem Königsbergschen Gelehrten und Politischen Zeitungen auf das Jahr 1764', Herder, *Sämtliche Werke*, I, 68–70.

17 Kurz, *Mittelbarkeit*, pp. 206–7; Eric L. Santner, *Friedrich Hölderlin: Narrative Vigilance and the Poetic Imagination* (New Brunswick: Rutgers University Press, 1986), pp. 35–8.

18 Richard Unger, *Hölderlin's Major Poetry: The Dialectics of Unity* (Bloomington: Indiana University Press, 1975), p. 13.

19 *Friedrich Schlegel's Lucinde and the Fragments*, trans. Peter Firchow (Minneapolis: University of Minnesota Press, 1971), p. 175.

20 Andrew Bowie, *Aesthetics and Subjectivity: From Kant to Nietzsche* (Manchester: Manchester University Press, 1990), p. 75.

21 See Bowie, *Aesthetics*, pp. 67–9; Dieter Henrich, 'Hölderlin über Urteil und Sein: Eine Studie zur Enstehungsgesichte des Idealismus', *Hölderlin-Jahrbuch*, 14, (1965-6), 73–96.

22 'How can I say: "I"! without self-consciousness? Yet how is self-consciousness possible? In opposing myself to myself, yet in recognizing myself as the same in the opposed regardless of this separation. Yet to what extent as the same? I can, I must ask in this manner; for in another respect it [the "I"] is opposed to itself. Hence identity is not a union of object and subject which simply occurred, hence identity is not = to absolute Being.' Friedrich Hölderlin, *Sämtliche Werke*. Grosse Stuttgarter Ausgabe, 8 vols, ed. Friedrich Beißner (Stuttgart: Kohlhammer, 1943-85), IV:1, p. 217.

All further references will be incorporated into the main text. Translations from Hölderlin's prose are taken, unless otherwise stated, from *Essays and Letters on Theory*, trans., ed. Thomas Pfau (Albany: State University of New York Press, 1988).

23 Bowie, *Aesthetics*, p. 71.

24 Theodor W. Adorno, 'Parataxis: On Hölderlin's Late Poetry', in *Notes to Literature*, 2 vols, ed. Rolf Tiedemann, trans. Shierry Weber Nicholsen (New York: Columbia University Press, 1992), II, 109–49, p. 137.

25 Dieter Henrich, *Hegel im Kontext* (Frankfurt am Main: Suhrkamp, 1971) p. 12.

26 See also Adorno, 'Parataxis', p. 110. For Hölderlin, composition is under-

stood in terms close in many ways to the concept of mediation in the Hegelian speculative dialectic that he helped formulate. For Hegel also, composition must be conceived as a complex process in which the singular moods and experiences of the writer must be negated in their immediacy if they are to achieve determination in a general or universal form capable of recognition by others. In the *Phenomenology of Spirit*, trans. A. V. Miller (Oxford, Oxford University Press 1977), Hegel dismisses the 'sky-rockets of inspiration' for true insights 'won through the labour of the Notion' (p. 43).

27 Friedrich Hölderlin, *Poems and Fragments*, trans. Michael Hamburger (Cambridge: Cambridge University Press, 1980), p. 251.

28 The topic of internalized leadership suggests only a 'he'.

29 See *German Aesthetic and Literary Criticism: Kant, Fichte, Schelling, Schopenhauer, Hegel*, ed. Simpson, pp. 11ff..

30 'On Naive and Sentimental Poetry', in *German Aesthetic and Literary Criticism: Winckelmann, Lessing, Hamann, Herder, Schiller and Goethe*, ed. Nisbet, pp. 180–232, p. 218.

31 Simon Critchley, 'Il y a – A Dying Stronger than Death (Blanchot with Levinas)', *Oxford Literary Review*, 15 (1993), 81–131, p. 125.

32 Schegel, *Ideas*, Fragment 131, *German Aesthetic and Literary Criticism: The Romantic Ironists and Goethe*, ed. Kathleen Wheeler (Cambridge: Cambridge University Press, 1984), p. 58.

33 Schelling, *The Unconditional in Human Knowledge: Four Early Essays (1794–1796)*, (1795; 2nd edn 1804), trans. Fritz Martin (Lewisburg: Bucknell University Press; London: Associated University Presses, 1980), p. 182.

34 Joseph L. Esposito, *Schelling's Idealism and Philosophy of Nature* (Lewisburg: Bucknell University Press; London: Associated University Presses, 1977), p. 21.

35 'Manes, the all-experienced, the seer, astonished by Empedocles' speeches, and by his mind, says that he is the one who was called and through whom the world was being at once destroyed and renewed' – Hölderlin's note for the third version, *Poems*, p. 366.

36 Lacoue-Labarthe, 'The Caesura of the Speculative', p. 76.

37 See Franz Gabriel Nauen, *Revolution, Idealism and Human Freedom: Schelling, Hölderlin and Hegel and the Crisis of Early Idealism* (The Hague: Martinus Nijhoff, 1971), pp. 45ff.

38 Schelling, *Ideas for a Philosophy of Nature* [1797; 2nd edn 1803], trans. Errol E. Harris and Peter Heath (Cambridge: Cambridge University Press, 1988); *System of Transcendental Idealism* (1800), trans. Peter Heath (Charlottesville, University Press of Virginia, 1978); Andrew Bowie, *Schelling and Modern European Philosophy: An Introduction* (London: Routledge, 1993), p. 45.

39 Arthur Schopenhauer, *The World as Will and Representation*, 2 vols, trans. E. F. J. Payne (New York: Dover, 1969), II, 408–9.

40 See Burwick, *Poetic Madness*, pp. 30-6.

41 Eduard von Hartmann, *Philosophy of the Unconscious: Speculative Results according to the Inductive Method of Physical Science* (1869), trans. William Chatterton Coupland (London: Kegan Paul, Trench, Trubner & Co., 1931), pp. 275–86.

42 For von Hartmann in France see James, *Dream, Creativity*, pp. 215, 218.

43 See, for instance, Francis Galton, *Inquiries into Human Faculty and its Development* (London: Macmillan, 1883) pp. 203–7; Théodule Ribot, *Essay on the Creative Imagination* [1900], trans. Albert H. N. Baron (Chicago: Open Court, 1906); and the discussion given in the introduction to this study of work connected to Harding's *An Anatomy of Inspiration*.

44 Martin Vöhler, 'Hölderlins Longin Rezeption', *Hölderlin-Jahrbuch*, 28 (1992–3), 152–72.

45 *Aristotle, Horace, Longinus: Classical Literary Criticism*, trans. T. S. Dorsch (London: Penguin, 1965), p. 126.

46 See Lawrence J. Ryan, *Hölderlins Lehre vom Wechsel der Töne* (Stuttgart: W. Kohlhammer, 1960).

47 See Ryan, *Holderlin's Lehre*.

48 See Gottfried Willems, 'Der Dichterische Enthusiasmus und die Macht der Negativität: Über Hölderlins Elegie *Brot und Wein*', *Jahrbuch der Deutschen Schillergesellschaft*, 32 (1988), 116–49.

49 Stanley Corngold, 'Hölderlin and the interpretation of the self', *Comparative Criticism*, 5 (1983), 187–200, p. 194.

50 Rainer Nägele, 'The Discourse of the Other: Hölderlin's Ode 'Stimme des Volks' and the Dialectic of the Enlightenment', *Glyph*, 5 (1979), 1–33, p. 8.

51 Peter Bürger, *Theory of the Avant-Garde*, trans. Michael Shaw (Minneapolis: University of Minnesota Press, 1984), p. 58.

52 Bowie, *Aesthetics*, p. 72; see also Lange, *Der Kalkulierte Wahnsinn*, pp. 223–6.

53 Hegel, in an early text on tragedy, writes: 'Tragedy [consists] in this: that moral nature separates the inorganic from itself in the form of fate, so as not to get involved with it, and confronts it; and, by recognizing it in a struggle, becomes reconciled with the divine being, which is the unity of both' (From Jeremy Adler, ed. 'On tragedy: 'Notes on the Oedipus' and 'Notes on the Antigone', trans. Adler, *Comparative Criticism*, 5 (1983), 205–44, p.220).

54 Hölderlin, Letter to Neuffer, 3 July, 1799; VI, 339, trans. modified.

55 Christopher Fynsk also contrasts Hölderlin's work on tragedy with Heidegger's appropriation of Hölderlin. See his *Heidegger: Thought and Historicity* (Ithaca and London: Cornell University Press, 1986), p. 181.

56 This theory that tragedy 'occurs at specific moments of historical change' anticipates the more recent thesis that it arises when an 'epistemic change' sets in, Adler, translator's introduction to Hölderlin, 'On tragedy', pp. 213–4.

CHAPTER 6

The fantasy crowd 2: Shelley's
A Defence of Poetry

L' âme n'a toute sa force qu'en s'abandonnant. (Madame de Staël)

Several salient features have emerged of the Romantic conception of inspiration, in Germany and Britain: the recuperation of notions of fanatical enthusiasm or *Schwärmerei* and their association with mass social feeling; the connection between inspiration and suicide; the notion of the creative as a form of supra-rationality critical of merely ratiocinative forms of consciousness; the status of inspiration as a residual orality; the dream of a faculty or technique with the status of a performative that ensures its own value; and, finally, concomitant anxieties about finding a readership or audience. All these are prominent in what is perhaps the best known inspirational aesthetic in post-Renaissance literature, P. B. Shelley's *A Defence of Poetry*.

Written in 1821 but not published until 1840, this gap of twenty years between composition and appearance is a significant factor in the reputation and image of this text. In 1821, the contexts of transgressive claims to authority and images of an ambivalently powerful mass feeling would have been easily legible to Shelley's contemporaries. By 1840, such contexts seem to have become invisible, and give way to a celebration of the artist as a quasi-divinity, hero of refined subjective states – an image of Shelley that has only been fully revised in recent decades.

Shelley writes:

> Poetry is not like reasoning, a power to be exerted at the determination of the will. A man cannot say, 'I will compose poetry.' The greatest poet even cannot say it: for the mind in creation is as a fading coal which some invisible influence, like an inconstant wind, awakens to transitory brightness: this power arises from within, like

the colour of a flower which fades and changes as it is developed, and the conscious portions of our natures are unprophetic of either its approach or its departure. Could this influence be durable in its original purity and force, it is impossible to predict the greatness of the results: but when composition begins, inspiration is already on the decline, and the most glorious poetry that has ever been communicated to the world is probably a feeble shadow of the original conception of the poet. I appeal to the greatest Poets of the present day, whether it be not an error to assert that the finest passages of poetry are produced by labour and study.[1]

This passage instantiates Shelley's recurrent revisionist strategy in relation to religious modes of thought. Narratives of religious conversion, such as St Paul's experience on the road to Damascus, are being rewritten as a conversion to Shelley's ardent brand of atheism and republicanism.[2] 'Hymn to Intellectual Beauty' (pp. 93–5) and the Introduction to *Laon and Cythna*[3] similarly depict scenes of intense elation and of self-dedication to ideals of liberty. Jean Hall observes that 'Remarkably, the author of *The Necessity of Atheism* chooses to defend poetry by characterizing it as a religion, and writing an inspirational essay meant to kindle our belief in the holiness of the human imagination'.[4] Lord Byron remarked that Shelley's campaign against institutional Christianity went hand in hand with great admiration for 'Scripture as a composition'. This is almost the first appearance in English of a phrase analogous to 'the Bible as literature'.[5] Yet Shelley's 'pagan' revisionism does not fully account for the claims about inspiration in *A Defence of Poetry*. Shelley is making an empirical claim and elaborating a philosophy of composition – 'I appeal to the greatest Poets of the present day ...'.

Coleridge and de Staël

A Defence of Poetry is a remarkable act of auto-legitimation in which the notion of inspiration serves several functions. Shelley returns to the most ardently anti-individualist formulations of inspiration to be found in Plato and assimilates them to a communitarian ethic opposed to the utilitarian ideology of the first industrializing society – inspirational poetry touches others as a kind of latent revolutionary *fête*. At the same time, inspiration functions as the ideal of a performative that ensures its own value, and provides Shelley with a strategy whereby a radical and socially-alienated poet may envisage or project an audience or posterity.

Seemingly spontaneous composition, and its implications for

the study of the mind, are a recurrent concern of Shelley's in 1821, his fourth year of exile in Italy and the year in which he wrote *A Defence* against his friend T. L. Peacock's utilitarian attack on poetry, 'The Four Ages of Poetry' (1820).[6] In January Shelley witnessed with fascination the performance of one Tommaso Sgricci, an Italian *improvvisatore*.[7] The *improvvisatori* maintained in a literate culture some of the techniques of traditional oral composition. Utilising formulae, set speeches adaptable for several purposes and other mnemonic devices, the *improvvisatori* performed a kind of verbal conjuring act. They would appear to compose, spontaneously and to order, large poetic works such as Sgricci's 'The Death of Hector' which Shelley watched with fascination, drafting an enthusiastic review. Shelley seems to have been less interested in Byron's comment that 'There is a great deal of knack in these gentry ... their poetry is more mechanical than you suppose' (Dawson, p. 19) than in finding in Sgricci's act 'a marvellous exhibition of the power of the human mind' (Dawson, p. 27). The encounter with Sgricci seems to have been decisive in Shelley's conception of the unconscious, unintentional nature of creative processes.

For the exiled Shelley improvisation offers a seductive model of an immediate and reciprocal relation to an audience. His review also instantiates the Romantic tendency to ascribe to hidden psychic powers effects that a modern critic would be more inclined to refer to an automatism in language. Sgricci is said to create 'ideas more rapidly than the human reason would ever have combined them' (Dawson, p. 28), and 'he scarcely seemed conscious of the words dictated to him by some superior power' (Dawson, p. 27). It is the *Ion* again, without the irony. Like Ion, Sgricci is a gifted mimic, a histrionic manipulator of affects upon a crowd. Shelley's hyperbolic review, however, deploys the terminology of genius. Sgricci projects himself and his auditors into a communal space of impassioned common-feeling:

> His gestures, the tone of his voice, his countenance completely directed by the living force of inspiration and continually expressing the various movements of soul of the characters, communicated to the soul of the spectators the passions that he was representing and by which his soul was by turns penetrated. (Dawson, p. 27)

In February or shortly after Shelley embarked on a translation of the *Ion* and the *Symposium*.[8] He repeatedly employs the language of those dialogues in *A Defence of Poetry*, which he sent to his publisher in March.[9]

Like Wordsworth's *The Prelude*, Shelley's *Defence* combines conceptions of enthusiasm and contagious rhetorical power with new German ideas of the creative as the supra-rational, partly transmitted through Coleridge. Shelley's interest in Sgricci fed into an attempt to revise Coleridge's idealization of the process of composition in terms removed from the older man's religious and political conservatism. In *Peter Bell the Third* (written 1819) (pp. 321–47, 336–7), Shelley depicts Coleridge in language almost identical to the account of the inspired poet in *A Defence of Poetry*. Nevertheless there are also striking divergences between Shelley's theory of inspiration and that in *Biographia Literaria* (1817).[10] Coleridge had argued, against Wordsworth's literalist doctrine that poetry should imitate 'the real language of men' in a state of passion, that the passion definitive of poetry is *sui generis*. Poetic passion, as experienced by a poet during composition, is not a duplicated or worked-up version of feelings that occur elsewhere in life. It is *sui generis*; it is imitative in Coleridge's sense of an essentializing mirror, rather than a mere photographic copy. It thus demands (*pace* Wordsworth) its own particular transformation of language.

The corollary of this view is a valorization of the act of composition as a psychical metamorphosis of huge import. Normal perception and self-communion are defamiliarized: 'the very *act* of poetic composition *itself* is, and is *allowed* to imply and to produce, an unusual state of excitement' (Coleridge's emphasis).[11] Coleridge understands this state in terms of the post-Kantian ideal of a union of *ars* and *ingenium* – it is the free play of all the faculties of the mind delighting in the exercise of their mutual harmony. The imagination is 'first put in action by the will and understanding and retained under their irremissive, though gentle and unnoticed controul' (*Biographia*, II, p. 16) It reveals itself as a principle of polarity, expressing and yet reconciling opposites. These include 'judgement ever awake and steady self-possession, with enthusiasm and feeling powerful or vehement' (II, p. 17). In the act of composition the poet thus becomes a rare instance of unalienated humanity: 'The poet, described in *ideal* perfection, brings the whole soul of man into activity, with the subordination of its faculties to each other, according to their relative worth and dignity' (II, p. 16). Inspiration also retains its seeming effect of something for nothing: 'the Effort required bears no proportion to the activity enjoyed.'[12] There is no overwhelming *ecstasis* or loss of consciousness, but an unifying act of imaginative power.[13]

Shelley likewise sees the passion of poetry as *sui generis*. He also argues that the state of mind associated with it composes the psyche and its perceptions into a condition compared to which the familiar world is a chaos. For Shelley, however, this power is intermittent, capricious and not the property of the conscious psyche. In the 'intervals of inspiration' the poet suffers a psychological backlash, 'abandoned to the sudden reflux of the influences under which others habitually live' (p. 507). The famous image of the fading coal describes poetry as a self-differing linguistic energy that metamorphoses itself in its very appearance. The wind, traditional image for poetic *afflatus*, remains also an image of caprice. Shelley's is a theory of poetry as a 'self-displacing energy'[14] that sets off a series of generative, associative and disseminatory effects in the imaginations of readers. Inspiration appears as a drive that defamiliarizes the received and worn associations of language and which forms, in metaphor, newly liberating connections and integrations of thought. These enact a synthetic power which would resemble Coleridge on imagination more closely were its agency not so fleeting and its results not so open-ended; for these are liable both, on the one hand, to become reified and static in the form of worn stereotypes and conceptions or, on the other, to be newly defamiliarized and configured in accordance with Shelley's notion of human perfectibility as an infinite process, with no fixed term or goal.

Shelley's essay also differs from Coleridge in the minutiae of its attention to the social and political conditions of poetic power. Like Coleridge, Shelley ascribes creativity to an innate power ('this power arises from within' (p. 504)) Yet this power depends on circumstantial conditions to an unprecedented degree in Shelley's theory, a relation well expressed in the image of a fire under the intermittent influence of the wind (no flame without oxygen). Elsewhere he argues that in Greece, source of literature 'the finest the world has ever produced',[15] conditions were such that it was impossible for any one with some talent to produce work with technical flaws. In *A Defence of Poetry* the enthusing impulse is so crucial a trigger or stimulus for the success and continuation of invention that inspiration seems almost the whole of the composing process. Yet Shelley asserts the enormous labour required for poetry, even if periods of composition themselves may be involuntary and spontaneous.[16]

The most striking difference between Shelley and Coleridge is that, whereas Coleridge valorizes the process of composition as a form of psychic autonomy, for Shelley inspiration remains both heteronomic and transgressive. Concerned to maintain an Anglican orthodoxy by distancing himself from any metaphysics that might be construed as pantheist, Coleridge needs to defend a certain integrity of the psyche against the danger of its being subsumed in some further principle. For Shelley, however, inspiration transgresses the principle of individuality and obliterates the workings of conscious reason or understanding. Inspiration is the overwhelming of an individual by forms of language that displace intentionality and which speak in the place of and faster than their seeming author. It is the expression of a potential, transfigured subjectivity, one that does not pre-exist the act of expression but which is instituted by it. This is, for Shelley, the enunciation briefly, not of what one is, but of what one may be or might become in a transfigured mode of community. It is an elusive and unforgettable cross-over in time, between the limited present and a possible liberated future.

Finally, in stressing the passivity and receptivity of the poet, Shelley seems to be deliberately deploying a 'feminizing' vocabulary. Nigel Leaske connects Shelley's recurrent imagery of electricity to his experiments with 'mesmerism' or animal magnetism. He argues that 'Shelley's poetics sought to privilege a spontaneous, vocalized word based on the model of the *improvvisatore* as a feminised, "sensitive" alternative to a Coleridgean poetics of the will ...'.[17]

By comparison with Coleridge's sophisticated German ideal of inspiration as the union of *ars* and *ingenium* ('*spontaneous* impulse and *voluntary* purpose' (*Biographia*, II, p. 65)), Shelley's notion of inspiration may seem like a curiously literal return to Plato, or even a case of being duped by the *improvvisatori*. In fact, what Shelley has done is to take over a more contemporary discourse on 'enthusiasm' and recast it in the vocabulary of the Platonic dialogues. Shelley's reversion to the more prestigious term, 'inspiration', conceals his proximity to the notion of enthusiasm both in the sense of mass feeling and in the sense of ardent sentiment established by Lord Shaftesbury.[18]

Let us examine this hidden concept of 'enthusiasm' more closely. In offering a theory of inspiration that addresses the status of the writer and the place of poetry amidst the uncertainties and chaos of post-revolutionary Europe, *A Defence of Poetry* aligns itself, more than to any other contemporary text, with de Staël's *De l'Allemagne*,[19] especially its closing chapters on enthusiasm. Although Shelley was defensive about meeting her,[20] De Staël was at this time, along with Goethe, Europe's most celebrated living writer. Hers is the book that introduced throughout Europe the German and now dominant sense of the term 'Romantic' (Isbell). *De l'Allemagne* was a *cause célèbre*, widely reviewed on its reissue in London in 1813, after it had been confiscated and pulped by Napoleon, forming as it does an exalted image of Germany (then occupied) as the homeland of values antithetical to those of imperial France.[21]

Although de Staël's brand of sentimental Protestantism is not Shelley's, a broad strategy of argument is similar in both writers. De Staël makes the customary distinction between enthusiasm and fanaticism. Enthusiasm, she reminds the reader, means 'god within us' (V, p. 188). She then defines it in terms that graft it into the debate against notions of self-interest as the main determinant of human action: 'Everything which makes us sacrifice our own welfare or our life is almost always enthusiasm of some kind, for the straight road of egoistical reasoning must always take itself as the end of all its exertions' (V, pp. 188–9). Opposed to mundane passion, which is centered on personal concerns, enthusiasm is *ec-static*, a feeling of 'the interest and beauty of all things' (V, p. 204). Enthusiasm (de Staël) or inspiration (Shelley) is an extreme form of happiness, an enlightening force opposed to any sort of material gratification. It integrates all the forces of the soul in a way that anticipates, however briefly, a more enlightened state of society.[22] Shelley writes:

> We are aware of evanescent visitations of thought and feeling sometimes associated with place or person, sometimes regarding our own mind alone, and always arising unforeseen and departing unbidden, but elevating and delightful beyond all expression: so that even in the desire and the regret they leave, there cannot but be pleasure, participating as it does in the nature of its object. It is as it were the interpenetration of a diviner nature through our own; but its footsteps are like those of a wind over a sea, which the coming calm erases, and whose traces remain only as on the wrinkled sand which paves it. (p. 504)

For Shelley the 'unalloyed' joy (p. 501) associated with poetic composition is *sui generis* yet his list of analogous states – 'virtue, love, patriotism, friendship' (p. 505) – might serve as a summary of more general instances of enthusiasm in de Staël or her precursor, Shaftesbury. In effect Shelley marries the commonplace notion of enthusiasm as the *ec-stasis* of the psyche in the act of creation with notions of enthusiasm from the tradition of moral sentiment. For Shelley, as for de Staël, poetic inspiration forms part of an attack on 'the principle of self'. 'The enthusiasm of virtue, love, patriotism, and friendship is essentially linked with such [poetic] emotions; and while they last, self appears as what it is, an atom to a universe' (p. 505).[23] The familiar evanescence and unreliability of enthusiasm also appears in de Staël's account (V, p. 216) as it does of course in Shelley's image of the fading coal.

In sum, Coleridge's notion of the passion of composition as a synthetic, essentializing power has been adapted in *A Defence of Poetry* to a notion of enthusiasm as an overwhelming, unwilled, capricious and trans-individual and 'feminizing' infusion of emotional energy, and recast in the prestigious language of the *Ion* and the *Symposium*.[24]

The subtext of mass psychology

Despite its proximity to *A Defence of Poetry*, aspects of de Staël's account are also antipathetic to Shelley's thinking, especially her traditional association of enthusiasm with the mass psychology of war, and the self-sacrificial heroics of the battlefield. Enthusiasm can overwhelm the principle of self so completely that at one point de Staël suddenly turns into that twentieth-century enthusiast Georges Bataille, writing of the glory of a suicidal self-expenditure: 'War ... always gives some people the joys [*joiussances*] of enthusiasm: the intoxication of a day of battle, the singular pleasure of exposing oneself to death when to love life is the command of our whole nature – this must, again, be attributed to enthusiasm' (V, pp. 192–3). This is a frightening image of a drive that possesses the will itself as an intense desire for personal annihilation. It is an image remote from Shelley's ideals though not so remote from aspects of his work in *Alastor* (pp. 69–87) or the nightmarish *The Triumph of Life* (pp. 453–70). *Alastor* (1816) depicts the tragic insanity of a young poet possessed by the vampiric image of a female soul-mate. He is seen as the victim of a mysterious 'Power' possessing his will and which the poem's narrator personifies as death itself (ll. 412–20, 675–6).[25]

This aspect of enthusiasm recalls the text to which *A Defence of Poetry* is a reply. Peacock's 'The Four Ages of Poetry' (1820) gives a slightly tongue-in-cheek attack on poetry as an irrational cult of feeling, the tool of demagogues and fanatics who wish to lead 'multitudes by the nose' (p. 201). The 'frame of mind which poetry inspires, or from which poetry can emanate' (p. 209), Peacock claims, robs its recipients of their capacity for rational judgement. Poets, once falsely 'regarded as portions and emanations of divinity'

(p. 201), are potentially anti-social, and playing with fire: 'The highest inspirations of poetry are resolvable into three ingredients: the rant of unregulated passion, the whine of exaggerated feeling, and the cant of factitious sentiment' (p. 209). As Peacock reminds us, the association of enthusiasm with sectarianism and crowd behaviour was still a very active one in Shelley's time. Attacks on Shelley assimilated him to the stereotype of the crazy and dangerous enthusiast with, as in Hazlitt's portrait of him, 'fire in his eye, a fever in his blood, a maggot in his brain, hectic flutter in his speech, which marks out the philosophic fanatic.' Hazlitt continues: 'As is often observable in the case of religious enthusiasts, there is a slenderness of constitutional stamina.'[26]

Shelley's desire to answer Peacock may also have related to a need to put to rest his own ambivalence about poetry and irrationalism.[27] In much of Shelley's work notions of 'sympathy' and 'enthusiasm' feed into what reads partly as an attempt to idealize some of the most striking and powerful features of mass psychology. For all Shelley's aristocratic sensibilities and his fear of people en masse as a source of violence, bigotry and superstition, they are a recurrent and often crucial feature in his work. Shelley regards with ambivalence and forced optimism the sense of power and of the possibility of seemingly miraculous transformation that are known in large gatherings, the behaviour of crowds, or merely the highly charged psychic atmosphere of periods of national crisis. Images of a general transformation, of some mass emotional force, a wind, ubiquitous spirit, a light or atmosphere, are among the commonest in Shelley's work. The 'Ode to Liberty' (pp. 229–36) opens by presenting the poet as the genuine representative of popular feeling, which is also his inspiration:

> A glorious people vibrated again
> > The lightning of the nations: Liberty
> From heart to heart, from tower to tower, o'er Spain,
> > Scattering contagious fire into the sky,
> Gleamed. My soul spurned the chains of its dismay,
> > And in the rapid plumes of song
> > Clothed itself, sublime and strong ...

Shelley's poetry often deploys subjects from Greek myth. But he disrupts the received associations of Hellenism and classicism by incorporating elements of Bacchic maenadism, with its anti-hierarchical connotations of liberating mass-feeling and sexual freedom.[28]

In the 'Ode to the West Wind' (pp. 221–3) the forces of revolutionary change are depicted as a creative-destructive wind sweeping through Europe and lifting the storm-clouds 'Like the bright hair uplifted from the head/Of some fierce Maenad' (ll. 20–1). The poet's prayer is to channel and temper this energy to something more assuredly creative, even though it may obliterate him in the process. Like several of Hölderlin's texts the ode forms a striking consideration of *poiesis* as personal annihilation (ll. 63–71): by associating the violence of the storm with impassioned Maenads, Shelley recalls the *sparagmos* or tearing to pieces of Orpheus. Also like Hölderlin's, Shelley's odes were conceived as close imitations of Greek odes. The odes of both writers project their source as a poetic voice engulfed in a communal, oral performance with ritual qualities.[29] Thomas Medwin's account of Shelley in an inspired state suggests how such a projection was empowering for this poet: 'his eyes flashed, his lips quivered, his voice was tremulous with emotion, a sort of ecstacy came over him, and he talked more like a spirit or an angel than a human being' (*Life*, pp. 27–8).

Shelley, then, sees a writer's creativity in symptomatic terms. It is the manifestation of social, trans-individual energies. A writer is a volcano whose work gives vent to pent-up social aspirations or frustrations. In a letter Shelley describes Wordsworth and Byron as deriving the energies of composition 'from the new springs of thought and feeling which the great events of our age have exposed to view.'[30] In 'Marianne's Dream' (written in 1817) Shelley seems to be making fun of Coleridge's 'Kubla Khan' and its defensive Preface of 1816, partly to highlight the older poet's apostasy from some of his political ideals in the 1790s.[31] Shelley implies that Coleridge's supposedly visionary poem is 'prophetic' (a prophecy of war) only in the sense of a symptomatic manifestation of accumulated mass energies.

Poets, Shelley argues, are the harbingers and transmitters of mass psychological change in which 'the cloud of mind is discharging its collected lightning' (Preface to *Prometheus Unbound*, p. 134). Shelley merges received tropes for rhetorical power such as contagion, lightning, electricity, heat and fire with the newly-political connotations of such imagery in an age of revolutionary unrest. The passage on inspiration in *A Defence of Poetry* recalls the power of the two poets/popular leaders and revolutionaries in *Laon and Cythna*. The poet/demagogue Laon declares:

> I will arise and waken
> The multitude, and like a sulphurous hill,
> Which on a sudden from its snows has shaken
> The swoon of ages, it shall burst and fill
> The world with cleansing fire ... [32]

Laon and Cythna are imagined to be gifted with such eloquence that they are capable of charging vast crowds with a radical enthusiasm. More orators than poets, they are brilliant workers upon mass psychology. As a crowd of millions congregates on a day of liberation, the hearts of the assembled multitude tremble 'Like ten thousand clouds which flow / With one wide wind as it flies!'[33] The communal feeling appears as a spirit of Liberty descending on the city and traversing its inhabitants like a possessing physical force, bringing a psychic transformation which may seem almost miraculous:

> To hear the restless multitudes for ever
> Around the base of that great Altar flow,
> As on some mountain-islet burst and shiver
> Atlantic waves; and solemnly and slow
> As the wind bore that tumult to and fro,
> To feel the dreamlike music, which did swim
> Like beams through floating clouds on waves below,
> Falling in pauses, from that Altar dim
> As silver-sounding tongues breathed an aereal hymn.
>
> To hear, to see, to live, was on that morn
> Lethean joy! so that all those assembled
> Cast off their memories of the past outworn ... [34]

For Shelley the release of repressions in mass psychology need not be the licence to violent passion feared by Le Bon and Freud. It frees potential according to an ultra-liberal, anarchist view of human nature as inherently benevolent but perverted by flawed institutions. In *Laon and Cythna* this brief release is premature, its fragility an analogue to the course of the French Revolution, the subject of Shelley's Preface. Faith in human potentiality, 'self-esteem', gives way to 'self-contempt' and superstition as the monarchists launch a counter-attack, induce mass panic, followed by plague and a social breakdown that sees Laon and Cythna martyred to placate the supposed anger of a vengeful god. Another text of 1817, the essay 'On Christianity', describes early Christianity in a similar way: 'After the transitory glow of enthusiasm had faded from the minds of men precedent and habit resumed their empire, broke like a universal deluge on one shrinking and solitary island.'[35]

Shelley's study of mass psychology matches closely the syndrome traced in David Hume's essay, 'Of Superstition and Enthusiasm.'[36] Hume applies this dichotomy to the analysis of large religious movements. Enthusiasm, whether in the '*anabaptists* in GERMANY, the *camisars* in FRANCE, the *levellers* and other fanatics in ENGLAND, and the *covenanters* in SCOTLAND' (pp. 148–9), is an irrationalism contemptuous of 'the common rules of reason, morality, and prudence' (p. 149). It is 'naturally accompanied with a spirit of liberty' (p. 149). It may have a 'fury like that of thunder and tempest' but is short-lived and may be cathartic. Superstition, on the other hand, endures and fits people 'for slavery' (p. 150), based as it is on a sense of guilt and abjection. Moreover, '*superstition is an enemy to civil liberty, and enthusiasm a friend to it*. As superstition groans under the dominion of priests, and enthusiasm is destructive of all ecclesiastical power' (p. 149).

Laon and Cythna reads then as a Godwinian tract, a cautionary tale of the need for gradualism in psychic and institutional reform, as opposed to the short-lived and illusory effects of mass psychology. It thus gives us a framework in which to place the more subtle, complex, and philosophically-grounded irrationalism of the action of poetry in *A Defence*. There it becomes an agent of a change that is genuinely and lastingly liberatory.

The tempering of poetic enthusiasm

For Shelley, the space of composition is no secluded interiority, like, for example the association of composition and contemplative retreat to be found in the younger Pliny or Seneca or in Young's *Conjectures on Original Composition*. It is a site of warring historical forces. Shelley's cousin, Thomas Medwin, wrote that 'It was one of [Shelley's] fanciful notions that what we call talent is in some degree magnetic, or epidemic, that spirits catch from each other a particle of the *mens divinior*.'[37] Describing the resurgence of the creative arts in Italy in the age succeeding Dante, Petrarch and Bocaccio, Shelley writes that in England 'Chaucer caught the sacred inspiration' (p. 500). This is the transmission of an effluence which 'at once connects, animates and sustains the life of all' (p. 493).

In his essay 'Of the Rise and Progress of the Arts and Sciences', David Hume argues that although the attempt to find general laws to account for individual creativity is fraught with difficulties of principle and practice, they must somehow relate to the general state of the taste, genius and spirit of their society:

> The mass cannot be altogether insipid, from which such refined spirits are extracted. *There is a God within us,* says Ovid, *who breathes that divine fire, by which we are animated* [Fast. lib. vi 5]. Poets, in all ages, have advanced this claim to inspiration. There is not, however, any thing supernatural in the case. Their fire is not kindled from heaven. It only runs along the earth; is caught from one breast to another; and burns brightest, where the materials are best prepared, and most happily disposed.[38]

The principle of the contagiousness of passion does a lot of surreptitious work here (Hume could have referred to his study of sympathy in *A Treatise of Human Nature* (1739)).[39] *A Defence of Poetry* may also be placed in a series of texts that situate enthusiasm or its cognates in terms that anticipate the modern psychology of group behaviour. This fact is partly disguised by Shelley's strategy of translating, or translating back, the terminology of mass enthusiasm into that of Platonic notions of inspiration. 'Enthusiasm' appears elsewhere in Shelley's prose in both an individual and communal sense, usually with a positive connotation. Plato himself, for instance, is said to be fired with 'the Pythian enthusiasm of poetry' and this, 'melted by the splendour and harmony of his periods', makes his language 'one irresistible stream of musical impressions.'[40] The Preface to *The Revolt of Islam* (as *Laon and Cythna* was retitled) reads: 'It is the business of the Poet to communicate to others the pleasure and the enthusiasm arising out of those images and feelings, in the vivid presence of which within his own mind consists at once his inspiration and his reward.'[41] Other examples of the use of the term in this individual sense could be cited, but Shelley also frequently uses the term for mass movements of mind. The idealized sect of gnostics in Shelley's unfinished story of 1814 'The Assassins', for example, are described as experiencing 'the enthusiasm of overwhelming transport.' Responding to the beauty of their surroundings 'The epidemic transport communicated itself through every heart with the rapidity of a blast from heaven.'[42]

Shelley is trying to reconcile a notion of enthusiasm in the normative idealistic sense at work in de Staël and Shaftesbury with attributes of enthusiasm as crowd psychology, especially its epidemic qualities.[43] *A Defence of Poetry* thus does not follow Coleridge in arguing for a 'deep' or metaphysical correlation between imaginative energies in human beings and principles of productivity in the universe in general. Shelley's frame of reference remains historical and political. Inspiration transgresses current social and institutional determinations of the self and affirms human perfectibility.[44] Shelley works out a detailed theory of literature and literary history based on their dialectical relation to institutions. He redeploys the Enlightenment view that the arts flourish only in conditions of relative political liberty in a theory of the developments and vicissitudes of the 'public mind' as the great mass of thought, opinion and aspiration that both sustains and is sustained by the educational and governmental institutions of its time.[45] The energies of mass psychology are thus, ideally, tamed, directed, refined and stabilized by a relative moral gradualism in the dialectical interaction of social energies and forms of governmental and other institutions.

William Blake's stance as an inspired prophet compares fruitfully with Shelley's doctrine of inspiration. Blake's work has been read in relation to the tradition of enthusiasm as seditious prophecy, dating from the wars of religion but coming to new life amidst the radicalism and popular millenarianism of the 1790s.[46] The power of prophecy, as in the careers of unhinged demagogues (like Richard Brothers and Joanna Southcote), is that of a 'dangerous enthusiasm', a contagious irrationalism that may transport the poor and the desperate. Blake's work often forms a sophisticated reworking of this radical, lower-class tradition. He appropriates the popular tradition of seditious prophecy in the articulation of his own metaphysical-historical system. This is one source of Blake's oratorical and prophetical voice: 'The cloud bears hard on Albion's shore / Filled with immortal demons of futurity. / In council gather the smitten Angels of Albion' (*Europe: A Prophecy*, ll. 63–5).[47] The example of Blake, however, shows us just how much farther Shelley is from this popular tradition. In *A Defence of Poetry* poetry is prophetic but the specific historical content of a prophetic text, such as predictions of the violent end of a royal dynasty, is not Shelley's concern. This is rather the general efficacy of poetry as the agent of liberating psychic forces. Some of the undesirable social connotations of enthusiasm with mass feeling and the battlefield are tempered, as in their transmutation into Shelley's image of poets as creating forms of manners and opinion which 'copied into the imaginations of men, become as generals to the bewildered armies of their thoughts' (p. 495)[48]

These mass energies are also countered in Shelley's thinking by the weight he gives to the notion of 'sympathy'. In other texts, whenever Shelley is analyzing the factors that make for ease in composition, the reference is to notions of sympathy. Like enthusiasm, this term is one in which some of the attributes of religious and Platonic notions of inspiration have been secularized as a philosophically-grounded principle of communicability.[49]

For Shelley as for Hume's *Treatise of Human Nature* (if not the later *Enquiries Concerning Human Understanding and Concerning the Principles of Morals*),[50] sympathy is less a particular passion or affect than it is the principle of communication between one person's feelings and another's. We do not simply imagine or represent to ourselves another's feeling and, by thinking of ourselves in a similar situation, come to feel something akin – the theory of sympathy given by Adam Smith and James Beattie.[51] There is a real 'transition of passion' (p. 385). The mere 'idea' of a passion transforms itself to an 'impression', i.e 'the very passion itself', and produces 'an equal emotion, as an original affection' (p. 316). Sympathy, as the communicability of feeling, becomes for Hume the basis of sociability in general, grounded in the notion of a universal human nature: 'The minds of all men are similar in their feelings and operations ... As in strings equally wound up, the motion of one communicates itself to the rest' (p. 576). For Shelley poetry incorporates a principle of sympathy: it 'compels us to feel that which we perceive, and to imagine that which we know' and 'It transmutes all that it touches, and every form moving within the radiance of its presence is changed by wondrous sympathy to an incarnation of the spirit which it breathes' (p. 505). It is a principle of enthusiastic intensification as well as of duplication: poetry 'multiplies all that it reflects' (p. 491). Moreover, 'the pleasure resulting from the manner in which [poets] express the influence of society or nature upon their own minds, communicates itself to others, and gathers a sort of reduplication from that communication' (p. 482). As a mode of sympathy with people in distant ages or countries, poetic inspiration is inherently levelling, a latent *fête*, testimony to the aspiration that 'The only perfect and genuine republic is that which comprehends every living being.'[52]

The transitivity and the paradoxy of inspiration

In several letters of his last years Shelley complains of the difficulty of putting pen to paper when so uncertain of the effect he may produce. 'It is impossible to compose except under the strong excitement of assurance of finding sympathy in what you write.'[53] Seeking sympathy with unborn posterity, he writes, is an uncertain impetus to writing. The sympathetic link between power of composition and the chances of sensitive reception becomes Shelley's rationale for the transitivity of inspiration. 'On the Devil and Devils' confesses that 'No poet develops the same power in the heat of composition when he feels himself insecure of the emotions of his readers, as in those where he knows that he can command their sympathy.'[54] Sympathy as a 'want or power' is not just a principle of communicability: it is also the demand that one's own feelings find recognition in others. This is not merely out of a desire for reciprocity; it follows from Shelley's argument that our identity is a relational one: 'Neither the eye nor the mind can see itself unless reflected upon that which it resembles' (p. 491). No wonder then that great poetry is seen as arising from periods of social crisis in which 'there is an accumulation of the power of *communicating and receiving* intense and impassioned conceptions' (p. 508, emphasis added). Even the claim that 'Poetry ever communicates all the pleasure which men are capable of receiving' (p. 493), otherwise close to a truism, suggests the same two-way logic. The magnet, image of inspiration from the *Ion*, becomes in Shelley an image for the combined sympathetic power of giving and receiving: for the magnet expresses perfectly a principle of transitivity. The train of influence is not the transmission of power through discrete individuals (divinity–poet–rhapsode–auditors): it is a matter of the precarious survival, since ancient Greek times, of cultural conditions sufficient to sustain in poets, readers and auditors a continuous, if sometimes perverted, sensibility to the poetic.

Notions of sympathy, then, underlie Shelley's extreme version of the transitivity of inspiration. Passions undergone during composition are held to be duplicated in the affect of the inspired/inspiring text on others, even to the degree that descriptions of the two things are interchangeable. The effect of Bacon's language is described in terms identical to those of the genesis of a work: it is 'a strain which distends, and then bursts the circumference of the hearer's mind, and pours itself forth together with it into the universal element with which it has perpetual sympathy' (p. 485). To read great poetry is not to parse or interpret a textual cipher, it is to be deindividualized by a transformative and quasi-oratorical force, and thrown into a space of ravishing communal energies. On one occasion the word 'read' is simply substituted by 'feel': 'It is impossible to feel [the verses of the Provençal trouvères] without becoming a portion of that beauty which we contemplate' (p. 497). The transitivity of inspiration is made the more plausible here by figures that construct the means of communication as oral (we read of the 'hearer's mind'; elsewhere Shelley talks of 'auditors' (p. 486)). Inspiration remains, once again, a case of residual orality working as a fantasy of immediate communication. Its effects – of unifying, energising and persuading – all recall the rhetorical tradition.

We come now to the most extraordinary feature of *A Defence of Poetry*: that in crucial passages it is not possible to tell whether Shelley is writing of the process of composition or of reception, or of both at once. This is so pervasive a feature that, rather like observers of the famous drawing of the duck/rabbit, critics have simply and at once read several passages one way or the other, without suspecting an alternative. Take, for instance, the sentence: 'Poetry is ever accompanied with pleasure: all spirits on which it falls, open themselves to receive the wisdom which is mingled with its delight' (p. 486). Is this the idea that poetic composition takes place as an unexpected event (falling upon its chosen spirits), or an account of the unexpected chances of reading or hearing? It could equally easily be either. The next sentence embraces both possibilities: 'In the infancy of the world, *neither poets themselves nor their auditors* are fully aware of the excellence of poetry: for it acts in a divine and unapprehended manner, beyond and above consciousness' (p. 486, emphasis added). In the next paragraph Shelley argues that 'poetry acts to produce the moral improvement of man' by its force of defamiliarization and by its transmission of sympathy. This argument would clearly be a stronger defence of poetry if applied to the multitude of readers or auditors, as opposed to the relatively few poets; yet conception and reception are described once more in an interchangeable way: 'Poetry acts in another and diviner manner [compared to the reasonings of ethical science]. It awakens and enlarges the mind itself by rendering it the receptacle of a thousand unapprehended combinations of thought' (p. 487). This could be simply about the reader or auditor yet as the paragraph continues so does the doubleness. Many critics read the following extract as simply about the poet at work, missing the duck for the rabbit:[55] 'Poetry enlarges the circumference of the imagination by replenishing it with thoughts of ever new delight, which have the power of attracting and assimilating to their own nature all other thoughts, and which form new intervals and interstices whose void forever craves fresh food' (p. 488). The very next sentence makes slightly fuller sense applied to the reader or auditor: 'Poetry strengthens that faculty which is the exercise of the moral nature of man, in the same manner as exercise strengthens a limb.' The next, however, explicitly returns us to composition: 'A poet therefore would do ill to embody his own conceptions of right and wrong ... in his poetical creations.' In sum, as in Wordsworth, the workings of the poetical faculty upon its material during composition seem curiously homologous with accounts of the workings of that same poetry upon an audience. Much of what is described of the imagination as an internal activity seems to be constructed – through the principle of the transitivity of inspiration – upon an ideal of the effect of inspired language upon others.

Let us take another example. Shelley's claim that poetry 'subdues to union, under its light yoke, all irreconcilable things' may initially recall Coleridge's argument that the imagination manifests itself as a principle of polarity which reconciles opposites. Shelley writes that poetry marries 'exaltation and horror, grief and pleasure, eternity and change.' Is Shelley describing, however, the work of composition upon its materials or the effect of a completed text upon others? Poetry

> marries exultation and horror, grief and pleasure, eternity and change; it subdues to union under its light yoke all irreconcilable things. It transmutes all that it touches, and every form moving within the radiance of its presence is changed by wondrous sympathy to an incarnation of the spirit which it breathes; its secret alchemy turns to potable gold the poisonous waters which flow from death through life; it strips the veil of familiarity from the world, and lays bare the naked and sleeping beauty, which is the spirit of its forms. (p. 505)

The rhapsodic abstracted language enables this passage to embrace, simultaneously, the action of the poetic faculty upon its materials, its effects upon a poet's psyche while composing and, thirdly, the affect of a completed text upon its recipients. By conflating such disparate elements as manifestations of one self-duplicating energy or series of energies, Shelley thus manages to sustain the traditional idealization of inspiration as a kind of performative that ensures its own truth, a scene of production whose forceful effect on others is somehow inherent to it.

To claim inspiration is also to claim a form of charismatic power or authority. It may also name a discrepancy between what a writer knows or may intend and what he or she does or achieves. Unlike Wordsworth, Shelley stresses inspiration as a principle incompatible with full self-knowledge or self-possession. Yet the claim that poets perform more than they can consciously represent to themselves, that they are 'unacknowledged legislators', bears on not one but several aspects of the notion of inspiration at work in *A Defence*, aspects uneasily blended together.

The difficulty is that Shelley wants to maintain some of the traditional aspects of inspiration – its affirmation of a certain privileged state of mind that somehow guarantees the quality of its results and hence an audience – at the same time as confronting situations that bear witness to an increasing sense of alienation from a possible audience. Insecurities about audience may be implicit in the way he appropriates the metaphor of composition as gestation. Shelley argues that the 'intuition and instinct' of poetry are analogous to the way a piece of sculpture or painting develops 'under the power of the artist as a child in the mother's womb' (p. 504). This image tends, like all idealizations of the 'mystery of creativity', to describe a cultural practice in naturalizing terms. Here the appropriation of female creativity is surely defensive – a fantasy of internalization in which the value as well as the material genesis of the work of art is not a matter of the uncertainties of publishing, audience response etc., but has the inherent finality of a biological process. Increasingly, as *A Defence* draws to a close, the notion of inspiration looks like an attempt to rationalize away the poet's lack of power over both the conditions of production and of the reception of his or her work.

If texts, for Shelley and other Romantics, do more than their writers plan or foresee, this is in part because possibilities of audience cannot be foreknown as easily as in periods with a more unified literary culture. The Romantics were faced with several mutually-antagonistic and fragmented publics, unknown and unpredictable.[56] Shelley's experience of exile and of occasional vilification in the reviews would have been sufficient testimony to the fact that what one writes will not necessarily match at all the performative effects that others will read. Other aspects of textual performativity, however, are more open to Shelley's idealizations:

> A great poem is a fountain for ever overflowing with the waters of wisdom and delight; and after one person and one age has exhausted all its diverse effluence which their peculiar relations enable them to share, another and yet another succeeds, and new relations are ever developed, the source of an unforeseen and an unconceived delight. (p. 500)

Does the future generation render conscious a process that was already there in composition, or is that seeming process an effect of hermeneutic distantiation, of reading from a different historical perspective? Shelley's association of inspiration with unconscious effects may simply engage with a poet's lack of control over even the immediate future of his or her texts. At the same time, this notion blends in an unclear way with what also seem to be notions of unconscious creativity or productivity. The following passage combines both possibilities: poetry 'acts in a divine and unapprehended manner, beyond and above consciousness; and it is reserved for future generations to contemplate and measure the mighty cause and effect in all the strength and splendour of their union' (p. 486).

One aspect of Shelley's thinking on how texts transcend intention relates to their historicity. A poem, in retrospect, may seem imbued with and formed by the 'spirit of [its] age' in a way the individual writer cannot foresee or control. The general social forces from which individual creativity is charged may even contradict the express programme of the writer:

> It is impossible to read the compositions of the most celebrated writers of the present day without being startled with the electric life which burns within their words. They measure the circumference and sound the depths of human nature with a comprehensive and all-penetrating spirit, and they are themselves perhaps the most sincerely astonished at its manifestations, for it is less their spirit than the spirit of the age. Poets are the hierophants of an unapprehended inspiration, the mirrors of the gigantic shadows which futurity casts upon the present, the words which express what they understand not; the trumpets which sing to battle and feel not what they inspire: the influence which is moved not, but moves. Poets are the unacknowledged legislators of the World. (p. 508)

In effect inspiration here is predicated on the act of reading. To be inspired by a text becomes (transitively) the ascription to its writer, who may well be dead, of an inspiration unfelt at the time of composition. This is clearly a very different notion from that of an overwhelming *ecstasis* given earlier, as well as the image of creation as pregnancy.

Shelley affirms the utility of poetry through an impassioned Platonic vocabulary – a strategic anachronism and one that was surely misguided in so far as it led to emasculating readings of Shelley and his supposed 'Platonism' for generations. The anachronism, however, may almost have been unavoidable if Shelley wanted to express a notion of the poetic as 'timeless' in a more complex way than as an immutable idea or eternal form. The temporality of the poetic, for Shelley, is anachronistic in a non-pejorative sense, i.e. open and futural in the mode of an event still in the process of happening, not yet determined. A poem may be timeless in the sense of something-yet-to-come, prophetic in the sense of opening to a future in which it will speak. This is how Shelley reads Dante, Milton, Plato etc. (p. 500). Like 'man' in the essay 'On Life', the poetic is inherently and affirmatively anachronistic, 'not what [it] is but what [it] has been and shall be' (p. 476). Poetry which finds its measure 'now' is only the product of those 'apes of humanity who make mouths in the glass of time',[57] unlike those writers who are, famously, 'the mirrors of the gigantic shadows which futurity casts upon the present' (*A Defence*, p. 508). Poetic inspiration is seen as a reaching out to others across large stretches of space and time, not (as in Wordsworth) as a sublime Power, but out of a self-sacrificing impulse of love. Again this is an idea also found in de Staël's work on enthusiasm: for her it is the writer's joy when inspired to project a bond of sympathy with other, as yet unknown souls.[58] Ingeniously then, Shelley recuperates the uncertainty of finding an audience for his work in terms of his notion of human perfectibility. The discrepancy between what a poet is conscious of and what the poetry does or may effect in its incalculable future is seen to affirm the poetical faculty as a principle of potentiality; it transcends its immediate historical context and looks towards a recovered community of readers in the future.

Shelley emerges as a theorist of anachronism as a creative principle, one that points to the finitude of an individual's creative act as part of a greater communal subjectivity, 'that great poem, which all poets, like the co-operating thoughts of one great mind, have built up since the beginning of the world' (p. 493). The transgressive dissolution of the individual in inspiration can thus be recuperated and made meaningful by being seen as part of a larger narrative of consciousness. The development of this communal subject is idealized in terms of a rhapsode's immediate relation to an audience: 'The past, like an inspired rhapsodist, fills the theatre of everlasting generations with ... harmony' (pp. 494–5).

Conclusion

A Defence of Poetry is an extraordinarily comprehensive and thorough idealization of the poetic act. Nevertheless, Shelley's own work elsewhere must make us question, even on his own terms, the idealization of enthusiasm as inspiration in *A Defence of Poetry*. *Laon and*

Cythna is not Shelley's only text to depict the dangerous and unreliable movements of mass or individual enthusiasm. *Alastor* (1816) and *The Triumph of Life* (composed 1822) both concern imaginative processes as a trangressive, violent force of passion that energizes or enthuses its victims for a brief time and then abandons them to exhaustion and debility. The most damning counter-statement to *A Defence* however, is the fragmentary 'On the Devil and Devils'. This contains an argument about poetic composition that collides head on with those in *A Defence*:

> Misery and injustice contrive to produce very poetical effect, because the excellence of poetry consists in its awakening the sympathy of men, which among persons influenced by an abject and gloomy superstition, is much more easily done by images of horror than of beauty. It requires a higher degree of skill in a poet to make beauty, virtue, and harmony poetical, that is, to give them an idealized and rhythmical analogy with the predominating emotions of his readers, than to make injustice, deformity, and discord and horror poetical. There are fewer Raphaels than Michael Angelos. Better verses have been written on Hell than Paradise ... No poet develops the same power in the heat of his composition when he feels himself insecure of the emotions of his readers, as in those where he knows he can command their sympathy.[59]

I repeat this last sentence, quoted earlier, because its logic, despite Shelley's attack on superstition and debased taste, is clearly that poetic power is amoral, and not inherently tending to perfectibility. This grim passage brings Shelley closer to Diderot's association of poetic creativity and social violence in his *De la poésie dramatique* (1758),[60] or to arguments that the vivacity of Homer's poetry is inseparable from the relative barbarism of his times, or to Hazlitt's association of poetry with the rhetoric of sensationalism and domination in his famous essay on *Coriolanus*.[61] Shelley's truncated career forbids any last word as to how successfully he would have managed to continue to idealize the energies of enthusiasm, or even to settle for himself the question of its status.

Finally, the reception of *A Defence of Poetry* demonstrates how by the time of its publication in 1840 readers had lost sight of the particular lineage of thought to which it belonged. Enthusiasm and its cognates had fed into debates about such issues as the nature of the social bond, the political responsibility of the poet, the ethics of communication. However, when it appeared in 1840, *A Defence* became part of an idealizing, sentimentalizing reading of Shelley as a Platonizing lyricist and utopianist. This may be partly because of Shelley's decision to translate many qualities associated with the ambivalent term 'enthusiasm' into a superficially Platonic notion of 'inspiration'. Ironically, Shelley's carnivalesque and anti-individualistic theory of inspiration fed into an idealization of the person of Shelley himself according to individualistic notions of the artist as cultural hero, a tendency intensified by the influence of German transcendentalism and the commercially-backed cult of Lord Byron. In a review of 1843 Shelley is celebrated for his 'benignant and glorious nature'. He is said to stand upon 'the mountain tops of the century in which he lived.'[62] Shelley as the self-possessed Wordsworth: it is an ironic triumph.

Notes

1 *A Defence of Poetry*, *Shelley's Poetry and Prose*, ed. Donald H. Reiman and Sharon B. Powers (New York: Norton, 1977), pp. 478–508, pp. 503–4. All references to Shelley's work are to this edition unless otherwise specified.

2 See, for instance, Timothy Webb, *Shelley: A Voice not Understood* (Manchester: Manchester University Press, 1977), pp. 157–90.

3 *The Complete Works of Percy Bysshe Shelley*, 10 vols. Julian edition (London: Ernest Benn, 1926–30), I, 235–408.

4 Jean Hall, 'The Divine and Dispassionate Senses: Shelley's *Defence* and Peacock's *The Four Ages of Poetry*', *Keats-Shelley Journal*, 41 (1992), 135–63, p. 139.

5 David Norton, *A History of the Bible as Literature*, 2 vols (Cambridge: Cambridge University Press, 1993), II, 164.

6 'The Four Ages of Poetry', in *Romantic Critical Essays*, ed. D. Bromwich (Cambridge: Cambridge University Press, 1987), pp. 199–211.

7 See Paul Dawson, 'Shelley and the "Improvvisatore" Sgricci: An Unpublished Review', *Keats Shelley Memorial Bulletin*, 32 (1981), 19–29.

8 James A. Notopoulos, *The Platonism of Shelley: a Study of Platonism and the Poetic Mind* (Durham, North Carolina: Duke University Press, 1949), p. 462; Dawson, p. 22.

9 Fanny DeLisle, *A Study of Shelley's* A Defence of Poetry: *A Textual and Critical Evaluation*, 2 vols (University of Salzburg, 1974), I, 2–3.

10 Samuel Taylor Coleridge, *Biographia Literaria: Or Biographical Sketches of My Literary life and Opinions* [1817], 2 vols, ed. James Engell and W. Jackson Bate (Princeton, New Jersey: Princeton University Press, 1983). Early draft material for *A Defence* contains a passage that seems to be an endorsement of Coleridge's attack on associationism as the principle mechanism of mental action: see DeLisle, *A Study of Shelley's* A Defence of Poetry, II, 592.

11 Coleridge, *Biographia*, II, 56.

12 A note of Oct.–Nov.1811, *The Notebooks of Samuel Taylor Coleridge*, 4 parts

in 8 vols, ed. Kathleen Coburn (London: Routledge, 1957–90), III, 4111.

13 For Coleridge on inspiration in biblical texts see Anthony Harding, *Coleridge and the Inspired Word* (Kingston and Montreal: McGill-Queen's University Press, 1985); Frederick Burwick, *Poetic Madness and the Romantic Imagination* (University Park: Pennsylvania State University Press, 1996), pp. 36–58.

14 Tilottama Rajan, *The Supplement of Reading: Figures of Understanding in Romantic Theory and Practice* (Ithaca and London: Cornell University Press, 1990), p. 278. See also Jerrold E. Hogle's invaluable 'Shelley's Poetics: The Power as Metaphor', *Keats-Shelley Journal*, 31 (1982), 159–91.

15 Shelley, 'On the Revival of Literature', *Complete Works*, VI, 213–15, p. 214.

16 Thomas Medwin, *The Life of Percy Bysshe Shelley* ed. H. B. Forman (London: Oxford University Press, 1913), p. 347.

17 Leaske, '"Shelley's Magnetic Ladies": Romantic Mesmerism and the Politics of the Body', in *Beyond Romanticism: New Approaches to Texts and Contexts 1780–1832*, ed. Stephen Copley and John Whale (London: Routledge, 1992), p. 59. Later in nineteenth-century Britain the image of the improviser was to be applied to women poets. See Angela Leighton, *Victorian Women Poets: Writing Against the Heart* (Charlottesville: University of Virginia Press, 1992), pp. 33ff.

18 See Hans H. Schulte, 'Zur Geschichte des Enthusiasmus im 18. Jahrhundert', *Publications of the English Goethe Society*, N.S. 19 (1969), 85–122, esp. pp. 97–8.

19 De Staël, *De L'Allemagne,* 5 vols, ed. La Comtesse Jean de Pange and Simone Balayé (Paris: Librairie Hachette, 1958–60).

20 See *Shelley and his Circle, 1773–1822*, 8 vols to date, ed. Kenneth Neill Cameron, Donald H. Reiman and Doucet Devlin Ficsher (Cambridge, Mass: Harvard University Press, 1961–), IV, 721.

21 See John Claireborne Isbell, *The Birth of European Romanticism: Truth and Propaganda in Stael's* De l'Allemagne (Cambridge: Cambridge University Press, 1994).

22 See Simone Balayé, *Madame de Stael: Ecrire, Lutter, Vivre* (Geneva: Librairie Droz, 1994), pp. 137–54). Diderot had employed a similar concept of '*enthousiasme*' as the passion of self-sacrifice against the arguments of Helvetius (*Oeuvres Philosophiques* ed. Paul Vernière (Paris: Garnier, 1956), p. 573).

23 Shelley would also have known de Staël's depiction of the heroine of her novel *Corinne: ou L'Italie* (1807) as an *improvvisatrice* composing on the theme of Italy and freedom, *Oeuvres Complètes de Madame La Baronne de Staël*, 17 vols (Paris: 1820), VIII–IX, VIII, 54–61; *The Letters of Percy Bysshe Shelley*, 2 vols, ed. Frederick L. Jones (Oxford: Clarendon Press, 1964), II, p. 68.

24 Shelley's saturation in Plato is such a cliché of criticism that it hardly needs illustration. For a detailed account see Notopoulos, *The Platonism of Shelley*. For specific textual resemblances in *A Defence* see DeLisle, *A Study of Shelley's* A Defence of Poetry, I, 241, 260–1; II, 350–1, 372, 374, 512, 520, 544, 550–1, 560, 578.

25 See Timothy Clark, *Embodying Revolution: The Figure of the Poet in Shelley* (Oxford: Clarendon Press, 1989), pp. 95–142.

26 *The Complete Works of William Hazlitt*, 21 vols, ed. P. P. Howe (London: J. M. Dent, 1931), VIII, 148. Hazlitt's notorious description of Shelley recalls his attack on methodists, 'On the Causes of Methodism' (*Works*, IV, 57–61). See also A. W. Cafarelli, 'Byron and the Pathology of Genius', in *Rereading Byron*, ed. A. Levine, R. N. Keane (New York: Garland, 1993), pp. 205–21.

27 A similar tension is legible in Emerson's essay 'Inspiration' in *Letters and Social Aims* (Boston and New York: Houghton, Mifflin and Co, 1876), pp. 269–97). There we find a Coleridgean, transcendentalist reading of inspiration in terms of a notion of Nature as the breath of God and a distinction between the merely discursive or sense-bound understanding and the insights of an intuitive reason when the human mind suddenly works in the full harmony of its faculties. Yet this idealization sits uneasily next to passages that carry over some of the more anti-individualistic aspects of enthusiasm. Like Shelley, Emerson takes enthusiasm back to Plato (the Seventh Letter in this case, though the metaphor of the bees used by Emerson also suggests the *Ion*):

> [Plato] said ... 'The man who is his own master knocks in vain at the doors of poetry.' The artists must be sacrificed to their art. Like bees, they must put their lives into the sting they give. What is a man good for without enthusiasm? and what is enthusiasm but this daring of ruin for its object? (pp. 274–5)

By the end of the essay, however, Emerson has abandoned this rhetoric of heroic self-expenditure in favour of the less disturbing notion of a regained psychic autonomy : the soul 'Itself is the dictator; the mind itself the awful oracle' (p. 297). In contrast to Shelley's feminism Emerson valorizes inspiration in strongly masculinist terms as 'the spermatic words of men-making poets' (p. 294). For Emerson as for Shelley not the least of the effects of substituting the prestigious Latin term 'inspiration' for the more dubious 'enthusiasm' is that some of the more destructive overtones of the Greek word drop out.

For Emerson's explicit appropriation of the claims of religious enthusiasts to his 'transcendentalism' see David S. Lovejoy, 'Shun Thy Father and All That: The Enthusiasts' Threat to the Family', *The New England Quarterly*, 60 (1987), 71–85, pp. 78–81.

28 Michael Rossington, 'The Bacchic in Shelley', in *Beyond Romanticism*, ed. Copley and Whale, pp. 101–17.

29 See Michael Erkelenz, 'Unacknowledged Legislation: The Genre and Function of Shelley's "Ode to Naples"', in *Shelley: Poet and Legislator of the World*, ed. Betty T. Bennett and Stuart Curran (Baltimore: Johns Hopkins University Press, 1996), pp. 63–72.

30 To Charles Ollier, 15 October 1819, Shelley, *Letters*, II, 127.

31 See Timothy Clark and Mark Allen, 'Between Flippancy and Terror: Shelley's "Marianne's Dream"', *Romanticism*, 1 (1995), 90–105.

32 Shelley, *Works*, I, 278, Canto II, ll. 118–22.

33 Shelley, *Works*, I, 323; Canto V, ll. 473–4.

34 Shelley, *Works*, I, 319–20; Canto V, ll. 361–72.

35 *The Prose Works of Percy Bysshe Shelley*, 1 vol. to date, ed. E. B. Murray (Oxford: Clarendon Press, 1993), pp. 246–71, p. 269.

36 David Hume, *Essays, Moral, Political, and Literary*, 2 vols, ed. T. H. Green and T. H. Grose (London: Longmans, Green and Co., 1875), I, 144–50.

37 Thomas Medwin, *Memoir of P. B. Shelley* (London, 1833), p. 38.

38 Hume, *Essays*, II, 174–177, 177

39 Hume, *A Treatise of Human Nature: Being an Attempt to Introduce the Experimental Method of Reasoning into Moral Subjects*, ed. L. A. Selby-Bigge, rev. P. H. Nidditch (Oxford; Clarendon Press, 1978).

40 'On the Symposium', Shelley, *Works*, VII, 161. The discourse of enthusiasm here becomes what was to be a familiar *topos* of privileged moments of being, moments of fullness and harmony.' For the 'epiphanic' moment in Romantic and post-Romantic writers, see Ashton Nichols, *The Poetics of Epiphany: Nineteenth-Century Origins of the Modern Literary Moment*, (Tuscaloosa: University of Alabama Press, 1987).

41 Shelley, *Works* I, 240.

42 Shelley, *Prose*, ed. Murray, pp. 124–39, p.129.

43 'A Philosophical View of Reform', contains comparable uses of the term, *Works*, VII, 15, 18. There Shelley argues also that it is the duty of the patriotic reformer to induce an enlightened enthusiasm among the populace: 'The true patriot will endeavor to enlighten and to unite the nation and animate it with enthusiasm and confidence' (p. 48)—a description that still seems to carry over the implicit rhetorical model of an orator's influence upon a massed group. Another account reads as a schema for the millenarian action of *Prometheus Unbound* (1820), and one answer to the dilemma posed by *Laon and Cythna*: 'If the majority are enlightened, united, impelled by a uniform enthusiasm and animated by a distinct and powerful apprehension of their object, – and full confidence in their undoubted power – the struggle is merely nominal' (p. 47). In *Prometheus Unbound* too the tyrant Jupiter is less violently deposed than suddenly recognized as impotent.

44 Close to *A Defence of Poetry*, here, is once again a work by Madame de Staël, her *De la littérature considerée dans ses rapports avec les institutions sociales* (1800), *Oeuvres Complètes*, IV. Like de Staël, with some differences I have discussed elsewhere, Shelley adapts the theory of perfectibility to an account of literary history, giving particular prominence to the effects of the relative liberation of women in modern Europe. See Clark, *Embodying Revolution*, pp. 58–64.

45 See Clark, *Embodying Revolution*, pp. 44–92.

46 See Jon Mee, *Dangerous Enthusiasm: William Blake and the Culture of Radicalism in the 1790s* (Oxford: Clarendon Press, 1992).

47 '*Europe: A Prophecy*', in *The Poems of William Blake*, ed. W. H. Stevenson and David V. Erdman (London: Longman, 1972), pp. 223–41.

48 See also Delisle, *A Study of Shelley's* A Defence of Poetry, II, 374.

49 John Mullan observes that in the eighteenth century, 'sympathy' 'could be synonymous with "enthusiasm"', *Sentiment and Sociability: The Language of*

Feeling in the Eighteenth Century (Oxford: Clarendon Press, 1990), p. 120.

50 Hume, *Enquiries Concerning Human Understanding and Concerning the Principles of Morals*, 3rd edn, ed. L. A. Selby-Bigge, rev. P. H. Nidditch (Oxford: Clarendon Press, 1975).

51 See Mullan, *Sentiment and Sociability*, pp. 43–7; Volume 2 of James Beattie, *Elements of Moral Science*, 2 vols (London: William Creech, 1790).

52 'On Christianity', Shelley, *Prose*, ed. Murray, p. 264.

53 To John Gisborne, 18 June 1822, *Letters*, II, 434–7, p. 436.

54 Shelley, *Works*, VII, 87–104, p. 101.

55 For example, Hogle, 'Shelley's Poetics', pp. 170–1; Rajan, *The Supplement of Reading*, p. 288.

56 See Jon P. Klancher, *The Making of English Reading Audiences 1790–1832* (Madison: University of Wisconsin Press, 1987).

57 To Leigh Hunt, 2 March 1822; Shelley, *Letters*, II, 393–5, p. 394.

58 De Staël, *De l'Allemagne*, V, 219. A manuscript reading of this passage writes of the poet being projected 'into the world's space and the centuries towards certain unknown friends, who, had they met you, would have loved you' (p. 219, var. A).

59 Shelley, *Works*, VII, p. 101.

60 Diderot, *Oeuvres Esthétiques* (Paris: Garnier, 1968), pp. 179–287, 261.

61 Hazlitt, *Works*, IV, 215–6.

62 Parke Godwin, in *Shelley: The Critical Heritage*, ed. J. E. Barcus (London and Boston: Routledge and Kegan Paul, 1975), pp. 395–409, p. 408, p. 409.

CHAPTER 7

Inspiration and the romantic body: Nietzsche and H.D.

Nietzsche: The birth of tragedy

Claims to inspiration have always comprised an ambivalent rhetoric of gender – prophetic authority suggests a strong, confident 'masculine' stance, yet at the same time a language of dispossession and of receptivity to an external force may seem to 'feminize' a male writer or to present a woman writer with just the sort of abject stance she may wish to repudiate. In the past hundred years, concepts of inspiration have become inceasingly a debate about forms of power invested in the gendered psyche or body. This chapter considers two comparable if contrasting theories of inspiration both of which focus upon the gendered body, the first by Friedrich Nietzsche, the second by the American poet Hilda Doolittle (H.D.).

Inspiration, in the German Romantic-idealist tradition, is closely related to concepts of the tragic. Both notions concern the antinomies of freedom and necessity, of the relation of human nature to some broader principle of life. In Schelling's *System of Transcendental Idealism*, inspiration is a creative reconciliation of these antinomies and a benign version of their conflict in the tragic. In Nietzsche's *The Birth of Tragedy* (1872) inspiration and tragedy are also inextricable. The destruction of the tragic hero enacts a transcendence of individuality in 'an augury of restored oneness'.[1]

As in Hölderlin, though with none of Hölderlin's minute attention to matters of technique, Nietzsche valorizes the process of composition and performance as one positioned uncertainly between suicidal obliteration and self-transcendence. For Hölderlin this involved a speculative recuperation of notions of enthusiasm and *Schwärmerei*. *The Birth of Tragedy* forms a defence of Richard Wagner's conceptions of communal art and the psychological transformations of the *Fest*. In both cases, the super-subjectivity of the inspired psyche is seen to partake of the force of an unalienated communal body. 'The artistic power of the Folk', Wagner writes, '[thrusts] itself forward with all the necessity of a nature-force.'[2] Wagner envisages the composite art work of the future, as not only conjoining differing arts in one but as a reunification of all the forces of the psyche. Performance would thus be the realization of 'the impulse that urges from *Life* into the work of art ... the impulse to bring the unconscious, instinctive principle of Life to understanding (*verständniss*) and acknowledgement as Necessity' (p. 197). Analogously, Nietzsche argues that the origin of tragic drama was in the overwhelming of the individual psyche in the communal rites of Dionysus:

> The Dionysian excitement is capable of communicating this artistic gift to the multitude, so they can see themselves surrounded by such a host of spirits while knowing themselves to be essentially one with them. This process of the tragic chorus is the *dramatic* proto-phenomenon: to see oneself transformed before one's own eyes and to begin to act as if one had actually entered into another body, another character. This process stands at the beginning of the origin of drama ... Here we have a surrender of individuality and a way of entering into another character. And this phenomenon is encountered epidemically: a whole throng experiences the magic of this transformation. (p. 64)

In *The Ages of the World* (1813) Schelling had seen Dionysus as a symbol of the unconscious productivity of nature identified also with the 'divine madness' of the ancients.[3] His *The Philosophy of Revelation* (1841–2) also opposes the creative insanity of the Dionysian to a reflective principle of form, the Apollonian: 'Not at different moments but at the same moment to be simultaneously drunk and sober is the secret of true poetry [*Poesie*]. This distinguishes the Apollonian enthusiasm from the simply Dionysian enthusiasm.'[4] The young Nietzsche conceives the origin of tragic drama in similar terms. It is a communal space of composition which is one of struggle between the opposing principles of the Apollonian and Dionysian, conceived in Schellingian terms. Nietzsche's argument forms a late member of the romantic tradition against which he was to react so vehemently. It is not without cliché: e.g. 'the genius in the act of artistic creation coalesces with [the] primordial artist of the world' (p. 52).

Like Schelling's, Nietzsche's Apollonian principle is one of restraint. Without it the energies of the Dionysian would break out in violence and the collapse of all social order. Nietzsche refers to the religious excesses of the German middle ages: 'singing and dancing crowds, ever increasing in number, whirled themselves from place to place under this same Dionysian impulse' (p. 36). The Apollonian principle, however, allows the spectator a sense of the enhancement of individual power through a dream-like participation in the Dionysian, without the loss of all individuality. Thus the Dionysian reveller 'sees himself as a satyr, *and as a satyr, in turn, he sees the god*' (p. 64). It is a dream which the dreamer recognizes as such, but consciously allows to unfold. '[W]e must', writes Nietzsche, 'understand Greek tragedy as the Dionysian chorus which ever anew discharges itself in an Apollinian world of images' (pp. 64–5). The Apollonian effects what the later Nietzsche, and also Freud, call a 'sublimation' of the sexual energies of the Dionysian, as opposed to their mere repression by a third princple of narrow ratiocination which Nietzsche terms 'the Socratic'. In sum, *The Birth of Tragedy* combines German Romantic conceptions of inspiration as a conjunction of spontaneous enthusiasm and intentional virtuosity with conceptions of the origins of art in communal ritual.[5] Unlike the notions of sober inspiration defended by Hölderlin and Schelling, however, this state provides for Nietzsche only an aesthetic, not an ethical, justification of human life.

The conception of Zarathustra

Nietzsche's view of a communal psyche as the interaction of three conflicting principles reads as a theory of creativity transitional between that of the *Naturphilosophie* of Schelling, von Hartmann and others, and Freud's economic model of the psyche. It also bears out Michel Foucault's argument about the place of sexuality in modern thinking: 'we demand that it tell us our truth, or rather, the deeply buried truth of that truth about ourselves which we think we possess in our immediate consciousness.'[6] Nietzsche criticizes the dominant idealizations of Hellenic civilization for overlooking the basis of Dionysian art in 'orgies' and the mysteries of sexuality (*Birth of Tragedy*, p. 39). Wagner's account of the creative process is also an instance of a form of thinking that has become as potent a myth about cultural production as that of the mysterious muse. Wagner sees the masculine, poetic understanding as fructifying the feminine, musical element of feeling: '*This procreative seed is the poetic intent, which provides music, that gloriously loving woman, with the subject matter that she must bear.*'[7] D. H. Lawrence's *Study of Thomas Hardy* (written 1915; published 1936)[8] also deploys a gendered cosmogony. He sees the creative act as a form of marriage between a male will-to-motion and intellect and a female will-to-inertia and the bodily. Such notions of sexuality form a late version of *Naturphilosophie*. They take traditional stereotypes about gender to apply them, in a pseudo-explanatory way, to what are taken to be universal natural or psychic polarities.

Nietzsche's early conceptions of art and mass communal feeling anticipate and to a large degree structure his later thinking on inspiration in terms of individual physiology, the various drives of the body. In 1878, he writes in a fragment about the artist as sublimating sexual impulses[9] – the first use of the term *Sublimieren* in the sense later to be familiar in Freud. Nevertheless, compared to Wagner, *The Birth of Tragedy* is reticent and ambivalent in ascribing any specific gender to the rival principles it depicts. Nietzsche pointedly omits reference to the maenads so prominent in the myths of Dionysus and to the god's *sparagmos* or being torn to pieces by women.[10] In the late text, *Ecce Homo* (written 1888), however, many of the Romantic-idealist features of inspiration in *The Birth of Tragedy* reappear as features of an unusually empowered masculine physiology. His account is of the conception of his own *Zarathustra*:

Has anyone at the end of the nineteenth century a clear idea of what poets of strong ages have called *inspiration* [*Inspiration*]? If not, I will describe it. – If one had the slightest residue of superstition left in one's system, one could hardly reject altogether the idea that one is merely incarnation, merely mouthpiece, merely medium of overpowering forces. The concept of revelation – in the sense that suddenly, with indescribable certainty and subtlety, something becomes *visible*, audible, something that shakes one to the last depths and throws one down – that merely describes the facts. One hears, one does not seek; one accepts, one does not ask who gives; like lightning, a thought flashes up, with necessity, without hesitation regarding its form – I never had any choice.

A rapture whose tremendous tension occasionally discharges itself in a flood of tears – now the pace quickens involuntarily, now it becomes slow; one is altogether beside oneself, with the distinct consciousness of subtle shudders and of one's skin creeping down to one's toes; a depth of happiness in which even what is most painful and gloomy does not seem something opposite but rather conditioned, provoked, a *necessary* in such a superabundance of light; an instinct for rhythmical relationships that arches over wide spaces of form – length, the need for a rhythm with wide arches is almost the measure of the force of inspiration, a kind of compensation for its pressure and tension.

Everything happens involuntarily in the highest degree but as in a gale of a feeling of freedom, of absoluteness, of power, of divinity. – The involuntariness of image and metaphor is strangest of all; one no longer has any notion of what is image or a metaphor: everything offers itself as the nearest, most obvious, simplest expression. It actually seems, to allude to something Zarathustra says, as if the things themselves approached and offered themselves as metaphors ('Here all things come caressingly to your discourse and flatter you: for they want to ride on your back. On every metaphor you ride to every truth. ... Here the words and wordshrines of all existence open up before you; here all being wishes to become word, all becoming wishes to learn from you how to speak').

This is *my* experience of inspiration; I do not doubt that one has to go back thousands of years in order to find anyone who could say to me 'it is mine as well.' – (*Ecce Homo*)[11]

This passage presents inspiration in terms of extremes of both self-affirmation and, simultaneously, of a transgression of personhood. Nietzsche reproduces the crucial features of inspiration from the Romantic-idealist tradition – those of self-transcendence, the sudden access of power, the gift of speech, the reconciliation of the seeming antinomy of freedom and necessity[12] – but he now understands these in physiological terms that undercut that tradition: 'The *body* is inspired [*begeistert*]: let us keep the "soul" out of it' (*Ecce Homo*, p. 302). Inspiration is a brief and overwhelming breach of the barriers that normally separate the body's disparate drives or selves. Thus they achieve a state of mutual enhancement and intensification, experienced as a revolutionary self-overcoming.

Nietzsche's account of inspiration in terms of the body is offered as a demystification. Nevertheless, many attributes of Schelling's notion of the unconscious productivity of nature reappear in the way Nietzsche describes physiological energies. The Romantic-idealist conception of inspiration as the reconciliation of antinomies remains, not as a metaphysical but as a psychological ideal,[13] that of a privileged interaction of conscious and unconscious.

To be inspired in Nietzsche's sense is to find oneself pitched into a space of composition in a ferment so intense as to transform everything in the environment into latent textual material, each percept and word triggering in turn new and compelling images and ideas: '"all things come caressingly to your discourse and flatter you: for they want to ride upon your back ... all existence here wants to

become words, all becoming here wants to learn speech from you –
" '. The text in process has uniquely holistic qualities: 'The whole
of *Zarathustra* I came to me' (p. 298). Such holism is not a novel
claim, but Nietzsche does not see it in terms of the organicism or
inherent finality of Schelling or von Hartmann. It makes up an
amplification and transformation of physiological rhythms into the
formal and semantic relationships of an emergent work. It is the
dance of a physiology coming to language.

Some of Nietzsche's most radical arguments find summary
expression in this conception of inspiration. Firstly, it enacts his
attack on the false valuation of consciousness as an agent.
Consciousness is merely epiphenomenal: 'a thought comes when
"it" wishes, and not when "I" wish, so that it is a falsification of the
facts of the case to say that the subject "I" is the condition of the
predicate "think" ... even the "it" contains an *interpretation* of the
process, and does not belong to the process itself. One infers here
according to the grammatical habit: "Thinking is an activity; every
activity requires an agent; consequently –"'.[14] Second, the false unity
of this 'it' must be further resolved into the heterogeneous drives
and agencies of the body. Consciousness is only a product, and a
very fragile one, of this diverse play of affects. The overwhelming
sense of freedom and power undergone in inspiration is not in any
way a matter of the individual conscious will. The will itself is the
product of the very forces with which it feels so in accord. The
sense of a reconciliation between freedom and necessity is an illusory result of this common source: 'he who wills believes with a fair
amount of certainty that will and action are somehow one; he
ascribes [falsely] the success, the carrying out of the willing, to the
will itself, and thereby enjoys an increase of the sensation of power
which accompanies all success' (*Beyond Good and Evil*, section 19, p.
26).

Nietzsche's argument may be read as a variant on a recurrent
nineteenth-century view of the creative process as a kind of supra-
rationality, one which, while related to madness and illness, is *sui
generis*, and which forms a critique of received conceptions of
normality. Baudelaire writes in his *Journaux Intimes* of inspiration as
a deliberately contrived delirium that can be called up at will, but
from which it may not be so easy to return to 'normality': 'I have',
he records, 'cultivated my hysteria with joy and terror.'[15] For
Nietzsche the space of composition is similarly transgressive. It is a
solitude, but not the high-Romantic solitude of a poetic consciousness working under the *aegis* of some higher principle of value such

as 'Nature', 'God', or '*Geist*'. Composition is an experiment upon *all* received determinations of value. In *Zarathustra* II we read:

> 'And life itself told me this secret : "Behold," it said, "I am that *which must overcome itself again and again.*
>
> "To be sure, you will call it will to procreate or impulse towards a goal, towards the higher, more distant, more manifold: but all this is one ... Whatever I create and however much I love it – soon I have to oppose it and my love ... "'[16]

It is the privilege Nietzsche gives to the body which distinguishes his conception from other notions of inspiration as a cultivated form of anti-rationality. *Ecce Homo*'s account of inspiration recalls Nietzsche's positive valorization of illness. Bodily disorientation may tear apart those bogus idealizations of life that accompany the modern over-valuation of consciousness. Individual consciousness, for the later Nietzsche, is a function merely of our social being. It is developed from the need to have an image of oneself in relation to the group. One's mundane self-consciousness, therefore, is correspondingly limited, and something to be overcome.[17] Inspiration trangresses this herd self, tearing it out of its limitations. The ancient *topos* of the madness of genius finds a new basis here, transvalued against a Platonic-Christian civilization and morality repeatedly diagnosed as themselves degenerate and diseased. Inspiration marks a supreme moment in the economy of the body's drives and strengths. The conception of *Zarathustra* occurs as an interlude in Nietzsche's chronic sickness, an euphoric period of '*great health*' (*Ecce Homo*, p. 298) followed by an exhausted relapse after 'the tremendous squandering of all defensive energies which is the presupposition of every *creative* deed' (p. 304).[18]

Freud conceives sublimation in the creative artist as a successful displacement and refinement of otherwise repressed sexual or destructive drives, as 'the only alternative to repression and neurosis.'[19] Nietzsche, however, might well have seen too normative a notion of 'health' at work in Freud's concept, reminiscent as it is of Hegel's idea of sublimation as a process which supposedly frees the mind from enslavement to the physiological (Berthold-Bond, p. 205). For Nietzsche the transformation undergone by the artist has for aim a transvaluation of the accepted distinction between health and sickness. In a note collected in *The Will to Power* we read 'The concept of normal health ... must be given up' (Section 812). Nietzsche looks back to Baudelaire's affirmation of decadence and anticipates the celebration of mental illness in the surrealists.

Whereas Freud was to remain committed to a scientific positivism, Nietzsche reads our fundamental metaphysical notions as expressions of the needs of the human body. Such a radical understanding of the belief in substance or the applicability to the universe of the principles of logic renders inspiration a transvaluation of 'reality' itself, a metaphorizing drive that tears open and defamiliarizes all we might accept as merely given. Likewise, 'there is no *essential* difference between waking and dreaming ... our moral judgements and evaluations too are only images and fantasies based on a physiological process unknown to us'.[20]

Nietzsche attacks the status of concepts of inspiration in the bourgeois religion of art. He also caricatures Romanticism in terms that repeat older conceptions of *Schwärmerei* as a pathology or disease, the effect of a weak constitution (*Daybreak*, section 538). Rousseau, Byron and also – by 1881 – Wagner are fanatics whose demagoguery allows them a grandiose self-conception merely on the basis of leading crowds by the nose: 'fanatics [*die Fanatiker*] are picturesque; mankind would rather see gestures than to listen to *reason*' (*The Anti-Christ*, section 54).[21] Romantic idealism is no more than the diseased escapism or utopianism of the *Schwärmer*. Yet Nietzsche's work is in many respects a culmination of the Romantic arguments about inspiration as a creative revolution in the mundane economy of the self. The following extract from *Human all too Human* recalls the high-Romantic idealization of enthusiasm or the 'good minute'.[22] This Nietzsche resembles nothing more closely than the Emerson of 'Inspiration' minus the transcendentalism:

> – Everyone has his good days where he discovers his higher self; and true humanity demands that everyone be evaluated only in the light of this condition and not in that of his working-day unfreedom and servitude ... Many live in awe and abasement before its ideal and would like to deny it: they are afraid of their higher self because when it speaks it speaks imperiously. It possesses, moreover, a spectral freedom to come or to stay away as it wishes; on this account it is often called a gift of the gods, whereas in reality it is everything else that it is a gift of the gods (of chance): this however is man himself.[23]

This reads as an extreme version of the appropriation of the heteronomy of inspiration or enthusiasm to a form of individualism. In effect, Nietzsche is giving an 'aestheticised' concept of an individual life as making up, for each of us, an intense space of composition in which what we must create and recreate is ourselves and the values that affirm our lives. The over-man of the future is to live in a continuous state of inspiration.

One result of this view is a peculiarly agonistic relation to one's own writings. If we turn back to the passage from *Ecce Homo* we find that the issue is not that of a self pre-existent to inspiration achieving self-representation, even in some state of heightened ability. Rather, a transformed super-subject or *Übermensch* is instituted by the advent of words and images that one's consciousness, in this transformed state, can merely register. This state maintains a maximized transgression of the original, mundane self, with a maximized realization of a briefly instituted super-self. The latter, alone, could claim to be 'author' of the text. To describe this state Nietzsche, appropriately, quotes 'himself' in the guise of his mask, Zarathustra, the eponymous hero of the text whose genesis he is describing. In *Beyond Good and Evil* we read: 'the "work", whether of the artist or the philosopher, invents the man who has created it, who is supposed to have created it; "great men", as they are venerated, are subsequent pieces of wretched minor fiction' (section 269).

Philosophy itself must be demystified as a material practice of writing. The essence of language, for Nietzsche, is rhetorical power, and this is true even of the slyly pretended neutrality of a philosophical treatise. Nietzsche's own philosophical writing, accordingly, must strive always to the status of a discourse of maximized force. Henry Staten writes:

> Nietzsche's discourse on power is itself an exercise of power. Because Nietzsche appeals to no instituted authority or canons of demonstration, the constative value of his discourse depends entirely on the persuasiveness of its claim of autarky, or, more precisely, on its enactments of the motions of that very power concerning which it speaks. Where there is no appeal to some additional authority, only the discourse *of* power can be a discourse *on* power. (*Nietzsche's Voice*, p. 33)

The ideal is thus that of a performative that ensures its own value and which brings into being, by the power of its own act, the ear capable of hearing it. In effect, inspired writing becomes a philosophical model, the articulation of the will-to-power. Nietzsche, in the figure of Zarathustra, collapses into each other the figures of philosopher, artist and prophet. (See also *Beyond Good and Evil*, section 292.)

Transgression and publication

'Dionysian' creativity, freed from the service of 'higher' values, and become its own end and object, forms a notion of self-creation and re-creation that is, necessarily, also continuously annihilating. Ultimately, it is indistinguishable from a transgressive death drive: 'The genius – in his works, in his deeds – is necessarily a prodigal: his greatness lies in the fact that *he expends himself*... The instinct of self-preservation is as it were suspended' (*Twilight of the Idols*, section 44). Here Nietzsche perhaps recalls, and contests, the appro-priation of suicidal *Schwärmerei* by the Romantic-idealist tradition. This irresistible drive differs from that of the Romantic in that its creativity, though destructive, is an expression of strength and abundance. It is not the pathology of an escapist consciousness but a drive as involuntary 'as a river's bursting its banks is involuntary' (ibid). This is the Nietzsche celebrated in Georges Bataille's *On Nietzsche* (1945), the figure who sees that 'Extreme states, either individual or collective, once were motivated by ends' some of which 'have lost their meaning (expiation and salvation)', and who will now celebrate such states for themselves.[24] Such ecstasy or *Rausch* would be ultimately the realization of a nihilistic monism: the *ecstasis* of a transcendence that abolishes transcendence.

What prevents the bleakness of such a notion being dominant in Nietzsche's conception of inspiration is his recuperation of its energies in terms of an exalted image of wholeness, unity and total-ity. That is, the energies that transgress and undo the finite, mundane self are also the creation of a textual mask, a 'Zarathustra', who will exist as an historical force across vast distances of space and time. There is, then, a doubleness in Nietzsche, one which reappears in his legacy: Bataille's nihilistic extremism on the one hand is matched on the other by a poetics of virile self-creation in Valéry or W. B. Yeats's doctrine of the mask.

Let us look in this respect at Nietzsche's account of his reading his 'own' work in *Ecce Homo*. The title itself is already indicative of the issue of self-transcendence through composition and publica-tion; 'Behold the man' is the title of a book, not the denotation of a person. Nietzsche idealizes the world projected in his texts in terms of the mountain air of their conception:

> Those who can breathe the air of my writing knows that it is an air of the heights, a *strong* air. One must be made for it. Otherwise there is no small danger one will catch cold in it. The ice is near, the solitude tremendous – but how calmly all things lie in the light!

> How freely one breathes! How much one feels *beneath* oneself!
>
> Philosophy, as I have so far understood and lived it, means living voluntarily among ice and high mountains – seeking out everything strange and questionable in existence ... (p. 218)

Who is 'one' here but the reader, including the writer himself as breather of the air of his own work, a traveller through its landscape? It is a weird image of self-reading, as the being taken up into the heights projected by one's own writing. Nietzsche speaks of his work throughout *Ecce Homo* not as attempts to articulate a thought or a system of thought already in mind but as moments of self-overcoming perpetuated in textual form, as the irruption of a 'phantasmatic author' whom Nietzsche himself encounters only as a reader more initiated than others. Of *Zarathustra*, for instance, he says: 'Above all, one must *hear* aright the tone that comes from this mouth, the halcyon tone, lest one should do wretched injustice to the meaning of its wisdom ...' (*Ecce Homo*, p. 219). It is a matter of having 'ears for Zarathustra', not 'ears for Nietzsche' (p. 220).

Nietzsche's ideal of self-overcoming is that of a virile power which spurns all 'slavish' need for the opinions of others. This ideal, however, cannot but be contaminated by the forms of 'reactive' or servile thinking it would reject. If Nietzsche's notion of a supremely self-sufficient affirmation is to have any substance that distinguishes it from solitary fantasy, it is necessarily mediated through the response of others.[25] The mere fact of publication is in itself testimony to the need for such mediation. Moreover, the image of others is implicitly at work in the very constitution of the super or over self that is encountered in inspiration; for the sense of power and supremacy is necessarily an image of effect, and an anticipation of future history, viz. the work creating the figure who wrote it. Few writers or thinkers' sense of themselves are more bound up with a sense of posterity and their posthumous life than is Nietzsche's. In *Human All too Human*, section 209, Nietzsche writes: '*Joy in age*. – The thinker, and the artist likewise, whose better self has taken refuge in his work, feels an almost malicious joy when he sees how his body and his spirit are being slowly broken down and destroyed by time: it is as if he observed from a corner a thief working away at his money-chest, while knowing that the chest is empty and all the treasure it contained safe' (p. 97).[26] Publication is both self-transcendence and self-perpetuation. The privilege that Nietzsche accords to inspiration as a purely bodily state, however, remains an attempt to ground the source of value of such writing in the properties of a mysterious source. Staten reminds us of a truth that Nietzsche may not be so ready to accommodate: 'the power of a discourse is ultimately dependent on an audience,' i.e. 'whatever power is felt as power by an actual audience' (*Nietzsche's Voice*, p. 33). Despite his expertise in demystification Nietzsche passes over the social and technological conditions of self-overcoming and writes of it as if it were more purely a matter of personal bodily strength.

H.D.

Although much in the account of the inspiration of *Zarathustra* is particular to Nietzsche, the passage also instantiates a way in which inspiration was often to be conceived in the twentieth century. Unusual creativity is seen as the result of an harmonious, non-repressed or otherwise privileged relation between the body and the mind. Nietzsche's valorization of the body aligns him, despite his overt misogyny, with twentieth-century women writers who appropriate the discourse of creativity in terms that privilege the female body. I turn, for the rest of this chapter, to the work of the American modernist H.D. (Hilda Doolittle) whose work has become one of the most celebrated examples of this counter-mythology.

Half a century before the work of Helène Cixous and Luce Irigaray on an *écriture feminine*, H.D.'s 'Notes on Thought and Vision' both elaborates and practises a modernist gynopoetics.[27] Composed in 1919 for the sexologist Havelock Ellis but first published in the 1982, 'Notes' blends such genres as the religious meditation, the essay, the prose poem and the aphorism. The H.D. of 'Notes' remains within the Romantic tradition of Coleridge and Emerson.[28] At the same time, she transvalues the creative in ways that affirm the gendered body, especially that of the woman.

Although 'Notes' arose in response to a 'vision' that over-whelmed H.D. spontaneously, its text offers a late version of the Romantic concept of inspiration as a cultivated delirium which is simultaneously a theory of creativity and a practical contestation of predominant conceptions of normality and the rational. This state of supra-rationality H.D. terms the 'over-mind', a unique state that combines sensitized intelligence and heightened bodily awareness. Like the states aspired to in theories of inspiration as a psychic discipline, the 'over-mind' combines intellectual virtuosity and emotional spontaneity. Similarly, it is also a theory of sublimation.

The artist is seen as cultivating, and instrumentalizing the energies and images of sexuality. One of the 'over-mind' 's conditions is the impetus and energy given the artist by an erotic relationship.

> We must be 'in love' before we can understand the mysteries of vision ...
> We begin with sympathy of thought.
> The minds of the two lovers merge, interact in sympathy of thought.
> The brain, inflamed and excited by this interchange of ideas, takes on its character of over-mind ...
> The love-region is excited by the appearance of beauty of the loved one, its energy not dissipated in physical relations, takes on its character of mind, becomes this womb-brain or love-brain ...
> (p. 95)

The erotic here is a source of creative powers conceptualized in terms of a vitalist and still even *Naturphilosophische* notion of the body as the source of creative energies that are inherently insightful or attuned to the cosmos. H.D.'s text stands out, however, for avoiding the crass sexual determinism of related conceptions of creativity in D. H. Lawrence (or Wagner). Although, for instance, she speaks of the 'over-mind' in terms of a 'vision of the womb or love-vision' (p. 95) she also traces creative energies to 'the corresponding love-region of a man's body' (p. 94).

As with Nietzsche's notion of inspiration, the 'over-mind' induces a crisis of the whole perceptual system. H.D. compares the 'over-mind' to a jelly-fish placed over the brain, a uterine covering whose sensors stretch throughout the body and into the environment. Thus 'things about me appear slightly blurred as if seen under water ... thoughts pass and are visible like fish swimming under clear water' (pp. 93–4). Objects and events in the environment take on a defamiliarized, proto-symbolic quality, transitional between the condition of a merely posited reality and the mode of being of a work of art. They give out 'electric' forces and cryptic messages (pp. 97–8) as if already latent with a more holistic, connotative mode of being.

Although she was to become a patient or student of Freud, H.D. is closer to Nietzsche in her view of inspiration as a transvaluation of the real. In her *Tribute to Freud* the phrase 'symptom or inspiration' appears twice, and affirms a revaluation of 'illness' as a privileged perspective that must challenge received norms of health and of reality.[29] From Freud's viewpoint H.D.'s visionary or dream experiences suggest a severe dysfunction; for H.D. the perceptual crisis associated with poetic composition has visionary status. H.D. gives the 'over-mind' a prominent place in her religious conception of the poet as a redemptive figure.

> The Galilean conquered because he was a great artist, like da Vinci.
>
> A fish-basket, upturned on the sand, or a candle in a candlestick or a Roman coin with its not unbeautifully wrought head of a king, could excite him and give him ideas, as the bird or boy's face or child's yellow hair gave da Vinci ideas ('Notes', p. 98)

A recurrent figure in H.D. is the would-be writer, usually a woman, struggling to achieve the self-transformation that both causes and results from successful composition, At issue is often the ideal of a lost language of integrity and power, both archaic and 'feminine', whose status is that of a performative that ensures its own value and answer: 'There, the very speaking of words, conjured up proper answering sigil.'[30] The space of composition may incite a crisis of identity that the writer will employ almost as part of a personal therapy. Like her contemporaries the surrealists, H.D. appropriates the practice of 'automatic writing' from the cult of spiritualism and exploits it as a means of access to an unconscious, conceived as the site of hidden powers and the recovery of occluded identities.[31] For Raymonde, the protagonist of the central section of *Palimpsest* (1926), the experiment with automatic writing forms a painful re-encounter, one newly emergent line at a time, with the past and its scars: 'Inspiration was more like a festering splinter than a rush of wings.'[32]

Writing in a memoir on her play *Hippolytus Temporizes* (composed between 1920 and 1925) H.D. describes the experience of composition in terms that recall 'Notes':

> The stanzas and lines run on and into the abstract – realized by rock and shale and snow and wind and foam and storm. I was realizing a self, a super-ego, if you will, that was an octave above my ordinary self – and fighting to realize it.[33]

The term 'super-ego' here is less Freud's than her own 'over-mind' – the predominance of the prefix 'super' and 'over' in H.D.'s work at this time bespeaks Nietzsche's influence. Composition induces and sustains the 'over-mind' state from which it also derives. Within this transformation the emergent text is felt to open out as a yet unarticulated 'abstract'.[34] This may be a 'Wordless, non-signi-fying ... a kind of unconscious for the play's text' (Wenthe, p. 116). Such a text is a palimpsest not in the sense of combining two discourses but two radically different modes of signification, that of the discursive meaning on the one hand, and, on the other, rhythm, 'music', and non-discursive, physiological modes. Such a conjunc-tion enacts that union of body and conscious mind that both produces and is produced by the 'over-mind' of inspirational creativity as it sublates both. Composition is a psychic rite of passage in which the authority figure 'H.D.' emerges from Hilda Doolittle.

H.D. has been held to anticipate Julia Kristeva's influential *Revolution in Poetic Language* (1974).[35] H.D.'s theory and practice seem to instantiate Kristeva's argument that avant-garde texts have been the occasion for deconstruction of the subject or agent of writing. In Lautréaumont, Mallarmé, Joyce and the texts of surreal-ism, Kristeva claims, an unconscious 'semiotic chora', composed of heterogeneous pre-Oedipal drives, manifests itself in rhythm and in other effects that transgress the public codes of semantics and syntax. This seems very obviously relevant to H.D. Readings of H.D. in relation to the pre-Oedipal have become a critical ortho-doxy.[36] However, there are objections to this view and to Kristeva's theory. Those writers she describes belong to the tradition of writing from out of an artificially cultivated delirium. They are calculating on inspiration as a form of irrationality or supra-ratio-nality that is *sui generis*, i.e. it is only partially intelligible in those terms with which psychoanalysis would describe hysteria, say, or the pre-Oedipal. Wolfgang Lange writes, contra Kristeva: 'The madness of modern art and literature does not come from the unre-strained desire of the body, is not an infantile act ... The madness of the artist is an artificial one, as far removed from the passions which inflame the heart as from the truth which satisfies the reason.'[37] Similarly in H.D., the 'over-mind' is not the irruption into the writer's intentionality of an infantile drive but is *sui generis*. The language that dictates itself to the writer from out of such a state results from a cultivated relation of body and mind, psyche and text. H.D.'s theory may be compared, contra Kristeva, to contemporary work such as T. S. Eliot's 'Tradition and the Individual Talent' (1919)[38] or Paul Valéry's contemporary reflections on inspiration as *improvisation du degré supérieure*, i.e. the hard-won harmonization and automatization of trained habits of intellect and poetic technique when integrated with structures of passion and desire, producing thus an exalted sense of release, power and serendipity.[39] For H.D.

also 'There is no way of aiming at the over-mind, except through the intellect' (p. 95). Madness and eroticism have been appropriated and transformed by intellectual discipline: 'a certain amount of detachment' (p. 99) is one of the conditions of the over-mind state. Hipparchia, the would-be poet of the first part of *Palimpsest* (1926), describes 'the perfected ecstacy where body having trained its perceptions, finds itself the tool of sheer intoxicating intellect' (p. 77) – an account that inverts the terms of the Kristevan reading. Furthermore, the 'over-mind' is as much a product of the space of composition as it is an agency within it: 'When a creative scientist, artist or philosopher has been for some hours or days intent on his work, his mind often takes on an almost physical character. That is, his mind becomes his real body. His over-mind becomes his brain' (p. 93). For the H.D. of 'Notes', inspiration is a moment of totalization, as in the German Romantic tradition. It is the culmination of the act of composition as a psychic discipline whose aim is a newly-emergent state, a temporarily sustained subject of enunciation whose language involves the co-working of all the levels of the psyche ('There are three states of manifestations – sub-conscious mind, conscious mind, over-conscious mind' (p. 107)).

Better known than H.D.'s 'Notes on Thought and Vision', T. S. Eliot's 'Tradition and Individual Talent' (1919) forms a comparable instance of a theory of inspiration as a cultivated technique. Successful composition, for Eliot, arises from a *sui generis* affective state achieved through discipline and study of the texts of tradition, one in which the writer's mind is metamorphosed into an impersonal medium whose products transcend the status of mere self-expression. Such a process is a continual 'self-sacrifice' that is yet self-transcendence (*Selected Essays*, p. 17). For a woman writer to appropriate the discourse of inspiration, however, especially in the form of a poetics of totalization, forms a cultural statement of a kind very different from that of any man in the same tradition. The H.D. of 'Notes' is coming to terms with her own previous experience of inspiration as one often of trauma, a fearful dispossession of the self. 'Notes' offers a feminist poetics of self-empowerment in answer to the ambivalent sense of inspiration as sexual possession found in H.D.'s early collections.[40]

To return to Kristeva, however, it would be caricaturing her thinking to see it merely as about the irruption of an 'infantile act' into the process of composition. Her later work on melancholy and the *imaginaire du pardon* gives full attention to the unique status of composition as a psychic crisis. Such work reads as a late member of the tradition of conceiving inspiration as the harmonizing of *ars* and *ingenium*, body and culture, impulse and technique. At the frontiers of emotion, she argues, 'writing arises through the surpassing of affectivity toward the effectivity of signs.' This is not the repression of affect, but (again) its 'sublimation'. The crucial factor in sublimation is the discipline of giving to affect a representational form that opens itself to the absolving and comprehending acknowledgement of an other. Here Kristeva does full justice to the modes of empowerment made available to the writer by the fact that composition, however solitary, is ultimately a public act. Writing transposes affects 'for an other in a third relation, imaginary and symbolic. And it is because it is pardon that writing is transformation, transposition, translation.'[41]

Kristeva and H.D. form late practitioners of the originally German Romantic programme of calculated inspiration, both revisionist and feminist. For H.D., rewriting myths such as that of Isis and Osiris, the process of writing is the reconstitution of a fragmented female identity.[42] The psychic discipline sketched in 'Notes' anticipates H.D.'s later poetic practice of dramatizing the space of composition as the crucible of an alchemical transformation, an experiment practiced upon the psyche of the poet herself. In 'Tribute to the Angels' (1945) in *Trilogy* the allotropic change undergone in composition is compared to the emergence of a butterfly from the cocoon of a 'worm' or caterpillar. It is a revisionist version of a poet's encounter with a muse:

> she carries a book but it is not
> the tome of ancient wisdom,
>
> the pages, I imagine, are the blank pages
> of the unwritten volume of the new;
>
> all you say, is implicit,
> all that and much more;
>
> but she is not shut up in a cave
> like a Sibyl; she is not
>
> imprisoned in leaden bars
> in a coloured window;
>
> she is Psyche, the butterfly,
> out of the cocoon.[43]

This scene is a specular one, an image of inspiration as both transvaluation and auto-legitimation. The recovered maternal deity is seen both as the origin of psychic power in the discipline of composition, yet also as its end or purpose in the confirmation of the woman poet herself as a visionary or prophetic figure to the public. Within the terms suggested in Chapter One, this may confirm that 'H.D.' – as opposed to Hilda Doolittle – is a 'phantasmatic author' in the sense outlined in the first chapter, i.e. that transformed sense of self, an imaginary subjectivity, encountered in the space of composition and constructed out of an anticipated relation to an audience.[44] In Nietzsche's words. '[t]he "work" ... invents the person who has created it.' This transformation, however, H.D. presents as the achievement of contact with an inner and divine power, in accordance with the familiar dream of inspiration.

To conclude, both H.D. and Nietzsche belong to the Romantic tradition concerning the creative, however seemingly demystified in terms of the body. The space of composition is still being understood primarily in terms of some deeper, inherently authoritative kind of productivity to which the writer has privileged access in the process of composition. Such theories tend to deny the degree to which the space of composition is a heterogeneous cultural arena: they trace the text to a source or sources with mysterious properties that entail the recurrent dream of inspiration – of access to a mode of language that will somehow create its own value and its impact on others. The orthodox reading of this aspect of H.D. is to see her work as a visionary reading of the pre-Oedipal or 'maternal.' It remains a source of controversy, however, just how far valorizations of the 'semiotic' or pre-Oedipal still belong to the inspirational tradition which they claim to demystify, tracing, as they do, the value of the text to its source in some seemingly privileged aspect of the psyche.

Notes

1 Nietzsche, *The Birth of Tragedy* and *The Case of Wagner*, trans. Walter Kaufmann (New York: Random House, 1967), p. 74.

2 Wagner, 'The Art-Work of the Future' [1849], in *The Art-Work of the Future and Other Works*, trans. William Ashton Ellis (Lincoln: University of Nebraska Press, 1993), pp. 69–213, p. 175.

3 Schelling, *Die Weltalter*, in *Sämmtliche Werke*, ed. K. F. A. Schelling, I Abteilung Vols 1–10; II Abteilung Vols 1–4 (Stuttgart: J. G. Cotta'scher, 1856–61), Vol. 8, 195–344, p. 337.

4 Schelling, *Philosophie der Offenbarung*, 2 vols, *Sämmtliche Werke*, 2te

Abteilung, III–IV, IV, p. 25. For detailed discussion of the genealogy of Nietzsche's distinction of the Apollonian and Dionysian in German Romanticism see Max L. Baeumer, 'Nietzsche and the Tradition of the Dionysian', trans. Timothy F. Sellner, in *Studies in Nietzsche and the Classical Tradition*, ed. James C. O'Flaherty *et al.*, 2nd edn (Chapel Hill: University of North Carolina Press, 1979), pp. 165–89.

5 Maria A. Simonelli demonstrates how much of Nietzsche's notion of the Dionysian is owing to classical scholars, yet, unlike them, Nietzsche does not mention how far the cult of Dionysus was bound up with anti-authoritarian and potentially rebellious activity. See Henry Staten, *Nietzsche's Voice* (Ithaca and London: Cornell University Press, 1990), p. 85. In effect 'it seems clear that he has consciously depoliticized it' (Staten, p. 85).

6 Foucault, *The History of Sexuality* (London: Penguin, 1987), p. 69.

7 Wagner, *Opera and Drama*, trans. Edward Evans, 2 Vols (London: W.M. Reeves, n.d.), I, 418, translation modified.

8 Lawrence, *Study of Thomas Hardy and Other Essays* (Cambridge: Cambridge University Press, 1985).

9 Nietzsche, *The Will to Power*, trans. Walter Kaufmann and R. J. Hollingdale (New York: Vintage, 1968), section 677. For sublimation in Nietzsche see Walter Kaufmann, *Nietzsche: Philosopher, Psychologist, Antichrist* (Princeton: Princeton University Press, 1974), pp. 218–27, esp. 219.

10 Henry Staten has analyzed this in terms of Nietzsche's virulent misogyny and his ambivalence about the violent transgression of individuality, *Nietzsche's Voice*, pp. 117–19.

11 Nietzsche, *On the Genealogy of Morals*, trans. Walter Kaufmann and R. J. Hollingdale. And *Ecce Homo*, trans. Walter Kaufmann (New York: Random House, 1969), pp. 300–1.

12 See Nietzsche, *Beyond Good and Evil: Prelude to a Philosophy of the Future*, trans. Walter Kaufmann (New York: Random House, 1966), section 213.

13 Nietzsche also effectively deconstructs the distinction between the psychological and the metaphysical.

14 Nietzsche, *Beyond Good And Evil*, section 17, p. 24.

15 Baudelaire, *Oeuvres Complètes*, 2 vols, ed. Claude Pichois (Paris: Gallimard, 1975), I, 658, 668.

16 Nietzsche, *Thus Spoke Zarathustra*, trans. R. J. Hollingdale (London: Penguin, 1969), p. 138.

17 Nietzsche, *The Gay Science: With a Prelude in Rhymes and an Appendix of Songs*, trans. Walter Kaufmann (New York: Random House, 1974), p. 354.

18 For the idea of a 'creative illness' in the nineteenth century, see Henri F. Ellenberger, *The Discovery of the Unconscious: The History and Evolution of Dynamic Psychiatry* [1970] (London: Fontana, 1994), pp. 447–9, also 39, 210, 216. Such metamorphic illnesses read as further appropriations of traditional conversion narratives – think of the metaphor of illness as spiritual crisis in Dickens for instance.

19 See Daniel Berthold-Bond, 'Hegel, Nietzsche, and Freud on Madness and the Unconscious', *The Journal of Speculative Philosophy*, 5 (1991), 193–213.

20 Nietzsche, *Daybreak: Thoughts on the prejudices of morality* [1881], trans. R. J.

Hollingdale (Cambridge: Cambridge University Press, 1982), pp. 119–20.

21 Nietzsche, *Twilight of the Idols* [1889]. Nietzsche, *The Anti-Christ* [1895], trans. R. J. Hollingdale (London: Penguin, 1968), p. 173.

22 Robert Browning, 'Two in the Campagna', *Poetical Works 1833–1894*, ed. Ian Jack (London: Oxford University Press, 1970) pp. 757–9, 759.

23 Nietzsche, *Human, all too Human: A Book for Free Spirits* [1878], trans. R. J. Hollingdale (Cambridge: Cambridge University Press, 1982), p. 197.

24 Bataille, *On Nietzsche*, trans. Bruce Boone (New York: Paragon House, 1992), Sylvère Lotringer, introduction, p. xxxii; see also pp. 41–2.

25 See Robert B. Pippin, *Modernism as a Philosophical Problem: On the Dissatisfactions of High European Culture* (Oxford: Basil Blackwell, 1991), pp. 108–11.

26 Contrast, by way of irony, this extract from *Human, all too Human* (section 375): '*Posthumous fame.* – To hope for the recognition of a distant future makes sense if one assumes that mankind will remain essentially unchanged and that all greatness is bound to be felt as great, not only in a single age but in all ages. This, however, is an error ...,' p. 148.

27 H.D., 'Notes on Thought and Vision', in *The Gender of Modernism: A Critical Anthology*, ed. Bonnie Kime Scott *et al.* (Bloomington: Indiana University Press, 1990), pp. 93–109.

28 See Kathleen Crown, 'H.D.'s Jellyfish Manifesto and the Visible Body of Modernism', *Sagetrieb*, 14 (1995), 217–41, p. 233.

29 H.D., *Tribute to Freud* [1956] (Manchester: Carcanet, 1985), p. 47, p. 51.

30 H.D., *Her* [written 1927] (London: Virago, 1984), p. 62.

31 For the experiments with automatic writing of nineteenth-century psychologists such as Frederick Myers, Pierre Janet and William James, see Ellenberger, *The Discovery of the Unconscious*, pp. 120–1, pp. 385–7.

32 H.D., *Palimpsest* [1926], (Carbondale and Edwardsville: Southern Illinois University Press, 1968) p. 149.

33 *Compassionate Friendship*, p. 28; requoted from William Wenthe, '"The Hieratic Dance": Prosody and the Unconscious in H.D.'s Poetry', *Sagetrieb*, 14 (1995), pp. 113–40, p. 115.

34 H.D. had originally written 'infinite' (Wenthe, p. 116).

35 Kristeva, *Revolution in Poetic Language*, abridged, trans. Margaret Waller (New York: Columbia University Press, 1984).

36 See, for instance, Wenthe, '"The Hieratic Dance": Prosody and the Unconscious', p. 132; Claire Buck, *H.D. and Freud: Bisexuality and a Feminine Discourse* (Hemel Hempstead: Harvester Wheatsheaf, 1991), p.46; Deborah Kelly Kloepfler, *The Unspeakable Mother: Forbidden Discourse in Jean Rhys and H.D.* (Ithaca: Cornell University Press, 1989), p. 96, p. 107.

37 Wolfgang Lange, *Der Kalkulierte Wahnsinn: Innenansichten, ästhetischer Moderne* (Frankfurt: Taschenbuch, 1992), p. 178. Judith Butler, in *Gender Trouble: Feminism and the Subversion of Identity* (London; Routledge, 1990), writes that Kristeva's notion of 'the predicscursive maternal body is itself a production of a given historical discourse, an effect of culture rather than its secret cause' (pp. 80–1).

38 T. S. Eliot, *Selected Essays* (London: Faber & Faber, 1932), pp. 17–20.

39 Compare Valéry's contemporary reflections on Leonardo, 'Introduction à

la mèthode de Léonardo de Vinci' [1919], *Oeuvres*, 2 vols (Paris: Pléiade, 1957), I, 1153–233, esp. p. 1210–1. H.D. mentions Leonardo in similar terms in 'Notes', esp. p. 104. See also Havelock Ellis, *The Dance of Life* (Boston: Houghton Mifflin, 1923), p. 113; W. N. Ince, *The Poetic Theory of Paul Valéry: Inspiration and Technique* (Leicester: Leicester University Press, 1961), pp. 111–16.

40 Helen Sword, *Engendering Inspiration: Visionary Strategies in Rilke, Lawrence, and H.D.* (Ann Arbor: University of Michigan Press, 1995), pp. 119–72

41 Kristeva, *Soleil noir: dépression et mélancholie* (Paris: Gallimard, 1987), p. 226.

42 See Buck, *H.D. and Freud*, p. 149.

43 H.D., *Trilogy* (Manchester: Carcanet, 1973), p.103.

44 One should not underestimate the sense of empowerment, and identity made possible to a woman writer like H.D. by the simple fact of being able to anticipate publication. As was argued in the first chapter, such anticipation is an imaginary factor in the space of composition (in Lacan's sense of the imaginary) that may render it the site of new and potentially empowering forms of subjective identification. As H.D. worked through her writing block in her sessions with Freud in the early 1930s, the ambivalence between 'symptom' and 'inspiration' is resolved for H.D. by increasing interpretation of her dreams and disturbed 'visionary' experience in proleptic terms, as the anticipation of a public statement. H.D.'s account of her later sessions with Freud marks her identification with – or would-be appropriation of – Freud's social authority [his *Sieg-Mund* or 'mouth of victory'). She sees a vision of the goddess Niké or Victory:

> I drop my head in my hands; it is aching with this effort of concentration,but I feel that I have seen the picture. I thought, 'Niké, Victory,' and even as I thought it, it seemed to me that this Victory was not now, it was another Victory; in which case there would be another war. When that war had completed itself ... I personally (I felt), would be free, I myself would go on in another winged dimension. (*Tribute to Freud*, pp. 55–6).

CHAPTER 8

Surrealism, inspiration and the mediations of chance in André Breton

we want nothing whatever to do with those, either large or small, who use their minds as they would a savings bank (*Second Manifesto of Surrealism*)

One evening ... before I fell asleep, I perceived, so clearly articulated that it was impossible to change a word, but nonetheless removed from the sound of any voice, a rather strange phrase which came to me without any apparent relationship to the events in which, my consciousness agrees, I was then involved, a phrase which seemed to me insistent, a phrase, if I may be so bold, *which was knocking at the window*. I took cursory note of it and prepared to move on when its organic character caught my attention. Actually, this phrase astonished me: unfortunately I cannot remember it exactly, but it was something like: 'There is a man cut in two by the window,' but there could be no question of ambiguity, accompanied as it was by the faint visual image of a man walking cut half way up by a window perpendicular to the axis of his body. Beyond the slightest shadow of a doubt, what I saw was the simple reconstruction in space of a man leaning out of a window. But this window having shifted with the man, I realized that I was dealing with an image of a fairly rare sort, and all I could think of was to incorporate it into my material for poetic construction. No sooner had I granted it this capacity than it was in fact succeeded by a whole series of phrases, with only brief pauses between them, which surprised me only slightly less and left me with the impression of their being so gratuitous that the control I had then exercised upon myself seemed to me illusory and all I could think of was putting an end to the interminable quarrel raging within me (*Manifesto of Surrealism*).[1]

This account is not from Ghiselin's *The Creative Process* or Shrady's *Moments of Insight* though it could well have been. All the classic items of a narrative of inspiration are there – here as a dream-experience triggering fluent composition and presented in the form of a secularized conversion narrative. The author, André Breton, has been working, unsuccessfully, on the problem of the relation between the psyche and poetic imagery posed for him by the poetics of Pierre Reverdy, as well as reading Freud. Suddenly, a solution comes to him out of the blue. As soon as Breton starts to incorporate it into thoughts for a possible project, it releases a whole series of further phrases, both seemingly gratuitous and mildly frightening in their strength of possession. Out of this experience, Breton tells us, came those experiments with writing that were to become surrealism, one of the most crucial aesthetic movements of the twentieth century.

In the surrealist programme announced in the first and second manifestos (1924, 1930), characteristics traditionally associated with inspiration, notably its apparent gift of something for nothing, its seemingly radical transformation of the psyche and its questioning of boundaries between writer and environment, become part of an explicit programme to transform human society: 'Surrealism is inspiration recognised, accepted and practiced. Not as an inexplicable visitation but as a faculty put into operation' (Louis Aragon).[2]

Although surrealism is now seen mainly as an aesthetic venture, it took for its general ambition a liberation of language – to revolutionary effect – from utilitarian and instrumental conceptions. Outside the aesthetic domain surrealist thought has been least eradicable in its conviction that what most of us take for the real world is a construct of forms of often oppressive discourse. 'He was our Goethe' wrote Foucault when Breton died in 1966.[3] It is a short step from Breton's attack on members of the psychiatric profession as servants of an exploitative and degrading conception of reality, 'La Médicine Mentale Devant le Surrealisme' (1930) ['Mental Medicine confronted with Surrealism'],[4] to Foucault's own *Madness and Civilization* (1961).[5] Like that of several other members of the surrealist group, Breton's background was in psychiatry. One of his duties during the First World War was that of deciding between true and false cases of madness in the trenches.[6]

The surrealists and other avant-garde movements of the early twentieth century represent a decisive break with the very conception of art inherited from previous decades. Rather than accepting the categories that define artistic production at this time, such as its supposed autonomy from material practice, the dichotomy of high and low art, the aesthetic and the utilitarian, the surrealists set out to transform the very way art is institutionalized in bourgeois society, trying to destroy the division between the artistic sphere and practical reality.[7] The very institution of literature is under attack as that sphere within which even the most revolutionary content is already neutralized by being part of a work of art. Inspiration is to be put at the service of freedom and of the reconciliation of humanity and world, art and life:

> Everything tends to make us believe that there exists a certain point of the mind at which life and death, the real and the imagined, past and future, the communicable and the incommunicable, high and low, cease to be perceived as contradictions. Now, search as one may one will never find any other motivating force in the activities of the Surrealists than the hope of finding and fixing this point. (*Second Manifesto*, pp. 123–4)

The question that has been repeatedly asked of this surrealist ideal is this: is the ideal of liberty in the name of which surrealism would both negate and transform social reality only a projection upon the social and political realm of modes of being carried over from the realm of the aesthetic? We will return to this question.

On several occasions, Breton refers to 'inspiration' as a term to be reclaimed,[8] though the term does not appear in the first manifesto of 1924. In the *Second Manifesto* of 1930 Breton calls on those drawn to surrealism to study 'the most complex mechanism of "inspiration"' with a view to dissociating it from notions of the sacred and to making it 'submit' to human power (p. 161). Moreover, inspiration is to be affirmed as a force that discredits the bogus individualism implicit in the notion of 'author' in the interests of making creative power available to everyone, a communism of genius. Breton attacks 'literary types' when they write about dreams because they limit themselves 'to exalting the resources of the dream at the expense of those of action, all to the advantage of the socially conservative forces that discern in it, and quite rightly, a precious distraction from rebellious ideas.'[9] Among other attitudes to dreams dismissed by Breton are those that defend 'the "creative imagination"' (*Communicating Vessels* (1932), p. 10). Elsewhere Breton, with Paul Eluard, affirms the connection of inspiration with moral luck, the receipt of personal credit for something for which one did not seem responsible ('Notes sur la poesie,' *Alentours* III (1920–4) (*Oeuvres*, I, 1017)). The *Second Manifesto* also drops any inverted commas around 'inspiration' to define it, familiarly, as a compulsive force of possession that has met the supreme needs of expression in any time or place; Breton also endorses the traditional opinion that it makes available powers that mere talent, hard work or discursive rationality cannot attain. It is of another order altogether:

> We can easily recognize it by that total possession of our mind which, at rare intervals, prevents our being, for every problem posed, the plaything of one rational solution rather than some other equally rational solution, by that sort of short circuit it creates between a given idea and a respondent idea (written, for example). Just as in the physical world, a short circuit occurs when the two 'poles' of a machine are joined by a conductor of little or no resistance. In poetry and in painting, Surrealism has done everything it can and more to increase these short circuits. It believes, and it will never believe in anything more whole-heartedly, in reproducing artificially this ideal moment when man, in the grips of a particular emotion, is suddenly seized by this something 'stronger than himself' which projects him, in self-defense, into immortality. (pp. 161–2)

This is an elusive, mildly contradictory passage, partly repeating an argument about imagery from the first manifesto (p. 37). The legacy of associationism is still apparent. Inspiration appears here in a context of problem-solving. The contrast between a step by step procedure and a sudden intuitive leap recalls the thought of Henri Poincaré.[10] The first part of the extract presents us with a notion of how inspiration has hitherto announced itself: when rational, procedural methods of reasoning or composition happen to lead to an impasse (e.g. two equally rational solutions present themselves, creating a paralysis), a jump or short circuit takes place, a jump inseparable from the breakdown of one sort of order and the sudden affirmation of another, surreal one. In trying to produce these jumps 'artificially' surrealism must be a programme of producing and intensifying breakdowns in the narrow order of reason. *L'Amour fou* (1937) will go so far as to call inspiration a 'technique',[11] just as the *Second Manifesto* called it a 'complex mechanism'. However, the passage from the *Second Manifesto* also presents us with the contradiction that runs like a rift through the surrealist project: how can one programme or instrumentalize something which is defined partly by its incalculability and its freedom from control? Why, moreover (and this must be left obscure for a time) is the person possessed by inspiration said to be projected 'in self-defence' into an immortalizing creative act (p. 162) ['*ce 'plus fort que lui' qui le jette, à son corps défendant, dans l'immortel*'] (*Oeuvres*, I, 809), as if the act itself of writing were a kind of protection from the compulsion that seizes the writer?

Expressly aligned with the Romantic movement (*Second Manifesto*, p. 153), the surrealist movement was the fullest attempt to realize a programme of calculated inspiration. At the same time, such ambitions of totalization and liberation are driven to a point at which they transgress themselves, opening upon anti-romantic and anti-humanist notions of inspiration such as we will encounter in the work of Blanchot and Derrida.

Automatic writing

Most surrealist attempts to programme inspiration assault the narrowly rational by conducting experiments with chance. The apparent randomness of automatic writing is the best known. There are also surrealist games with chance such as 'Le cadavre exquise' ['the exquisite corpse'] (*Oeuvres*, I, 1726) or 'L'un pour l'autre' (in this one entity is seen as lying, potentially, within another, producing an effect that is a kind of collage in motion, e.g. a lion's mane appearing within the flame of a match;[12] in another experiment one person writes down a question ('*Qu'est-ce que le baiser?*' ['What is kissing?'] while another, ignorant of the question to which it relates, composes an answer ('*Une divagation, tout chavire*' ['A raving, everything capsizes'] (*Oeuvres*, I, 945–8, p. 945)). Surrealism's scientific pretensions appear in this introduction of the notion of *experiment* into the field of writing. There were also imitations of madness or hysteria, as in Breton and Eluard's *L'Immaculée Conception* (1930) [*The Immaculate Conception*] (*Oeuvres*, I, 841–84), or the writing out of states of hypnosis, the transcription of dreams and experiments with thought transference.

What is meant by 'chance' in these experiments? Several possible constructions of 'chance' may be said to be at issue. Often, to ascribe something to chance is to discount it. Chance may interfere in an experiment – a window blows open – disrupting the fixed order of controls that enable an experiment to seem a reliable contributor of data to some regime of knowledge. 'Chance' is the nuisance that must be expelled from the domain of a knowledge in order for that knowledge to be able to function, and to isolate those laws assumed, as a founding postulate of the domain, to be inherent to it. To ascribe something to chance, then, may be to perform an act of exclusion, one necessary to the autonomy of the regime at issue and the functioning of its internal laws. Every regional field may be said to have its defining stereotomy, or 'science of the cut',[13] viz. its rules of demarcation and self-constitution. 'Chance' in this context is either an absolute property of the world, uneliminable even in some hypothetical union of the sciences, or an effect of human finitude, resulting from the need to divide up cognitive labour.

Such a notion of finitude is something that surrealism set out to challenge, modelling itself partly on that new science that seemed to be successfully conquering domains previously abandoned to chance, namely psychoanalysis. What once seemed mere chance within certain boundaries may actually make sense from another perspective. 'Chance' may be the something for nothing of an inspired event, a serendipity affirmed by the surrealists against a social order based on a means and end rationality and an ethic of work: 'There is no use being alive if one must work. The event from which each of us is entitled to expect the revelation of his own life's meaning – that event which I may not yet have found, but on whose path I seek myself – is not earned by work.'[14] As with the emergence of psychoanalysis from Freud's self-analysis, surrealism must attempt both to found itself and, at the same time, to try to overcome the contingency and the arbitrariness of this self-positing in the name of a general programme of verifiable results. The first manifesto, appearing over a collective signature, is such an act of auto-foundation. It defines surrealism as if it were quoting from a dictionary in which it already appears. This both acknowledges and wittily defies surrealism's status as a still-fictive institution in a perpetual state of crisis as to its own nature and status (while psychoanalysis did not die with Freud, it is still an open question whether or not surrealism died with Breton in 1966):

> SURREALISM, *n.* Psychic automatism in its pure state, by which one proposes to express – verbally, by means of the written, or in any other manner – the actual functioning of thought. Dictated by thought, in the absence of any control exercised by reason, exempt from any aesthetic or moral concern. (p. 26)

Breton's 'dictionary' definition is already a definition of 'automatic writing' as inaugurated in *Les Champs magnétiques* [*Magnetic Fields*] in 1919 (*Oeuvres*, I, 53–105), the experiment most crucial to surrealism, at least up to the reassessment taking place in

Communicating Vessels (1932). As the phrase already announces, 'automatic writing' inaugurates a practice that takes up many ideas from parapsychology. However, in 1934 in 'Le Message Automatique', looking back over the history of the 'continual misfortune' that had befallen this project by the early 1930s (*Oeuvres*, II, 380), Breton remains passionate that automatic writing be firmly dissociated from any associations with nineteenth-century spiritualism.[15] It may reveal new powers of the mind, but these are entirely immanent. Surrealism is both an atheism and a humanism, looking to the work of Freud and, before Freud, to F. W. H. Myers whose Romantic psychology affirming a subliminal self of hidden powers is often far closer to Breton's formulations than Freud's work on the unconscious and the genealogy of neuroses.[16]

What stereotomy constitutes the coherence of the surrealist programme? Immediate verbal expression, with minimal intervention by the writer as a conscious agent, is identified with a lifting of repression and access to hidden psychical powers, described as the real or actual functioning of thought. Leaving the production of written images to chance, language itself becomes a kind of neutralized space, freed from the instrumentalizing demands normally made upon it and newly sensitive to the appearance of disparate and unexpected phrases and images in which the hidden laws of personal desire will become readable. Automatism can be read as the culmination of an aspect of French Romanticism, taking up Rimbaud's programme of a derangement of all the senses to deliver the writer's habitual self over to a realm in which 'I' is an other. Each text is thus a scene of encounter between the conscious ego, the affirmation of its desire and thus also the possible *toi* towards whom it is drawn – hence the deep analogy for Breton between poetry and love.[17] Two further assumptions, however, are at work here. The first is that free thought, so defined, is accessible at all – might not the automatic really be the realm of cliché, prejudice and conventional formulae instead? Automatism, while taking up the notion of the *furor poeticus*, is now linked to values of immediacy and novelty that invert the associations of automatism in oral culture. A second assumption is that such unbound psychic energy can achieve immediate verbal expression without distortion, an assumption markedly at odds with Freud, for whom the unconscious is never the object of unmediated observation.[18]

In the actual practice of automatic writing such presuppositions translate themselves into the imposition of strenuous conditions upon the experiment itself: this is to be set up in accordance with a very peculiar and strict stereotomy. To achieve the ideal of an immediacy in which psychic life and linguistic transcription may be identified, all chance influences impinging on the writer must be closed off. No preconception or interference from consciousness are to be allowed, no sort of contamination of imagery from the environment. The ideal is a mechanical verbo-auditive dictation in which the writer only becomes aware of the results *après coup*, or after the event. This is to be an act of writing that is not at the same time a reading. Michel Beaujour, writing from the perspective of the mid and early 1970s, a time at which Derrida's work had become known and at which Breton had come under heavy attack from the *Tel Quel* group for his idealism and his naive readings of psychoanalysis (see Houdebine),[19] sees surrealist automatism as marking a crucial episode in the uncertain emergence of Western culture from its sources in orality: 'As an extreme, romantic negation of rhetoric (which is an inveterate residue of oral culture) surrealism reduces the graphic trace to the transitory status of a document and denies the specificity of writing ("by means of the written or in any other manner").'[20] Writing is to be a pure act, one without the accompaniment of any mediating consciousness, a war machine against the literary. The surrealist celebration of the repressed, the criminal and the insane renders the act of writing a kind of Sadian crime. Jean Paulhan called it an act of 'terror', evoking the Terror of 1793. Its 'method was characterized by an explosion of old meanings from within, a wrenching of words into a new language that spoke from the body, from overfulness, a language rooted in a desire for literary freedom often metaphorically evoked as a desire to "lose one's head"',[21] Reading, on the other hand, seems to be identified entirely as an agent of censorship and dilution: 'All that results from listening to oneself, from reading what one has written, is the suspension of the occult, that admirable help' (*Manifesto of Surrealism*, p. 33). If I really want to know about my day to day self, Breton writes, I can always read the newspaper.

This view of self-reading as ideological censorship is matched by the virulence of Breton's rejection of mimetic art as well as his reluctance to see inspired poets, such as Rimbaud, described as visionaries. This is not just to deny that they have any sort of access to some supra-mundane sphere but also, more pointedly, that they have any premonition of what they are writing. For Breton there should be no realm internally perceived by the poet which is then transcribed: this would make their writing a species of description: 'verbal inspirations are infinitely richer ... than visual images' ('Le

Message Automatique', *Oeuvres*, II, 389). The reality of desire is held to enact itself in freed language. No gap of representation is to be admitted: Rimbaud and others no more understand what they are writing than does the first reader who comes to the text, 'The "illumination" comes afterwards' (*Oeuvres*, II, 389). In sum the ideal of automatic writing as blind dictation puts to work, in the strictest terms, a dichotomy of external and internal, of the intra-psychic and extra-psychic, self and other. It does so, however, to be able to affirm, at a later stage, an 'illumination' of a surreal realm whose distinction is precisely to overturn and sublate these same divisions.

A second aspect of the stereotomy that sets up the practice of automatic writing concerns the far vaguer boundaries to be observed between the psychic and the linguistic. Breton's dilemma here is that he needs both to conflate these realms and to maintain their separation. He has to confer existential or psychic status upon language in order to bear out the possibility that liberated language, with its novel combinations, may be proclaimed a revelation or enactment of hidden powers of mind, rather than just the play of the signifier. At the same time he cannot subscribe to a view of language as merely or simply expressive: there has to be a minimal, even if only temporary discrepancy between the unpredictable or seemingly aleatory movements of the signifier, with their effects, and the psyche, in order for liberated language to retain the possibility of novelty or surprise – the spark of revelation.

The ideal of automatic writing as a dialectic of gain and loss bears out Breton's pervading Hegelianism: the psyche surrenders itself to the signifier and to apparent effects of chance, only to reclaim and sublate this opposition of mind and language in the interests of an expanded notion of reality and consciousness, the surreal.[22] Philosophy itself, however, will be *surclassé* or sublated [*aufgehoben*] in this project (*Oeuvres*, I, 795, nt 1, p. 1603). Much of what is most problematic and fascinating in the surrealist enterprise inheres in the tension between the movement of surrender and the movement of recuperation. When stressing the genesis of writing, what he sometimes calls 'inspiration', Breton stresses discontinuity, the unassimilable, the unthinkable, that which resists – if only for a time – all mediation. It is what we might now term a poetics of the event, one that would reject everything that is ritualized or a matter of convention in the practice of writing.[23] Accordingly Breton professes a contempt for the realist novel, which he caricatures as the working out of predictable recipes, clichés and stereotypes (*Manifesto of Surrealism*, p. 7). In his essay on symbolism, 'Le

Merveilleux contre le mystère' (1936),[24] Breton also takes issue with Mallarmé's practice of rendering his verse mysterious by a carefully-crafted obscurity and difficulty. This is an art in which the poet, retaining control, risks nothing, unlike the surrealist whose artistic practice is a deliberate surrender of the ego to *le merveilleux*: 'It is not the fear of madness which will oblige us to leave the flag of imagination furled' (*Manifesto of Surrealism*, p. 6).

Surrealist practice presents itself as radically heteronomic, opening itself to the chances and the risks of inspiration, yet the tone of this last quotation already suggest complications. Its stridency and use of military imagery are characteristic of Breton's work throughout. A virile rhetoric of conquest and exploration, oddly reminiscent both of the war and of sexual conquest, dominates the manifestos and cuts across the notions of self-abandonment being celebrated there.[25] Moreover, when stressing the movement of recuperation into the surreal Breton writes in ways that signal his close relation to notions of the Romantic imagination. The surreal text is a novel and wonderful synthesis of once seemingly disparate elements: it unifies the real and the imaginary, dream life and waking life. It points towards an apotheosis familiar in late Romantic or Symbolist poetics.

Aspects of Breton's work draw back from the idea of writing as the effraction of a pure act to affirm the more familiar association of inspiration with orality. The *Second Manifesto* still speaks of inspiration in traditional terms as a voice that dictates to the poet. Although Breton is still discussing the realm to which automatic writing gives access in the following extract, the ground seems to have shifted in ways that are unacknowledged:

> we still know as little as we ever did about the origins of the *voice* which it is everyone's prerogative to hear, if only he will, a voice which converses with us most specifically about something other than what we believe we are thinking, and upon occasion assumes a serious tone when we feel most light-hearted or deals in idle prattle when we are unhappiest. (*Second Manifesto*, p. 158)

Breton locates this voice within the poet. This location, which may seem obvious, is actually highly problematic. 'Voice' is an anthropomorphic trope, one that may be said to work to maintain the stereotomy defining surrealist ambitions, excluding chance effects that would contaminate them. The notion of voice protects the assumption of a relatively unified source dictating to the poet as messenger. It also elides the possibility of a lack of continuity between source and affect. 'Voice' anthropomorphizes the source or sources of writing, so privileging the idea that meaningful communication of some sort is taking place through the poet. The invariable mystificatory aspect in the notion of inspiration as traditionally conceived (the inner voice, contact with some daemonic being or person) is already at work here. Equally important is the imputation implicit in the trope that this voice is an agent separate from both the poet and the reader or audience:

> For Breton, it is essential that the surrealist voice manifests itself as a dictation of thought; it is essential that the experimenter, or medium, does not feel identified with the dictating thought ... It is a separate entity, which is not a human being but which dictates none the less ; it is a 'spirit', or a mythical being that is manifesting its presence. (Roger Champigny)[26]

No less than Socrates, Breton seems to need a relatively separate, identifiable source behind the effects that manifest themselves through the text. On analysis, one could even say that Breton does not really break from an instrumentalist notion of language; he merely alters – albeit drastically – the field within which it is imagined to function. Thus the true place of enunciation is now imagined to be other than the conscious ego of the poet, and the true referent is not the empirically real but the super-real. Contrariwise, Breton does not entertain the possibility that desire and inspiration might themselves be contradictory in their essence, or that their realization might be impossible except through a practice of unforeseen heterogeneity. Automatic writing may be imaged as a dangerous *katabasis* or descent to the underworld, yet Breton never really puts the unity of the subject at issue.[27]

Let us turn briefly to some of the results of experiments with automatic writing – 'poems' as they are usually called. Pure automatism is surely an impossible idea. The very fact that the results from 1922–3 are published as a radical book of poetry, fragments and dream transcriptions, *Clair de terre* [*Earth-light*] (*Oeuvres*, I, [147]–189) already demonstrates how mediated such writing is and how quickly, despite itself, surrealism is in danger of becoming merely an aesthetic movement, rather than a rejection of the very understanding of the institution of art dominant in bourgeois society. What does it mean, for instance, to give a piece of automatic writing a title, a question dormant here though raised against Philippe Soupault in the first manifesto (*Manifesto of Surrealism*, p. 24)? In the texts of *Clair de terre* Breton seems to be employing automatism itself as a theme, as a trope that gives accessible meaning to the results of automatism as a method. It is a minimal but surely decisive gesture whose implications do not seem to have been fully grasped in the early twenties. One might crudely compare it to the simple act of holding a mirror vertically next to a randomly generated shape: all at once a form of seemingly meaningful symmetry takes wing. Analogously, in 'Ligne brisée' the emergent writing is represented as addressing the poem's speaker, seeming to taunt him with its limitations.[28] Images of the prison and the penitentiary are recurrent. Elsewhere the experience of automatism is envisaged as a trial for the poet's humanism, or as a source of alternate comedy and frustration.[28] Fantastic experiences of seeming self-dispersal or loss in a bizarre medium are sometimes celebrated (('I am the pawn of no sensory power'), 'Tournesol', pp. 38–9); at other times such ecstasies are treated ambivalently ('Plutôt la vie', Oeuvres, pp. 176-7). In sum, the surrealist ideal of automatism as both immediacy and continuity, thus treated thematically, is broken or mediated as its very condition of appearance. Jean-Luc Steinmetz goes so far as to claim that automatic writing was often nourished by unconscious alexandrines![29]

In L'Amour fou Breton outlines another notion of inspiration as a 'technique'. The generation and the recognition of chance events in the environment may act as a space of composition for the constructions of fantasy and novel images:

> Leonardo, inviting his students to copy their paintings from what they could see (remarkably arranged and appropriate for each of them) when they stared at an old wall for a period of time, is still far from being understood. The whole problem of the passage from subjectivity to objectivity is implicitly resolved there, and the implications of this resolution are fuller of human interest than those of a simple technique, even if the technique were that of inspiration itself. (p. 86)

This technique is closely related to those outlined in Max Ernst's 'Inspiration to Order'[30] and Salvador Dali's idea of a paranoiac criticism.[31] It is not confined to painting. The poet too can generate surprising effects from out of an attitude of passive receptivity to whatever forms desire may project upon 'some grid of a particular texture' (L'Amour fou, p. 86).[32]

A passage in the first manifesto also bears decisively on the issue of generating textual effects through secondary mediation and chances that involve others, a practice that becomes dominant in

Nadja and *L'Amour fou*. Breton describes and celebrates a familiar effect of dialogue, that the speaker cannot control the effect which his or her language may have on an interlocutor. Even the most ordinary remark bears the potential for working as an unforeseen stimulus and may become only a point of departure for an unforeseeable response. Breton envisages a mode of surrealist dialogue that would exploit to the full this potentially creative slippage at work in all language. Such a surrealist dialogue, the basis of work with Soupault in *Les Champs magnétiques*, would be free from all obligations of politeness:

> The remarks exchanged are not, as is generally the case, meant to develop some thesis, however unimportant it may be; they are as disaffected as possible. As for the reply that they elicit, it is, in principle, totally indifferent to the personal pride of the person speaking. The words, the images are only so many springboards for the mind of the listener (*Manifesto of Surrealism*, p. 35).

Tensions in the workings of inspiration in surrealist experiments (immediation or mediation?) become legibly acute in some works of Antonin Artaud, who broke from the group at the end of the twenties. Artaud is relentlessly opposed to the mode of inspiration at work in Breton's dialogue with Soupault, that movement of language in which it seemed to Artaud that even as I speak, my words and their sense are stolen from me, a strange double thus usurping my body: 'my thought abandons me at every step – from the simple fact of thought to the external fact of its materialization in words.'[33] Derrida's essay 'La Parole Soufflé'[34] traces some of the fortunes of this drama of inspiration as theft, powerlessness. Artaud must, in the interests of immediacy, and the ideals of his extreme vitalist programme, set out to destroy inspiration:

> The generosity of inspiration, the positive irruption of a speech which comes from I know not where, or about which I know (if I am Antonin Artaud) that I do not know where it comes from or who speaks it, the fecundity of the *other* breath [*souffle*] is unpower: not the absence but the radical irresponsibility of speech, irresponsibility as the power and origin of speech. (*Writing and Difference*, p. 176)

A sense of an irresponsibility at work in language, skewing the unity of enunciation, is what led Socrates to propose the idea of inspiration in the *Ion*. Now it leads Artaud to denounce it. That passage in which Breton describes the surreal 'voice' inside the poet in his second manifesto is also, despite Breton's programme, close to an acknowledgement of such an *irresponsibility* in the origin of speech: 'No one', writes Breton, 'when he expresses himself, does anything more than come to terms with the possibility of a very obscure reconciliation between what he knew he had to say and nonetheless said' (*Second Manifesto*, p. 159). One only needs to remember Breton's own experiments with dialogue, let alone the work of Jacques Lacan (an early admirer of the surrealists), to realize how fragile the supposed interiority of the voice has become here. It may be read as the *effect* of the collision of unexpected signifiers rather than their source. The 'inner' poetic voice that surrealism would liberate becomes very like that of the movement of slippage in reading or being-read, dispossessing the authorial ego and affirming possibilities of meaning beyond the horizon of the anticipated. Surrealism as a programme cannot proclaim itself as the liberator of the one without becoming simultaneously the liberation of the other. Much of the stridency of Breton's writing comes from the continual effort to draw a line between two apparently separate phenomena: these are arbitrariness as the freedom that allows for surrealist desire to affirm itself (chance sublated into the surreal) and arbitrariness as the very vulnerability to dissemination inherent in the mere legibility of the sign (chance as possibility of misconstruction).

The ambiguities and ambivalence at work in Breton's various notions of inspiration may be related to the equivocal place *reading* has in the economy of surrealist textual production. On the one hand reading is associated with repression and censorship, all that threatens the flow of automatic writing. However, this banishment of the empirical act of self-reading cannot be all. The text has to be read at some point, in order for desire itself to be legible and affirm itself. At that point the appeal to notions of reading is merely implicit, as if the act were natural or immediate. Nevertheless, much of how surrealist inspiration is understood, as mysterious or as withstanding easy conceptualization, may be said to lie in the way in which effects resulting from laws of textual construction that actually lie in the reader or in conventions of reading are projected into a virtual or *phantasmatic subject* of writing.

Breton's presentations of the results of surrealist practice bear this out. Breton's revolt from an aesthetics of *mimesis* is far from total, but recuperates the mimetic in the interests of a different, surreal reality. All the images from the work of Reverdy cited as 'surrealist' in the first manifesto in fact bear a relatively easy phenomenological or referential reading.

In the brook, there is a song that flows ...

Day unfolded like a white tablecloth ...

The world goes back into a sack. (p. 36)

Breton's interest is in the way such images cannot be calculated in advance. The fortuitous juxtaposition of terms that strike the poet and produce a 'spark', is an experience in which the poet is fundamentally passive. The poet is thus essentially a reader, the first reader, and the effect produced stems from the way the emergent image is processed to make an unforeseen connection. The images that Breton most values are those 'arbitrary to the highest degree' ['*le degré d'arbitraire le plus elevé*'] (*Oeuvres*, I, 338). This really means, we learn, those that take 'the longest time to translate into practical language' (*Manifesto of Surrealism*, p. 38). An image then is forceful to the degree that it first resists and then gives itself to received modes of reading. Nevertheless, Breton does not seem to show much awareness that conventions of textual reception are historically determined and are at least as decisive as conventions of textual production. The convention at issue in his account of the surrealist image is that of unifying discrepant elements by trying to resolve them as mimetic in the ordinary sense. As William R. Paulson observes, the very way we read today when least self-conscious still often reflects, unwittingly, the domination of norms of construction from the Romantic tradition:[35] we read with a view to unification, to drawing together elements before us according to the maximum number of internal relations to be found between them, constructing an inherent teleology or guiding 'intention' as we do so. The force of the surrealist image may be understood, then, from a perspective opposite to Breton's, not as expressing some mysterious creative realm to be tapped and affirmed, but as arising from the effects projected by a double relation of resistance and accommodation to post-Romantic conventions of reading in terms of multeity in unity. The surreal is a *phantasmatic author* in the sense outlined in the first chapter.

Unable always to see the crucial mediating role played by reading in its revolutionary programme, or its ideal of introspective self-discovery, surrealism itself becomes vulnerable to effects of 'mere' chance. Automatic writing seems to become prey to writers who are said only to run their pen over the surface of the page to gather mere startling images 'more or less arbitrarily' (*Second Manifesto*, p. 158), or to writers who subordinate sense to sound, governed by 'only the empty carapaces of words' ('Surrealist Situation of the Object' (1935)).[36] Surrealist writing, Breton insists, should not be merely idiosyncratic in personal ways, but universal, 'poetry must be understood by everyone' (*Manifestoes of Surrealism*, p. 262). Hence Breton's repeated redrawings of the boundaries as to what surrealism 'really' is, the expulsions from the group, the insistence that surrealist phenomena be read now this way, now that, that they not be taken out of context, etc. The surrealist manifestos, once published over a collective signature, are now part of Breton's *oeuvre* alone.

The practice of inspiration, in the surrealist experiments, is simultaneously an idealistic theory of inspiration and, despite itself, the contestation of that theory's coherence and of surrealism itself. It is not the affirmation of a surreal realm in which distinctions of self and other, conscious and subliminal, are overcome. It seems to be more a chiasmatic structure of dispossession in which the very act of writing is inevitably contaminated in unpredictable ways by reading, considered as a necessary element in the structure of the text, opening the space of inspiration as one of novel effects of meaning but also one of conflict, powerlessness and misrecognition. Inspiration reveals a contradiction at the heart of the surrealist project of surpassing human reification and alienation. The apparent plausibility of the surreal as a realm or event that affirms itself in the space freed for it by automatism or chance stems from an ignorance of the degree to which meaning is at once a matter of relations to others, to conventions of reading, and not a making outward of some hidden force or realm. The surreal is thus constituted as an effect of the very alienation, the absence of relationship, it seeks to overcome.

The drive of pure im-mediation

A second aspect of surrealist inspiration may now be considered. I turn now to closer examination of one of Breton's most forceful texts, 'Toujours pour la première fois' ['Always for the first time']:[37]

> Toujours pour la première fois
> C'est à peine si je te connais de vue
> Tu rentres à telle heure de la nuit dans une maison oblique à ma fenêtre
> Maison tout imaginaire

C'est là que d'une seconde à l'autre
Dans le noir intact
Je m'attends à se que ce produise une fois de plus la déchirure fascinante
La déchirure unique
De la façade et de mon coeur

[Always for the first time
I scarcely know you by sight
You return at some hour of the night to a house oblique to my
window
A totally imaginary house
It is there that from one second to the next
In the inviolate darkness
I anticipate the fascinating tearing up once more
The unique tearing up
Of the facade and my heart]

The poem, from *L'Air de l'eau* (1934), stems from a period in which Breton was not using automatic techniques *per se*, but exploiting them to catalytic effect within more consciously held literary frameworks. In *Point du jour* Breton endorses a psychoanalytic study of automatic writing (one of whose authors was Lacan) which points out how certain frames of reference, fixed beforehand, always seem to mediate and control the potential chaos of automatic images (*Oeuvres*, II, 328–9).[38] Breton argues that a poet must maintain a minimal sense of direction in the act of writing. It is a matter of the overall form and direction of the poem (*Oeuvres*, II, 326–31). Breton is gradually giving up the ideal of automatic writing as a pure mnemotechne: it is necessarily mediated by the ways we read. This minimal sense of direction prevents automatic writing from dispersing itself as a disparate clash of different discourses, a possible result of surrealist experimentation that Breton seems to see as illegitimate *a priori*, presumably because it would be at odds with its programme of reuniting the human personality.

The frames of mediation at work in 'Toujours pour la première fois' are principally those provided by the generic conventions of the lyric. Thus one assumes, by force of this convention, that the two poles of the fictive speech-act that make up a lyric, 'I' and 'you', refer throughout to the same human figures, not to conflicting groups or even to someone completely different on each occurrence (a possibility that the title and the concluding lines invite us to consider nevertheless). Breton's text may be traced as a field of interaction between the discursive rules of the love-lyric and the transgressive/destructive drives released through automatism.

Breton reacted against Freud's reductive scientism and defended inspiration as irreducible to it (*Communicating Vessels*, pp. 10–23). The poem too instantiates an aspect of Breton's difference from Freudian psychoanalysis. For Freud, love, or 'falling-in-love', is crucially a repetition or re-enactment of an emotional pattern inscribed in childhood. For Breton too, the beloved is mediated by a series of remembered scenes and locations, notably that in the middle of the poem of the women picking jasmine in a field one dawn near Grasse. Breton, however, is committed to a romantic conception of *eros* as a path to the 'supreme point' of surrealist freedom, and is drawn to the experience of love as one that seems to rewrite the past, unravelling a sense, *après coup*, that everything then had been leading to the present. If there is a sense of re-cognition, it is one that looks back from out of the future of what is being recalled. The present, in this view, is what repeats itself 'now' retrospectively in the past. (Elsewhere Breton modifies Villon's 'Where are the snows of yester-year?' to 'Where are the snows of tomorrow?')[39] A reading of this poem as a scene of backward recognition, however, would be only a partial one. For one thing, every image in the text is set at an angle, is 'out of true' as the English has it. There is also a disconcerting and exciting sense that these scenes are not quite, or not yet, scenes of recognition, for the event is still in the process of revealing itself, from out of the future, and always for the first time.

In an early section of *L'Amour fou* Breton writes about how he has always identified certain aesthetic sensations before landscapes or works or art with that of erotic pleasure ('like the feeling of a feathery wind brushing across my temples', p. 8). These differ only in degree. Both express that spark of *convulsive beauty* which may enact or harbinger the surreal, reconciling that which is mutually attractive through their opposed natures (p. 124 nt.). This recuperation of the potential heterogeneity of automatic writing through a notion of *eros* may be an idealization however, as we shall see. The text proceeds by virtue of a simple trope, that of identifying the force of the loved woman's presence with that of the continuous event enacted in automatic writing as one which leaves the next line always unpredictable. This is almost the poem's explicit programme – 'I've found the secret/Of loving you/Always for the first time.'

Let us look in more detail at lines 1 to 8. These enact the poem's opening of itself to the advent of the adored woman as an event in the lover's psyche. It merges inner and outer space in problematic ways. The force of this advent is represented as being to compel a series of images which succeed one another such that each affirms the merely temporary adequacy of its predecessor. Stamos Metzidakis writes that Breton's poetry is a striving to be *original* in a double sense, both that of novelty and in the sense of a quest to liberate language from utilitarian ends and return it to its origins. Thus the origin is 'simultaneously the point of departure and the destination for surrealist poetry.'[40] The force of the lover's approach, necessitating such a train of imagery, renders her an originary muse figure – the effect achieved is that the compulsion which drives the act of writing and the approach to the beloved addressed in the poem are one.

Surrealist poetry extends a tendency traced in late nineteenth- and early twentieth-century French verse of making levels of figuration (what is literal, what metaphorical? etc.) increasingly hard to decide.[41] Automatic writing often deploys a series of figures in which what seemed metaphorical in one line has become quasi-literalized in the next as its principle frame of reference. Breton sets up (in the third line) what seems briefly a scene of description in which the poet, almost like a voyeur, watches his lover enter at night into a house 'oblique to my window.' This sense of outwardness, however, is immediately reversed. It is a 'totally imaginary house', positing a sense that the whole thing is happening in the watcher's mind. However, further possibilities disrupt what might otherwise be a tame psychic allegory – is it maybe the woman who imagines the house or the both of them? The next line performs a further involution by placing the 'I' inside the imagined house. This does not, to my mind, produce what might be termed a Chinese-doll effect, viz. the poet doubling as observer and observed in a potentially endless series. The effect of each successive line is partly to dissolve or undo the world posited by the previous one, in a verbal collage that is too rapid to allow a totalizing framework to endure in the reader's mind:

> C'est la que d'une seconde à l'autre
> Dans le noir intact
> Je m'attends à ce que se produise une fois de plus la déchichure fascinante
> La déchirure unique
> De la façade et de mon coeur.

The violence of this scene is indicative of the technique of this text throughout. By this point 'levels' of figuration have become so uncertain, so interfused with an ongoing effect of metamorphosis, that it is not only as if both the façade of a house and and a human heart could tear like brittle paper; what seems torn is the whole thing, the poem and its page themselves. ('In reality', writes Aragon, 'all poetry is surrealist in its movement.')[42] The poem is this continual act of tearing itself up – 'To participate in a surrealist poem is to consent to its movement, to surrender one's totalizing impulse to the very spur of writing's moment.'[43] The basic trope of 'Toujours pour la première fois' is this act of tearing up conventions of representation and figurative structures, yet also recuperating this violence, according to lyric convention, as the violence of surrealist eros.

Breton has set up a textual dynamic in which, each line negating the world posited by the previous one, the poem's act becomes recuperable as a species of quest whose object, as in Browning's 'Life in a Love', must be 'Ever / Removed':[44]

> *Plus je m'approche de toi*
> *En réalité*
> *Plus la clé chante à la porte de la chambre inconnue*
> *Où tu m'apparais seule*
> *Tu es d'abord tout entière fondue dans la brillant*
> *L'angle fugitif d'un rideau*

> [The closer I come to you
> In reality
> The more the key sings at the door of the unknown room
> Where you appear alone before me
> At first you coalesce entirely with the brightness
> The elusive angle of a curtain]

Doors and curtains: these both trope and make explicit the distance, delay or discrepancy at the heart of the process set up. Identifying the beloved's force with the effraction of the act of writing itself, the poem finds that that act itself can never be written, any more than a stream can flow back over its own bed. By the time the poem reaches the scene with women picking jasmine one feels that almost any scene of memory, acting as a veil for the lover's presence (both, that is, indicating and concealing it) would be imbued with a peculiar fascination simply by virtue of its positioning in the text and by its seeming arbitrariness and opacity. The effect is that the brilliant angled curtain obscuring the woman's presence becomes a field of flowers:

> *C'est un champ de jasmin qui j'ai contemplé à l'aube sur une route des*

environs de Grasse
Avec ses cueilleuses en diagonale
Derrière elles l'aile sombre tombante des plantes dégarnis
Devant elles l'équerre de l'éblouissant

[It is a field of jasmine I gazed on at dawn on a road near Grasse
With the diagonal slant of its women picking
Behind them the dark falling wing of the plants stripped bare
Before them a T-square of dazzling light]

The effraction of writing, for Breton, seems inseparable here from a form of male sexuality, for this is the excitement of an act of unveiling that seems also to defer and prolong itself by its own act. It is a scene of a dazzlement and revelation manifesting itself in a movement that is also the promise of a greater *éblouissement* to come – for it is merely an aspect of the veil or screen that is losing its flowers.

The central section of the poem then manages an effect of unexpected calm and tenderness. It is as if the violence inherent in the writing were turned upon itself, holding itself off so as to create a temporary, fragile and ambivalent episode of stasis. The woman appears poignantly weak, almost unbearably vulnerable in the midst of unspoken, sinister destructive possibilities, a violence identifiable throughout as inseparable from what might be termed the drive of writing itself, even as this is troped as the erotic. Here it is imaged as an external threat in the environment, the branches, for instance, that seem about to scratch her in the forest, the image of a hunt, or of rocking-chairs on a deck or bridge ... This analysis could go on to trace how the poem's final return to its first line enacts an attempt at formal closure at odds with the dynamic of the writing itself, but I hope that my argument now seems clear. A second aspect of surrealist inspiration is this: a violent force of effraction in which automatism is part of a continual movement of *déchirure* and transgression that is at once mediated as a condition of its appearance by the norms of the frame in which it announces itself.

Automatic writing seems to manifest a force that will be more explicitly realized and described in Blanchot's work on writing as a transgressive 'search for immediation.'[45] Writing for Blanchot is 'the greatest violence, for it transgresses the law, every law, and also its own' (p. xii). Yet this violence is never 'pure' or immediate – Breton's poem is far more than the meaningless babble or the mutism in which Bataille tried to see a certain authenticity, or those painful marks of bodily excoriation that Artaud affirmed as a material writing traversing the body. The use of the lyric as mediating frame enables Breton to affirm a textual event that both trangresses and renews the love-poem, albeit at the risk of opening it to manifestations of a barely suppressed violence. The woman, as a muse figure mediating the *merveilleux* and subject to the effraction of writing as a kind of romanticized Sadian crime, is in danger of becoming as fragmented as the women of many surrealist paintings.[46] The poem, exposing itself to the continual possibility of fragmentation, puts intense pressure on the two poles ('I' and 'you') that hold it all together and maintain its legibility as a lyric. The codes of recognition and identity are continually transgressed, and yet this force of transgression is continually reclaimed and so renewed: 'From the fusion without hope of your presence and your absence / I have found the secret / Of loving you / Always for the first time.'

The poem bears out the intense surrealist drive towards a pure freedom ('Never freedom except for freedom' ('Non-lieu', *Poems*, pp. 54–5)). At the same time it demonstrates how such a drive towards the immediate is close to a desire for self-immolation. Self-transcendence may be akin to suicide. In 'Vigilance' we read:

> I head for the room where I am lying
> And set fire to it
> So that nothing will remain of the consent wrung from me
> *(Poems*, pp. 78–9)

Examination of the manuscripts of *Les Champs magnétiques* leads A. Joufroy to write of an '*écriture suicide*'.[47] The notion of the affirmation of a hidden surreal identity does not seem to be borne out by these texts. Carolyn Dean, writing on surrealism in general, concludes:

> If the true self was to be found in the unbinding of subjectivity, in otherness or crime, then the confounding of the self with its own unravelling was epistemologically complete. Thus the surrealist quest for an 'unmediated unity' between the self and crime had the peculiar effect of dissolving the self.[48]

When the surrealist Prometheus is unbound, nothing is left but the pile of bandages that made up his body.

The streets as space of composition

Inspiration has traditionally named a quasi-mythical account of the genesis of the poetic through an encounter with another being, often a muse or a deity of some sort. Some Romantic writers attempt both to internalize and appropriate this scene of genesis as an individual power. While Breton is clearly writing in this Romantic tradition, a third discernible aspect of the practice of surrealist inspiration also marks a decisive break from it. This break is also affirmed in the way surrealism was a collective enterprise, involving experiments with dialogue, thought-transference or games such as 'Le cadavre exquise'. Such a practice places enormous strain on the idealization of inspiration and on surrealist expectations of opening up a realm of untapped power. The unity of the self becomes increasingly impossible to defend and something like the radical anti-humanist notion of inspiration explicit in Blanchot and Derrida begins to become legible. Writing becomes the space of a plural word, one in which any act of utterance is instantly and unpredictably mediated by the presence of another or of others. It is a novel opening up of intersubjective space, not simply as a gap to be traversed in representation, but as an aleatory space of composition in which surprising effects of language may emerge from a plural site of enunciation without an author.

Not unlike experiments with dialogue or shared authorship (as in Breton and Eluard's *L'Immaculée Conception*), Breton's *Nadja* (1928) and *L'Amour fou* (1937), though penned by one man, also enact this notion of communication as an opening to the unforeseen through relation with an other. In *La Confession dédaigneuse* (1924) Breton writes that at a certain period of his life he never left his home to go out without saying a farewell to all the memories accumulated there, all that might be felt to perpetuate an identity. He continues: 'The street ... with its disquiets and glances; I caught there as nowhere else the wind of eventuality' (*Oeuvres*, I, 193–202, p. 196).

Nadja and *L'Amour fou* enact an unprecedented mode of writing whose provenance is a new experience of the streets as a space of inspiration and mediation to the unknown. Paris is not primarily a social or political entity in these texts. *L'Amour fou* makes no mention of political events at the time of its narration in which the surrealists were involved.[49] The streets are a theatricalized dream-space, one usually entered at dusk: it is a space whose usual emotional charge has been neutralized, that is say one in which objects and passers-by possess equal and floating interest until some unexpected encounter or coincidence charges the whole scene with latent possibilities of 'meaning'. For Breton, to move through the city's streets in this way is to open oneself to the dialectic already at work in other surrealist experiments: 'his drifting across Paris is abandonment to destiny, but also *conquest* of that destiny.'[50]

What sort of texts are *Nadja* and *L'Amour fou*? Neither 'fiction' nor 'autobiography' seem adequate as generic headings. Breton's writing here, which can sometimes seem to be merely mundane narrative or anecdote, is actually doing something unprecedented. *Nadja* and *L'Amour fou* are anatomies of surrealist inspiration that cut across traditional stereotomies, opening themselves from out of a space between, while embracing the psychic and the extra-psychic, the literary and the historical. Writing takes on a dialectical relation to life itself, in the process of being lived – the first part of *Nadja* appeared before the happening of events which were later to be written in subsequent parts. The actual writing of the text is affirmed as part of the writer's own exploration of the events he is living. Breton is writing an anti-novel, one whose heterogeneous elements, he claims, do not produce any predictable or foreknown sum. Both *Nadja* and *L'Amour fou* transcribe 'real' events and would lose a lot of their interest if the reader did not remember that these remarkable coincidences and meaningful encounters are, to a problematic degree, not the concoctions of a novelist. Yet 'real' earns its inverted commas here, and not solely because our only means of access to these events is discursive. If literary texts are definable partly as those in which a thetic relation to reference, if not reference itself, has been suspended then Breton, drifting through actual streets, has already practised a 'phenomenological conversion of the gaze'[51] in this manner. It renders the neutralized urban space a literary one, a space of signs, of latent symbolism and cross-referencing. Blanchot writes of Breton encountering events in the real which nevertheless find their site only 'in the space opened by this movement of writing' (*The Infinite Conversation*, p. 421). 'Literariness' becomes a condition of real events. Albert Py observes that Breton's activity as a *flaneur* follows the broad pattern that may be traced in automatic writing: Expectancy – Encounter – Revelation.[52]

Nadja opens with the question '*Qui suis-je?*' The street is itself a space of composition in the sense already defined, a space of self-reading, a non-linear space of mysterious phantasmatic agencies, of *après coup* constructions and of leaps of recognition. Breton is, like the writer described in chapter one, engaged in an act that may transgress or transform the subject of that act, rendering the work itself a fracture or hiatus in any linear conception of self-expression or representation. It is again a matter of 'experiences that possess the potential to break in their very occurrence with the limits whereby they might be understood or conceptualised' (ch. 1).

Breton's own quest is analogous to what John Ashbery says of the act of writing itself: 'If I did not write, I would have no idea of what I have to write. I suppose that I write so as to find what I have to write.'

On 4 October 1926 Breton encounters a strangely made-up young woman, Nadja (her own name for herself, the beginning of the word meaning hope in Russian), an 'always inspired and inspiring creature who enjoyed being nowhere but in the streets, the only region of valid experience for her' (*Nadja*, p. 113). Then follow a series of encounters: some are arranged, others the result of uncanny coincidence as when, for instance, Nadja's trajectory, taken purposely to avoid a planned rendezvous with Breton, leads her straight to him in another street. Other experiences and coincidences are 'petrifying', presenting the sense that life is a cryptogram to be deciphered. Nadja herself lives on the edge of insanity, continually mimicking historical or mythical figures such as Madame de Chevreuse or Mélusine. She is a drifter, forced to practise occasional prostitution to survive. Her conversation mixes bizarre profundity with a triteness that increasingly irritates Breton. At the same time involvement with the infatuated Nadja seems to frighten him. He resists her attempt to stage a love death: Nadja had put her hands over Breton's eyes while he was driving, pressing his foot further down on the accelerator while moving to kiss him (*Nadja*, pp. 152-3). 'Self-preservation' (*Nadja*, p. 20) is a concern that recurs in the book.

We have traced in various surreal experiments a syndrome of self-abandonment and recoil. Madness is being surrendered to, but deliberately, so it is also being controlled, as in the appropriative simulations of insanity in *L'Immaculée Conception*. Surrealist experiments read as a delicate balancing act between fragmentation, chaos on the one hand and intense reconciliation and repair on the other; it is a pattern that resembles a *war neurosis*. Alina Clej has read Breton's experimentation in *Nadja* and elsewhere as reproducing 'the delirium' of World War One, its 'deadly mechanism' (Clej, p. 843). The space of composition is the site of a peculiar war game, a 'staging of an 'appearance-as-disappearance', in which the controlled, manipulated danger becomes a source of pleasure' (Clej, p. 843). The notion of 'convulsive beauty', is introduced at the very end of *Nadja*, framed by an account of a probable plane-crash. In *L'Amour fou* it is an eroticized explosion, 'veiled-erotic, fixed explosive' (p. 20). Nadja's own advent is staged in an image of eroticized war: 'Last of all, now, the tower of the Manoir d'Ange [where

Breton was writing] explodes and a snowfall of feathers from its doves dissolves on contact with the earth of the great courtyard, once paved with scraps of tiles and now covered with real blood' (*Nadja*, p. 60).

The *Second Manifesto* is itself marked by a strong ambivalence as to inspiration. As we saw, it is said to project the person it seizes '*in self defence, into immortality*' (p. 162, emphasis added). This act is defensive, and oddly ambiguous: 'immortality' suggests a kind of fame or glory quite at odds with surreal ideals of a communism of genius; to be thrown into immortality also of course suggests a violent death. The passage continues:

> If he were lucid, awake, he would be terrified as he wriggled out of this tight situation. The whole point for him is not to be free of it, for him to go on talking the entire time this mysterious ringing lasts: it is, in fact, the point at which he ceases to belong to himself that he belongs to us (p. 162).

I take 'us' here to refer to the surrealists as readers of the work that is being conceived. The passage is slightly obscure, but it seems that by 'talking' here Breton means that the artist continues creating so as to surrender to the mysterious ringing. Moreover, by doing so, he or she avoids the terror that would accompany this experience if it were undergone in lucid self-consciousness. The possession inherent to inspiration has a traumatic element, one only overcome, paradoxically, by an intensification of the very surrender whose exigency is yet what makes the experience traumatic in the first place. In the huge sentence that follows this ambivalent passage, Breton claims that this surrender to automatism may open new secrets of human nature, provided the artist does not give way to the temptation to turn back 'for reasons of self-preservation' (p. 163).

Nadja exemplifies this structure of fascination with self-immolation and then recoil. The principle of reconstruction there is the sense of purposeful teleology that Breton constructs out of these bizarre and frightening experiences. Breton's treatment of chance consists above all in aestheticizing it. The notion of 'objective chance', formulated after *Nadja* was written, looks to Breton's dialogue with Freud and attempts to reconcile surrealist ideology with the demands of dialectical materialism. Nevertheless the hidden debt to aesthetics is massive and more decisive. Contingent events are subject to a mode of reflective judgement that, as a condition of being able to place their contingency under some more general rule, assumes a certain purposiveness. Such a Kantian principle of purposiveness works in the interrelations Breton sets up between various elements in *Nadja*. Nadja's strong eye make-up, for instance, the first thing he notices about her (and which marks her at once as a figure of a kind of theatre), forms part of a series of references to eyes. The eyes form what would be called, in a simpler and more purely literary work, a recurrent symbol or motif, and this is what Roger Cardinal calls them in his study of *Nadja*,[53] surely eliding a crucial difference. Breton's procedure is to attach strong importance to some detail or other that strikes him, such as the eyes, rendering this detail the first in a series formed by subsequent phenomena that may seem related, or by memories that now seem to realign themselves in the space of composition in process. All produce a sense that they present 'all the appearance of being a signal, without our being able to say precisely which signal' (*Nadja*, p. 19).

'Objective chance', with its peculiar effect of collapsing the real and the literary into each other, places the artist in an overall dream-like context, an oneiric theatre in which the ego is only one member of a cast that includes mere things as well as people. This is all affirmed explicitly by Breton, yet it is also implicitly at odds with the *ex cathedra* stance of the narrating voice. Breton's dogmatic and sometimes oratorical pose as narrator reveals an intense defensiveness about the realm opened up by the ambiguous status of his project. Breton would be, but cannot be, both actor and spectator in the scene of the text's unfolding, for it is once again the aleatory effects of reading and of being read that are at issue in Breton's inability not to try to lay down the law of interpretation for his text. What could be less like an openness to the unexpected and the aleatory that the following statement, for example: 'from the first page of this book to the last, my faith will certainly not have changed' (*Nadja*, p. 151)?

A third aspect of surrealist inspiration then is mainly latent as a source of anxiety, a radically anti-fictional practice that opens up a new and potentially uncomfortable notion of chance. Neither ascribing the strange encounters of these texts to 'mere chance', nor, as Breton does, drawing on the aesthetic tradition to construct, surely too hastily, some new order out of them, surrealist chance could become the name for an affirmed crisis in the boundaries between realms or discourses, the opening out of their stereotomies. Chance would thus remain an event, or a series of events, to be traced as cutting across these boundaries, without sublating them in some imaginary surreal order. The work resulting from such an experience would be one that opened itself to unprecedented and unforeseeable modes of 'coherence', in which the desire for unification, purposiveness and meaning – the whole literary tradition and its conventions of reading – would be subject to revision and trangression by contradiction and heterogeneity, without at the same time becoming merely fragmentary or meaningless (for these terms still affirm, dialectically, a lost overall harmony that ought instead to be at issue). The cohabitation of heterogeneous orders in *Nadja* and *L'Amour fou* opens itself to such innovation and experiment, yet Breton also recoils from it.

This is a latent possibility in the surrealist experiment that fascinates Blanchot and which is taken up in his own concept of inspiration:

> An *experience* that is ... not only an experimentation (the action of writing on life), but an experience of that which does not obey the reigning order of experience, and, without taking the form of a new order, holds itself between the two – between the two orders, two times, two systems of signification or of language: the ordeal, therefore, of what is given neither in the arrangement of the world nor in the form of the work, and thus announcing itself on the basis of the real as *derangement*, and the basis of the work as *unworking* (*The Infinite Conversation*, p. 417)

Breton shies away from this ordeal. The epilogue to *Nadja* opens with an acute sense of failure. Nadja, we hear with an excruciating apparent casualness, has been confined to a mental institution. The whole episode with Nadja is now offered finally as a mere signal, pointing to the unnamed woman who is the addressee of the text's conclusion.[54] Breton brings off a merely traditional kind of formal closure, giving both life and art a spurious autonomic status. This internalizes and totalizes all the vectors that play across this very peculiar, hybrid space of composition into an inherent teleology leading to 'X', the woman celebrated in the epilogue, whom Breton had met since completing the two previous sections. Again Breton's construction of hidden purposes at work in the coincidences of *Nadja* owes more to Romantic aesthetics than it does to Freud. Such an idealization dominates *L'Amour fou*, rendering it a far less interesting text than the earlier, more adventurous *Nadja*.[55] The self-realization toward which the protagonist is drawn is one which will unite freedom and necessity, mind and chance, life and art – all in short that a certain idealist tradition tries to claim as the state supposedly realized either in, or in the making of, great works of art – the surreal as an all-harmonizing form of relation.

Notes

1 André Breton, *Manifestoes of Surrealism*, trans. Richard Seavert and Helen R. Lane (Ann Arbor: University of Michigan Press, 1972), pp. 2–22. All further references in main text.

2 Louis Aragon, *Traité du style* (Paris: Editions Gallimard, 1928), pp. 187–9.

3 Quoted in Gérard Legrand, *André Breton en son temps* (Paris: Le Soleil noir, 1976), p. 9.

4 *Point du Jour* [1934] In *Oeuvres Complètes*, 2 vols to date, ed. Marguerite Bonnet (Paris: Editions Gallimard, 1988–92), II, 265–392, pp. 322–5.

5 Michel Foucault, *Madness and Civilisation*, trans. Richard Howard (New York: Pantheon, 1965).

6 See *Entretiens 1913–1952* (Paris: Editions Gallimard, 1952), pp. 19–31; see Alina Clej, 'Phantoms of the Opera: Notes Towards a Theory of Surrealist Confession – The Case of Breton', *MLN*, 104 (1989), 819–44, p. 840.

7 See Peter Bürger, *Theory of the Avant-garde*, trans. Michael Shaw (Minneapolis: University of Minnesota Press, 1984).

8 Breton, 'Pour Dada', *Les Pas perdus* (1924), in *Oeuvres*, I, 193–308, p. 239; 'Le Message Automatique', in *Le Point du Jour*, *Oeuvres*, II, 375–92, p. 378.

9 Breton, *Communicating Vessels*, trans. Mary Ann Caws and Geoffrey T. Harris (Lincoln and London: University of Nebraska Press, 1990), p. 7.

10 Judith Schlanger, *Invention Intellectuelle* (Paris: Fayard, 1983), pp. 36–42.

11 Breton, *Mad Love* [*L'Amour fou*, 1937], trans. Mary Ann Caws (Lincoln and London: University of Nebraska Press, 1987), p. 86.

12 See Mary Ann Caws (ed.), *About French Poetry fron DADA to 'Tel Quel': Text and Theory* (Detroit: Wayne State University Press, 1974), p. 35.

13 I take this term from Derrida, 'My chances/*Mes Chances*: A Rendezvous with Some Epicurean Stereophonies', in *Taking Chances: Derrida, Psychoanalysis, and Literature*, ed. Joseph H. Smith and William Kerrigan (Baltimore: The Johns Hopkins University Press, 1984), pp. 1–31, p. 11.

14 Breton, *Nadja*, trans. Richard Howard (n.p.: Grove Press, 1960), p. 60.

15 Such a gesture of dissociation also applies to any lingering religiosity in the concept of inspiration, as was apparent, for example, in Victor Hugo's use of spritualism; see Keith Aspley, 'Visions and Voices: The Nature of Inspiration from Romanticism to the Birth of Surrealism', in *Poetry in France: Metamorphoses of a Muse*, ed. Keith Aspley and Peter France (Edinburgh: Edinburgh University Press, 1992), pp. 154–68.

16 See Jean Starobinski, 'Freud, Breton, Myers', *Les Critiques de notre temps et Breton*, ed. Marguerite Bonnet (Paris: Gamier frères, 1974), pp. 48–59.

17 Paule Plouvier, *Poétique de l'amour chez André Breton* (Paris: José Corti, 1983) p. 37.

18 Claude Abastado, 'Ecriture automatique et instance du sujet', *Revues des Sciences Humaines*, 56, No. 184 (October–December 1981), 59–75. p. 69.

19 Jean-Louis Houdebine, 'Méconnaissance de la psychanalyse dans le discours surréaliste', *Tel Quel*, No. 46 (1971), 67–82.

20 Michel Beaujour, 'La Poétique de l'automatisme chez André Breton', *Poétique*, 7 (1976), 116–23, p. 123.

21 See Carolyn J. Dean, *The Self and its Pleasures: Bataille, Lacan, and the History of the Decentered Subject* (Ithaca: Cornell University Press, 1992), pp. 213–4.

22 See *Entretiens*, pp. 153–4.

23 Plouvier, *Poétique de l'amour*, p. 79.

24 In Breton, *La Clé des champs* (Holland: Jean-Jacques Pauvert, 1967), pp. 7–13.

25 Consider: 'Nothing, in fact, can any longer prevent this country [language] from being conquered. The hordes of words which, whatever one may say, Dada and Surrealism set out to let loose ... are not of a kind to withdraw again for no good purpose. They will slowly but surely make their way into the silly little towns and cities of literature' (*Second Manifesto*, p. 152).

26 Robert Champigny, 'Analyse d'une définition du Surréalisme', *PMLA*, 81 (1966), 139–44, p. 143.

27 These issues are at the heart of the vituperative dispute between Breton and Georges Bataille. See Jean-Loius Houdebine, 'L'Ennemi du Dedans: Bataille et le surréalism: éléments, prises de parti', in *Bataille*, ed. Philippe Solers (Paris: U.G.E., 1973), pp. 153–191; John Lechte, 'Surrealism and the Practice of Writing, or The 'Case' of Bataille', in *Bataille: Writing the Sacred*, ed. Carolyn Bailey Gill (London: Routledge, 1995), pp. 117–32.

28 *Poems of André Breton: A Bilingual Anthology*, trans., ed. Jean-Pierre Cauvin and Mary Ann Caws (Austin, Texas: University of Austin Press, 1982), pp. 86–7. See Michael Sherringham, 'Breton and the Language of Automatism: Alterity, Allegory, Desire', *Forum for Modern Language Studies*, 18 (1982), pp. 142–58.

29 Jean-Luc Steinmetz, *La Poésie et ses raisons: Rimbaud, Mallarmé, Breton, Artaud, Char, Bataille, Michaux, Ponge, Tortel, Jaccottet* (Paris: José Corti, 1990), p. 101.

30 Brewster Ghiselin (ed.), *The Creative Process: A Symposium* (Berkeley: University of California Press, 1952), pp. 64–71.

31 See Breton's account of this in 'What is Surrealism?' (1934), in *Theories of Modern Art: A Source Book by Artists and Critics*, ed. Herschel B. Chipp *et al.* (Berkeley: University of California Press, 1966), pp. 410–27, pp. 415–16.

32 See Gérard Durazoi, *Artaud: l'alienation et la folie* (Paris: Libraire Larousse, 1972) pp. 81–90.

33 Antonin Artaud, *Oeuvres complètes*, 26 vols (Paris: Editions Gallimard, 1961), I, 20.

34 Derrida, *Writing and Difference*, trans. Alan Bass (Chicago: University of Chicago Press, 1978), pp. 169–95.

35 William R. Paulson, *The Noise of Culture: Literary Texts in a World of Information* (Ithaca and London: Cornell University Press, 1988), pp. 155–71.

36 In *Manifestoes of Surrealism*, pp. 255–78, p. 262.

37 *Poems*, pp. 108–10 (translation modified).

38 J. Lévy-Valensi, Pierre Migault, Jacques Lacan, 'Écrits "inspirés": schizo-graphie', *Annales médico-psychologique* (December 1931) 508–22.

39 Mary Ann Caws, 'The Poetics of a Surrealist Passage and Beyond',

Twentieth Century Literature, 21 (1975), 24–36, p. 28.

40 Stamos Metzidakis, 'Breton and Poetic Originality', in *André Breton Today*, ed. Anna Balakian, and Rudolf E. Kuenzli (New York: Willis Locker & Owens, 1989), pp. 28–35, p. 33.

41 Graham D. Martin, 'A Measure of Distance: The Rhetoric of the Surrealist Adjective', *Forum for Modern Language Studies*, 18 (1982), 108–25.

42 Aragon, *Traité du style*, p. 189.

43 J. Gratton, 'Runaway: Textual Dynamics in the Surrealist Poetry of André Breton', *Forum for Modern Language Studies*, 18 (1982), 126–41, p. 127.

44 Robert Browning, *Poetical Works 1833–1864*, ed. Ian Jack (London: Oxford University Press, 1970), p. 632.

45 Blanchot, *The Infinite Conversation*, trans. Susan Hanson, (Minneapolis and London: University of Minnesota Press, 1993), p. 9.

46 Mary E. Eichbauer, 'The Surrealist Muse and the Sister Arts: René Char's "Artine"', *Paragraph*, 12 (1989), 124–38.

47 See Abastado, 'Écriture automatique', p. 63.

48 Dean, *The Self and its Pleasures*, p. 219.

49 Jean Gaulmier,'Remarques sur le thème de Paris chez André Breton', *Les Critiques de notre temps et Breton*, ed. Bonnet, pp. 130–38, p. 133.

50 Gaulmier, 'Remarques' p. 138.

51 Jacques Derrida, '"This Stange Institution called Literature": An Interview with Jacques Derrida', in Derrida, *Acts of Literature*, ed. Derek Attridge (London: Routledge, 1992), p. 45.

52 Albert Py, 'De l'Amour et du comportement lyrique chez André Breton', in *Hommages à Marcel Raymond* (Paris: Corti, 1967), pp. 265–74, p. 267.

53 Cardinal, *Breton: Nadja* (London: Grant & Cutler, 1986), pp. 16–17.

54 Breton's use of Nadja recalls perhaps the sexist early twentieth-century doctrine of the *femme inspiratrice*: 'Biographies of an author would be divided into periods according to the women who had inspired him successively' (Ellenberger, p. 294).

55 See also 'Le Château étoile', *Minotaure*, No. 1, p. 33.

CHAPTER 9

Octavio Paz and *Renga*: the dispersal of inspiration?

One of the most adventurous, peculiar and thought-provoking poetic and theoretical enterprises of modern times has yet to receive its due. In late March and early April 1969, four poets gathered in the basement of a hotel in Paris. Then followed five days of collective writing, producing a quadri-lingual work, *Renga*, modelled on the Japanese 'renga' or chain-poem. *Renga* is written in the (Mexican) Spanish of Octavio Paz, the (British) English of Charles Tomlinson, the French of Jacques Roubaud and the Italian of Edoardo Sanguineti.[1]

Renga is not primarily a poem or a theory of poetry, neither is it criticism: it is a situation, an *experiment* with the act of composition. It enacts the surrealist ambition of incarnating the poetic in a historical situation. The concept of experiment, in surrealism and *Renga*, is precise. Modern poetry, Paz writes, has become experimental in ways comparable with the natural sciences: '[The poet's] body and his psyche, his entire being, are the "field" in which all sorts of transformations take place. Modern poetry is an experimental process whereby the knowing subject is the object of knowledge'.[2] Composition, whether or not one uses drugs like Baudelaire or Henri Michaux, has often been, since Romanticism, an experiment upon the nature of the psyche.

When it first appeared in English translation in 1972, a reviewer hailed *Renga* immediately as a modern classic (*Shanti*, 1973, 36–7). Since then two articles have appeared (one of them by the author of this study)[3] and *Renga* has long gone out of print. Nevertheless, *Renga* is one of the most extraordinary experiments with the act of writing as a crisis in subjectivity to be found in Western literature even though, in the face of its own extremism, it retreats into Romantic and surrealist cliché on occasions.

What brings these four poets together, apart from a common friendship with Paz, is a shared valorization of the act of composition itself as a valuable transformation of the psyche. For Tomlinson, the poetic act is the practice of a minute phenomenology of perception. Poetic contemplation must be a purging of the ego if it is to be able to do justice to the otherness and inhuman allure of the object world. Much of *Renga* reads as a dialogue between Tomlinson and the others on this issue: '*Surreal Narcissus / the river and the buildings are passing you by!*' (*Renga*, p. 76). For Roubaud, who is also a mathematician, the poetic act is also one of ascesis. His prizewinning poem *E* (1967), based on the Japanese game of Go, had dramatized the relative marginality and bafflement of a detached consciousness caught up in a combinatorial textual mechanism that projects multiple, overlapping and conflicting voices. In effect, Roubaud sets up a kind of textual machine that deploys what might be termed a 'structuralist' notion of inspiration which sees the poem's seeming speaker as merely the intersection and effect of the impersonal laws and combinatorial possibilities of language. For Sanguineti, modern Europe forms a kind of debased museum culture in which the poet, treating all discourses as if they were dead languages (including those that make up a personal identity), must attempt to burn through the debris and postcards to a lost core of integrity. In effect, all four of *Renga*'s poets, Paz most of all as we shall see, bring with them a conception of inspiration found in many of the writers discussed in this study so far – the process of composition is seen as a crisis and revision of the determinations that define simultaneously both the nature of one's personhood and the properties of the emergent work of art.

Octavio Paz is the mastermind behind *Renga*, the one who gathered the other three poets together. *Renga* is dedicated to André Breton. Paz had met Breton on coming to Paris after World War Two, and had been associated, without total commitment, with the surrealist group. One route into *Renga* is through the essay Paz wrote as an obituary to Breton and which appeared in *La Nouvelle Revue Française* in 1967.[4] This essay anticipates some of the tensions inherent in *Renga*'s conception, since Paz draws parallels between certain oriental notions and practices, especially in Buddhism, and surrealism. He writes of the surrealist conception of poetry (though the account applies also to his own practice):

> Poetry does not save the 'I' of the poet, it dissolves it in the vaster and more powerful reality of speech. The practice of poetry requires abandonment, renunciation of the 'I.' It is sad that Buddhism did not interest [Breton]: that tradition too destroys the illusion of the 'I,' though not for the benefit of language but of

> silence ... I am reminded of Buddhism because I believe that 'auto-
> matic writing' is rather like a modern equivalent of Buddhist
> meditation; I do not think it is a method for writing poems, nor is
> it a rhetorical recipe: it is a psychic exercise, a convocation and an
> invocation to open the floodgates of verbal flow. (p. 68)

Breton saw surrealist practice as directing itself towards a 'supreme
point' that resolved oppositions between the real and the imaginary,
mind and world. This is taken up by Paz in an interview: 'For me,
eroticism and poetry, which are identical ... have perhaps the only
way to arrive at this point. In eroticism as in poetry, the two opposites that we are made of – death and life – one of them in this
moment disappears.' There is a transcendence of the opposition
between life and death: 'in love we are possessive but in the same
way we are not possessive any longer. The man, as "I", as "me",
disappears as in poetry.'[5] Such a view was also confirmed for Paz by
living in the East.

This assimilation of an extremely vague notion of the orient or
of Buddhism to these rather clichéd Romantic and surrealist notions
already suggests limits to *Renga*'s experiment in multiculturalism.
Renga's orientalism is only a superficial facet of an experiment that
more clearly joins that list of texts from the Romantics onwards
whose concern is the act of writing itself as a philosophical act. At
the same time, Paz has set up in *Renga* a situation that necessarily
transcends, exceeds and negates much in his own programme.

In Japan, a renga was a collective poem written according to a
great number of strictly-imposed rules governing the movement of
the poem as it passed from person to person down the chain. In the
preface to Tomlinson's parallel English version of *Renga*, Roubaud
analyzes these prescriptions, which govern both form and subject
matter. In his introduction to *Renga* Paz writes, however: 'We have
no intention of taking over a [Japanese] genre, but rather of putting
into operation a system for the production of poetic texts' (p. 20).

The relation between the West-European renga and its
Japanese model is throughout an elusive, problematic and fascinating one. Roubaud sums up the principles of the Japanese renga in
the introduction (p. 33). The European renga translates the Japanese
form into a series of quasi-sonnets. Why the sonnet? Firstly it is a
pan-European form, still alive in the four literary cultures involved
in *Renga*. Secondly, the sonnet, in most of its varieties, articulates or
divides itself in ways that recall the Japanese renga, principally in the
relation of octave to sestet. *Renga*'s sonnets are actually of varying
length, but the text overall forms a kind of sonnet sequence of

twenty-seven parts. It can be read in two ways; either in the order of composition (five days of writing, producing six texts a day) or as the text is actually bound in book form, as a series of four sequences each of which is started by one poet in turn, who also ends the series with a single-authored sonnet entirely in his own language (apart, that is, from Sanguineti).

The experiment, Paz claims, is antipathetic to basic Western assumptions about the act of writing:

> The practice of the renga implies the negation of certain cardinal western notions, such as the belief in the soul and the reality of the I. The historic context in which it was born and developed did not know of the existence of a creator god and denounced the soul and the I as pernicious illusions. (p. 23)

Paz's essay affirms the notion, now rather stale, of the 'death of the author.' For Paz, *Renga* is affirmed as a discipline that incorporates Buddhist conceptions of the dissolution of the ego. The subversion which *Renga* brings to any thought of property in relation to the poetic voice is evident at once.

In the four sequences of quasi-sonnets there is an extraordinary interference between the four voices/languages, as each voice both takes up from the one before in the chain and lends itself to the one afterwards: '*I have become four voices that encircle / a common object, defining a self / lost in a spiral of selves, a naming*' (p. 94). What Nicholas Carbo writes of Roubaud's *E* applies equally to *Renga*: 'Unusual effects are achieved by combining the stratagem with the chance occurence within an unfamiliar and contrapuntal setting, in which the slightest change or addition alters fragile relationships between parts, and in turn alters the whole.'[6] Both texts, in effect, set themselves up as machines that exploit, to the maximum, the explosive, inspirational effects of the space of composition. This is 'a system for the production of poetic texts' (Paz, *Renga*, p. 20), 'a movement in which calculation prepares for the appearance of chance' (p. 21).

Renga is an experiment, one that even offers itself as an object of study to the ethnologist – this is how Western poets write and behave under these unaccustomed conditions. For instance, *Renga* breaks the taboo that, in the West, tends to associate writing with privacy and interiority: 'I write in front of the others, the others in front of me. Something like undressing in a café, or defecating, crying before strangers.' (Paz, *Renga*, p. 25). This side of *Renga* recalls an aspect of surrealism that Paz does not mention, the so-called 'ethnographic surrealism' practised by Bataille and Michel Leiris in the journal *Documents* in the late 1920s. This used a technique of ironic collage in which Western artefacts, texts or images were simply juxtaposed with material from other cultures. The overall effect was of a mutual defamiliarization, the European material no longer serving as a kind of supposedly universal metalanguage for humanity in general. Even though Paz's universalism seems less interesting than such a practice of collage, the experiment set up with the four poets transcends his programme. *Renga* is situated in the divide between the conflicting legacies of surrealism: the one which aims to transcend cultural alienation in some recovered form of unity and the other which opens up its own cultural context to unpredictable forms of transgression, revision or ironization.[7]

For someone coming to *Renga* for the first time, the most accessible and initially memorable part of the text is Paz's introduction, especially that long section in which he gives an impressionistic account of writing *Renga*:

> *Les mots font l'amour* [André Breton] on my page, on my bed. Beautiful and terrifying promiscuity of language. Embrace becomes struggle, struggle dance, dance a wave of the sea, the wave a wood. Dispersion of signs. Concentration of insects, black, green, blue. Ants on the paper. Volcanoes, scattered archipelagos. Ink: stars and flies. (pp. 25–6)

Many of these images actually recur in *Renga* itself, the ants, the trees, the achipelagos, the flies, the struggle that is part erotic and part destructive. Paz is quietly suggesting an interpretation of *Renga*. The poem is to be read as the record, perhaps also the enactment, of a form of peculiar and extreme experience – the struggle of the act of writing itself as a kind of purgative rite of passage. Paz's introduction to *Renga* may be compared to the account of inspiration in a chapter of that name in his *The Bow and the Lyre* (1956; rev. 1967). It is worth quoting at length:

> Here is the poet before the paper. It does not matter whether or not he has a plan, if he has meditated for a long time about what he is going to write, or if his consciousness is as empty and blank as the immaculate paper that alternately attracts and repels him. The act of writing involves, as the first movement, a separating oneself from the world, something like throwing oneself into the void. Now the poet is alone. All that was his everyday world and his usual preoccupations a moment ago, disappears. If the poet truly

wishes to write and not to perform a vague literary ceremony, his act leads him to break away from the world and to interdict everything – not excluding himself. Then there are two possibilities: everything can turn to vapor and disintegrate, lose weight, float, and finally dissolve; or else, everything can close and turn aggressively into an object without meaning, matter that is unseizable and impenetrable to the light of significance. The world opens: it is an abyss, an immense yawn; the world – the table, the wall, the goblet, the remembered faces – close and becomes a wall without fissures. In both cases, the poet is left alone, without a world to lean on. It is time to create the world anew and to name again with words that menacing external vacuity: table, tree, lips, stars, nothing. But the words have evaporated too, they have slipped away. We are surrounded by the silence that precedes the word. Or the other side of silence: the senseless and untranslatable murmur, 'the sound and the fury,' the prattle, the noise that does not say anything, that only says: nothing. In being left without a world, the poet has been left without words. Perhaps, at that instant, he recoils and draws back: he wishes to remember language, to take from within it all that he learned, those beautiful words with which, a moment before, he made his way in the world and which were like keys that opened every door for him. But there is no longer a backward, there is no longer a within. The poet thrown forward, tense and attentive, is literally outside himself. And like him, the words are beyond, always beyond, put to flight as soon as he grazes them. Thrown out of himself, he will never be able to be one with the words, one with the world, one with himself.[7]

This passage from the pre-orientalist Paz combines Romantic, surrealist and existentialist ideas. The dissolution of the personality recalls Sartre on human freedom, the argument that we have no determinate being. Existentialism with its emphasis on the historicity, contingency and ungrounded character of human finitude provides a attractive way of articulating the crisis of subjectivity undergone in composition. For Paz, inspiration is nothing other than an experience of the structure of aspiration inherent to the very temporalizing of consciousness, a 'mortal leap' into being itself. It opens upon the space that precedes, as it were, any particular determination of the self as such and such, the emptiness of a potentiality. Such existentialism is a basis of Paz's difference from Breton: 'The difficulties experienced by spirits such as Novalis and Breton [in conceptualizing inspiration]', he writes:

may perhaps lie in their conception of man as something given, that is, as the master of a nature: poetic creation is an operation during which the poet plucks or extracts certain words from within him. Or, if one utilizes the opposite hypothesis, from the substratum of the poet, at certain privileged moments, words pour out. Now, there is no such substratum, man is not a thing and even less a static, motionless thing, in whose depths lie stars and serpents, jewells and viscous animals' (p. 158).

This existential argument, however, forms for Paz only part of a more familiar dialectic of self-dissolution then reconfiguration through the mediation of some more fundamental principle. The breakdown of received determinants of the self is also an encounter with that 'constitutive otherness' that is yet our own being, an as yet faceless muse calling on us to become what we may be: 'we can come out of ourselves, *go beyond ourselves to the encounter of ourselves*' (p. 161).

Paz's argument in 'Inspiration' is Nietzschean in its conception of the space of composition as a kind of desert, a solitude in which all received determinations fall away and make possible a violent but creative transvaluation. For Paz, however, such a crisis is understood as a return to an originary, undetermined being as source of all enunciation. 'Anterior to creation, the poet as such does not exist. Nor after it. He is a poet because of the poem. The poet is a creation of the poem as much as the poem is a creation of the poet' (p. 151). Paz offers *Renga* as a meditation that returns poetry and language itself to their sources, towards an original *poiesis* or an *Ür-Sprache*. All poems, according to Paz, 'say the same thing. They reveal an act that is repeated ceaselessly: that, the incessant destruction and creation of man, his language and his world' (p. 161). The writer, becoming other, 'recognises his original being, prior to the fall or the plunge into the world, prior to the split into self and "other"'. Tomlinson seems to be recalling such ideas when he writes of

> this subterranean Babel, babble and beginning place, place that for the first time is weighed and heard incarnate, as word on word.

(p. 88)

This idea recurs in the text in the motif of the poets' discovering America, another 'melting pot', as in the sonnet of which Tomlinson is sole author at the end of section III. *Renga* is messianic in the high modernist tradition. It presents itself as attempting a mutual ascesis that will open upon linguistic utopia, a place of revitalized language and relationship. If inspiration, in its Romantic form, has often been utopianist in its anticipation of a renewed sense of community in the future, *Renga*, by making each poet both writer and audience simultaneously, would try to incarnate such a renewal in its own present. Paz could also be recalling his account of the Mexican *fiesta* as a communal place and event in which 'past and future at last are reconciled' and the barriers of individuality break down (*El laberinto de la soledad*).[8]

Let us look now at a full section of *Renga*, relating it to these questions of language and translation. This is the weirdly beautiful section II:5:

> *(mi distendo sopra il tuo corpo, come queste parole*
> *sopra il secondo verso di un sonetto rovesciato:*
> *ti stringo con le deboli dita di queste mie parentesi)*
>
> *je te serre sans force avec de l'ozone avec de la paille*
> *je répète ta musique au début de chaque laisse*
> *jour à jour (les nuits sont cette* canso capfinida*)*
>
> *abres y cierras (paréntesis) los ojos como este texto*
> *da, niega, da (labios, dientes, lengua) sus sentidos:*
>
> in this branchwork labyrinth of glance and feature,
> these liners that are life-lines,
> these veins vines.

(p. 64)

> [(I stretch myself out over your body, like these words
>   along the second line of a sonnet inside out:
>   I grasp you with the weak fingers of these brackets of
>   mine)
>
> I grasp you without force with ozone with straw
> I repeat your music at the start of each *laisse*
> day by day (the nights are this *canso capfinida*)
>
> you open and close (brackets) your eyes, and this text
> gives, denies, gives (lips, teeth, tongue) its meanings
>
> in this branchwork labyrinth of glance and feature
> these lines that are life–lines,
> these veins vines.]

(p. 65).

The first thing one notes is the difficulty of *Renga*, not just a certain linguistic obscurity not unknown in modern poetry but a perplexity as to the very mode of reading – symbolic, surrealist? – one ought to try to perform. European literature has no established rubric for the reading of a chain-poem and one cannot, overnight, hope to internalize the conventions at work when a Japanese reads a renga, even assuming that would be one pertinent solution. One question is this: Does one read each section, one at a time, as a self-contained unit, and then move on to the next one, seeing, for example the French section above as an answer of some sort to the Italian section before it, then the Spanish as an answer to those two and so on? Alternatively, does one assume the whole poem here forms a coherent whole such that one can read the first section with reference to the last, to which it might seem to be leading, although one might remember that the last section did not yet exist when the first was written? Having no inherited means of reading a chain-poem, a Western reader will oscillate between reading *Renga* in ways constructed by two more familiar genres, the dialogue on the one hand and the lyric on the other. What one actually reads (at least in the case of a literate Westerner) is constructed, to an undecidable degree, by the oscillation between these genres. This is also, of course, the problem faced by each writer at each point of the chain.

The section of *Renga* just quoted is, at first reading, the most high Romantic and utopian of *Renga*'s sections. It moves through each of the four voices, exploiting the image of writing as love and love as an act of writing, until it affirms what seems to be a trans-individual unity. The poets and/or the lines of their poem are like branches or twigs on one vine tree (*'these lines that are life-lines / these veins vines'*). In this process the word 'you' – the addressee of each section, already indeterminate in line one (is it the poem or some other lover, or both at once?) – gathers, as it moves forward, a host of possible senses. The plurality and indeterminacy of this 'you', as a multiple and unstable figure projected by this bizarre space of composition, clearly divorces and distinguishes it from the traditional relation of male poet to mediating female muse. 'You' is, most apparently, the poem itself, the lover whose invocation is an act of love on the part of each poet. Alternatively, the addressee is another of the four poets, the one from whom the section concerned has been received or the one to whom it will pass on . Hence Roubaud, receiving the poem from Sanguineti, identifies the Italian with his language: *'je te serre sans force avec de l'ozone avec de la paille / je répète ta musique au début de chaque laisse ...'* (*canso* is

Provençal for madrigal; *capfinida* I am still unable to trace). This section, then, admits of a simple interpretation in terms of self-reference; the whole poem, or event, is a '*branchwork labyrinth of glance and feature.*' In Paz's section the poem becomes a figure of sexual dalliance or flirtation, a simultaneous giving and denying of meaning: '*abres y cierras (paréntesis) los ojos como este texto / da, niega, da (labios, dientes, lengua) sus sentidos.*' Finally, in Tomlinson's section, the poem and poets become branches of one tree.

However, numerous aspects of sonnet II:5 are recalcitrant to the utopian reading to which the last section directs us. The poem repeatedly engages with the possibility of meaninglessness. The suggestion of sexual dalliance is figured in terms of bodily organs of communication '(*labios, dientes, lengua*)' – meaning reduced to physical movement. The analogy of watching someone speaking an unfamiliar tongue too quickly inevitably suggests itself here as the very situation *Renga* repeatedly confronts and intensifies. This is not a return to the sources of language, but a foregrounding of the fragility of the act of positing meaning upon a potential chaos.

The reduction of meaning to non-cognitive sensory phenomena (language to noise, writing to shapes, reading to seeing) is also an issue in the functioning of parentheses in this section. Parentheses become, as well as the familiar marks of punctuation, the closed fingers of a weird embrace in this act of writing/love. They are also eyelids opening and closing. Both these figures depend upon the physical appearance of parentheses on the page rather than on their grammatical function. Both uses could be called self-reflexive, though in a rather peculiar way. Sanguineti's lines, in which parentheses are said to be like the fingers of an embrace clasping the lover, are themselves in parenthesis: '(*mi distendo sopra il tuo corpo, come queste parole / sopra il secondo verso di un sonnetto rovesciato:/ti stringo con le deboli dita di queste mie parentesi*).' By implication, the poem itself is what is grasped in the weak fingers of the brackets – the parentheses to be seen at either end of the three lines as well as read within them as the word *parentesi*. Brackets do have the shape of grippers. This interchange of self and/as other is peculiarly apt to the plurivocity of *Renga*. Moreover, Sanguineti's section is this twisting movement, rather than being simply about such a movement: the second line of a sonnet turned inside out. This actually says no more than, for example, the stock opening of a child's letter – 'I am writing this letter to you.' This intransitive movement of language says only its own act. It is not a meditation on the sources of language except in the sense of making a game out of the contingencies of physical marks and the layout of the page.

Paz's section, comparing parentheses to the eyelids of the poem's phantasmatic and unspecified lover, is, if anything, more virtuoso than Sanguineti's. The word '*paréntesis*', appearing as the only content of the parentheses, makes this phrase another movement between act and description. It is a fluttering movement, like the blinking of eyelids, that both gives and denies meaning, since the only characteristic of this meaning is the fluttering of (non) reference itself (reference without a referent). Again, brackets on the page are the shape of an eye in profile. Similarly, in Paz's second line, the terms in parenthesis '(*labios, dientes, lengua*)' enact an analogous hiatus, for the physical organs of utterance supplant here any spoken meaning. It is a reduction of signification that seems to acknowledge the recurrent eclipse of writing by physical, non-signifying marks, and simultaneously, the *impossibility* of not reading or positing a meaning of some sort, even if this is taking the poem as being about its own status or the event that conditions it ('Nor does the knowledge of this impossibility make it less impossible').[9] In fact the very virtuosity of section II:5 suggests also resistance to the disorienting and multiplicitous space of composition that opens between the poets, precisely by so thoroughly and cleverly thematizing and personifying its effects – a defensive trope that we also observed in the practice of automatic writing (p. 202). Like Breton's '*Toujours pour la première fois*', this section also illustrates the resources of the love lyric as a genre capable of recuperating contingent effects of the signifier in psychological terms.

It is not difficult to be critical of *Renga*'s programme – all the poets are men, three of the four languages are Romance languages, none are Eastern European etc. Other tensions may be traced in a section of Paz's introduction where he writes about how he would like to spread the practice of rengas among other poets, to 'all the idioms of the West' (p. 28). Paz excludes non-Western poets from the project in the interests of a shared tradition. He wants to maintain a certain coherence or unity in the renga, based on that common horizon, yet he does not seem to see that these notions of coherence and unity, unless articulated further, can only remain European aesthetic notions that it would surely have been more interesting to put at stake (even assuming that European culture does have the kind of unity Paz ascribes to it).

Renga is also a testament to discord, one that may seem to expose any act of reading or composition as both an act of power and a negotiation with the possibility of meaninglessness. By affirming translation as a mechanism of poetic creation, Paz's introduction directs us less to the separate sections of *Renga* than to the movement from one to the other (p. 20). This is 'translation' not as the would-be faithful reproduction of a text in another language, but as the element of interaction between the four poets as readers of each others' work in the movements of the chain in a multi-lingual space of composition. Trans-lation envelops each section as its multi-readability in relation to three non-native speakers. In addition, since no one language serves as a frame of reference within which to situate the others, every language in *Renga* is 'foreign', outside its native ground. Likewise, no national identity is predicated for the reader; 'it makes *all* readers equally foreigners, together' (Edwards, p. 120). This has two effects, which are paradoxical in their complementarity. First, when a language is juxtaposed to the others it seems to come into its own – Italian seems all the more Italian for its placement next to English, French and Spanish. Second, in *Renga*, as each native-language speaker reads/translates/interprets/the foreign text passed to him by his predecessor, his language becomes like a palimpsest of incalculable depth, continually fading. There are interference patterns, especially at the levels of sound and accent. In section IV:1 'French' comes very close to coming to pieces so overwhelming have become the 'patterns of interference' from the preceding languages. It is like the 'noise' of information theory. What emerges is not the dominance of any one language over the others, or some shared originary language, but a hybrid creole working through each. This clamour without an author imposes its rhythm across linguistic divisions in a resonance of sounds and letters.

The trope of language

What is most striking in *Renga* is that it repeatedly engages with what Marc Redfield has called (speaking of the work of Paul de Man) the 'trope of language' – the trope whereby certain marks or sounds are taken as language, eliding the possibility that they may have been generated meaninglessly.[10] Such a trope, evidently, is constitutive of language as language and enables meaning to emerge from out of the substratum of the act of enunciation.

De Man's argument is that the positing that something is a

language, is referential, is (a) a necessary condition for meaning and interpretation and (b) an act that always remains tainted by a certain violence and contingency.[11] *Renga* actually serves to clarify these abstruse points, partly because it reminds us that the phrase 'trope of language' is a misnomer. It should be the trope of a language. A series of marks or sounds is posited as Spanish, as French, as English but not, of course, all three at the same time. In *Renga*, however, where each language switches at every third or fourth line to another, this act of positing, normally barely perceptible, imposes itself unignorably in the disjunctive movement, for example, from French to Italian to Spanish in a single sentence. The effect is not of a singular positing of language; the disjunctions are plural and diverse (English after French is not the same as English after Italian, nor Spanish before French the same as Spanish before English). The question, 'which language?', is never closed. Oddly de Man, with his concern for effects of power in language, barely touches on the question of translation. Nevertheless, as *Renga* suggests, the movement from one tongue to another may in itself register the non-cognitive substrate of language.

This also reminds us that, despite the idealistic universalism of Paz's preface, languages must at some point be mutually exclusive and even in an antagonistic relation to each other. It is also possible to argue that languages are mutually exclusive in so far as each is, implicitly, the positing of a community of speakers and hence a claim to territory.

The final fascinating aspect of Paz's experiment is the least conspicuous: *Renga* is a text written almost entirely *in situ*. It thus raises issues about a poem's 'setting', Paris and the underground room as a rendezvous of four languages. The 'setting' of a text is normally a projection of language; the landscape near Tintern Abbey was not where Wordsworth composed his famous poem, despite the fictional scene of enunciation given in the text. In *Renga*, however, the text offers itself repeatedly as a space of composition presented as a form of possible utopia, a new-found land or encounter of differing languages. This unique realm is also seen to metamorphose the immediate environment of the poem. The four poets also open themselves to the chances that present themselves in their environment, contingencies such as a man looking for a lost suitcase who bursts into the hotel basement where the poets are working (Introduction, pp. 24–5; section III:3). The etymology of 'contingency' suggests a site where two places, frontiers, or orders *touch*, to unpredictable effect. These chance effects and happenings

from out of the city come to be personified as a muse, characterized, familiarly, as an unpredictable female figure. This uncertain
agency in a space of composition also embraces the environment as
a kind of latent calligraphy:

> The city also became Persephone, rousing from its darkness into a
> season of possibilities. It became woman, the other, the outside, but
> the outside in the process of being metamorphosed, (while resisting
> metamorphosis) by the conditions of our waking dream.
>
> (Tomlinson, p. 38)

The metamorphosis takes two forms. On the one hand, language is
tending to become itself a mere thing. There are numerous images
of insects on the page: 'Dispersion of signs./Concentration of
insects, black, green, blue./Ants on the paper' (Paz, Introduction,
p. 25); 'Across my page run graceful mice in their ring-a-roses' (Paz,
p. 45). At the same time the environment projected by the poem is
one in which things also take on the status of a peculiar writing.
Take Tomlinson's contribution to the first sonnet:

> *the gestureless speech of things unfreezes*
> *as the shadow, gathering under the vertical*
> *raised lip of the column's fluting, spreads*
> *its inkstain into the wrinkles of weathered stone*: (p. 42)

In this unstable space of composition, meaning both threatens to
abandon writing as a series of mere shapes and also extends itself to
render objects the particles of an alien writing: the environment
becomes '*a frame of nearnesses / surrounding things half-seen: thick,
bare / calligraphy and confusion of boughs on air*' (Tomlinson, p. 70).

One effect of this simultaneous deficiency and claustrophobia
of meaning is that it is impossible to decide on the import of certain
figures of speech in the poem. For instance, might the phrase 'traffic
of syllables in search of a home' (Paz, p. 73) be a metaphor for the
Parisian afternoon traffic rather than for the circulation of syllables
in the text? Is writing the tenor or the vehicle here? This floating
effect between modes of signification is ubiquitous in *Renga* and the
major source of its difficulty. The border between what one might
read as referring to objects and what referring to signs blurs in
renewed and multiple tropes of language. *Renga* is a space of criss-
crossing borders, less a no-man's-land than an overcrowded frontier
in which lines of demarcation have formed a Moebius structure.
There is only a difference in degree, not kind, between the inter-
lingual puns in *Renga* (for example, Roubaud's '*poisse*' ('makes

sticky') become Tomlinson's *'poise'* in section IV:2) and what may be hypothesized as the passage from things or sounds into the oscillating creole of the poem, as in the following extract:

> (*Rumor de río en cadenas: el metro.*
> *Yo piense en ríos de lado nácar*
> *que sobre immensas páginas de polvo – Punjab, Bihar,*
> *Bengala – esciben su discursu insensato ...*)

> [(Rumble of a river in chains: the metro.
> I think of rivers of nacreous mud,
> over immense pages of dust – Punjab, Bihar,
> Bengal – scribbling their senseless discourse ...)]

$$(\text{I:5; pp. 50–1})$$

Once again this passage seems to offer itself in terms of the trope of language (the sound of the metro, the onomatopoeic words – *Rumor de río en cadenas* – and then the image of the rivers as foreign writers 'scribbling their senseless discourse'). The oscillation at work throughout *Renga* may seem to be particularly legible here, giving the Parisian environment, as a source of contingencies, something of the status of a latent fifth language or participant. *Renga* blurs notions of agency in a multi-lingual space in which boundaries between contingency and intentionality become impossible to draw.

In conclusion, *Renga*'s experiment with the act of composition recalls the ambivalence already traced in surrealist practice. Its modernist ideal of a return to the purity of a lost beginning gives way to a 'post-modern' crisis of legitimation, a space of composition that maximizes the sense of uncertainty as to agency and principles of construction, or interpretation. The Romantic or surrealist idealism of a utopian or festive originary language breaks down. *Renga* becomes, despite itself, an instantiation of the possible radical practice adumbrated at the end of the last chapter: 'an experience of that which does not obey the reigning order of experience ... the ordeal ... of what is given neither in the arrangement of the world nor in the form of the work, and thus announcing itself on the basis of the real as *derangement* and the basis of the work as *unworking*' (Blanchot).

Blanchot's work, for the second time, has been presented in terms of possibilities opened up but largely foreclosed by surrealist experimentation. It is time to look at Blanchot on inspiration more closely.

Notes

1 *Renga: A Chain of Poems*, trans. Charles Tomlinson (London: Penguin, 1979). This edition includes introductions by Claude Roy, Paz, Tomlinson and Roubaud.

2 Paz, *Alternating Current* [1967], trans. Helen Lane (New York: Seaver Books, 1990), p. 74.

3 Michael Edwards, 'Collaborations', in *Charles Tomlinson: Man and Artist*, ed. Kathleen O'Gorman (Columbia: University of Missouri Press, 1988), pp. 104–24. Timothy Clark, '*Renga*: Multi-Lingual Poetry and Questions of Place', *Sub-Stance* 68 (1992), 32–45.

4 Reprinted as 'André Breton, or the Search for the Beginning', in Paz, *On Poets and Others*, trans. Michael Schmidt (New York: Seaver Books, 1986), pp. 66–78.

5 Requoted from J. H. Matthews, review of *Selected Poems of Octavio Paz* (1963), *Comparative Literature Studies*, 2 (1965), pp. 97–100, p.100.

6 Nicholas Andrew Carbo, 'The Poets of "*Renga*": Octavio Paz, Jacques Roubaud, Edoardo Sanguineti, and Charles Tomlinson', Diss. New York University, 1976, p. 119.

7 Paz, *The Bow and the Lyre: The Poem: The Poetic Revelation and History* [2nd edn, 1967], trans. Ruth L. Simmons. (Austin: University of Texas Press, 1973), p. 159.

8 See Jason Wilson, *Octavio Paz: a Study of his Poetics* (Cambridge: Cambridge University Press, 1979), p. 51.

9 Paul de Man, *The Rhetoric of Romanticism* (New York: Columbia University Press, 1984), p. 118.

10 Redfield, 'Humanizing de Man', *Diacritics*, 19:2 (Summer 1989), 35–53.

11 Paul de Man, *The Resistance to Theory* (Minneapolis: University of Minnesota Press, 1986), p. 42.

CHAPTER 10

Contradictory passion: inspiration in Blanchot's *The Space of Literature* (1955)

People do not understand what a temptation there is, if you cannot bear anything not very good, to transfer your operations to a region where form is everything. Perfection of a certain kind may be there attained, or ar least approached, without knocking yourself to pieces, but to attain or approach perfection in the region of thought and feeling, and to unite this with perfection of form, demands not merely an effort and a labour, but an actual tearing of oneself to pieces, which one does not readily consent to (although one is sometimes forced to it) unless one can devote one's whole life to poetry. (Matthew Arnold, letter to his sister, September, 1858).

In *The Space of Literature* (1955; trans. 1982)[1] Maurice Blanchot offers what is surely the fullest, least idealizing and most detailed theory of literary inspiration in Western literature, vindicating in the process the fruitfulness of this ancient and peculiar concept. By definition inspiration finds its provenance outside or beyond the consciousness of the writer; in Blanchot the outside from which inspiration comes is, counterintuitively, both the emerging work itself and, literally, nowhere. Inspiration forms a complex and contradictory passion, one that does not belong to the writer, but takes possession from out of nothing.

The pivotal section of *The Space of Literature*, 'Inspiration' (pp. 163–87), is the culmination of a series of studies that take issue with the way post-Romantic writers (especially Valéry, Mallarmé, Kafka and Rilke) valorize the act of writing as giving access to a unique realm of human possibility. The Romantic tradition of attempting to appropriate inspiration as a form of human power may be said to come to an end in Blanchot, and though the Romantic tradition has continued with many writers, it must be seen as doing so as an anachronism. Blanchot's argument also provides an account of the paradoxical and contradictory mode of being of the literary work that remains unsurpassed in its detail and in the rigour with which it traces the emergence of the work in its singularity. Blanchot's study presupposes throughout a certain valorization of the unique and the original in relation to the literary work of art. At the same time, he can be seen as taking these Romantic and modernist criteria of value to a radical extreme at which they undergo a qualitative transformation, one which justifies the increased recognition of Blanchot's place in the genealogy of deconstruction.[2] What remains so striking about *The Space of Literature*, however, is the way this transformation takes place, not through concern with critical problems of interpretation, but through a relentless meditation on the crisis of subjectivity undergone by the writer in the process of writing.

The Space of Literature invites its reader to participate in a deepening series of engagements with literary inspiration, moving almost stage by stage between general meditations on the writer's predicament and close readings of Kafka, Mallarmé and Rilke respectively, and especially of their thinking on the relations between the act of writing and death. My purpose here in schematizing the account of inspiration to emerge from this process (sometimes even from passages widely separated) cannot but repeat Blanchot's own unavoidable distortion in presenting in narrative form a topic whose force and complexity is precisely to resist a linear presentation.

Blanchot seeks to elucidate what he terms the characteristic features of a writer's 'experience', traceable as the work itself. This is not a reference to some sort of biographical decoding, however. To read the work by reference to the extra-literary is, for Blanchot, not only problematic as a possibility, but it also makes up a denial of the real force of the literary. This demands that one be attentive to the work as the site of the writer's engagement and struggle with writing itself and the existential space (provisionally speaking) projected by the work-in-process. For Blanchot the emergent work is placed in a peculiar dialectic between its inherent demands and constraints and their effect upon the writer, whose relation to the work is one of inevitable misconstruction, for literary inspiration is incalculable, a series of unanticipated leaps.

Literature as a limit-experience

In *The Infinite Conversation* (1969) Blanchot outlines the notion of a 'limit-experience':

> The limit-experience is the response that man encounters when he has decided to put himself radically in question. This decision involving all being expresses the impossibility of ever stopping, whether it be at some consolation or some truth, at the interests or the results of an action, or with the certitudes of knowledge and belief.[3]

In *The Space of Literature*, literary inspiration is precisely such a limit-experience, an experience of insecurity that enacts a crisis in the relation to beings as a whole. Blanchot's notion of literature as a total experience has been interpreted and contextualized in various ways; in terms of his complex relation to Levinas[4] and to Bataille,[5] his repudiation of aspects of Heidegger's thinking[6] and the labyrinthine relation between his work and Derrida's.[7] *The Space of Literature* in particular, is a transgressive reworking of Martin Heidegger's work on the affective in *Being and Time* (1927) and elsewhere,[8] especially his paper 'The Origin of the Work of Art' (1950).[9] Blanchot recalls directly the extraordinary philosophical privilege which Heidegger gives to certain affective states, fundamental moods which he sharply, if problematically, distinguishes from mere personal feeling by their quasi-transcendental status in disclosing the totality of being. The later Heidegger characterizes fundamental moods in historical terms, as both determined by and determining the epochality of being. 'Astonishment', for instance, was such a state for the Greeks (philosophy itself finding its provenance in this transport and the questioning it provokes);[10] while doubt and the desire for certainty, hence control, are determinants in post-Cartesian Europe. For Blanchot, however, the literary passion as a limit-experience, while it emerges in a pure form only in the relatively recent past, is both acultural and ahistorical. In this respect he remains always closer to the early Heidegger who describes anxiety (*Angst*) in *Being and Time* as a shattering of human being, a crisis of the human essence. Anxiety is a mood in which whomever it possesses is anxious not about any particular item or aspect of life, but about the totality of existence as the question of its own contingency, and about death as the possibility of the impossibility of existing. Anxiety is thus less an expression of individual subjectivity than, as the (self)questioning of its very essence, its *syncope*, paralysis. At its extreme this total question pitches *Dasein* beyond any sense of history, culture or environment, or anything that still serves to define *Dasein* as being-in-the-world. Hubert Dreyfus observes that Heidegger is justified when he writes not '*Dasein* is anxious' but, tautologically, 'anxiety is anxious.'[11] There is here neither 'you' nor 'I' only a 'someone' (cf. *Space of Literature*, p. 31). Similarly, literature as a total experience, for Blanchot, is 'foreign to all culture', possessing an 'a-cultural part ... to which one does not accommodate oneself easily' (*The Infinite Conversation*, p. 346).

Blanchot's is not the familiar claim that literature has some universal value that remains invariant across time. Rather, the literary is radically ahistorical as the bearer of a movement of transcendence that holds the text open as the question of its own nature, a question that any reading in terms of historical context could only foreclose.[12] Heidegger's notion of the *Grundbestimmungen* is adapted in two ways in *The Space of Literature*. Firstly it serves to demarcate the emergence of literature historically, in relation to a certain crisis in conceptions of history and of art. It is at the time of the Romantics and the German idealists, Blanchot argues, that literature ceases to fulfil any clear or agreed social function, becoming a 'thing of the past' in Hegel's provocative phrase. Literature becomes now its own question, the search for its own nature and origin. Blanchot asks: 'why, at the moment when through the force of the times art disappears, does it appear for the first time as a search in which something essential is at stake ... ?' (*Space of Literature*, p. 220). Blanchot takes up Hölderlin's characterization of his (and our) age as, for the poet, a *dürftiger Zeit*, 'time of distress' (*Space of Literature*, p. 38, p. 75, p. 83, p. 177, pp. 245–6) but does not read into this an implicit promise of renewal as Heidegger does.[13] For Blanchot the very concept of literature as its own question situates it in a perpetual crisis of belatedness. Literature becomes the institution of the limit-experience, which is also to say, one in which the nature of literature and received criteria of understanding become at stake anew in each work. *The Space of Literature* gives us then a seeming paradox, a notion of literature as a passion, but as a crisis in subjectivity that makes up a strong repudiation of any theory of art that would recuperate the work as an expression of writer's ideas, emotions or, *pace* Sartre, existential project.[14]

The work's emergence

I turn then to the other way in which Blanchot interprets the account of the poet's time as that of distress, his notion of literary inspiration in general; for '*The time of distress* designates the time which in all times is proper to art' (*Space of Literature*, p. 246). My concern here is less with Blanchot's specific readings of Kafka and others than with the general account of inspiration to emerge from them.

One could hardly be further from an aesthetic of *mimesis* than one is in Blanchot. The artist, even while gazing at the environment with a view to the art-work, does not see a realm of things to be imitated. If they are 'inspirational' in any way it is in so far as the exigency of the work is already in play as an perceptual *Stimmung*, determining what appears to the artist. The work might be called an emergent affect, without (as yet) determinacy in any subject or material:

> it is because, through a radical reversal, he already belongs to the work's requirements that, looking at a certain object, he is by no means content to *see* it as it might be if it were out of use, but makes of the object the point through which the work's requirements pass and, consequently, the moment at which the possible is attenuated, the notions of value and utility effaced, and the world 'dissolves.' (*Space of Literature*, p. 47)

The writer becomes involved with the drawing pull of the work-to-be-achieved as something which does not yet exist except as this peculiar exigency, drawing memories and perceptions into itself. Above all, the work begins to be a work when a stage is reached at which the linguistic structure is something other and more pressing than the mere externalization of personal effort or expression, when it takes on a certain force of speaking for itself, an authority whose law may dictate, impersonally, the work's future unfolding. It is the moment at which

> that which is glorified in the work *is* the work, when the work ceases in some way to have been made, to refer back to someone who made it, but gathers all the essence of the work in the fact that now there is a work – a beginning and initial decision – this moment which cancels the author ... (*Space of Literature*, p. 200)

This moment – if it can be called a moment – is elusive and scarcely definable, and Blanchot is certainly not outlining any sort of writer's guide! The writer's relation to the work is defined as no less than the impossibility of reading it; he or she oscillates anxiously between being too close to the work and being too alienated by it.

It appears either as a personal externalization only or as an object whose otherness defies further progress, for the work's emergent laws are neither necessarily always recognized nor submitted to. The writer's experience of the work is notoriously one of frustration, of repeated false starts along with sudden bursts of ease or insouciance. For Blanchot, clearly, the intentionalist fallacy is multiply fallacious. Even as the writer submits to its exigency, the work's coming-to-be remains a process of inevitable misconstruction and unanticipated effects. The writer's predicament is often the basis for a little recognized aspect of Blanchot's work, its humane comedy of understatement:

> It is true: the writer is willing to put the highest value on the meaning his work has for him alone. Then it does not matter whether the work is good or bad, famous or forgotten. If circumstances neglect it, he congratulates himself, since he only wrote it to negate circumstances. But when a book that comes into being by chance, produced in a moment of idleness and lassitude, without value or significance, is suddenly made into a masterpiece by circumstantial events, what author is not going to take the credit for the glory himself ... [and] see his own worth in that glory ... the working of his mind in providential harmony with his time?[15]

The work then should become, at some 'moment', an affirmation which takes on the force of projecting the law of its own continuing enunciation. This might be schematized as a first aspect of the complex, even contradictory, leap of inspiration in Blanchot. The writer relates to the work as much as the road to inspiration as to inspiration as the road to the work:

> one writes only if one reaches that instant which nevertheless one can only approach in the space opened by the movement of writing. To write, one has to write already. In this contradiction are situated the essence of writing, the snag in the experience, and inspiration's leap. (*Space of Literature*, p. 176)

Another of the contradictory tensions in inspiration concerns the work's relation to the reader. The quotation given earlier (*The Space of Literature*, p. 200), describing the moment when the text ceases to be something made and becomes a work, ends as follows: 'this moment which cancels the author is also the moment when, as the book opens to itself, the reading finds its origin in this opening.' Blanchot is not yet referring to reading in the sense of the act of an empirical agent, but as a structure in the economy of the emergent work. As soon as any mark is committed to paper it is immediately also read, working unpredictably beyond the author's horizon. This moment of escape is necessary to the work's transcendence of mere authorial self-expression:

> the work is a work only when it becomes the intimacy shared by someone who writes it and someone who reads it, a space violently opened up by the contest between the power to speak and the power to hear. (*Space of Literature*, p. 37)

This moment also brings dangers of its own. Composition is less a struggle between world and earth in Heidegger's terms than between writer, work, and reader. One danger here is this. A writer whose work is produced merely for a predetermined public betrays the nature of literary inspiration, no less than the writer who insists on still instrumentalizing language as self-expression. Blanchot argues that a work written only to be read can say nothing fundamentally new. Thus even as the writer is engaged by the work's emergent self-affirmation, pressing itself forward according to the law of its own emergent properties, he or she must resist not only the desire for self-expression but also the hypothetical reader for whom the words may already have another and alien signification; for both could foreclose the work's emergence on its own singular and unprecedented terms.

In *The Infinite Conversation*, that movement in writing whereby it always differs from itself, exceeding itself in an essential detour or errancy of sense, is identified simply as 'poetry' (p. 23). The poetic is that 'turning' in language whereby, for instance, a word alters in the movement of dialogue, even if the interlocutors merely repeat the 'same' word. In *The Space of Literature* Blanchot construes this force in language that always says more or other than what can be anticipated, and which can never be silenced by analogy with Levinas's notion of the *il y a* [the 'there is] – the idea of an anonymous and contentless affirmation, incessant existence without determinacy or subject.[16] Even as the writing moves about that point at which the work will achieve self-affirmation, cancelling authorial intention, the writer is engaged with a struggle with both the reader and also with this movement, always present in language, of errancy, of signifying without form. The demand made by the work on the writer is thus less to instrumentalize language in a certain way, than, suppressing the urge to personal expression, to impose a certain silence, form or limit upon that 'giant murmuring' upon which language opens (*Space of Literature*, p. 27) (a distant variant of that space of self-repeating formulae that was language for the oral poet). 'The tone [of a writer's oeuvre] is not the writer's voice, but the intimacy of the silence he imposes upon the word' (*Space of Literature*, p. 27). The writer then is at the crossroads of contradictory but simultaneous forces. These must be endured in the emergent work so as to produce a 'worklessness' [*désoeuvrement*] that is truly poetic, viz. something other than the product, the work, of its conditions of creation, but transcending them all. In *The Infinite Conversation* Blanchot goes so far as to risk the following formulation:

> I would even say that every important literary work is important to the extent that it puts more directly and more purely to work the meaning of this [poetic] turn; a turning that, at the moment when it is about to emerge, makes the work pitch strangely. This is a work in which worklessness, as its always decentered center, holds sway: the absence of work. (p. 32)

Blanchot's notion of the literary space thus differs radically from the phenomenological notion outlined in Georges Poulet's *The Interior Distance* (1952)[17] a study with which *The Space of Literature* is in dialogue (*Space of Literature*, pp. 43–4, p. 114). Blanchot does not see the work as an articulation of that intentional and affective field that makes up a writer's life-world. The literary space is one in which (like the Freudian unconscious) '[c]ontradictions do not exclude each-other ... nor are they reconciled' (*Space of Literature*, p. 130). It opens instead from out of the antagonistic exigencies of the writer, reader and work, bearing an affect that is *sui generis*, touching the writer finally as a mode of dispossession or dispersal. The literary is an experience of impossibility, the unpredictable result of contradictory factors almost entirely beyond authorial control. Yet these same factors are also the condition for the emergence of the work as something radically novel: 'it is the *impossibility of literature that preserves literature as a possibility*' (Simon Critchley, '*Il y a*', p. 87).

The desire of the origin

Apart from his giving an account of the emergence of the literary work unprecedented in its detail and patience, Blanchot's account deserves consideration for announcing aspects of arguments that have since become familiar in deconstructive criticism – the need to affirm the work as an emergent singularity which exceeds received criteria of interpretation and, as we shall see, the need to recognize an antagonism between the constative and the performative dimensions of the text. Blanchot's notion of inspiration may even seem unique, perhaps timely, in the way these notions are affirmed, which is not through discrediting the subjective element of literary production but by making the contradictory and paradoxical passion of writing (a double genitive) his very means of approach to what he terms the non-phenomenal space of literature. To illustrate this further let us consider in more detail that 'moment' in the work's coming-to-be that annuls the writer, allowing the work to affirm its exigency to emerge as a singular and impersonal affirmation. 'Inspiration' elaborates this in terms of the myth of Orpheus and Eurydice,[18] the avowed 'centre' of *The Space of Literature*. Everything decisive in the argument bears on this transformation; my presentation follows Blanchot's by consisting of a series of visits and revisits to it at increasing degrees of intensity.

The transformation is, above all, a matter of reversed intentionality. It is one in which the writer, no longer relating to the work as the correlate of his or her own intentional act, becomes *fascinated* by the work's emergent exigencies. These compel and possess authorial intention, reversing the vectors of effective action in the text's appearance. Language, no longer quite an instrument or a sign to be referred elsewhere, becomes in this movement not the language of imagery in the familiar sense but 'the image of language' (*Space of Literature*, p. 34). Jean Pfeiffer writes:

> One cannot comport oneself in front of the imaginary space, because we are not capable of doing anything with the image, since it precisely reverses the relation we are able to have with the object, for, far from being the possessor ... we are on the contrary the possessed.[19]

The language of the work is now become a language in which no one is expressed or addressed. Although there is a proximity between Blanchot's language here and Heidegger's, the work's force is not an event of phenomenological disclosure. Blanchot's account is more purely formal: the literary space is without content and without truth. Everything reverts to a peculiar kind of affirmation, that of a 'neutral word, which has always been said already, cannot stop its saying, and to which no hearing can be given' (*Space of Literature*, p. 51).

The work, however, is more than a merely formal object, a linguistic structure affirming its being as an impersonal artefact. Blanchot also expresses the force of reversed intentionality by describing the work as becoming a new form of passion. It is the passion, the search, for its own origin. The word 'origin' here has two aspects. Firstly, 'origin' means *Ursprung* as in Heidegger's *Der Ursprung der Kunstwerkes* ['The Origin of the Work of Art'] – origin in the sense of that whence something springs as what it is. For Heidegger, 'The artist is the origin of the work. The work is the origin of the artist' (p. 17) (i.e. it is only on the basis of an achieved work that an artist is an artist). For both work and artist, however, there is a deeper source; both find their origin in the essence of art in general. In Blanchot, however, despite his proximity to Heidegger's argument, the work does not spring from its origin any more than it is also, paradoxically, the search for this origin. The work is in quest of its source or essence. This is tantamount to saying that there is no general essence of art to be realized, either in the work or the artist; rather, in each work the question of its essential nature is open and at stake afresh. The literary, as a limit-experience, is the unfinishable crisis of its own question: 'The work always means: not knowing that art exists already, not knowing that there is already a world' (*Space of Literature*, p. 125), a position that anticipates much written more recently by J-F. Lyotard on the practice of the avant-garde, and on the sublime.[20] Moreover, this crisis may be another source of conflict between the demands of the artist and the exigency of the work. Whatever the artist may claim to know in theory or in general about art or literature, nevertheless, if it is to have any force, 'his work does not know it, and his search is ignorant of it' (*Space of Literature*, p. 56). If a writer is anxious while writing, it is partly out of 'the anxiety of this ignorance' (*Space of Literature*, p. 56). Blanchot writes, in respect of Valéry:

> Poetry is not granted the poet as a truth and a certainty against which he could measure himself. He does not know whether he is a poet, but neither does he know what poetry is, or even whether it is. It depends on him, on his search. And this dependence does not make him master of what he seeks; rather, it makes him uncertain of himself and as if nonexistent. Every work, and each moment of the work, puts everything into question all over again. (*Space of Literature*, p. 87)

It is thus that each text raises anew the question of the totality, both of art and experience. Moreover, the essence or source of the work cannot pre-exist the work itself. It lies in the future. Hence, for the writer and the reader, the work's mode of being is that of an

exigency, a passion, the appeal to be. As the maintenance and intensification of itself as a question, inspiration is a perpetual struggle
but one against, not for, security. For Blanchot the question 'why
write?' can become so intense, so acute, that the aridity of lack of
inspiration may become a limit-experience indistinguishable from
inspiration 'itself'.

'Inspiration' here may seem at odds with the notions suggested
in the first chapter (that inspiration is a psychic chiasmus in which a
plurivocal and potentially transgressive space of composition is
structured by possible relations to readers and codes of reading).
Blanchot's notion, on the other hand, affirms only all that is transgressive in the space of composition and which resists the place of
reading in the economy of the emerging work. This affirmation,
however, touches on the most problematic aspect of Blanchot's
work, i.e. his seeing in certain kinds of Romantic and post-
Romantic literature a manifestation of a literary essence supposedly
obscured by the previous subservience of literature to religious or
humanist ends. Today, he argues, 'The work is no longer innocent;
it knows whence it comes' (*Space of Literature*, p. 186). Literature's
supposed uselessness since the Romantics is said to manifest its
essentially a-cultural, *ec-static* nature, an argument that surely moves
too quickly past the multifarious kinds of cultural work that literary
texts have been made to perform over this period. Comparison with
Renga, for all its failings, also reveals just how Euro-centric
Blanchot's essentialist anti-essentialism remains. The limits of
Blanchot's approach are surely most apparent in his need to deny
much status to modes such as the realist novel or poetry in alexandrines, as opposed to those modes of writing which most easily
accommodate themselves to the notion of a limit-experience. In
fact, one might rejoin, Blanchot takes up certain conceptions of the
literary from aesthetic modernism and surrealism, and then pushes
them through to an extreme to produce a model of literary dynamics which he questionably takes to be an account of essential
questions about literature in general: the literary space as one of a
writer's encounter with, or evasion of, a certain essential meaninglessness.

Like Heidegger's essay on art, *The Space of Literature* seems to
employ a notion of causality that reads, at first sight, as one of *creatio
ex nihilo*, an apparent impossibility to which Blanchot holds fast as a
real paradox in the work's conditions of possibility. The paradox
can again be described as that of a linguistic event that seems to
establish itself, and to exist by virtue of its own pronouncement and

projection. The emergent work, for Heidegger, 'opens upon (and opens) the conditions of its own enunciation.'[21] It is through the work itself that there is cleared that open breach in the realm of things extant – a bringing forth of unconcealment – whereby the work itself appears as the thing it is:

> The event of its being created does not simply reverberate through the work; rather, the work casts before itself the eventful fact that the work is as this work, and it has constantly this fact about itself. The more essentially the work opens itself, the more luminous becomes the uniqueness of the fact that it is rather than is not. The more essentially this thrust comes into the Open, the stranger and more solitary the work becomes. ('The Origin of the Work of Art' pp. 65–6, trans. modified)

The passage already quoted on the work's force as a self-affirmation seems to recall and revise this argument (*Space of Literature*, p. 200). Blanchot differs from aspects of Heidegger's essay in two ways. Firstly, the work's exigency, for Blanchot, opens upon a literary space that has none of the historical, disclosive force that the artwork has in Heidegger as a mode of fundamental *Stimmung*. Secondly, Blanchot differs from Heidegger in the prominence he gives to the question of the affective in the movement of inspiration, a term absent from Heidegger, presumably because of its subjectivist associations. For Heidegger, the subjective existence of the writer is only of marginal importance to the emergence of the work. In a great work of art, he argues, 'the artist remains inconsequential as compared with the work, almost like a passageway that destroys itself in the creative process for the work to emerge' ('The Origin of the Work of Art', p. 40). '[D]estroys' is a strong word, yet it is left to Blanchot to pick up the implications of pain and risk-taking, often in terms that evince a proximity to the work of Georges Bataille and his notion of a pure expenditure, of abandonment to an experience intense beyond the possibility of being undergone.[22]

'Origin' in Blanchot's study carries then an affective dimension not prominent in Heidegger: it is the source of the work as the draw or pull of a point to which the work is tending. The phrase 'passion of the origin' names, among other things, a desire in the writer to possess the movement whence the work is coming forth. It is this passion, more than technical skill, that marks the writer as a writer. This is, again, a contradictory desire, since, as we saw, this movement itself already demands the writer's eclipse and the writer's imposition of silence upon the impersonal murmur of language.

The origin becomes attractive, fascinating, at the 'moment' when, escaping intentionality, the work begins to come, as it were, from itself, from its own exigency to be, emerging from a 'nowhere' which is yet the space the work projects in its unfolding; at the same time it becomes in this movement the quest for the point whence it is coming. Blanchot writes of Herman Melville: 'It is quite true that Ahab only encounters Moby Dick in Melville's novel. But it is equally correct to say that such an encounter is what enables Melville to write his novel.'[23]

> The central point of the work is the work as origin, the point which cannot be reached, yet the only one which is worth reaching.
>
> This point is the sovereign requirement. One can approach it only by means of the completed work, but one can complete the work only by means of the approach. (*Space of Literature*, pp. 54–5)

What can one say of this point? It is a virtual point, a 'vanishing point' (*Space of Literature*, p. 48), an unreality. It is replete with illusion for the writer. The writer is someone who, even while surrendering to the work's emergent demands, must also resist the seemingly magical power of the work's point of origin: 'the illusion that if one maintained contact with this point even as one came back from it to the world of possibility, "everything" could be done, "everything" could be said' (*Space of Literature*, p. 52; also p. 181). This delusion underlies, for Blanchot, the hubristic ambitions of the surrealists. Blanchot's notion of the 'origin' is a specific answer to Breton's concept of inspiration as the draw of a 'supreme point'. Nevertheless, the ambitions of 'automatic writing' also do nothing other, he argues, than give explicit form 'to the initial poetic demand' (*Space of Literature*, p. 179), viz. succumbing to the illusion that inspiration is a power to be gained or possessed, not dispossession and aridity. (This is the issue treated in Blanchot's readings of Kafka, Mallarmé and Rilke: each, even as he gives himself to the exigencies of the literary space, attempts to appropriate the movement of inspiration as a power, or to affirm it as a cultural value, and finds only, as in Blanchot's thoughts on death, the impossibility of possibility as the work's final goal and source). Moreover, it is precisely the surrender to the automatism in literary creation that produces so many second-rate works, those pale non-events always familiar in advance.

Risks and evasions

Needing to give way to inspiration, and yet resist its delusions, the writer remains in a position riven by contradiction. In this situation, deception, evasion and persons from Porlock are inevitable. *The Space of Literature* constitutes throughout an implicit answer to Sartre on writing and commitment. Elsewhere Blanchot writes that '[A]s soon as honesty comes into play in literature, imposture is already present. Here bad faith is truth, and the greater the pretension to morality and seriousness, the more surely will mystification and deceit triumph' ('Literature and the Right to Death', p. 28). Blanchot outlines several traps or risks in particular that beset the writer. One is 'that the author may want to maintain [during writing] contact with the world, with himself, with the language he can use to say "I"' (*Space of Literature*, p. 53). Contrary to the stereotype of the artist who flees to art to escape the complexities of mundane life, the world is the artist's temptation, for the sources of the literary are traumatic ('It is then that Rimbaud flees into the desert from the responsibilities of the poetic decision' (*Space of Literature*, p. 53)):

> The work requires of the writer that he lose everything he might construe as his own 'nature,' that he lose all character and that, ceasing to be linked to others and to himself by the decision that makes him an 'I,' he becomes the empty place where the impersonal affirmation emerges. (*Space of Literature*, p. 55)

In *The Infinite Conversation* Blanchot refers more explicitly to the risk of madness undergone by the writer (esp. *Space of Literature*, pp. 200ff) and the fates of Hölderlin, Nietzsche and Artaud. Denial of this risk could entail abandoning the work or alternatively (a second risk) renouncing the passion of the origin, that desiccating elation, and producing a work that is mere self-representation in some form, or material for a predetermined public. It is in relation to this evasion that, with what may seem extraordinary reductiveness, Blanchot situates here the whole tradition of the realist novel! He argues that 'The notion of characters, as the traditional form of the novel, is only one of the compromises by which the writer, drawn out of himself by literature in search of its essence, tries to salvage his relations with the world and himself' (*Space of Literature*, pp. 27; also pp. 202–3). This need not, however, be the sweeping dismissal it might seem: Blanchot is not implying that such novels are without value, but that their value is not wholly 'literary' in the sense at issue (but lies in terms, for example, of social analysis or psychological documentation). This must, however, raise questions about the circularity of Blanchot's own valuations. The section on Kafka (*Space of Literature*, pp. 57–83) traces the consequences of lifelong conflict between a writer's desire to use literature for certain ends (religious in Kafka's case) and the exigency of the literary passion itself. Nevertheless, *The Space of Literature* reads as an ironic culmination of the tradition of seeing the act of composition as a kind of spiritual heroism. For all Blanchot's stress on the separation of the literary from questions of value, there is still a lingering macho heroism in the way writers are said to risk their being in the acultural space of literature. Blanchot's account of Goethe's daring, joy and 'mastery' (*Space of Literature*, p. 52) and of the 'great heroic creators' (*Space of Literature*, p. 54) betrays an intense attachment to the Romantic tradition that is also the object of critique.

Other risks that beset the writer are said to be unavoidable, not a matter of bad faith or evasion. One is 'impatience', a term with a precise sense in Blanchot. He finds in it nothing less than 'the principle of figuration' itself (*Space of Literature*, p. 79), a necessary and decisive aspect of the literary process, albeit one at odds with the work's exigency to affirm itself, not 'as a language containing images or one that casts reality in figures', but as 'an image of language (and not a figurative language)' (*Space of Literature*, p. 34). The writer, striving with the elusive and indefinite space of the work in quest of its origin, may abandon the patience inherent to the work's unfolding, the requirement: 'that one never believe the goal is close or that one is coming nearer to it' (*Space of Literature*, p. 79):

> This demand for a premature dénouement is the principle of figuration: it engenders the image, or, if you will, the idol, and the curse which attaches to it is that which attaches to idolatry. Man wants unity right away. (*Space of Literature*, p. 79)

Any seizure of an image or symbol as what unifies the work, either by the writer or the reader (including the writer as reader of the work in process)[24] is to take as an end what is only intermediary. It is to attempt to give comfortable and definite form to the pull of the work's continuing fascination, unsuccessfully, for, despite the hope of closure, 'this representation, the image of unity, immediately reconstitutes the element of dispersion where [the writer] loses himself more and more' (*Space of Literature*, p. 79). The 'unity' so achieved is a spurious presentation of the origin. Nevertheless, such impatience is unavoidable, for its alternative is indolence, inactivity and indifference to the pull of the work – the writer's situation, once again, is a double bind.

These concepts are elaborated through Blanchot's reading of *The Castle* (1926), a reading which also provides a good example of his brand of formalism. He reads the actions and aberrations of the landsurveyor K. as enacting the writer's predicament between impatience and indolence as these become, paradoxically, frustratingly interchangeable:

> Scarcely having arrived, understanding nothing about this ordeal of exclusion in which he finds himself, K. sets out right away to get quickly to the end. He won't expend any energy on the intermediaries; in their regard he is indolent. This is probably to his credit: doubtless it demonstrates the force of his tense striving towards the absolute. But his aberration is not any the less glaring. It consists in taking for the end what is only an intermediary, a representation befitting his 'lights'. (*Space of Literature*, p. 79)

In K.'s absurd career, Blanchot suggests, Kafka is punishing an error which is also the writer's, that of wanting to hurry the story on before it has developed in all its possible directions. Yet this impatience is inevitable, for such a tracing is itself impossible. It is Kafka's resistance to this temptation of premature figuration that produces the scrupulous slow-motion exactitude of his writing, its hallucinatory detail, all that is inappropriately known as his realism.

Kafka's resistance highlights yet another of the contradictions endured by the writer. Shelley argues that 'when composition begins, inspiration is already on the decline'[25], for Blanchot, however, the writer needs to resist inspiration in order for composition to be able to begin or to continue. To be able to write at all the writer must take on and accept, however minimally, the demands of the reader:

> To the extent that to write is to snatch oneself back from the impossibility where writing becomes possible, writing assumes the characteristics of reading's demand, and the writer becomes the nascent intimacy of the still infinitely future reader. But it goes without saying that this power is nonetheless the power to write, only because of the opposition to itself which it becomes in the experience of impossibility. (*Space of Literature*, p. 199)

Without figuration, and the impatience it enacts, there would be no readable text at all; one can only write by 'resisting the pure need to write' (*Space of Literature*, p. 184). It is the intensity of Kafka's

THE THEORY OF INSPIRATION

patience, his very impatience with impatience as it were, that
prevents his work from being able to conclude.

The logic of Blanchot's argument is clearly that the notion of
a work that would be truly finished is incoherent – the more a
work affirms itself in singularity the less sure must become received
criteria that could say whether it is finished or not (*Space of
Literature*, p. 22). How, then, does any work come to a minimally
unsatisfactory stop? Throughout the composition, he argues, the
writer has to confront episodes of intense alienation from the work,
an experience in which the work's exigencies are known to persist,
yet inaccessibly, unfelt except as a force of repulsion: 'What the
author sees is a cold immobility from which he cannot turn away,
but near which he cannot linger' (*Space of Literature*, p. 54). The
writer will only re-enter the field of the work, if ever, through
another contingent and incalculable leap, 'through an inexplicable
manouevre, through some distraction or through the sheer exces-
siveness of his patience' (*Space of Literature*, p. 54; also p. 81). Finally,
however, a point may come at which the work can be continued
just as well from outside the circle of its fascination as from within
it; this is a point at which technical skill and craft may seem sufficient to complete the job. This however, is only an ideal, one 'never
altogether justified' (*Space of Literature*, p. 54).

The work is always a space of risk and misrecognition. For
Blanchot there is always an unbridgeable divide between what the
work does and what the writer can know or say. By situating inspiration in this gap between act and knowledge – the aspect which
Paul de Man picks up in his well-known but rather inaccurate essay
on Blanchot[26] – Blanchot can be said to be answering the post-
Romantic idealization of the act of writing by returning 'inspiration'
to an aspect of its ancient formulation in Plato's *Ion*. There the issue
was precisely the inability of the rhapsode Ion (and by implication
Homer's inability) to ground the undeniable effects of his discourse
in some theory or *techne*. It is the discrepancy between what we
would now term the performative and the constative dimensions of
Ion's performance that leads Socrates to the dubious compliment of
arguing that, since he doesn't know what he is doing, Ion must be
inspired. For Blanchot, however, the ignorance effective in inspiration is essential, not an object of irony.

A final risk undergone in writing is the decisive one, for it
relates to the writer's being borne by inspiration about as far as it
can go. It is, again, the risk that the work will be unachieved, but
not this time because the work demands the surrender of the ego.

The risk is that the work will come to seem unrealizable, impossible, or even of relative unimportance compared to that passion of the origin that carries the work, further perhaps than the work can bear. The aridity of inspiration comes to consist in 'the impossibility which the artist questions in vain', impelled outside of 'tasks, of acquired forms, and proven expressions' (*Space of Literature*, p. 182). The work then 'may return ever closer to [its] origin by renouncing its realization' (*Space of Literature*, p. 53).

This last risk, however, is essential to the work, even if as a result it may remain unfinished in some technical sense. Inspiration is both the origin of the work yet also, in its purest and most singular form, its paralysis and ruination, confronting the work with impossibility. Its exigency is stronger than the need that the work itself be finished: 'the work counts less than the experience of the search for it ... an artist is always ready to sacrifice the work's accomplishment to the truth of the movement that leads to it' (*The Infinite Conversation*, p. 397). This is the gaze of Orpheus – the moment at which, skilfully leading Eurydice up from the underworld by force of his art, Orpheus, through desire and a perverse impulse, cannot not look back at her, even at the cost of ruining his enterprise and losing her. The work may become a 'sacrifice' to inspiration, and inspiration itself becomes 'the gift par excellence' (*Space of Literature*, p. 175) in Bataille's sense of a giving so extreme that, giving itself, it breaks with any logic of restitution, or any economy of adequation or measure (see Comay). From the writer's perspective, inspiration is undergone as an experience of impossibility, of being thrown beyond the possibilities of language, beyond the law that governs the work, a *syncope* in which subjective consciousness is paralysed in the essential solitude of the work. Here Blanchot is somewhat hindered by the linear mode of the myth he is exploiting, for this moment should be also, simultaneously, the scattering of Orpheus at the hands of the Thracian women – 'Inspiration pronounces ... the certainty of his ruin' (*Space of Literature*, p. 174).

Sacrificing the work as possibility, this experience is yet a necessary one for the artist – a further contradiction. 'Not to look would be infidelity to the measureless, imprudent force of his movement', betraying inspiration itself; for 'Had he not looked at her, he would not have drawn her towards him' (*Space of Literature*, p. 172). In a sense, Orpheus has been turned toward Eurydice ever since the work got underway. Moreover, Orpheus, even as his art enables him to lead Eurydice forth from the underworld, never wants her in her day-time truth or everyday character; her fascination is her nocturnal obscurity, 'as the foreignness of what excludes all intimacy ... [he wants] to have living in her the plenitude of her death' (*Space of Literature*, p. 172). He wishes, impossibly, to possess the mysterious point from which the work is coming, even while continuing to surrender to its unapproachable allure, to combine act and knowledge. This is the moment at which the paradoxical nature of the act of writing, the contradictoriness of its passion – to give oneself to, and yet to possess, a force of dispossession – becomes intolerable ('only in the song does Orpheus have power over Eurydice. But in the song too, Eurydice is already lost, and Orpheus himself is the dispersed Orpheus' (*Space of Literature*, p. 173)). To look at Eurydice and to lose her is the exorbitant point and risk to which the work tends, at which it becomes impossible, and hence also the source whence it comes. This is, in short, Blanchot's definition of inspiration: 'To look at Eurydice, without regard for the song, in the impatience and imprudence of desire which forgets the law: *that* is *inspiration*' (*Space of Literature*, p. 173).

Blanchot says that this point of the gaze of Orpheus, where the emergence of the work becomes an impossibility, is where the work is 'consecrated' (*Space of Literature*, p. 174), finally set free from the writer, even as 'he frees himself from himself' (*Space of Literature*, p. 175). However, though the work surpasses itself in this movement, becoming united with its origin (*Space of Literature*, p. 174), this is certainly no guarantee of its success. 'It reaches, in that instant, its point of extreme uncertainty' (*Space of Literature*, p. 174). The gaze of Orpheus, in other words, is the 'moment' of the work's most intense self-realization as the crisis of its own question – 'for is there ever a work?' (*Space of Literature*, p. 174)

Although Blanchot's account is thoroughly traditional in the vehemence with which it depends on maintaining a strict distinction between the aesthetic and the instrumental, the result is scarcely a position of *l'art pour l'art*. Rather, from the retrospect of the late 1990s, *The Space of Literature* emerges as a text in which an extreme modernist aesthetic of defamiliarization, pushed through to its most extreme implications, becomes the trangressive drive that Blanchot names inspiration. Taking criteria of singularity and originality to an extreme, the work is no longer an aesthetic artefact, object of possible interpretation or historical classification: it becomes a crisis in historicity and in our criteria of understanding.

Notes

1 Blanchot, *The Space of Literature*, trans. Ann Smock (Lincoln: University of Nebraska Press, 1982).

2 See Gerald Bruns, 'Language and Power', *Chicago Review*, 34 (1984), 27–43; Timothy Clark, *Derrida, Heidegger, Blanchot: Sources of Derrida's Notion and Practice of Literature* (Cambridge: Cambridge University Press, 1992); Herman Rapaport, *Heidegger & Derrida: Reflections on Time and Language* (Lincoln: University of Nebraska Press, 1989).

3 Blanchot, *The Infinite Conversation*, trans. Susan Hanson. (Minneapolis: Minnesota University Press, 1993), pp. 203–4. See also *Le Livre à venir* (Paris: Gallimard, 1959), p. 284.

4 John Gregg, *Maurice Blanchot and the Literature of Transgression* (Princeton: Princeton University Press, 1994); Simon Critchley, '*Il y a* – A Dying Stronger than Death (Blanchot with Levinas)', *The Oxford Literary Review*, 15 (1993), 81–131; Joseph Libertson, *Proximity: Levinas, Blanchot, Bataille and Communication* (The Hague: Martinus Nijhoff, 1982).

5 See Joseph Libertson, *Proximity*; Steven Shaviro, *Passion and Excess: Blanchot, Bataille, and Literary Theory* (Tallahassee: Florida State University Press, 1990).

6 See Clark, *Derrida, Heidegger, Blanchot*; Emmanuel Levinas, *Sur Maurice Blanchot* (Paris: fata morgana, 1975).

7 See Clark, *Derrida, Heidegger, Blanchot*; Jacques Derrida, *Parages* (Paris: Galilée, 1986).

8 Martin Heidegger, *Being and Time*, trans. John Macquarrie and Edward Robinson (Oxford: Basil Blackwell, 1980).

9 Heidegger, 'The Origin of the Work of Art', in *Poetry, Language, Thought*, trans. Albert Hofstadter (New York: Harper & Row, 1971).

10 Heidegger, *What is Philosophy?*, trans. William Klubeck and Jean T. Wilde (London: Vision Press, 1963).

11 Hubert L. Dreyfus, *Being-in-the-World: A Commentary on Heidegger's* Being and Time, Division 1 (Cambridge, Mass.: Massachusetts Institute of Technology Press, 1991).

12 Blanchot diverges radically from Heidegger on *Angst* and death in one crucial respect. For Heidegger, the possibility of impossibility renews *Dasein*'s engagement with the world by returning it to the sense of itself as possibility. For Blanchot, on the other hand, the limit-experience, as it bears on the question of the totality, opens upon another understanding of death. Other than that death I can anticipate and in some sense extract meaning from, there is the reality of that death that intervenes between myself and my very act or thought, a passivity beyond any condition of being passive, dissolving the very 'I' that might have been supposed to undergo the experience (even if, as in suicide, death had seemed to be a thing I give myself, in an impossible reflexivity). This is, reversing Heidegger's formulation, the impossibility of possibility, 'what I cannot grasp, what is not linked to one by any relation of any sort' (*Space of Literature*, p. 104).

13 Heidegger, 'What are Poets for?' (1950), in *Poetry, Language, Thought*, trans. Hofstadter, pp. 91–142.

14 See Françoise Collin, *Maurice Blanchot et la question de l'écriture* (Paris: Editions Gallimard, 1971), pp. 190–221.

15 Blanchot, 'Literature and the Right to Death', in *The Gaze of Orpheus and Other Literary Essays*, ed. P. Adams Sitney, trans. Lydia Davis (New York: Station Hill, 1981), pp. 21–62, p. 29.

16 See Critchley, '*Il y a*', pp. 102–116.

17 Georges Poulet, *The Interior Distance*, trans. Elliott Coleman (Baltimore: Ann Arbor Paperback, University of Michigan Press, 1964).

18 Blanchot's use of the myth of Orpheus and Eurydice makes him vulnerable to critique of the kind Alice Jardine conducts in *Gynesis* against some avant-garde male writers for projecting upon woman the image of some desired otherness or outside to conceptual thought (Alice Jardine, *Gynesis: Configurations of Woman and Modernity* (Ithaca: Cornell University Press, 1983)). Helène Cixous argues that the writer in Blanchot is a male writer ('Blanchot, *The Writing of the Disaster*: Nothing is What There is', in *Readings* (Hemel Hempstead: Harvester, 1992), pp. 19–27). Karen Jacobs also argues that what Blanchot terms 'inspiration' is bound up with an aggressive form of male sexuality, one which exploits a female muse (Eurydice) as a mediating figure sacrificed to the demand's of a man's work (Karen Jacobs, 'Two Mirrors Facing: Freud, Blanchot and the Logic of Invisibility', *Qui Parle*, 4 (1990), 21–46).

19 Pfeiffer, 'La Passion de l'imaginaire', *Critique*, 229, 571–8, p. 577.

20 Jean-François Lyotard, 'The Sublime and the Avant Garde', trans. Lisa Liebmann, *Paragraph*, 6 (1985), 1–18.

21 Christopher Fynsk, *Heidegger: Thought and Historicity* (Ithaca: Cornell University Press, 1986) p. 137.

22 See Rebecca Comay, 'Gifts without Presents: Economies of "Experience" in Bataille and Heidegger', in *On Bataille*, *Yale French Studies*, 78 (1990), 66–89; Shaviro, *Passion and Excess*, pp. 83–108.

23 Blanchot, 'The Sirens' Song', in *The Sirens' Song*, ed. Gabriel Josipovici, trans. Sacha Rabinovitch (Sussex: Harvester, 1982), pp. 59–65, p. 63.

24 For Blanchot on reading see my companion article, 'The Impossible Lightness of Reading: Blanchot and the Communicational Model of Subjectivity', *Southern Review*, 28 (1995), 83–95.

25 *A Defence of Poetry*, in *Shelley's Poetry and Prose*, ed. Donald H. Reiman and Sharon B. Powers (New York: Norton, 1977), pp. 478–508, p. 504.

26 De Man 'Impersonality in Blanchot', in *Blindness and Insight*, 2nd edn (Minneapolis: University of Minnesota Press, 1983), pp. 60–78. De Man argues that Blanchot's work as a critic is directed to a reading of his work as a writer. However, in seeing the critical work as a 'preparatory' version for Blanchot's *récits*, de Man gets the chronology of Blanchot's work quite wrong – almost all the *récits* were written before 1950, the majority of the critical work afterwards (see Michael Holland, 'Towards a Method', *Sub-Stance*, 14 (1976), 7–17). Moreover, the coincidence of writing as an act and writing as critical knowledge is precisely what is affirmed as impossible throughout *The Space of Literature*.

Dictation by heart: Derrida's 'Che cos'è la poesia?' and Celan's notion of the *Atemwende*

Each time you happen to me all over again. (Wharton, *The Age of Innocence*)

In 1960 Paul Celan made an acceptance speech on receipt of the Georg Büchner Prize.[1] He was concerned to instantiate his under-standing of poetry (*Dichtung*), and he did this by setting a contrast between an ideal of poetry as a form of authentic speech and the mere theatrics and nauseating show of 'art' (*Kunst*). Celan refers to the closing scene of Büchner's French revolutionary play, *Danton's Death* (1835).[2] There, Danton, Camille Desmoulin and other revolutionaries have all been put to death. Each has died histrionically, and gone speechifying to the scaffold. Everything confirms Danton's grim sense of revolutionary events as a theatre, both terrible and banal, in which all actors are puppets. Lucille, a spectator of all this and Desmoulin's wife, suddenly cries out appalled: 'Long live the king!', an exclamation that leads to her immediate arrest and to inevitable execution. This cry, Celan observes, is not that of a royalist; it is simply a kind of suicidal word, a 'counterword', an assertion of something that testifies to the 'human' (*Menschliche*) in the face of a brutal absurdity, yet being itself absurd. This, says Celan, is *Dichtung*. It is also in his revisionist term for inspiration, an *Atemwende*, or a turning or reversal of the breath:

> Poetry is perhaps this: an *Atemwende*, a turning of the breath. Who knows, perhaps poetry goes its way – the way of art – for the sake of just such a turn? (*The Meridian*, p. 47)

Celan's conception of the *Atemwende* is very similar to Hölderlin's conception of 'infinite inspiration', a counter-rhythmic rupture or 'cesura' that affirms the freedom of an extreme moment in the neighbourhood of silence and the breakdown of language, insanity, or death. 'Poetry is the spasm or black-out [*syncope*] of language' (Philippe Lacoue-Labarthe).[3] For the Hölderlin of 'Remarks on "Antigone"', Antigone's language of defiance gave her over to death, no less than Lucille's does for Celan. If such language is that of a free act it is so only in the sense of a catastrophe, one in which received determinations of being and language break down, giving way to a kind of *syncope*. Yet that same catastrophe is also the beseeching of another, more authentic and absolutely singular form of speech. Celan gives another example of such a 'counterword', the remark of Reinhold Lenz, '"only, it sometimes bothered him that he could not walk on his head"' (*The Meridian*, p. 46). Philippe Lacoue-Labarthe writes of an 'existence suddenly "released" at the height of the catastophe, in the mortal's sudden revelation of himself as one whose existence rests upon the abyss – the bottomlessness – of the sky' (Lacoue-Labarthe, p. 16) Celan's reference clearly recalls an aphorism of Hölderlin on enthusiasm: 'One can fall upward just as well as downward.'

Paul Celan has haunted Derrida's thinking in poetics, especially in *Schibboleth* (1986)[4] and 'Che cos'è la poesia?' (1988).[5] These two thinkers, linked by a shared Jewishness, both try to articulate what an authentic poetic might be in the wake of the catastrophes of twentieth-century history, and in a culture completely in the thrall of a means-end rationality. For both, the poetic is not primarily an object of critical interpretation; it is an event in language considered as a matter of desire and beseeching. Both writers take up and radically reconfigure the terminology of inspiration, as in Celan's notion of the *Atemwende* or Derrida's of a dictation 'by heart'.

In *Schibboleth*, Derrida writes that his concern is with the poetic at this date: 'Not the essence of poetic modernity or postmodernity, not the essence of an epoch or a period in some history of poetry, but what happens "*today*" "*anew*" to poetry, to poems, what happens to them at *this* date' (emphasis added).[6] By isolating the poetic in terms of its eventhood, as something that happens, Derrida (with Celan) recalls Heidegger's argument that essence, in this field, has to be understood in a verbal sense.[7] The poetic has no stable essence in a manner of an entity present-at-hand. To connect the poetic with singularity in this way is to acknowledge the degree to which the question of the poetic is open in the manner of an event that must exceed definition – it is never inconceivable that, at any time, a new poem may arrive whose effect is precisely to discredit any general poetics already in existence. In 'Che cos'è la poesia?'

the poetic emerges as a structure of passion that both sets in motion, resists (and hence calls for) the interpretation it yet continues to exceed.

The fable of the hedgehog

Let us turn here to consider Derrida's text at some length, returning later to Celan. 'Che cos'è la poesia?' is another of Derrida's texts whose interest, initial difficulty and untranslatability lies in its breaking with received philosophical language. It enacts the poetic by the attempt to be itself poetic, in a qualified sense. The terms of Derrida's argument demand that, correspondingly, his text presents itself as part of a structure of dictation from a muse-like other.

It takes the form of two 'fables' that interconnect or interlace. One is a meditation on the idiomatic expression (said to be a 'poem' in miniature) *apprendre par coeur* ('to learn by heart'). The other is a fable of the hedgehog lying rolled up, for self-defence, in the middle of the road.

This is not the first time the lowly hedgehog has found itself at the heart of a provocative text on poetics. 'Che cos'è la poesia?' forms another episode in the massive if often implicit debate between modern post-Heideggerian poetics and Jena Romanticism.[8] By choosing to relate the poetic in terms of the fable of the hedgehog, Derrida cannot but be engaged with one of the best known of the *Athenaeum Fragments* (1798), no. 206. Friedrich Schlegel writes of the fragment form in relation to the idea of a transcendental poetry, a poetry that will have no empirical referent but would exist as the essential or the absolute poem, the self-presentation of poetic creativity (*poiesis*) itself. A fragment, in relation to such an ideal, would be paradoxically 'like a miniature work of art', 'entirely isolated from the surrounding world and ... complete in itself like a hedgehog.'[9] For Schlegel the hedgehog-fragment, in its isolation, its would-be perfect closure upon itself, figures the ideal of the Romantic text as unconditional, i.e. absolved of relation to anything but itself – *ab-solute*.

'Che cos'è la poesia?' shares with Schlegel the conviction that the poetic is inherently contradictory, existing as a practice of radical contradiction resistant to philosophical conceptualization.[10] Derrida, in a gesture of inversion however, locates the origin of the poetic in the desire for 'the absolute nonabsolute' (pp. 229–31)! This vertiginous phrase would express the poetic as that which is not unconditioned, that is to say it relates to otherness as well as to

itself. Further, as *absolutely* nonabsolute, the poetic would be definable in terms of a desire to relate *never* to itself or to itself *only* as to
otherness: the dream of a total singularity and novelty, pure eventhood (*Nous sommes encore une fois sans expérience antérieure, nouveaux
venus, épris. La rose!*).[11] It would be pure immediacy, experience
without precedent. At issue throughout is the best-known and most
widespread mode of inspiration: '*Tu aimes*/You love' (pp. 228–9).

The correlative of this notion of the poetic, from the reader's
view-point, is the ideal of a mode of reception that would not
subsume the poetic under this or that interpretation but preserve its
original force untranslated. Derrida considers this possibility through
meditation on the phrase *apprendre par coeur*:

> *Literally*: you would like to retain by heart an absolutely unique
> form, an event whose intangible singularity no longer separates the
> ideality, the ideal meaning as one says, from the body of the letter.
> In the desire of this absolute inseparation, the absolute nonabsolute,
> you breathe the origin of the poetic [*tu respire l'origine du poétique*].
> (pp. 229–31).

Apprendre par coeur expresses the dream of a total interiorization –
the poem is to become part of the spontaneity of one's affective life.
To take a text to heart in this way is to preserve it, to cherish it
within oneself, to renounce all mediation in order to interpret the
poem, if that were possible, in terms only of itself. Such a desire is
in-spiration ('you breathe the origin of the poetic'). In a recent
article on 'Quoting Poetry' William Flesch relates this experience to
what Longinus says of the sublime, that 'you feel that you have
written yourself what you have only heard or read.' Quotation
becomes inwardness, originality of feeling, even as this same passion
itself becomes a 'sense of quotation' – a dictating dictation – as 'you
will seek to inspire others with the same passion to quote these
things.'[12]

The rest of Derrida's text complicates these ideas considerably
by thinking through the implications and conditions of the (impossible) realization of this extreme modernist aesthetic.

First of all to learn by heart is also to learn by rote, to be
dictated, ventriloquized. It is to commit oneself to a mnemotech-
nique, to the automatism of signs that seem thus to supplant the
apparent immediacy of what is entrusted to them, possessing the
psyche they touch. Derrida's argument, ever since *Speech and
Phenomenon* deconstructed Edmund Husserl's attempt to exclude
signs from his conception of the 'interior' life,[13] is that the two

meanings of the phrase 'by heart' are indissociable. The two meanings might be said to condition and to contaminate each other:

> *Heart*, in the poem, 'learn by heart' (to be learned by heart), no longer names only pure interiority, independent spontaneity, the freedom to affect oneself actively by reproducing the beloved trace. The memory of the 'by heart' is confided like a prayer – that's safer – to a certain exteriority of the automaton, to the laws of mnemotechnics, to that liturgy that mimes mechanics on the surface, to the automobile 'that surprises your passion and bears down on you as if from outside: *auswendig*, 'by heart' in German. (p. 231).

The poem, as a would-be singular event, is in a double bind. It 'Reiterates in a murmur: never repeat ... ' (p. 233). The poetic takes place only at the risk of disappearing into the very economy of language which it needs and unsettles, those 'sentences that circulate risk-free through the interchanges and let themselves be translated into any and all languages' (p. 285). In its commitment to language, 'it gathers itself up, rolled up in a ball on itself, it is more threatened than ever in its retreat: it thinks it is defending itself and it loses itself' (p. 229).

The double movement enacted in the idiom *apprendre par coeur* is one that may seem familiar in Derrida's work. It also relates, however, less familiarly, to an argument that can be stated in terms of the contrast between two modes of obliteration or oblivion, and, again, the necessity of conceiving their mutual contamination.

Characterizing the matter of the poem's injunction to learn-by-heart, Derrida specifies it, surprisingly, as the phrase 'destroy me'. This, rather sensationally, enacts well the poem's contradictory conditions of being. Not only does it express the doubleness of the movement, *apprendre by coeur*, as the desire for singular preservation which is yet contaminated, as its very condition, by obliteration, it also expresses the paradoxy of the dream of a total interiorization, i.e. the drive to render the poetic event independent of any material support (paper, ink, any medium of archiving) and absolutely private: 'destroy me: or rather render my support invisible to the outside ... do what must be done so that the provenance of the mark remains from now on unlocatable or unrecognizable' (p. 227). The poetic, in the idea of its pure eventhood, could not be a *recog*nition of anything it does not itself institute, singularly, and for the first time – 'without external support, without substance, without subject, absolute of writing in (it)self' (p. 237). As Jean-Pierre

Richard writes of some of the implications of this extreme modernist aesthetic in the work of René Char:

> The matinal instant arises, effectively out of nothing but itself: being its own proper cause and proper end, it marks a rupture with every instant that has come before it, it freezes time, effaces the past. The primary charm of the awakening is indeed forgetting[14]

'[S]et fire to the library of poetics' (Derrida, p. 233).[15] This seemingly benign oblivion, without which no novelty nor event would be conceivable, is contaminated by the possibility of obliteration and disfigurement inherent in the very condition of language in the repeatability of the mark. Yet this threat is also, paradoxically, the poem's inspiration, the threat to which the injunction 'destroy me' is already a response. ('The ruse of the injunction may first of all let itself be inspired by the simple possibility of death, by the risk that a vehicle poses to every finite being' (p. 229)). The 'address, the retreat' of the poem is the hedgehog's movement inwards/outwards both to and from an ineluctable vulnerability. In an inversion then of Romantic conceptions of an infinite *poiesis*, the poetic is the experience of a radical finitude. The poetic cannot be conceived (as it is perhaps in Char) as a singular event that might be thinkable before or outside those complex conditions or contradictions. This *double bind is its mode of existence* – this risk, 'distress' (p. 231), or exposure.

Prose, we read in the last sentence of 'Che cos'è la poesia?', is the type of language that can respond, symmetrically, to philosophical questioning ('By announcing that which is just as it is, a question salutes the birth of prose'). Correspondingly, to hearken to the poetic is to attend to something which is not 'just as it is' but whose identity is unstable, wild, impatient of definition. It thus cannot be *known*: knowledge as such must be renounced if one is to perceive this creature that, unexpectedly, crosses the thoroughfares of communication from side to side. The poetic moves or disturbs obliquely; its space is one in which the language of identification and exchange is traversed by what cannot be simply said or thought.

In the phrase *apprendre par coeur* we seem to have returned to a formulation that was applied to the oral composition of the Homeric poet, with its technics of learning, composing and reciting 'by heart'. Yet Derrida's formulation is also as antithetical as can be to notions of the formulary in oral poetics, and even at odds with any material of transmission whatsoever ('[S]et fire to the library of poetics'). The double and contradictory syntax of the *apprendre par coeur* is the double bind of a would-be pure event. Inspiration in this text has become what Derrida calls the 'poematic experience', the dream of letting one's heart be traversed by a singular trait (repeating: 'never repeat'). Such inspiration is yet the experience of its own impossibility (a statement to be clearly distinguished from saying that the 'poematic experience' is merely impossible). Lacoue-Labarthe has argued in 'Catastrophe' that the poetic in Celan makes up an experience, not of the expression of subjectivity or affective consciousness, but their dispersal. The poetic is inseparable from the notion of an experience of total immediacy, one which consciousness, as the medium of identity, synthesis and mediation, could only undergo as a movement of powerlessness. Subjectivity conceived in terms of 'identity-to-self or presence-to-self of consciousness' must be reconfigured.[16]

The poetic happens upon subjectivity as its powerlessness or *ecstasis*: an experience of impossibility, of the poetic as a singular trait that both compels and resists the desire *apprendre par coeur*, its keeping as losing. 'Che cos'è la poesia?' enacts Derrida's argument on the constitution of subjectivity through, one might say, its deconstruction, its relation to alterity. Identity-to-self, as a structure of auto-affection, is necessarily constituted through otherness in a movement that prevents subjectivity being conceived except non-absolutely, as an impure *différance*, touched with a radical finitude. Elsewhere Derrida speaks of redefining conscious subjectivity in terms of a singularized I, definable as 'the finite experience of nonidentity to self, as the underivable interpellation coming from the other.'[17] The poetic is the interruption or injunction that, dislocating the notion of subjectivity as presence-to-self, is an experience of finitude; a *syncope*. Derrida's notion is of a turning in/from that is a catastrophe of discourse or 'art', an *Atemwende* in Celan's sense.

> the *poetic* ... you intend to speak about an *experience*, another word for voyage, here the aleatory rambling of a trek; the strophe that turns but never leads back to discourse, or back home, at least is never reduced to poetry – written, spoken, even sung. (p. 225).

The 'poematic experience' then precedes and conditions cognition as both 'benediction before knowledge' (p. 227) and as catastrophe.

'Ode to Psyche'

This issue is inseparable from questions of the formal status of Derrida's text. For 'Che cos'è la poesia?' is an ode. Comparison with odes of John Keats and of Celan demonstrates 'Che cos'è la poesia?' to be a complex post-Romantic, post-modern reconfiguration of the ode form. However, my working through Keats and Celan to Derrida is not meant as an elaboration of the genealogy of the ode. Rather, each writer is engaged in a poetic inquiry into the being or act of poetry. Each bears out Blanchot's statement, in response to the question 'Where is literature going?', 'literature is *en route* to itself, to its essence, which is to disappear'.[18] The 'poematic experience' of 'Che cos'è la poesia?' has so far been engaged only in relation to the notion of singularity. Reading it as an ode brings out three additional facets of the structure of Derrida's inspirational poetic. The first is the association of the poetic with enunciation in the mode of an address, appeal or apostrophe, as opposed to the language of constative or knowing statement. Secondly, the poetic is bound up with the paradoxy of speaking of the future – one cannot describe the future (there is no referent) one can only inhabit, or open oneself to, a hypothesis which one's language projects into a context that may never be there. Thirdly, in so far as the poetic is an extreme performative in 'Che cos'è la poesia?', it is understood as creating the very conditions of its reception. It cannot be anticipated. It is language, not as our instrument, but in the guise of seeming to anticipate us. As such, the poetic is to be affirmed as that which in any text resists interpretive closure. While it may not be grasped outside a historical context, it always exceeds that context.

These three facets of 'Che cos'è la poesia?' enable us to map it onto recurrent features of the ode. The ode frequently presents itself, as does this text, in the mode of apostrophe, often to a deity of some kind or, at least, to some figure on whom (as in 'Che cos'è la poesia?') the poem itself is said to depend. The ode may thus work performatively, giving itself as an act of dedication, worship or of supplication. It frequently opens itself to an imagined or projected future in which it may receive answer or acknowledgement ('O, Wind,/If winter comes can Spring be far behind?' (Shelley, 'Ode to the West Wind'); 'Come now again my lady, and set me free/From anxious troubles ... Be my ally in person!' (Sappho, 'Hymn to Aphrodite'); 'Bring for him/The crown, and bring the fillet of fine wool/And send forth upon wings this new-made song' (Pindar, 'Ishmian V'). Paul Fry argues that the ode has always tended to a certain reflexiveness.[19] The most startling aspect of Derrida's text, however, the notion of an apostrophe that brings into being its addressee, is only, I believe, a striking feature of some odes since the Romantic movement. Here the poetic practice of Keats and Celan is indispensable to help situate the paradoxy of the poetic in Derrida's ode.

Keats's 'Ode to Psyche' (1819)[20] is distinguished by its engagement with the nature of invocation and apostrophe as these relate to the poetic act itself. Keats revivifies the relation between the ode form and religious invocation yet he does so in a way that secularizes it, so destabilizing the genre itself.[21] The ode is also a prayer. It is not a case, however, of a literal revival of a pagan religion. As a prayer to a deity (Psyche) who is known to be a fiction and thus a projection of the text addressed to her, the 'Ode to Psyche' reflexively enacts a meditation on the question of poetic creation itself. The text invokes a figure, or rather an encounter, that is also its inspiration. It thus enacts a variant of the Romantic ideal of inspiration as auto-legitimation, a performative that underwrites itself.

Blanchot writes of the paradoxical temporality of the space of composition: 'It is quite true that Ahab only encounters Moby Dick in Melville's novel. But it is equally correct to say that such an encounter is what enables Melville to write his novel.'[22] For Keats, as for Celan and Derrida (see below), the poetic is bound up with the notion of such an encounter. The 'Ode to Psyche' opens:

> O Goddess! hear these tuneless numbers, wrung
>   By sweet enforcement and remembrance dear,
> And pardon that thy secrets should be sung
>   Even into thine own soft-conchèd ear:
> Surely I dreamed to-day, or did I see
>   The wingèd Psyche with awakened eyes.

The poem, even in its invocation, is itself a gift, an act of homage. Psyche, even as she is the occasion, inspiration and subject of the verse, is also its would-be recipient. The poet himself, figured as the mere vehicle of this movement of restitution and return, takes on initially a certain redundancy and abasement ('pardon that thy secrets should be sung/Even into thine own soft-conchèd ear'). These secrets are most probably love-secrets, for the poem invokes not Psyche alone, but an encounter with two figures, Psyche and Cupid, met in the suspension of an adoring embrace. Their realm is one of the pastoral forest, figured as an immediacy so remote from human knowledge that, as in the 'Ode on a Grecian Urn', it can only be pictured in terms of immobility, suspension:

> I wandered in a forest, thoughtlessly,
>   And, on a sudden, fainting with surprise,

> Saw two fair creatures, couchèd side by side
>   In deepest grass ...

> They lay calm-breathing on the bedded grass;
>   Their arms embraced, and their pinions too;
>   Their lips touched not, but had not bade adieu ...

The sense of the mortal's abasement and intrusion before the two divinities is partly undone by an implicit identification of the poet, whose poem is a love poem, with Cupid, a figure otherwise indeterminate in the ode ('The wingèd boy I knew').

The text enacts the poetic or creative process itself as a movement of self-transcendence or becoming, for the ode unfolds itself as the act of dedication to a deity which is both its inspiration and its projection: viz. at issue, is not some hypothetical pagan goddess, but the mind-in-creation in dialectic with itself. The final stanza moves towards the convergence and culmination of these differing vectors, towards a supreme movement of love and identification in which the poles relating, yet separating, text, addressee and muse would collapse upon each other in a total communicative act. The poem envisages the union of Psyche and Cupid taking place in the mind of the poet celebrating them. This conflation of poem and subject, inspiration and addressee, poet and audience, is anticipated in lines 46-48. There the poet aims to be 'Thy voice, thy lute, thy pipe'. Partaking both of the act of worship and its object he may become 'thy incense sweet / From Swinged censer teeming −/Thy shrine, thy grove, thy oracle ...' The temporality of the ode, then, is determinedly futural. It projects itself towards a conjunction with Psyche that would be at once the summation of a human poetic yet, at the same time, also its annihilation − for poetry itself as odal dedication or invocation could only be redundant once the poet has become the very voice of the goddess:

> And there shall be for thee all soft delight
>   That shadowy thought can win,
> A bright torch, and a casement ope at night,
>   To let the warm Love in!

The whole ode is itself, one might say, this window opening (*l'oeuvre est l'attente de l'oeuvre* (Blanchot)).[23]

Peggy Kamuf in her brief but forceful introduction to 'Che cos'è la poesia?' reminds us 'As always, Derrida works to abolish the distance between what he is writing *about* ... and what his writing is *doing*' (p. 221). As with Keats, the poetic in this text is indissociable from apostrophe, from the structure of address to a figure who is both the text's destination and its muse. Derrida's ode, however, invokes a 'you' who has neither name nor obvious identity. Who is being addressed here?

> It sees itself, the response [to the question, what is poetry?], dictated to be poetic by being poetic. And for that reason, it is obliged to address itself to someone, singularly to you but as if to the being lost in anonymity, between city and nature, an imparted secret, at once public and private, *absolutely* one and the other, absolved from within and from without, neither one nor the other (p. 223).

Once again this is a passage which sets out to resist that conceptual understanding which the poetic, performatively, puts at issue. This passage exemplifies what is the most perplexing aspect of 'Che cos'è la poesia?'. Although it is an exercise in poetics, it never utilizes the words 'writer', 'author' or even 'poet'. The word 'reader' also never appears! This is extraordinary, not to say a source of huge initial difficulty. Instead of using these familiar terms, Derrida's text, works, ode-like, through a reconfiguration of structures of address and apostrophe, moving through three poles in particular, 'you' (as in the citation just given), 'I' and 'other'. These terms or vectors become part of a Moebius-like (or hedgehog-like) topology of language; they play across and within the borders and limits of language. For all the apparent vagueness of terms like 'you', 'I' and 'other', the apostrophic / inspirational structure of Derrida's text enables a complex enactment of a poetic event, one whose multiplicity could not be said in the familiar vocabulary of poetics without considerable violence.

In linking the poetic with an address 'singularly to you' (p. 223) Derrida need not be directing the text to any particular empirical figure. Rather, it is the word or vocative 'you' itself that is being engaged. It is of importance as a moment in which the general system of language opens itself to an outside, viz. *you* is not only a general pronoun of the second person, it exposes language to the singularity of a reference each time unique, in the 'here' and 'now' of its occurrence. A poetic event, in its singularity, should only be addressed 'singularly to you': it singularizes its recipient with the impossible demand, *apprendre par coeur*.

A text which is addressed 'singularly to you' can be thought to singularize whoever happens upon it, in the time of that reading or encounter: yet, simultaneously, in so far as the word or call must function generally, be repeatable according to the established codes of the language, 'you' remains anonymous, indeterminate, empty in the mode of a merely abstract universal. These two senses, 'at once public and private', seemingly exclusive, are in fact conditions of each other. No singular address would be possible without the enabling laws or conventions governing the second person, just as those find their *raison d'être* in a singular address. *You* is both and simultaneously 'public and private, absolutely one and the other.' An impossible condition, it is also 'neither one nor the other', opening on elusive space within and yet beyond language, 'between city and nature'. Unobtrusively, it may be the most powerful word in the language, its equivocality the heart and the pathos of all lyricism (*O einer, o keiner, o niemand, o du* (Celan)).[24] In relation to the poetic itself, Derek Attridge writes:

> the poem has the power to speak to your most intimate feelings and thoughts, and at the same time to reveal how even these primitive depths are made possible by otherness and externality, always passing through the institutions of the law, that which is not you, which calls to you and without which 'you' could not come into being.[25]

However, to read the addressee of 'Che cos' è la poesia?' only in this meta-poetic way, as enacting the equivocal status of the vocative itself, must not be to elide other aspects. At times the text directs itself to an other who might seem to be merely the text's reader: yet elsewhere the text has the effect of a poetic self-communing. For example, in a discussion of the protocol that sets up the text's question ('what is poetry?'), we read 'if you respond otherwise depending on each case' or, later, 'since you intend to speak of an *experience*' (p. 225) – 'you' is surely here the writer himself in the mode of thought as a dialogue one conducts with oneself. (Unfortunately, in English, the use of 'you' as an informal version of the impersonal pronoun 'one', obscures completely the clear effect of address at work in the French.)

However, the writer's identity or subjectivity must be understood, not in terms of punctual self-identity, but as self-address, opening even in the heart a gap between addressor and addressee. Elsewhere we read: 'The "you", the word you, may be addressed to the other as well as to oneself as other, and *each time it overruns the economy of the discourse*' (emphasis added) (*Schibboleth*).[26] Thus, in 'Che cos'è la poesia?' the use of 'you' is not only or merely meta-poetic: it opens language to its conditions of possibility in what it cannot say, engaging the writer in the 'here'/'now' of the process of inscription, or rather the non-dialectical process of the writing becoming reading, becoming other, then relating back to 'itself' as other in a complex apostrophic movement of dictation - strope, antistrophe, systole, diastole.[27]

In Keats the obvious pun on the name Psyche acknowledges the poem's addressee as a creative process vehicled through the writer himself. The futural mode of the poetic in this text renders it a paradox: both an expression of subjectivity and its *ecstasis*, creative power as creative dispossession.[28] Moreover, the poem tends towards an impossible culmination in which the word 'Psyche' would no longer be a pun. Derrida's ode to psyche, on the other hand, affirms itself in the space of differal, the futural temporality that the Keats seeks to erase, a movement in which spacing, otherness, insist as the condition of an identity, even as they fracture its would-be circularity. This is the *daemonic*: the poem as a '"demon of the heart"' (p. 235). The poem 'can reflect language or speak poetry, but it never relates back to itself' (p. 235). The vector of the apostrophe curves outward, to the other, exposed, even as it curls towards itself in self-communing. In an inversion of Romantic conceptions of the transcendental imagination, the genesis of the poetic in Derrida emerges as the sur-prise within a fundamentally passive temporalization. It is self-relation as *différance*, language dictating itself in unexpected ways in the relay of 'I' and 'you', cutting across the rhythm of the heart-beat.

> The poetic, let us say it, would be that which you desire to learn, but from and of the other, thanks to the other and under dictation, by heart (p. 227).

Celan

In a powerful reading of Celan, Werner Hamacher argues:

> They [Celan's poems] move away from subjectivity ... by articulating the structure of self-reference as that of the speech-act, which, once released from its ties to the self and the logic of its positing, attains an altered relation to itself in the very movement of being released.[29]

This citation reinforces a point that has already been implicit in this chapter, that, while it is common to describe Celan's poems in terms of the 'hermetic lyric', the ode may often be a more specific, a more mobilizing term especially if it is also allowed to embrace the psalm. The poems are often elliptical odes, engaged in inspirational structures of dedication or invocation characteristic of odes since oral culture. Even Celan's well-known practice of writing to and from certain commemorated dates recalls the associations of the ode with occasion and supplication. Moreover, the reflexiveness inherent to the ode becomes in Celan (as Hamacher describes) a complex movement of poetic transformation that is radically anti-lyrical, at least in so far as one wants to hold on to a notion of the lyric as subjective expression rather than a heteronomic structure of inspiration by an other. Finally, Celan, like Keats, can be read as engaging with the complex relation of the poetic to the transcendent, often at issue in more traditional odes.

The hermetic nature of Celan's texts, as in Derrida's ode, often lies in their complex, elliptical deployment of apostrophe. Michael Hamburger writes:

> No feature of Celan's later poems is more characteristic of their openness and mysteriousness than their unidentified personal pronouns, the 'you' that can be the woman addressed in a love poem or an alter ego or a deity or only the amorphous, unknowable 'other' to whom all Celan's poems make their way; the 'he', 'she', or 'they' that enters a poem without any introduction or identification.[30]

As in Keats, but more elliptically, both Derrida and Celan engage with the poem's staging of apostrophe as tracing, in the text, its own conditions of possibility, and its finitude.

In his dialogue with the poetics of Martin Heidegger, Celan rewrites the thinker's notion of poetic language (*Dichtung*) as a structure of impersonal manifestation and gives a concept of poetry as a form of singular, even desperate address, destined towards the future, towards a barely conceivable addressee able to bear witness to the experience encrypted in or as the poem. Moreover, Celan's texts on poetics, *The Meridian* and his Bremen address of 1958, are engaged in a radical new understanding of the act of writing poetry in terms of the wagers of apostrophe. The Bremen address reads:

> A poem, being an instance of language, hence essentially dialogue, may be a letter in a bottle thrown out to sea with the – surely not always strong – hope that it may somehow wash up somewhere, perhaps on a shoreline of the heart. In this way, too, poems are *en route*: they are headed toward.

> Toward what? Toward something open, inhabitable, an approachable you, perhaps, an approachable reality.[31]

The 'Ode to Psyche' fits with some accuracy Friedrich Schlegel's definition of the romantic text as always futural, 'forever ... becoming and never ... perfected.'[32] In Keats the addressee is figured as the mythical Psyche, a projection of the text – the empirical reader, on whom the text depends for its very life, is not explicitly recognized. In Celan, the unknown addressee to whom a poem directs itself is not only a projection of the text but embraces the futural reader in the mode of an appeal-to-be (*La poésie ne s'impose plus, elle s'expose*).[33] It is *you* who may become the source and destination of the elliptical ode. Celan writes in *The Meridian*: 'The poem intends another, needs this other, needs an opposite. It goes towards it, bespeaks it' (*Collected Prose*, p. 49). This other is potentially anyone, anyone who, falling upon the poem, becomes thereby its addressee – 'For the poem, everything and everybody is a figure of this other toward which it is heading' (*Collected Prose*, p. 49). A Celan ode exposes its own fragile conditions of being in its hermetic structures of apostrophe.

Whereas the notion of inspiration has often comprised the dream of a performative that would somehow ensure its own value and response, the reworking of the discourse of inspiration in Celan and Derrida is very different: it openly acknowledges the lack of an assured response that received notions of inspiration seek to deny. Both writers engage with the poetic as an apostrophic/inspirational structure whose need for or beseeching of an other is inherent to it, not as a fantasy of command, but as fragile appeal. The poem is inspired, one might say, by its encounter with a reader who may not yet exist.

As in Keats's ode, both Celan and Derrida conceive the poem as an encounter. The latter two, however, stress the element of chance in the encounter,[34] for the encounter, even in the poem's inception, is with an other who is futural, and who might form, in Celan's phrase, a 'meridian' with the text's implicit or explicit addressee. Celan writes of an encounter as both the genesis of the poem and as that toward which it remains addressed:

> The poem is lonely. It is lonely and *en route*. The one who writes it stays with it.
>
> Does this very fact not place the poem already here, at its inception, *in the mystery of encounter* (p. 49: trans. modified).

The poetic event has a very peculiar, 'open' temporality: it is both the encounter towards which the poem directs itself, as apostrophe, and which, in so far as the poem's elliptical but determinate identity stems from being thus *en route*, already occurs as the force of the poem's inception. What is this encounter?

Critical thinking is so saturated with a vocabulary of representation, restitution and retrieval that the notion here that the muses might be beings of the future, not of the past, seems deeply counterintuitive. This, however, is at issue in Celan and in Derrida's reconfiguration of the ode, a mode of writing whose temporality, as we have seen, is often projective, futural. We can no longer say, with these poems, that poetry re-calls, re-counts or re-enacts, nor speak of the reader or interpreter as engaged on any form of recreation or research of meaning. Paul Davies, in a pathbreaking essay, writes of the notion of poetic prophecy he reads in an essay of Blanchot's on René Char: 'There is no "truth" contemporaneous with the poem that might one day verify what it says. With the word "prophetic" Blanchot wishes us to hear in this phrase "the speech of the future", a double genitive. The poem speaks of the future but it is also the future's speech. It opens us to a future in which it *will* speak.'[35] For Derrida, a futural poetics is not one possibility among others. It is inevitable, one's only option, given the implications of his deconstructive thinking on the nature of memory, and the arts of memory. In *Mémoires* (1986) he reaffirms Paul de Man's argument that '"the power of memory does not reside in its capacity to resurrect a situation or a feeling that actually existed, but is a constitutive act of the mind bound to its own present and oriented toward the future of its own elaboration".'[36] Memory is a constitutive act to the degree that it must destroy the very anteriority of the past in order to elaborate its figure in the present, and entrust it ('by heart') to the iterability of a code whose projective nature is inherently one of repetition, the effacement of any possible immediacy. This argument forms an explicit acknowledgement of something apparent since Rousseau and Wordsworth chose to stress the writer's solitariness as a condition of integrity, that a notion of inspiration engaged with the technics of writing must be oriented towards the future, the time of its response or recognition.

'Che cos'è la poesia?' accordingly, is marked by a striking use of the future tense: 'You will call a poem a silent incantation' (p. 233); 'You will call a poem from now on a certain passion of the singular mark' (p. 235). This is not a strident authoritarianism, but a performative commitment of the text underway ('here' and 'now' and to 'you') to the impossible inspiration – or inspiration of impossibility – *apprendre par coeur*.

In neither Celan nor Derrida is it a matter of addressing the futural 'you' as a reader who could be conceived as merely the passive recipient of the message. In 'Telepathy' and elsewhere Derrida has written about the possibility of a written performative: that is to say written marks whose incalculable efficacy may be to bring into being the addressee capable of reading them:

> I am not putting forward the hypothesis of a letter which would be the external occasion in some sense, of an encounter between two identifiable subjects – and who would already be determined. No, but of a letter which after the event seems to have been launched towards some unknown addressee at the moment of writing [cf. Celan's notion of the poem as a letter in a bottle], an addressee unknown to himself or herself if one can say that, and who is determined ... on receipt of the letter; this is then quite another thing than the transfer [*transfert*] of a message. Its content and its end no longer precede it.[37]

Is it a peculiar instance of this structure that, retrospectively, Celan's poetic practice so clearly anticipates Derrida's 'Telepathy' and 'Che cos'è la poesia?' The complex temporal and textual movement that Derrida designates by the phrase 'by heart' incorporates the notion of an incalculable written performative.

What a thinker in hermeneutics might read in terms of a 'fusion of horizons' between the worlds of text or reader, or in terms of Ricoeur's notion of appropriation (see his 'Appropriation'),[38] becomes both more complex, more creative but also more violent in Derrida's understanding of the poetic as a singular and singularizing apostrophe:

> Someone writes you, to you, of you, on you. No, rather a mark addressed to you, left and confided with you, is accompanied by an injunction, in truth it is instituted in this very order which, in its turn, constitutes you. Destroy me ... (p. 227).

The movement of poetic communication, or rather experience, cannot be fitted into a familiar tripartite division of a sender, a relay and a receiver. Rather, it is an event (the injunction: *apprendre par coeur*) which must be conceived as a relation prior to its relata, bringing what it relates into being by force of its own event. Hence we read that the mark is not 'accompanied by an injunction' but 'instituted in this very order' and this 'in its turn, constitutes you'. The poetic obviously does not constitute the addressee in his or her empirical being. It reconfigures identity in the *experience* of surprising the reader in the mode of having become the addressee projected by the text and as having, unforeseen, entered what Celan calls the other's time, that is the singular temporality, 'here', 'now', of the text in its multiple singularly. It interrupts, or cuts across, subjectivity conceived as a structure of possible self-return. The poetic, as the impossible demand for a singular event that would be not re-cognized but experienced as such an interruption of the possibility of mediation or relation, would thus make up what Derrida has called elsewhere a 'crazy relation' (*un rapport fou*), 'a relation without relation, one which comprehends the other in a certain relation of incomprehension. This is not ignorance, nor obscurantism nor resignation in front of any desire for intelligibility … it is … the condition of desire.'[39]

Derrida's anti-hermeneutic notion of *interruption* is alone adequate to conceptualize this movement. The hermeneutic ideal of a fusion of interacting worlds, mediated by a common tradition, gives way to the poetic as an interruption of any possibility of mediation or commensuration between opposing poles. Rather poem and recipient configure or reconfigure themselves, for a first time, in the space opened by or as the interruption, within which they are mutually constituted:

> To enter into a relation with the other, interruption must be possible: the relation [*rapport*] must be a relation of interruption. And interruption does not interrupt the relation of the other, it opens the relation to the other.[40]

An instance of such a movement might be said to be at work in forceful metaphor, considered not as a comparison between two terms based on pre-perceived similarity, but as an unanticipated event of juxtaposition whose *fiat* sets up the very relation that seems to justify it, a relation which is in its turn not the spark of surreal unification but an *interruption*, an event of reconfiguration of all the terms or poles of the metaphor ('you' and 'I').

One peculiar effect of writing of the poetic as a bizarrely futural performative is that, in 'Che cos' è la poesia?' it is often impossible to tell if what is at issue is the poetic in relation to the writing of a poem or to the reading of it! At issue in the studied avoidance of the basic terms of poetics ('poet', 'reader', etc.) is a deconstructive reworking of the distinction between what such poetics would call the 'process of composition' and an 'aesthetics of reception'. Two quotations may illustrate this. The first seems, at a cursory reading, to concern the scene of a text's reception:

> Thus the dream of *learning by heart* arises in you. Of letting your heart be traversed by the dictated dictation ... I call a poem that very thing that teaches the heart, invents the heart ... (p. 231).

The second seems to concern the temporality of composition:

> Without a subject: poem, perhaps there is some, and perhaps it *leaves itself*, but I never write any. A poem, I never sign(s) it. The other sign(s). The I is only at the coming of this desire: to learn by heart [*apprendre par coeur*]. (p. 237).

Justification for what might seem a damaging indeterminacy is that, in 'Che cos'è la poesia?', the poem is said to come from the text's addressee, as in the provocative and difficult sentence: 'You will call a poem a silent incantation, the aphonic wound that, of you, from you [*de toi*], I want to learn by heart' (p. 233). The very 'moment' of incision in language whereby a poetic event sets to keep or entrust itself (to conventions of language, readability) is also its wounding, its division as the risk of effacement in a movement whose repeatability is an opening to an other, a futural other to whom it is already indebted and to whom the impossible, singularizing apostrophe directs itself. Thus the apostrophe, the vocative 'you', is already a force in or rather *as* the very incision of the poetic mark in language. This is what 'Violence and Metaphysics' terms 'the wound or inspiration that opens speech' (p. 98). This wound constitutes the poetic in both its interruption of language and, by the same token, its risk, its entrusting itself to language, to readability, in the impossible demand of its appeal-to-be. The poetic is the chance of an event of interruption whose arrival constitutes its receiver, even as it simultaneously institutes itself and is contaminated, risking effacement, by the force of this reception. The event of the poetic is a two-way movement in which it makes no sense to say which pole has temporal precedence - whether this is the text's inception by its possible reception or its addressee's 'telepathic' projection by the text. Thus the poem can be said to be dictated by the addressee it simultaneously projects. This is also Derrida's version of Celan's notion of a text's apostrophic structure, as an *Atemwende*, a crisis of subjectivity and temporality.[41]

> The poem becomes dialogue – often desperate dialogue. Only the space of this dialogue can establish what is addressed, can gather it

> into a 'you' around the naming and speaking I. But this 'you' *comes about by dint of being named and addressed*; brings its otherness into the present. Even in the here and now of the poem – and the poem has only this one, unique momentary present – even in this immediacy and nearness, the otherness gives voice to what is most its own: its time (*The Meridian*, p. 50; emphasis added, trans. modified).

It is both contamination and experience – a fissure in the structure of subjectivity:

> Just this contamination, and this crossroads, this accident here. This turn, the turning round of *this* catastrophe. The gift of the poem cites nothing, it has no title, its histrionics are over, it comes along without your expecting it, cutting short the breath, cutting all ties with discursive and especially literary poetry. (Derrida, p. 235)

It is clear that this accident happens 'now' to 'you' in the time of reading. Celan's term, *Atemwende*, designates inspiration not as the bestowal of the breath or the spirit as much as its taking away – as a total defamiliarization of received determinations of the human and the real. The event of the poem takes on the complex multiplicity and temporality already traced in the terms 'you', 'here' and 'now'. A poem's images are 'What has been, what can be perceived, again and again, and only here, only now' (*The Meridian*, p. 51) (*Das einmal, das immer wieder einmal und nur jetzt and nur hier Wahrgenommene und Wahrzunehmende*).

If 'Che cos'è la poesia?' diverges in a major respect from the poetics of Celan, it is in its stress on the mortality and accidental nature of the poetic event. The possibility of effacement, of going astray, is *necessary* to the very structure of the event. The poem's status as only a message in a bottle cannot be regarded as an unhappy vicissitude only. For Derrida, the poetic comes from the other. Yet, as he argues elsewhere, to conceive this other as purely other ('altogether other': Celan) is, paradoxically, to risk effacing its alterity ('The point is that if one insists on holding a pure respect for this alterity without alteration (*cette altérité sans altération*), one always risks lending a hand to a lack of mobility, conservatism, etc, that is, an effacement of alterity itself').[42]

In conclusion, both Celan and Derrida rework the oldest notion in Western poetics – of the poem as dictation from another. They do so in ways that radically extend conceptions of the process of composition as a limit-experience. As in Blanchot the tradition of conceiving inspiration as a mode of power gives way to an affirmation of the writer's powerlessness. Yet, unlike Blanchot's account in

The Space of Literature, this limit-experience is potentially utopian, irenic. Inspiration remains the appeal of a barely conceivable mode of communality.
'The poem is lonely. It is lonely and *en route*.'

Notes

1 *The Meridian*, Speech on the Occasion of Receiving the Georg Büchner Prize, Darmstadt, 22 October, 1960. In Celan, *Collected Prose*, trans. Rosemarie Waldrop (Manchester: Carcanet, 1986), pp. 37–55.

2 Büchner, *Danton's Death; Leonce and Lena, Woyzeck*, trans. Victor Price (Oxford: Oxford University Press, 1971).

3 Lacoue-Labarthe, 'Catastrophe: A Reading of Celan's "The Meridian"', trans. Timothy Clark and Sylvie Gautheron, *Oxford Literary Review*, 15 (1993), 3–41, p. 14. See also Mark A. Anderson, 'The "Impossibility of Poetry": Celan and Heidegger in France', *New German Critique*, 53 (1991), 3–18.

4 Derrida, *Schibboleth: Pour Paul Celan* (Paris: Galilée, 1986). For an English translation by Joshua Wilner see *Midrash and Literature*, ed. Geoffrey Hartman and Sanford Budick (New Haven: Yale University Press, 1986), pp. 307–47.

5 Derrida, 'Che cos'è la poesia?', in *A Derrida Reader: Between the Blinds*, ed. Peggy Kamuf (London; New York: Harvester Wheatsheaf, 1991), pp. 221–37. All other references to Derrida are to this text unless otherwise specified. Originally published in a bilingual edition in the Italian journal *Poesia*, Derrida's text/performance is a response to the question 'what is poetry?' with which every issue of this journal opens. See also the brief discussion of drugs and inspiration in 'The Rhetoric of Drugs', in *Points: Interviews 1974–1994*, ed. Elisabeth Weber (Stanford: Stanford University Press, 1992) pp. 228–54, 238–40.

6 Modified trans. from extract in Derrida, *Acts of Literature*, ed. Derek Attridge (London; New York: Routledge, 1992), p. 379.

7 For a good general introduction to Celan's poetics see Véronique Foti, *Heidegger and the Poets: Poiesis, Sophia, Techne* (New Jersey; London: Humanities Press, 1992), pp. 78–110.

8 See Derrida, '*Istrice 2: Ick bünn all hier*', in *Points*, pp. 300–26; Timothy Clark, 'Transformations of German Romanticism: Blanchot and Derrida on the Fragment, the Aphorism and the Architectural', *Paragraph*, 15 (1992), 232–47.

9 Friedrich Schlegel, *Lucinde and the Fragments*, trans. Peter Firchow (Minneapolis: University of Minnesota Press, 1971), p. 189.

10 For Schlegel and contradiction see Gerald N. Izenberg, *Impossible Individuality: Romanticism, Revolution, and the Origins of Modern Selfhood, 1780–1802* (Princeton: Princeton University Press, 1992).

11 René Char, *Poèmes et prose choisis* (Paris: Editions Gallimard, 1957), p. 192.

12 William Flesch, 'Quoting Poetry', *Critical Inquiry*, 18 (1991), 42–63, p. 45.

13 Derrida, *Speech and Phenomenon and Other Essays on Husserl's Theory of Signs*,

ed., trans. David B. Allison (Evanston, Ill.: Northwestern University Press, 1973).

14 Richard, *Onze Études sur la poésie moderne* (Paris: Editions de seuil, 1964), p. 82.

15 The phrase recalls Rimbaud's boredom with the Louvre and his wanting to burn down the Bibliothèque Nationale.

16 '"Eating Well", or the Calculation of the Subject: An Interview with Jacques Derrida', in *Who Comes After the Subject*, ed. Eduardo Cadava, Peter Connor and Jean-Luc Nancy (London; New York: Routledge, 1991) pp. 96–119, p. 103.

17 '"Eating Well", p. 103. Derrida corroborates this notion with the proviso that the notion of subjectivity must be re-examined with a view to questioning its exclusive application to the human, as opposed to other animals.

18 Blanchot, *Le Livre à venir* (Paris: Editions Gallimard, 1959), p. 265.

19 Paul Fry, *The Poet's Calling in the English Ode* (New Haven: Yale University Press, 1980).

20 John Keats, *The Complete Poems*, ed. John Barnard (London: Penguin, 1973), pp. 340–2.

21 See Nathaniel Teich, 'The Ode in English Literary History: Transformations from the Mid-Eighteenth to the Early Nineteenth Century', *Papers in Language and Literature*, 21 (1985), 88–108.

22 Blanchot, 'The Sirens' Song', in *The Sirens' Song*, ed. Gabriel Josipovici, trans. Sacha Rabinovitch (Sussex: Harvester, 1982), pp. 59–65, p. 63.

23 Blanchot, *Le Livre à venir*, p. 236.

24 From 'there was Earth Inside Them ...' [*Es war Erde in Ihnen*], Celan, *Selected Poems: A Bilingual Edition*, trans. Michael Hamburger (London: Penguin, 1990), p. 152.

25 Attridge, ed., *Acts of Literature*, p. 22.

26 In *Midrash and Literature*, p. 339.

27 See Geoffrey Bennington's discussion of the 'countersignature' in Derrida, Bennington, *Jacques Derrida* (Paris: Editions de seuil, 1992) p. 153. In 'Violence and Metaphysics' Derrida writes: 'By definition, if the other is the other, and if all speech is for the other, no logos as absolute knowledge can *comprehend* dialogue and the trajectory towards the other. This incomprehensibility, this rupture of the logos is not the beginning of irrationalism but the wound or inspiration which opens speech and then makes possible every logos or every rationalism ' ('Violence and Metaphysics: An Essay on the Thought of Emmannuel Levinas', in *Writing and Difference*, trans. Alan Bass (Chicago: University of Chicago Press, 1994), pp. 79–153, p. 98).

28 Martin Aske's argument that the ode, by imagining an incorporation of Psyche into the poet's mind, is a celebration of 'the authority of the poet's own voice' must be tempered by consideration of the ode's futural temporality, its enactment of a structure of restitution that tends to abase the poet as anything other than vehicle or servitor (*Keats and Hellenism: An Essay* (Cambridge: Cambridge University Press, 1985), pp. 103–9).

29 Werner Hamacher, 'The Second of Inversion: Movements of a Figure through Celan's Poetry', trans. William D. Jowett, *Yale French Studies*, 69 (1985), 276–311, p. 303.

30 Introduction to Celan, *Selected Poems*, pp. 30–1.

31 Celan, 'Speech on the Occasion of Receiving the Literature Prize of the Free Hanseatic City of Bremen', in *Collected Prose*, pp. 34–5.

32 *Athenaeum Fragments*, no. 116, in *Friedrich Schlegel's* Lucinde *and the Fragments*, ed. Peter Firchow, p. 175.

33 Celan, *Collected Prose*, p. 29.

34 In the collection of conference papers on his work collected under the heading *Les Fins de l'homme* (Paris: Editions galilée, 1981), Derrida remarks in relation to a provisional definition of literature as a mode of language whose source and destination admits of indetermination in the act of ascribing meaning:

> La litterature, c'est une maniere d'écrire qui sans cesse fait apparaître l'indetermination pour donner une chance à l'envoi [le desir]. Un envoi peut donc ne pas arriver à destination, mais justement c'est dans ce drame, dans cette tragedie, que consiste l'origine ou la possibilité de la littérature. (p. 213)

35 Davies, 'A Linear Narrative? Blanchot with Heidegger in the Work of Levinas', in *Philosophers' Poets*, ed. David Wood. (London; New York: Routledge, 1990), pp. 37–69, p. 51.

36 Derrida, *Mémoires: For Paul de Man* (New York: Columbia University Press, 1986), p. 59. See also Derrida's discussion of the notion of Judaism as an apostrophic relation to a future to come, in *Archive Fever: A Freudian Impression*, trans. Eric Prenowitz (Chicago: Chicago University Press, 1995), pp. 72–4.

37 Derrida, 'Telepathy', trans. Nicholas Royle, *The Oxford Literary Review*, 10 (1988), 3–41, p. 21. See also Nicholas Royle's provocative study, *Telepathy and Literature: A Study of the Reading Mind* (Oxford: Basil Blackwell, 1991).

38 Ricoeur, 'Appropriation', in *Hermeneutics and the Human Sciences*, ed., trans. John B. Thompson (Cambridge: Cambridge University Press, 1981), pp. 182–93.

39 Derrida and Pierre-Jean Labarrière, *Altérités* (Paris: Editions Osiris, 1986), p. 82.

40 Derrida, *Altérités*, p. 82.

41 Consider the extraordinary temporality of the structure of the following short poem from *Fadensonnen* (1968), Celan, *Selected Poems*, pp. 274–5:

> You were my death
> you I could hold
> when all fell away from me

42 Derrida, *Altérités*, p. 31.

Conclusion

This study has attempted the rehabilitation of a crucial but slated term in poetics. Inspiration, in its simplest description as the notion of composition as dictation by an other, is both the oldest and the most contemporary theory of the genesis of the poetic.

The theory of composition, of which accounts of inspiration should be part, has been neglected for too long. Its discussion has been confined either to occasional articles by philosophers or to the specialized contexts of rhetoric and writing classes in the U.S. Consideration of the genesis of the poetic has become a lacuna in literary study, an empty space between ritual denigrations of romantic idealizations of the creative and forms of discursive and sociological analysis that usually evade the psychic dimensions of the composing process altogether.

We have traced the permutations of the notion of inspiration in a series of artists from a time-span of over two and a half millenia. Since the early nineteenth century poetic composition has recurrently been conceived and practised as a form of experimental knowledge, an experiment with the psyche or body of the writer. The archaic notion of inspiration as dictation from another was reconfigured in a humanist cult of an otherness supposedly within us, a source of hidden powers and transformations. Such attempts to locate some privileged inner source of authority, insight or transcendence often subserved a liberal rhetoric of self-liberation and self-discovery. Yet, as we saw, notions of inspiration as a performative that (impossibly) founds its own value, were often articulated in terms that contradict the express idea of self-legislation, *viz.* as a proleptic image of an emergent text's effect on others, a fantasy audience. Concepts of inspiration as a form of super-subjectivity or creativity in Wordsworth, Shelley, Hölderlin, Nietzsche and others still bespoke a constitutive need for a responding other which they seemed, on the surface, to deny. Romantic philosophies of compo-

sition internalized oral and rhetorical models of immediate communication to construct idealizing notions of the solitary act of written
composition that elide its heavily mediated nature and uncertain
effect. We have traced this Romantic valorization of the act of
composition, and the simultaneous culmination and collapse of this
tradition of thought and school of practice in Nietzsche, the surrealists and then Blanchot. The solitude of the act of composition,
newly valorized by existentialist conceptions of the emptiness of
'human nature', allowed conceptions of inspiration as an encounter
with death and indetermination, or, as in Derrida and Celan, an
explicit engagement with the mediated nature of the sign as consti-
tutively an appeal to others, in the incalculable future of a possible
response.

Inspiration has meant many different things at different times
and places. It has embraced diverse and contradictory images of
authority. It has related to forms of poetic practice as remote as oral,
formulaic composition and Celan's conception of the written poetic
sign as a forlorn 'message in a bottle'. Always, however, the term
has been a matter of contention. From Plato's ironies to the evasions
of the modern academy, 'inspiration' has been a focus of unease as
to whether it names something true and exciting about poetic
composition or a laughable form of old hat. Such unease, as we
have seen, may be symptomatic of the kinds of issues inspiration
raises about the nature of subjectivity and agency. The term seems
always to occupy a crucial, liminal, uncomfortable and often exas-
peratingly mobile place in conceptions of the process of the
composition: it names a space in which distinctions of self and other,
agency and passivity, inner and outer, the psychic and the technical
become deeply problematic.

A continuous thread running through this study has been the
close relation between conceptions of inspiration and varying techniques of composition, the forms of imaginary subjectivity that are
made possible by different technologies of communication and
potential audiences. Yet there is a contradiction between the kinds
of oral and written composition discussed in this study and the technology with which it was composed. New technologies of the sign
such as hypertext and the internet are beginning to change once
more the interrelations of the psychic and the technic, posing anew
questions of authority and agency in language. With the use of
complex and unpredicable programs, effects of meaning and
thought become increasingly detached from any evident or simple
intentional source, whether this is what might be termed the

program's author or authors or its readers or users. Bizarre claims have already appeared that some computer programs should be treated as a form of life. In this context we might turn for help to the study of inspiration in relation to earlier technologies of the sign. New controversies about inspiration are only just underway: of thought as dictation from an other, on effects of something for nothing in the relays of communication, on forms of imaginary subjectivity and the multiple agencies at work in the making of texts (some empirical, some phantasmatic, some the effects of chance) ...

BIBLIOGRAPHY: SELECTED
SECONDARY MATERIAL

Abastado, Claude. 'Ecriture automatique et instance du sujet'. *Revues des Sciences Humaines* 56, No. 184 (October–December 1981), pp. 59–75.

Abra, Jock. *Assaulting Parnassus: Theoretical Views of Creativity*. Lanham, MD: University Presses of America, 1988.

Abrams, M. H. 'The Correspondent Breeze: A Romantic Metaphor'. In *English Romantic Poets: Modern Essays in Criticism*. Ed. M. H. Abrams. New York: Oxford University Press, 1960, pp. 37–54.

Adkins, Arthur W. H. 'Orality and Philosophy'. *Language and Thought in Early Greek Philosophy*. Ed. Kevin Robb. La Salle, Il: The Hegeler Institute, 1983.

Adorno, Theodor W. 'Parataxis: On Hölderlin's Late Poetry'. In *Notes to Literature*. 2 vols. Ed. Rolf Tiedemann. Trans. Shierry Weber Nicholsen (New York: Columbia University Press, 1992), II, 109–49.

Allen, Jeffner, and Young, Iris Marion. *The Thinking Muse: Feminism and Modern French Philosophy*. Bloomington: Indiana University Press, 1989.

Allen, Michael J. B. *The Platonism of Marsilio Ficino: A Study of his Phaedrus Commentary, its Sources and Genesis*. Berkeley: University of California Press, 1984.

Anderson, Mark A. 'The "Impossibility of Poetry": Celan and Heidegger in France'. *New German Critique* 53 (1991), 3–18.

Ashbery, John. 'Pourquoi Écrivez-vous?'. *Libération*, March 1985.

Aspley, Keith. 'Visions and Voices: The Nature of Inspiration from Romanticism to the Birth of Surrealism'. In *Poetry in France: Metamorphoses of a Muse*. Ed. Keith Aspley and Peter France. Edinburgh: Edinburgh University Press, 1992, pp. 154–68.

Baeumer, Max L. 'Nietzsche and the Tradition of the Dionysian'. In *Studies in Nietzsche and the Classical Tradition*. Ed. James C. O'Flaherty, Timothy F. Sellner and Robert M. Helm. Chapell Hill: University of North Carolina Press, 1979, pp. 165–89.

Balakian, Anna, and Kuenzli, Rudolf E. (eds). *André Breton Today*. New York: Willis Locker, 1989.

Bataille, Georges. *Inner Experience*. Trans. Leslie Ann Boldt. Albany: State University of New York Press, 1988.

——On Nietzsche. Trans. Bruce Boone. New York: Paragon House, 1992.

Beaujour, Michel. 'La Poétique de l'automatisme chez André Breton'. *Poétique* 7 (1976), 116–23.

Berthold-Bond, Daniel. 'Hegel, Niezsche, and Freud on Madness and the Unconscious'. *The Journal of Speculative Philosophy* 5 (1991), 193–20.

Bevan, D. G. and Wetherill, P. M. (eds). *Sur la Genetique textuelle*. Amsterdam; Atlanta, Ga.: Rodopi, 1990.

Bialostosky Don H., and Needham, Lawrence D. (eds). *Rhetorical Traditions and British Romantic Literature*. Bloomington: Indiana University Press, 1995.

Blanchot Maurice. 'Literature and the Right to Death' [1949]. In *The Gaze of Orpheus and Other Literary Essays*. Trans. Lydia Davis. New York: Station Hill, 1981, pp. 21–62.

———*The Infinite Conversation* [1969]. Trans. Susan Hanson. Minneapolis and London: University of Minnesota Press, 1993.

———*The Sirens' Song*. Ed. Gabriel Josipovici. Trans. Sacha Rabinovitch. Sussex: Harvester, 1982.

———*The Space of Literature* [1955]. Trans. Ann Smock. Lincoln: University of Nebraska Press, 1982.

Boden, Margaret A. *The Creative Mind: Myths and Mechanisms*. London: George Weidenfeld and Nicholson, 1990.

Bonnet, Marguerite (ed.). *Les Critiques de notre temps et Breton*. Paris: Gamier frères, 1974.

Böschenstein-Schäfer, Renate. 'Die Stimme der Muse in Hölderlins Gedichten'. *Hölderlin-Jahrbuch*, 24 (1984–5), 87–112.

Bowie, Andrew. *Aesthetics and Subjectivity: From Kant to Nietzsche*. Manchester: Manchester University Press, 1990.

———*Schelling and Modern European Philosophy: An Introduction*. London: Routledge, 1993.

Bowra, C. M. *Inspiration and Poetry*. London: Macmillan, 1955.

Braudy, Leo. *The Frenzy of Renown: Fame and its History*. New York: Oxford University Press, 1986.

Brinkley, Robert and Hanley, Keith (eds). *Romantic Revisions*. Cambridge: Cambridge University Press, 1992.

Broughton, Irv. *The Writer's Mind: Interviews with American Authors*, 3 vols. Fayetteville and London: University of Arkansas Press, 1989.

Bürger, Peter. *Theory of the Avant-Garde*. Trans. Michael Shaw. Minneapolis: University of Minnesota Press, 1984.

Burke, Seán (ed.). *Authorship: From Plato to the Postmodern: A Reader*. Edinburgh: Edinburgh University Press, 1995.

Burwick, Frederick. *Poetic Madness and the Romantic Imagination*. University Park, PA: University of Pennslyvania Press, 1996.

Butler, Judith. *Gender Trouble: Feminism and the Subversion of Identity*. London: Routledge, 1990.

Canetti, Elias. *Crowds and Power*. Trans. Carol Stewart. London: Gollancz, 1962.

Carbo, Nicholas Andrew. 'The Poets of 'Renga': Octavio Paz, Jacques Roubaud, Edoardo Sanguineti and Charles Tomlinson'. Diss. New York University, 1976.

Carrouges, Michel. *André Breton et les données fondamentales du surréalisme*. Paris: Editions Gallimard, 1950.

Castor, Grahame. *Pléiade Poetics: A Study in Sixteenth-Century Thought and Terminology*. Cambridge: Cambridge University Press, 1964.

Cave, Terence. *The Cornucopian Text: Problems of Writing in the French Renaissance*. Oxford: Clarendon, 1979.

Champigny, Robert. 'Analyse d'une Definition du Surréalisme'. *PMLA* 81 (1966), 139–44.

Clark, Jonathan P. 'Beyond Rhyme or Reason. Fanaticism and the Transference of Interpretive Paradigms from the Seventeenth-Century Orthodoxy to the Aesthetics of Enlightenment'. *MLN* 105 (1990), 563–82.

Clark, Timothy. *Derrida, Heidegger, Blanchot: Sources of Derrida's Notion and Practice of Literature*. Cambridge: Cambridge University Press, 1992.

————*Embodying Revolution: The Figure of the Poet in Shelley*. Oxford: Clarendon Press, 1989.

Clej, Alina. 'Phantoms of the Opera: Notes towards a Theory of Surrealist Confession – The Case of Breton'. *MLN* 104 (1989), 819–44.

Corngold, Stanley. 'Hölderlin and the Interpretation of the Self.' *Comparative Criticism* 5 (1983), 187–200.

Critchley, Simon. 'Il y a – A Dying Stronger than Death (Blanchot with Levinas)'. *Oxford Literary Review* 15 (1993), 81–131.

Csikszentmihalyi, Mihaly. 'Society, culture, and person: A systems view of creativity'. *The Nature of Creativity*. Ed. Robert J. Sternberg. Cambridge: Cambridge University Press, 1988, pp. 325–39.

Curtius, E. R. *European Literature and the Latin Middle Ages*. Trans. Willard R. Trask. London: Routledge and Kegan Paul, 1953.

Dawson, Paul. 'Shelley and the "Improvvisatore" Sgricci: An Unpublished Review'. *Keats Shelley Memorial Bulletin* 32 (1981), 19–29.

Dean, Carolyn J. *The Self and its Pleasures: Bataille, Lacan, and the History of the Decentered Subject*. Ithaca: Cornell University Press, 1992.

de Rachewiltz, Siegfried Walter. *De Sirenibus: An Inquiry into Sirens from Homer to Shakespeare*. Cambridge, Mass: Harvard University Press, 1983.

Delatte, V. 'Les Conceptions de l'enthousiasme chez les philosophes présocratiques'. *L'Antiquité Classique* 3 (1934) 5–80.

Delègue, Yves. 'La Littérature ventriloque'. *Poétique* 18 (1987), 431–42.

DeLisle, Fanny. *A Study of Shelley's A Defence of Poetry: A Textual and Critical Evaluation*. 2 vols. University of Salzburg, 1974.

Derrida, Jacques. 'Force and Signification'. *Writing and Difference*. Trans. Alan Bass. Chicago: University of Chicago Press, 1978, pp. 3–30.

————'Plato's Pharmacy'. *Dissemination*. Trans. Barbara Johnson. Chicago: University of Chicago Press, 1981, 63–172.

————'This Strange Institution Called Literature'. An Interview with Jacques Derrida. In *Derrida, Acts of Literature*. Ed. Derek Attridge. London: Routledge, 1992, pp. 33–75.

————'"Eating Well", or the Calculation of the Subject: An Interview with Jacques Derrida'. In *Who Comes After the Subject*. Ed. Eduardo Cadava, Peter Connor, Jean-Luc Nancy. London; New York: Routledge, 1991, pp. 96–119.

————'*Istrice 2: Ick bünn all hier*'. In *Points: Interviews 1974–1994*. Ed. Elisabeth Weber. Stanford: Stanford University Press, 1992, pp. 300–26.

————'Qual Quelle: Valéry's Sources'. In *Margins of Philosophy*. Trans. Alan Bass. Chicago: University of Chicago Press, 1982.

————*Mémoires: for Paul de Man*. New York: Columbia University Press, 1986.

————*Schibboleth: Pour Paul Celan*. Paris: Galilée, 1986.

————'Violence and Metaphysics: An Essay on the Thought of Emmannuel Levinas'. In *Writing and Difference*. Trans. Alan Bass. Chicago: University of Chicago Press, 1994.

DeShazer, Mary K. *Inspiring Women: Reimagining the Muse*. New York: Pergamon Press, 1986.

Detienne, Marcel. *Les Maîtres de vérité dans la grèce archaîque*. Paris: Francois Maspero, 1967.

Dietrich, Bernard C. 'Oracles and Divine Inspiration'. *Kronos* 3 (1990), 157–74.

Dodds, E. R. *The Greeks and the Irrational*. Berkeley: University of California Press, 1951.

Durazoi, Gérard, and Lecherbonnier, Bernard. *André Breton: L'écriture surréaliste*. Paris: Libraire Larousse, 1974.

Durling, Robert M. *The Figure of the Poet in the Renaissance Epic*. Cambridge, Mass.: Harvard University Press, 1965.

Eichbauer, Mary E. 'The Surrealist Muse and the Sister Arts: René Char's "Artine"'. *Paragraph* 12 (1989), 124–38.

Ellenberger, Henri. *The Discovery of the Unconscious*. London: Fontana, 1994.

Engell, James. *Forming the Critical Mind: Dryden to Coleridge*. Cambridge, Mass.: Harvard University Press, 1989.

——*The Creative Imagination: Enlightenment to Romanticism*. Cambridge, Mass and London: Harvard University Press, 1981.

Entralgo, Pedro Lain. *The Therapy of the Word in Classical Antiquity*. Ed., trans. L. J. Rather and John M. Sharp. New Haven and London: Yale University Press, 1970.

Evans, Robert R. (ed) *Readings in Collective Behavior*. Chicago: Rand McNally and Co., 1969.

Faigley, Lynn. 'Competing Theories of Process: A Critique and a Proposal'. *College English* 48 (1986), 527–42.

Ferrari, G. R. F. 'Plato and Poetry'. *The Cambridge History of Literary Criticism*. I, Classical Criticism. Ed. George A. Kennedy. Cambridge: Cambridge University Press, 1989, pp. 92–148.

Fichte, Johann Gottlieb. 'On the Spirit and Letter in Philosophy'. In a series of Letters, 1794. Trans. Elizabeth Rubenstein. In Simpson (ed.), 74–93.

Flesch, William. 'Quoting Poetry'. *Critical Inquiry*, 18 (1991), 42–63.

Ford, Jennifer. *Coleridge on Dreaming: Romanticism, Dreams and the Medical Imagination*. Cambridge: Cambridge University Press, 1997.

Foti, Véronique. *Heidegger and the Poets: Poiesis, Sophia, Techne*. New Jersey; London: Humanities Press, 1992.

Foucault, Michel. *Madness and Civilisation*. Trans. Richard Howard. New York: Pantheon, 1965.

Fowler, R. L. *The Nature of Early Greek Lyric: Three Preliminary Studies*. Toronto: University of Toronto Press, 1987.

Fränkel, H. *Early Greek Poetry and Poetry: A History of Greek Epic, Lyric and Prose to the Middle of the Fifth Century*. Trans. M. Hadas and J. Willis. Oxford: Basil Blackwell, 1975.

Freud, Sigmund. *The Standard Edition of the Complete Psychological Works of Sigmund Freud*. 24 vols. Ed. James Strachey. London: Hogarth Press, 1953–74.

Fruman, Norman. 'Creative Process and Concealment in Coleridge's Poetry'. In *Romantic Revisions*. Ed. Robert Brinkley and Keith Hanley. Cambridge: Cambridge University Press, 1992, 154–68.

Fry, Paul. *The Poet's Calling in the English Ode*. New Haven: Yale University Press, 1980.

Ghiselin, Brewster, (ed.). *The Creative Process: A Symposium*. Berkeley: University of California Press, 1952.

Gilbert, Sandra M., and Gubar, Susan. *The Madwoman in the Attic: The Woman*

Writer and the Nineteenth-Century Imagination. New Haven and London: Yale University Press, 1979.

Gratton, J. 'Runaway: Textual Dynamics in the Surrealist Poetry of André Breton'. *Forum for Modern Language Studies* 18 (1982), 126–41.

Graves, Robert. *The White Goddess: A Historical Grammar of Poetic Myth*. London: Faber and Faber, 1948.

Grean, Stanley. *Shaftesbury's Philosophy of Religion and Ethics: A Study in Enthusiasm*. N.p.: Ohio University Press, 1967.

Gregg, John. *Maurice Blanchot and the Literature of Transgression*. Princeton: Princeton University Press, 1994.

Gubar, Susan. '"The Blank Page" and the Issues of Female Creativity'. In *Writing and Sexual Difference*. Ed. Elizabeth Abel. Sussex: Harvester Press, 1982, pp. 73–93.

Hamacher, Werner. 'The Second of Inversion: Movements of a Figure through Celan's Poetry'. Trans. William D. Jowett. *Yale French Studies*, 69 (1985), 276–311.

Harding, Anthony. *Coleridge and the Inspired Word*. Kingston and Montreal: McGill-Queen's University Press, 1985.

Harding, E. M. Rosamund. *An Anatomy of Inspiration*. Cambridge: W. Heffer & Sons, 1940.

Harshbarger, Scott. 'Robert Lowth's *Sacred Hebrew Poetry* and the Oral Dimension of Romantic Rhetoric'. In *Rhetorical Traditions and British Romantic Literature*. Ed. Don H. Bialostosky and Lawrence D. Needham. Bloomington: Indiana University Press, 1995, pp. 199–214.

Havelock, Eric A. *Preface to Plato*. Oxford: Basil Blackwell, 1963.

Hawes, Clement. *Mania and Literary Style: The Rhetoric of Enthusiasm from the Ranters to Christopher Smart*. Cambridge: Cambridge University Press, 1996.

Heffernan, James A. W. *Wordsworth's Theory of Poetry: The Transforming Imagination*. Ithaca and London: Cornell University Press, 1969.

Heidegger, Martin. 'The Origin of the Work of Art'. In *Poetry, Language, Thought*. Trans. Albert Hofstadter. New York: Harper & Row, 1971, pp. 17–87.

Henrich, Dieter. 'Eine Philosophische Konzeption entsteht: Hölderlins Denken in Jena'. *Hölderlin-Jahrbuch*, 28 (1992–3), 1–28.

Heyd, Michael. 'The Reaction to Enthusiasm in the Seventeenth Century: From Anti-Structure to Structure'. *Religion* 15 (1985), 279–89.

Hogle, J. E. 'Shelley's Poetics: The Power as Metaphor'. *Keats-Shelley Journal* 31 (1982), 159–91.

Houdebine, Jean-Louis. 'Méconnaissance de la psychanalyse dans le discours surréaliste'. *Tel Quel*, 46 (1971), 67–82.

Howell, Wilbur Samuel. *Eighteenth-Century British Logic and Rhetoric*. Princeton, N.J.: Princeton University Press, 1971.

Ince, W. N. *The Poetic Theory of Paul Valéry: Inspiration and Technique*. Leicester: Leicester University Press, 1961.

Irlam, Shaun Anthony. 'Unworlding and Otherworldliness: Enthusiasm, Epiphany, and Typology in the Poetry of James Thomson and Edward Young'. Diss. Johns Hopkins University, 1993.

Izenberg, Gerald N. *Impossible Individuality: Romanticism, Revolution, and the Origins of Modern Selfhood, 1780–1802*. Princeton: Princeton University Press, 1992.

Isbell, John Claireborne. *The Birth of European Romanticism: Truth and Propaganda in Stael's de l'Allemagne*. Cambridge: Cambridge University Press, 1994.

Jacob, Karen. 'Two Mirrors Facing: Freud, Blanchot and the Logic of Invisibility'. *Qui Parle* 4 (1990), 21–46.

Jaffe, Kineret S. 'The Concept of Genius: Its Changing Role in Eighteenth-Century French Aesthetics'. *Journal of the History of Ideas* 41 (1980), 579–99.

James, Tony. *Dreams, Creativity, and Madness in Nineteenth-Century France*. Oxford: Clarendon Press, 1995.

Jardine, Alice. *Gynesis: Configurations of Woman and Modernity*. Ithaca: Cornell University Press, 1983.

Kelley, Theresa M. *Wordsworth's Revisionary Aesthetics*. Cambridge: Cambridge: Cambridge University Press, 1988.

Koestler, Arthur. *The Act of Creation*. London: Picador, 1975.

Kris, Ernst. *Psychoanalytic Explanations in Art*. New York: International University Press, 1952.

Kristeva, Julia. *Revolution in Poetic Language*. Trans. Margaret Waller. New York: Columbia University Press, 1984.

——*Soleil noir: dépression et mélancholie*. Paris: Gallimard, 1987.

Kurz, Gerhard. *Mittelbarkeit und Vereinigung: Zum Verhältnis von Poesie, Reflexion und Revolution bei Hölderlin*. Stuttgart: J. B. Metzlersche Verlagsbuchhandlung, 1975.

Lacoue-Labarthe, Philippe. 'Catastrophe: A Reading of Celan's "The Meridian"'. Trans. Timothy Clark and Sylvie Gautheron. *Oxford Literary Review* 15 (1993), 4–41.

——*La Poésie comme expérience*. Paris: Christian Bourgois, 1986.

Lacoue-Labarthe, Philippe, and Nancy, Jean-Luc. *The Literary Absolute: The Theory of Literature in German Romanticism*. Trans. Philip Bernard and Cherly Lester. Albany: State University of New York Press, 1988.

Lange, Wolfgang. *Der Kalkulierte Wahnsinn: Innenansichten ästhetischer Moderne*. Frankfurt: Fischer Taschenbuch, 1992.

Leask, Nigel. '"Shelley's Magnetic Ladies": Romantic Mesmerism and the Politics of the Body'. In *Beyond Romanticism: New Approaches to Texts and Contexts 1780–1832*. Ed. Stephen Copley and John Whale. London: Routledge, 1992, pp. 53–78.

Lechte, John. 'Surrealism and the Practice of Writing, or The "Case" of Bataille'. In *Bataille: Writing the Sacred*. Ed. Carolyn Bailey Gill. London: Routledge, 1995, pp. 117–32.

Lernout, Geert. *The Poet as Thinker: Hölderlin in France*. Columbia, SC: Camden House, 1994.

Lettis, Richard. '"Hard Work": Dickens in the Writer's Chair'. *The Dickensian* 89 (1993), 5–24.

Levinas, Emmanuel. 'Reality and its Shadow'. *Collected Philosophical Papers*. Trans. Alphonso Lingis. Dordrecht: Martinus Nijhoff, 1987, pp. 1–13.

Lewin, Bertram D. *The Psychoanalysis of Elation*. New York: The Psychoanalytic Quarterly Inc., 1961.

Libertson, Joseph. *Proximity: Levinas, Blanchot, Bataille and Communication*. The Hague: Martinus Nijhoff, 1982.

Lipkowitz, Ina. 'Inspiration and the Poetic Imagination: Samuel Taylor

Coleridge'. *Studies in Romanticism* 30 (1991), 605–31.

Lord, Albert B. *The Singer of Tales.* Cambridge, Mass.: Harvard University Press, 1960.

McGahey, Robert. *The Orphic Moment: Shaman to Poet-Thinker in Plato, Nietzsche, & Mallarmé.* Albany: State University of New York Press, 1994.

Maddison, Carol. *Apollo and the Nine: A History of the Ode.* London: Routledge and Kegan Paul, 1960.

Magnuson, Paul. 'Wordsworth and Spontaneity'. In *The Evidence of the Imagination.* Ed. Donald H. Reiman. New York: New York University Press, 1978, pp. 101–18.

Manuel, Frank, E. *The Eighteenth Century Confronts the Gods.* Cambridge, Mass: Harvard University Press, 1959.

Mee, Jon. *Dangerous Enthusiasm: William Blake and the Culture of Radicalism in the 1790s.* Oxford: Clarendon Press, 1992.

Meissner, W. W. *Psychoanalysis and Religious Experience.* New Haven and London: Yale University Press, 1984.

Minnis, A. J. *The Medieval Theory of Authorship: Scholastic Literary Attitudes in the Later Middle Ages.* London: Scholar Press, 1984.

Moscovici, Serge. *The Age of the Crowd.* Cambridge: Cambridge University Press, 1985.

Murray, Penelope. 'Poetic Inspiration in Early Greece'. *Journal of Hellenic Studies* 101 (1981), 87–100.

Myerhoff, Barbara. 'The Transformation of Consciousness in Ritual Performance: Some Thoughts and Questions'. In *By Means of Performance: Intercultural Studies of Theatre and Ritual.* Ed. Richard Schechner and Willa Appel. Cambridge: Cambridge University Press, 1990.

Nagy, Gregory. 'Early Greek Views of Poets and Poetry'. *Cambridge History of Literary Criticism* I. Ed. G. Kennedy. Cambridge: Cambridge University Press, 1989, pp. 1–77.

——*Pindar's Homer: The Lyric Possession of an Epic Past.* Baltimore and London: The Johns Hopkins University Press, 1990.

Nash, Roger. 'The Demonology of Verse'. *Philosophical Investigations* 10 (1987), 299–316.

Nichols, Ashton. *The Poetics of Epiphany: Nineteenth-Century Origins of the Modern Literary Moment.* Tuscaloosa: University of Alabama Press, 1987.

Nisbet, H. B. (ed.). *German Aesthetic and Literary Criticism: Winckelmann, Lessing, Hamann, Herder, Schiller and Goethe.* Cambridge: Cambridge University Press, 1985.

Norton, David. *A History of the Bible as Literature.* 2 vols. Cambridge: Cambridge University Press, 1993.

Ong, Walter J. *Orality and Literacy: The Technologizing of the Word.* 1982; London: Routledge, 1988.

——*Rhetoric, Romance, and Technology: Studies in the Interaction of Expression and Culture.* Ithaca and London: Cornell University Press, 1971.

Owen, W. J. B. 'The Perfect Image of a Mighty Mind'. *The Wordsworth Circle* 10 (1979), 3–16.

——*Wordsworth as Critic.* Toronto and Buffalo: University of Toronto Press, 1969.

Oxley, William. *The Cauldron of Inspiration*. Salzburg: Universität Salzburg, 1983.

Pappas, Nickolas. 'Plato's *Ion*: The Problem of the Author'. *Philosophy* 64 (1989), 381–89.

Patey, Douglas, Lane. *Probability and Literary Form: Philosophic theory and literary practice in the Augustan age*. Cambridge: Cambridge University Press, 1984.

Paz, Octavio. *Alternating Current*. Trans. Helen Lane. New York: Seaver Books, 1990.

——'André Breton and the Search for the Beginning'. In *On Poets and Others*. Trans. Michael Schmidt. New York: Seaver Books, 1986, pp. 66–78.

——*The Bow and The Lyre*. 2nd edn. Trans. Ruth L. C. Simmons. Austin: University of Texas Press, 1973.

Pickering, Robert. 'Writing and the Page: Rimbaud, Mallarmé, Valéry'. *Modern Language Review* 87 (1992), 56–71.

Plimpton, George (ed.). *Women Writers at Work: The* Paris Review *Interviews*. New York: Viking, 1989.

——*Writers at Work: The* Paris Review *Interviews*. 1st Series. New York: Viking, 1958.

——*Writers at Work: The* Paris Review *Interviews*. 3rd Series. New York: Viking, 1967.

——*Writers at Work: The* Paris Review *Interviews*. 4th Series. New York: Viking, 1976.

——*Writers at Work: The* Paris Review *Interviews*. 7th Series. New York: Viking, 1986.

Poe, Edgar Allan. 'The Philosophy of Composition' [1846]. In *The Fall of the House of Usher and Other Writings*. Ed. David Galloway. 1967: London: Penguin, 1986, pp. 480–92.

Ponsford, Michael. '"Poetical Fury": The Religious Enthusiasts of the Late Seventeenth Century'. *Christian Scholar's Review* 16 (1986), 24–39.

Poulet, Georges. *The Interior Distance*. Trans. Elliott Coleman. Baltimore: Ann Arbor Paperback, University of Michigan Press, 1964.

Press, John. *The Fire and the Fountain: An Essay on Poetry*. London: Methuen, 1966. First published 1955.

Prickett, Stephen. *Words and The Word : Language, Poetics and Biblical interpretation*. Cambridge: Cambridge University Press, 1986.

Ribot, Théodore. *Essay on the Creative Imagination* [1900]. Trans. Albert H. N. Baron. Chicago: Open Court, 1906.

Richter, Jean Paul. *Horn of Oberon: Jean Paul Richter's School for Aesthetics* [1804]. Trans. Margaret R. Hale. Detroit: Wayne State University Press, 1973.

Riffaterre, Michael. 'Semantic Incompatibilities in Automatic Writing'. In *About French Poetry from DADA to "Tel Quel": Text and Theory*. Ed. Mary Ann Caws, Henri Peyre and Michael Beaujour. Detroit: Wayne State University Press, 1974, pp. [223]–41.

Rose, Mike. *Writers' Block: The Cognitive Dimension*. Edwardsville and Carbondale, Southern Illinois University Press, 1984.

Rossington, M. 'The Bacchic in Shelley'. In *Beyond Romanticism*, pp. 101–17.

Rothenberg, Albert. *Creativity and Madness: New Findings and Old Stereotypes*. Baltimore: Johns Hopkins University Press, 1990.

Russo, Joseph and Simon, Bennett. 'Homeric Psychology and the Oral Epic

Tradition'. *Journal of the History of Ideas* 29 (1968), 483–98.

Salman, Aktar. 'Hypomanic Personality Disorder'. *Integrative Psychiatry* 6 (1988), 37–52.

Sartre, Jean-Paul. *What is Literature?* Trans. Bernard Frechtman. New York: Philosophical Library, 1949; Harper Colophon Books, 1965.

Schindler, Walter. *Voice and Crisis: Invocation in Milton's Poetry.* Hamben, Connct.: Archon Books, 1984.

Schings, Hans-Jürgen. *Melancholie und Aufklärung: Melancholie und ihre Kritiker in Erfahrungsseelenkunde und Literatur des 18. Jahrhunderts.* Stuttgart: J. B. Mezlersche, 1977.

Schlanger, Judith. *L'Invention intellectuelle.* Paris: Fayard, 1983.

Segal, Charles. 'Eros and Incantation: Sappho and Oral Poetry'. *Arethusa* 7 (1974).

Shaviro, Steven. *Passion and Excess: Blanchot, Bataille, and Literary Theory.* Tallahassee: Florida State University Press, 1990.

Shrady, Maria. *Moments of Insight: The Emergence of Creative Ideas in the Lives of Great Men.* New York: Harper & Row, 1972.

Simpson David (ed.). *German Aesthetic and Literary Criticism: Kant, Fichte, Schelling, Schopenhauer, Hegel.* Cambridge: Cambridge University Press, 1984.

Starobinski, Jean. 'Freud, Breton, Myers'. *Les Critiques de notre temps et Breton.* Ed. Marguerite Bonnet. Paris: José Corti, 1983, pp. 48–59.

Staten, Henry. *Nietzsche's Voice.* Ithaca and London: Cornell University Press, 1990.

Steffan, Truman Guy. 'The Social Argument Against Enthusiasm (1650–1660)'. *Texas Studies in English* (1941), 39–63.

Stewart, Garrett. *Reading Voices: Literature and the Phonotext.* Berkeley: University of California Press, 1990.

Stone, P. W. K. *The Art of Poetry 1750–1820: Theories of Poetic Composition and Style in the Late Neo-Classic and Early Romantic Periods.* London: Routledge and Kegan Paul, 1967.

Strauss, Walter A. *Descent and Return: The Orphic Theme in Modern Literature.* Cambridge, Mass.: Harvard University Press, 1971.

Svenbro, Jesper. *Phrasikleia: An Anthropology of Reading in Ancient Greece.* Ithaca, N.Y.: Cornell University Press, 1993.

Sword, Helen. *Engendering Inspiration: Visionary Strategies in Rilke, Lawrence and H.D..* Ann Arbor: University of Michigan Press, 1995.

Tigerstedt, E. N. *'Furor Poeticus:* Poetic Inspiration in Greek Literature before Democritus and Plato'. *Journal of the History of Ideas* 31 (1970), 163–78.

Tucker, Susie I. *Enthusiasm: A Study in Semantic Change.* Cambridge: Cambridge University Press, 1972.

Valéry, Paul. *The Art of Poetry.* Trans. Denise Folliot. New York: Panther Books, 1958.

Verdenius, W. J. 'The Principles of Greek Literary Criticism'. *Mnemosyne* 36 (1983), 14–59.

Vernant, Jean-Pierre. *Mythe et pensé chez les Grecs: Etudes de psychologie historique.* 2 Vols. Paris: Francois Maspero, 1971.

Vöhler, Martin. 'Hölderlins Longin Rezeption'. *Hölderlin-Jahrbuch,* 28 (1992–3), 152–72.

Wallas, G. *The Art of Thought.* London: Cape, 1926.

Wasserman, Earl. 'The Sympathetic Imagination in Eighteenth-Century Theories of Acting'. *Journal of English and Germanic Philology*, 46 (1947), 264–72.

Weisberg, Robert W. *Creativity, Genius and Other Myths: What You Mozart, Einstein, Picasso Have in Common.* New York: W. H. Freeman and Co., 1986.

Wenthe, William. '"The Hieratic Dance": Prosody and the Unconscious in H.D.'s Poetry'. *Sagetrieb* 14 (1995), 113–40.

Wheeler, Kathleen (ed.). *German Aesthetic and Literary Criticism: The Romantic Ironists and Goethe.* Cambridge: Cambridge University Press, 1984.

Willcox, Joel F. 'Ficino's Commentary on Plato's *Ion* and Chapman's Inspired Poet in the *Odyssey*'. *Philological Quarterly* 64 (1985), 195–209.

Willems, Gottfried. 'Der Dichterische Enthusiasmus und die Macht der Negativität: Über Hölderlins Elegie *Brot und Wein*'. *Jahrbuch der Deutschen Schillergesellschaft*, 32 (1988), 116–49.

Wilson, Jason. *Octavio Paz: A Study of His Poetics.* Cambridge: Cambridge University Press, 1979.

Woolfe, Sue, and Grenville, Kate. *Making Stories: How Ten Australian Novels were Written.* St. Leonards, NSW: Allen and Unwin, 1993.

INDEX

Note: 'nt' after a page reference indicates the number of a note on that page.